SPIRITUAL REFORMERS IN THE 16TH & 17TH CENTURIES

Rufus Matthew Jones, the great American Quaker philosopher, was born in South China, Maine in 1863. He received his B.A. degree from Haverford College in 1885, an A.M. in 1886, and an LL.D. in 1922. During his lifetime he was professor of philosophy at Haverford College, a trustee of both Bryn Mawr College and Brown University, a member of the Appraisal Commission of Foreign Missions in the Orient, and a member of the Dominican Republic Settlement Association. From 1917 to 1927, and again from 1934 to 1944, he was chairman of the American Friends Service Committee for European Relief which was founded in 1917 largely through his efforts. He was serving as honorary chairman in 1947 when the Committee was awarded the Nobel Peace Prize. Among his many books are PRACTICAL CHRISTIANITY, SOCIAL LAW IN THE SPIRITUAL WORLD, QUAKERISM, A RELIGION OF LIFE, STUDIES IN MYSTICAL RELIGION, HAVERFORD COLLEGE — A HISTORY AND AN INTERPRETATION, RE-THINKING RELIGIOUS LIBERALISM, and NEW EYES FOR THE INVISIBLES. He died in 1948 at Haverford.

SPIRITUAL REFORMERS

in the

16TH AND 17TH CENTURIES

By RUFUS M. JONES

GLOUCESTER, MASS.

PETER SMITH

1971

PREFACE

In my *Quakers in the American Colonies* I announced
the preparation of a volume to be devoted mainly to
Jacob Boehme and his influence. I soon found, however,
as my work of research proceeded, that Boehme was no
isolated prophet who discovered in solitude a fresh way of
approach to the supreme problems of the soul. I came
upon very clear evidence that he was an organic part of
a far-reaching and significant historical movement—a
movement which consciously aimed, throughout its long
period of travail, to carry the Reformation to its legitimate
terminus, the restoration of apostolic Christianity. The
men who originated the movement, so far as anything
historical can be said to be " originated," were often
scornfully called " Spirituals " by their opponents, while
they thought of themselves as divinely commissioned
and Spirit-guided " Reformers," so that I have with good
right named them " Spiritual Reformers."

I have had two purposes in view in these studies.
One purpose was the tracing of a religious movement,
profoundly interesting in itself, as a great side current
of the Reformation. The other purpose was the discovery of the background and environment of seventeenth
century Quakerism. There can be little doubt, I think,
that I have here found at least one of the great historical
sources of the Quaker movement. This volume, together
with my *Studies in Mystical Religion*, will at any rate

furnish convincing evidence that the ideas, aims, experiences, practices, and aspirations of the early Quakers were the fruit of long spiritual preparation. This movement, as a whole, has never been studied before, and my work has been beset with difficulties. I have been aided by helpful monographs on individual " Reformers," written mainly by German and French scholars, who have been duly credited at the proper places, but for the most part my material has been drawn from original sources. I am under much obligation to my friend, Theodor Sippell of Schweinsberg, Germany. I am glad to announce that he is preparing a critical historical study on John Everard and the Ranters, which will throw important light on the religious ideas of the English Commonwealth. He has read my proofs, and has, throughout my period of research, given me the benefit of his extensive knowledge of this historical field. I wish to express my appreciation of the courtesy and kindness which I have received from the officials of the University Library at Marburg. William Charles Braithwaite of Banbury, England, has given me valuable help. My wife has assisted me in all my work of research. She has read and re-read the proofs, made the Index, and given me an immense amount of patient help. I cannot close this Preface without again referring to the inspiration of my invisible friend, John Wilhelm Rowntree, in whose memory this series was undertaken.

HAVERFORD, PENNSYLVANIA,
January 1914.

CONTENTS

INTRODUCTION

CHAPTER I

CHAPTER II

CHAPTER III

CHAPTER IV

CHAPTER V

CHAPTER VI

CONTENTS

CHAPTER XV

BENJAMIN WHICHCOTE, THE FIRST OF THE " LATITUDE-MEN"   288

CHAPTER XVI

JOHN SMITH, PLATONIST—" AN INTERPRETER OF THE SPIRIT "   305

CHAPTER XVII

THOMAS TRAHERNE AND THE SPIRITUAL POETS OF THE SEVENTEENTH CENTURY   320

CHAPTER XVIII

CONCLUSION   336

INDEX   351

WITHIN thy sheltering darkness spin the spheres ;
Within the shaded hollow of thy wings.
The life of things,
The changeless pivot of the passing years—
These in thy bosom lie.
Restless we seek thy being ; to and fro
Upon our little twisting earth we go :
We cry, " Lo, there ! "
When some new avatar thy glory does declare,
When some new prophet of thy friendship sings,
And in his tracks we run
Like an enchanted child, that hastes to catch the sun.

And shall the soul thereby
Unto the All draw nigh ?
Shall it avail to plumb the mystic deeps
Of flowery beauty, scale the icy steeps
Of perilous thought, thy hidden Face to find,
Or tread the starry paths to the utmost verge of the sky ?
Nay, groping dull and blind
Within the sheltering dimness of thy wings—
Shade that their splendour flings
Athwart Eternity—
We, out of age-long wandering, but come
Back to our Father's heart, where now we are at home.

EVELYN UNDERHILL in *Immanence*, p. 82.

INTRODUCTION

WHAT IS " SPIRITUAL RELIGION "

I

THERE is no magic in words, though, it must be confessed, they often exercise a psychological influence so profound and far-reaching that they seem to possess a miracle-working efficacy. Some persons live all their lives under the suggestive spell of certain words, and it sometimes happens that an entire epoch is more or less dominated by the mysterious fascination of a sacred word, which needs only to be spoken on the house-top to set hearts beating and legs marching.

"Spiritual" has always been one of these wonder-working words. St. Paul, in Christian circles, was the first to give the word its unique value. For him it named a new order of life and a new level of being. In his thought, a deep cleavage runs through the human race and divides it into two sharply-sundered classes, "psychical men" and "pneumatical men"—men who live according to nature, and men who live by the life of the Spirit. The former class, that is psychical men, are of the earth earthy ; they are, as we should say to-day, *empirical*, parts of a vast nature-system, doomed, as is the entire system, to constant flux and mutability and eventually to irretrievable wreck and ruin ; the natural, psychical, corruptible man cannot inherit incorruption.[1] On the other hand, the pneumatical or spiritual man

[1] I Cor. xv. 50.

" puts on " incorruption and immortality. He is a member of a new order ; he is " heavenly," a creation " not made with hands," but wrought out of the substance of the spiritual world, and furnished with the inherent capacity of eternal duration, so that " mortality is swallowed up of life." [1]

This word, thus made sacred by St. Paul's great use of it to designate the new race of the saved, was made the bearer in the Johannine writings of a no less exalted message, which has become a living and indissoluble part of the religious consciousness of the Christian world. " Eternal life "—or, what in these writings is the same thing, " life "—comes through the reception of the Spirit, in a birth from above. " That which is born of the flesh is flesh, and that which is born of the Spirit is Spirit." [2] When the Spirit comes as the initiator of this abundant life, then we " know that we abide in Him and He in us, because He hath given us of His Spirit," and it becomes possible for the Spirit-led person to be guided " into all the truth," to " love even as He loved," and to " overcome the world." [3] Here, again, the human race is divided into those who have " received of the Spirit," and those who have not so received ; those who are " born from above " and those who have had only a natural birth ; the twice-born and the once-born ; those who are " of the Spirit," *i.e.* spiritual, and those who are " of this world," *i.e.* empirical.

The Gnostic Sects of the second century had one common link and badge ; they all proposed a " way," often bizarre and strange-sounding to modern ears, by which the soul, astray, lost, encumbered, or imprisoned in matter, might attain its freedom and become *spiritual*. Most of the Gnostic teachers, who in their flourishing time were as thick as thistle-downs in summer, conceived of man as consisting of two " halves " which corresponded with two totally different world-orders. There was in man, or there belonged to man (1) a visible body, which

[1] 2 Cor. v. 1-4.   [2] John iii. 6.
[3] 1 John iv. 13 ; John xiii. 34 and xvi. 13 ; 1 John iv. 4.

was again dichotomized, and believed to be composed, according to many of the Gnostics, of a subtle element like that of which they supposed Adam in his unfallen state was made, which they named the *hylic* body, and a sheath of gross earthly matter which they called the *choical* body.[1] There was also (2) another, invisible, " half," generally divided into lower and higher stories. The lower story, the psychical, was created or furnished by the Demiurge, or sub-divine creator of the natural system, while the top-story, or pneumatical self, was a *spiritual seed* derived from the supreme spiritual Origin, the Divine Pleroma, the Fulness of the Godhead. Those who possessed this spiritual seed were " the elect," " the saved," who eventually, stripped of their sheath of matter and their psychical dwelling, would be able to pass all " the keepers of the way," and rise to the pure spiritual life.

The Montanists launched in the second century a movement, borne along on a mountain-wave of enthusiasm, for a " spiritual " Church composed only of " spiritual " persons. They called themselves " the Spirituals," and they insisted that the age or dispensation of the Spirit had now come. The Church, rigidly organized with its ordained officials, its external machinery, and its accumulated traditions, was to them part of an old and outworn system to be left behind. In the place of it was to come a new order of " spiritual people " of whom the Montanist prophets were the " first fruits,"—a new and peculiar people, born from above, recipients of a divine energizing power, partakers in the life of the Spirit and capable of being guided on by progressive revelations into all the truth. To be " spiritual " in their vocabulary meant to be a participator in the Life of God, and to be a living member of a group that was led and guided by a continuously self-revealing Spirit. This Spirit was conceived, however, not as immanent and resident, not as the in-

---

[1] They found their authority for this outer sheath of body in the text which says : " The Lord God made for Adam and for his wife coats of skins, and clothed them."—Gen. iii. 21.

dwelling and permeative Life of the human spirit, but as foreign and remote, and He was thought of as " coming " in sporadic visitations to whom He would, His coming being indicated in extraordinary and charismatic manifestations.

This type of " spiritual religion," though eventually stamped out in the particular form of Montanism, reappeared again and again, with peculiar local and temporal variations, in the history of Christianity.[1]   To the bearers of it, the historic Church, with its crystallized system and its vast machinery, always seemed " unspiritual " and traditional. They believed, each time the movement appeared, that *they* had found the way to more abundant life, that the Spirit had come upon them in a special manner, and was through them inaugurating a higher order of Christianity, and they always felt that their religion of direct experience, of invading energy, of inspirational insights, of charismatic bestowals, and of profound emotional fervour was distinctly " spiritual," as contrasted with the historic Church which claimed indeed a divine origin and divine " deposits," but which, as they believed, lacked the continuous and progressive leadership of the Spirit. They were always very certain that their religion was characteristically " spiritual," and all other forms seemed to them cold, formal, or dead. In their estimates, men were still divided into spiritual persons and psychical persons—those who lived by the " heart " and those who lived by the " head."

Parallel with the main current of the Protestant Reformation, a new type of " spiritual religion " appeared and continued to manifest itself with mutations and developments, throughout the entire Reformation era, with a wealth of results which are still operative in the life of the modern world. The period of this new birth was a time of profound transition and ferment, and a bewildering variety of roads was tried to spiritual Canaans and new Jerusalems, then fondly believed to

---

[1] Many of these historical reappearances are considered in my *Studies in Mystical Religion.*

be near at hand. It is a long-standing tragedy of history that the right wing of a revolutionary or transforming movement must always suffer for the unwisdom and lack of balance of those who constitute the left, or extreme radical, wing of the movement. So it happened here. The nobler leaders and the saner spirits were taken in the mass with those of an opposite character, and were grouped under comprehensive labels of reproach and scorn, such as " Antinomians," " Enthusiasts," or " Anabaptists," and in consequence still remain largely neglected and forgotten.

The men who initiated and guided this significant undertaking—the exhibition in the world of what they persistently called "spiritual religion "—were influenced by three great historic tendencies, all three of which were harmoniously united in their type of Christianity. They were the Mystical tendency, the Humanistic or Rational tendency, and the distinctive Faith-tendency of the Reformation. These three strands are indissolubly woven together in this type of so-called spiritual Religion. It was an impressive attempt, whether completely successful or not, to widen the sphere and scope of religion, to carry it into *the whole of life*, to ground it in the very nature of the human spirit, and to demonstrate that to be a man, possessed of full life and complete health, is to be religious, to be spiritual. I propose, as a preliminary preparation for differentiating this special type of " spiritual religion," to undertake a study, as brief as possible, of these three underlying and fundamental strands or tendencies in religion which will, of course, involve some consideration of the inherent nature of religion itself.

For my present purpose it is not necessary to study the twilight history of religion in primitive races nor to trace its origins in the cradle-stage of human life. Anthropologists are rendering a valuable service in their attempts to explore the baffling region of primitive man's mind, and they have hit upon some very suggestive clues, though so far only tentative ones, to the psychological experiences and attitudes which set man's feet on the

momentous religious trail. At every stage of its long
and devious history, religion has been *some sort of life-
adjustment to realities which were felt to be of supreme
importance either to the individual or to the race,* and it
becomes thus possible for the scientific observer to note
a developmental process and to discover a principle
which links it in with a universal scheme of evolution.

But religion can never be adequately treated either
in terms of racial origins or of biological history, though
there can be no doubt whatever that there are genetic
and biological factors to be considered. Nor, again, can
religion be adequately and exhaustively dealt with by
the psychological method of investigation. The psychological studies of religion in recent years have greatly
enriched our knowledge of the range and scope and
power of man's psychic nature and functions, of his
instincts, desires, valuations, needs, yearnings, beliefs,
and modes of activity and behaviour, and particularly
of the important influence which the social group has
exercised and still exercises in the furtherance of religious
attitudes and ideals. But the psychological method has
obvious and inherent limitations. Like any other natural
science, psychology is limited to description and causal
explanation of the phenomena of its special field, which
in this case is states of consciousness. It does not
pretend, or even aspire, to pronounce upon the ultimate
nature of consciousness, nor upon the moral significance
of personality. Psychology is as empirical as any other
science. It modestly confines its scope of research to
what *appears* in finite and describable forms. It possesses
no ladder by which it can transcend the empirical
order, the fact-level. The religion which the psychologist reports upon is necessarily stripped of all transcendental and objective reference. Its wings are
severely clipped. It is only one of man's multitudinous
reactions in the presence of the facts of his time and
space world. It is nakedly subjective and *works*, not
because there is Something or Some One beyond, which
answers it, and corresponds with its up-reach, but only

because undivided faith-attitudes always liberate within the field of consciousness energy for life-activity.

We need not blame the psychologist for this radical reduction of the age-long pretensions of religion. If he is to bring religion over into the purview of the scientific field, he can do nothing else but reduce it. Science can admit into its world nothing that successfully defies descriptive treatment. The poet may know of flowers which " can give thoughts that do often lie too deep for tears," but science discovers no such flowers in its field. Its flowers are amazingly complex, but they call for no handkerchief. They are merely aggregations of describable parts, each of which has well-defined functions. The " man " whom science studies is complicated almost beyond belief. He is an aggregation of trillions of cells. He is such a centre of vibrations that a cyclone is almost a calm compared to the constant cyclic storms within the area of man's corporeal system. His " mental states " have their entries and exits before " the foot-lights of consciousness " and exhibit a drama more intricate than any which human genius has conceived. But each " state " is a definite, more or less describable, *fact* or *phenomenon*. For science, " man's " inner life, as well as his corporeal bulk, is an aggregate of empirical items. No loophole is left for freedom—that is for any novel undetermined event. No shekinah remains within for a mysterious " conscience " to inject into this fact-world insights drawn from a higher world of noumenal, or absolute, reality. " Man " is merely a part of the naturalistic order, and has no way of getting out of the vast net in which science catches and holds " all that is."

There is, I repeat, no ground for blaming the psychologist for making these reductions. His science can deal only with an order of facts which will conform to the scientific method, for wherever science invades a field, it ignores or eliminates every aspect of novelty or mystery or wonder, every aspect of reality which cannot be brought under scientific categories, *i.e.* every aspect which cannot be treated quantitatively and causally and

arranged in a congeries of interrelated facts occurring
according to natural laws. The only cogent criticism
is that any psychologist should suppose that his scientific
account is the " last word " to be spoken, that his reports
contain all the returns that can be expected, or that this
method is the only way of approach to truth and reality.
Such claims to the rights of eminent domain and such
dogmatic assertions of exclusive finality always reveal
the blind spot in the scientist's vision. He sees steadily
but he does not see wholes. He is of necessity dealing
with a reduced and simplified " nature " which he constantly tends to substitute for the vastly richer whole
of reality that boils over and inundates the fragment
which submits to his categories. We do well to gather
in every available fact which biology or anthropology or
psychology can give us that throws light on human
behaviour, or on primitive cults, or on the richer subjective and social religious functions of full-grown men.
But the interior insight got from religion itself, the rich
wholeness of religious experience, the discovery within
us of an inner nature which defies description and baffles
all plumb-lines, and which *can draw out of itself more than
it contains*, indicate that we here have dealings with a
type of reality which demands for adequate treatment
other methods of comprehension than those available
to science.

In the old Norse stories, Thor tried to empty the
famous drinking-horn in the games of Utgard, but to his
surprise he found that, though the horn looked small,
he could not empty it, for it turned out that the horn
was immersed in the limitless and bottomless ocean.
Again he tried to lift a small and insignificant-looking
animal, but, labour as he might, he could not lift it, for
it was grown into, and was organic with, the whole world,
and could not be raised without raising the very ground
on which the lifter stood ! Somewhat so, the reality of
religion is so completely bound up with the whole personal
life of man and with his conjunct life in the social group
and in the world of nature ; it is, in short, so much an

affair of man's whole of experience, of his spirit in its
undivided and synthetic aspects, that it can never be
adequately dealt with by the analytic and descriptive
method of this wonderful new god of science, however
big with results that method may be.

The interior insight, the appreciation of religion, the
rich and concrete whole of religious consciousness, is,
and will always remain, the primary way to the *secret*
of religion—religion in its " first intention "—as the
experience of time-duration is the only possible way to
the elemental meaning of time. It has in recent years
in many quarters become the fashion to call this " interior
insight," this appreciation of religion from within,
" mysticism " ; and to assume that here in mysticism
we come upon the very essence of religion. This conclusion, however, is as narrow and as unwarranted as is
the truncation of religion at the hands of science. The
mystical element in religion is only one element in a
vastly richer complex, and it must not be given undue
emphasis and imperial sway in the appreciation of the
complete whole of " spiritual religion." We must, too,
carefully discriminate *mystical experience* from the elabo-
rate body of doctrines and theories, historically known
as " mysticism," which is as much an *ism* as are the other
typical, partial, and more or less abstract formulations
of religion.

Mysticism for the mystic himself is characterized by
a personal experience through which the ordinary limitations of life and the passionate pursuits of the soul are
transcended, and a self-evident conviction is attained
that he is in communion, or even in union, with some
self-transcending Reality that absolutely satisfies and
is what he has always sought. " This is He, this is He,"
the mystic exclaims : " There is no other : This is He
whom I have waited for and sought after from my childhood ! " [1]

The experience is further characterized by the inrush

---

[1] Isaac Penington, " A True and Faithful Relation of my Spiritual Travails,"
Works (edition of 1761), i. pp. xxxvii.-xxxviii.

of new energies as though a mysterious door had been
pushed open—either out or in—admitting the human
spirit to wider sources of life. " Fresh bubblings from
the eternal streams of Life flowing into the soul " is the
way the recipient often describes it. All the deep-lying
powers of the inward self, usually so divergent and con-
flicting—the foreground purposes defeated by background
inhibitions, and by doubts on the border,—become
liberated and unified into one conscious life which is not
merely intellectual, nor merely volitional, nor solely
emotional, but an undivided whole of experience, intensely
joyous, enriched with insight and pregnant with deeds
of action. As in lofty experiences of appreciation of
beauty, or of music, or when the chords of life are swept
by a great love, or by a momentous moral issue, the
spirit rises in mystical experience to a form of consciousness which no longer marks clock-time and succession of
events, whether outward or inward. It may afterwards
take hours or days or weeks or even years to spread out
and review and apprehend and adjust to the experience
—" the opening," to use George Fox's impressive word—
but while it is *there* it is held in one unbroken synthetic
time-span. It is, to revive a scholastic phrase, a *totum
simul*, an all-at-once experience, in which parts, however
many, make one integral whole, as in a melody or in a
work of art ; so that the mystic has a real experience of
what we try to express by the word Eternity. It feels
as though the usual insulations of our own narrow personal
life were suddenly broken through and we were in actual
contact with an enfolding presence, life-giving, joy-
bringing, and light-supplying.

In instances where the intensity is great, unusual
psychological phenomena appear. Sometimes voices are
heard, or sounds " like a mighty rushing wind " ; sometimes there are automatic visions of light, or of forms or
figures, as, for instance, of Christ, or of a cross ; sometimes automatic writing or speaking attends the experience ; sometimes there are profound body-changes of a
temporary, or even permanent character ; sometimes there

is a state of swoon or ecstacy, lasting from a few seconds to entire days. These physical phenomena, however, are as spiritually unimportant and as devoid of religious significance as are the normal bodily resonances and reverberations which accompany, in milder degrees, all our psychic processes. They indicate no high rank of sainthood and they prove no miracle-working power. The significant features of the experience are the consciousness of fresh springs of life, the release of new energies, the inner integration and unification of personality, the inauguration of a sense of mission, the flooding of the life with hope and gladness, and the conviction, amounting in the mind of the recipient to certainty, that God is found as an environing and vitalizing presence— as the recipient already quoted reports his conviction : " I have met with my God ; I have met with my Saviour. I have felt the healings drop upon my soul from under His wings." [1]

If *everybody* had experiences of that sort there would be no more doubt of the existence of an actual spiritual environment in vitalizing contact with the human spirit than there now is of an external world with which we correspond. There is *a priori* no reason against the reality of such an inner spiritual universe. It is precisely as conceivable that constructive and illuminating influences should stream into our inner selves from that central Light with which our inmost self is allied, as that objects in space and time should bombard us with messages adapted to our senses. The difference is that we all experience the outer environment and only a few of us experience the inner. The mystic himself has no doubt— *he sees*, but he cannot give quite his certainty of vision to any one else. He cannot, like " the weird sisters " of Greek story, lend out his eye for others to see with. He can only talk about, or write about, what he has seen, and his words are often words of little meaning to those who lack the vision.

---

[1] Isaac Penington's *Works*, i. pp. xxxvii.-xxxviii.

II

But the very characteristics of mystical religion which give it its self-evidence and power at the same time mark limits to its scope and range. It is and must be primarily and essentially first-hand experience, and yet it is an experience that is by no means universal. It is not, so far as we can see from the facts at hand, an experience which attaches to the very nature of consciousness as such, or indeed one which is bound to occur even when the human subject strains forward all the energies of his will for the adventure, or when by strict obedience to the highest laws of life known to him he *waits* for the high visitation. Some aspect is involved over which the will has no control. Some other factor is implied besides the passion and the purity of the seeking soul. The experience " comes," as an inrush, as an emergence from the deeper levels of the inner life, but the glad recipient does not know how he secured the prize or how to repeat the experience, or how to tell his friend the way to these " master moments " of blessedness.

There are numerous persons who are as serious and earnest and passionate as the loftiest mystical saint, and who, in spite of all their listening for the inner flow of things, discover no inrushes, feel no invasions, are aware of no environing Companion, do not even feel a " More of Consciousness conterminous and continuous with their own." Their inner life appears impervious to divine bubblings. The only visitants that pass over the threshold of their consciousness are their own mental states, now bright and clear, now dim and strange, but all bearing the brand and mark of temporal origin. This type of experience must not, therefore, be insisted on as the only way to God or to the soul's homeland. Spiritual religion must not be put to the hazard of conditions that limit its universality and restrict it to a chosen few. To insist on mystical experience as the only path to religion would involve an " election " no less inscrutable and pitiless than that of the Calvinistic system—an " election " settled for each person by the peculiar psychic structure of his inner self.[1]

There is another limitation which must always attach to religion of the purely mystical type. In so far as it is an *experience* of the inward type, it is indescribable and incommunicable. That does not mean or imply any lessened value in the experience itself, it only means that it is very difficult to mint it into the universal coinage of the world. The recovery of faith, after some catastrophic bankruptcy of spiritual values, as with Job or Dante or Faust, cannot be described in analytic steps. The loss of faith in the rationality of the universe, the collapse of the " beautiful world " within, can be told step by step ; the process of integration and reconstruction, on the other hand, always remains somewhat of a mystery, though it is plain enough that a new and richer inner world has been found. So, too, with Mysticism. The experience itself may, and often does, bring to the recipient an indubitable certainty of spiritual realities, revealing themselves within his own spirit, and, furthermore, it is often productive of permanent life-results, such as augmented conviction, heightened tone of joy, increased unification of personality, intense moral passion and larger conquering power, but he, nevertheless, finds it a baffling matter to draw from his mystical experience concrete information about the nature and character of God, or to supply, from the experience alone, definite contributions that can become part of the common spiritual inheritance of the race.

>   The soul
> Remembering how she felt, but *what* she felt
> Remembering not, retains an obscure sense
> Of possible sublimity.[2]

---

[1] The exact and sharply-defined " ladders " of mystic ascent which form a large part of the descriptive material in books on Mystical Religion are far from being universal ladders. Like creeds, or like religious institutions, they powerfully assist certain minds to find the way home, but they seem unreal and artificial to many other persons, and they must be considered only as symbolisms which speak to the condition of a limited number of spiritual pilgrims.

[2] Wordsworth's " Prelude," Bk. ii.

There can be, I think, no doubt that the persons whom we call mystics have enormously added to the richness of our conception of God, or that they have made impressive contributions to the capital stock of our religious knowledge. But I question whether these increments of knowledge can be fairly traced to " information " which has entered the world through the secret door of mystical " openings." The conception of God by which we live, and our knowledge of eternal life, are in the main not formed of the material which has mysteriously dropped into the world by means of " sudden incursions," or " oracular communications " through persons of extraordinary psychical disposition. What we get from the mystic, or from the prophet, is not his " experience " but his interpretation, and as soon as he begins to *interpret*, he does so by means of the group-material which the race has gathered in its corporate experience through the ages. The valuable *content* of his message, so far as he succeeds in delivering one, the ideas with which his words are freighted, bear the marks of the slow accumulations of spiritual experience, and they reveal the rich and penetrative influence of the social group in which the mystic's inner life formed and ripened. They have a history as all ideas do.

The real fact of the matter is, that the great mystics are religious geniuses. They make their contribution to religion in ways similar to those in which the geniuses in other fields raise the level of human attainments and achievements. They swiftly seize upon and appreciate the specific achievements of the race behind them ; they are profoundly sensitive to the aspirations of their time and to the deep-lying currents of their age ; they are suggestible in an acute degree, through heightened interest, to certain ideas or truths or principles which they synthesise by such leaps of insight that slow-footed logic seems to be transcended. Then these unifying and intensifying experiences to which they are subject give them irresistible conviction, " a surge of certainty," a faith of the mountain-moving order, and an increasing dynamic of life which, in the best cases, is manifest in thoughts and words and deeds.   Their mystical experience seldom supplies them with a new intellectual content which they communicate, but their experience enables them rather to *see* what they know, to get possession of themselves, and to fuse their truth with the heat of conviction.   The mystical experience is thus a way of heightening life and of increasing its dynamic quality rather than a way to new knowledge.

The *negative way*, which has been such a prominent and prevailing characteristic of historical mysticism that many writers have made it the distinct and sufficient differentia of mysticism, has often produced intensity and depth, but it is, nevertheless, a mark of the limitation of this type of religion.   The indescribable and undifferentiated character of mystical experience is no doubt partly responsible for the emphatic place which negation has held in mysticism.   The experience itself, which seems like " a flight of the alone to the Alone," can be told in no words except those of negation.   " The mortal limit of the self " seems loosed, and the soul seems merged into that which it forever seeks but which having found it cannot utter.   But the type of metaphysics through which most of the great mystics of history have done their thinking and have made their formulations is still further responsible for the excessive negativity of their systems.

There is, of course, a negative element or aspect in all genuine religion.   No person can grow rich in spiritual experience or can gain an intimate acquaintance with a God of purity and truth without negating the easy ways of instinct, the low pursuits of life which end in self, the habits of thought and action which limit and hamper the realization of the diviner possibilities of the whole nature. Sometimes the eye that hinders must be plucked out or the right hand cut off and thrust away for the sake of a freer pursuit of the soul's kingdom.   There is, too, a still deeper principle of negativity involved in the very fibre of personal life itself.   No one can advance without

surrender, no one can have gains without losses, no one
can reach great goals without giving up many things in
themselves desirable.   There is "a rivalry of mes"
which no person can ever escape, for in order to choose
and achieve one typical self another possible self must
be sternly sacrificed.   In a very real sense it remains
forever true that we must die to live, we must die
to the narrow self in order to be raised to the wider
and richer self.

But the *negative way* of mysticism is more rigorous
and more thorough in its negation than that.   Its negations "wind up the hill all the way to the very top."
Even the *self* must be absolutely negated.   "The self,
the I, the me and the like, all belong to the evil spirit.
The whole matter can be set forth in these words : Be
simply and wholly bereft of self."   "The I, the me, and
the mine, nature, selfhood, the Devil, sin, are all one and
the same thing." [1] Not only so, but all *desire* for any
particular thing, or any particular experience must be
utterly extirpated.   "Whatever Good the creature as
creature can conceive of and understand is something
this or that," and therefore not the One Real Good. [2]
"So long as thy soul has an image, it is without simplicity,
and so long as it is without simplicity it doth not rightly
love God. [3] "Divine love can brook no rival."   He who
seeks God must "rid himself of all that pertains to the
creature."   He that would find the absolute Good must
withdraw not only beyond all his senses, but beyond all
desires, into an inner "solitude where no word is spoken,
where is neither creature nor image nor fancy."   "Everything depends," Tauler counsels us, "upon a fathomless
sinking into a fathomless nothingness. . . . God has
really no place to work in but the ground where all has
been annihilated. . . . Then when all forms have ceased,
in the twinkling of an eye, the man is transformed. . . .
Thou must sink into the unknown and unnamed abyss,
and above all ways, images, forms, and above all powers,

[1] *Theologia Germanica*, chaps. xxii. and xliii.
[2] *Ibid.* chap. liii.   [3] *Meister Eckhart*, Pfeiffer, p. 320. 20.

lose thyself, deny thyself, and even unform thyself.[1]
The moment the will focusses upon any concrete aim as
its goal, it must thereby miss that Good which is above
and beyond all particular " things " that can be conceived
or named.

But the *negative way* winds up farther still.   It ends
in the absolutely negative Silent Desert of Godhead
" where no one is at home."   Its way up is the way of
abstraction and withdrawal from everything finite.   He
whom the soul seeks cannot be found in anything " here "
or " now " ; He must be " yonder."   " It is by no means
permitted," says one of the great experts in negation,
" to speak or even to think anything concerning the
super-essential and hidden Deity. . . . It is a Unity above
mind, a One above conception and inconceivable to all
conceptions, a Good unutterable by word." [2]   " Thou
must love God," Eckhart says, " as not-God, not-Spirit,
not-person, not-image, but as He is, a sheer, pure, absolute
One, sundered from all two-ness and in whom we must
eternally sink from nothingness to nothingness." [3]   God,
the Godhead, is thus the absolute " Dark," " the nameless
Nothing," an empty God, a characterless Infinite.   " Why
dost thou prate of God," Eckhart says, " whatever thou
sayest of Him is untrue ! "   The rapt soul at the end of
his road, at the top of the hill, only knows that every
finite account is false and that the only adequate word
is an everlasting Nay.

> Whatever idea your mind comes at,
> I tell you flat
> God is *not* that.[4]

The great mystics have always saved themselves by
neglecting to be consistent with this rigorous negation
and abstraction.   In their practice they have cut through
their theory and gone on living the rich concrete life.

---

[1] Tauler's Sermons. See especially Sermons IV. and XXIII. in Hutton's
Inner Way.
[2] *The Divine Names* of Dionysius the Areopagite, chap. i. sec. i.
[3] *Meister Eckhart*, Pfeiffer, p. 320. 25-30.
[4] Quoted in W. H. J. Gairdner's *The Reproach of Islam*, p. 151.

But the theory itself is a false theory of life, and it leads
only to a God of abstraction, not to the God of spiritual
religion.   The false trail, however, is to be charged, as I
have said, not so much to mystical experience as to the
metaphysics through which the mystics, not only of
Christian communions, but of other faiths, were compelled
to do their thinking.   There was no other way of thinking
known to them except this way of negation.   The Infinite
was the not-finite ; the Absolute was precisely what the
contingent was *not*.   The perfect was free of every mark
of imperfection.   Behind all manifestations was the
essential Substance which made the manifestations.
The completely Real was above all mutation and process.
" For one to assign," therefore, " to God any human attributes," as Spinoza, the supreme apostle of this negative
way has said, " is to reveal that he has no true idea of
God."   It has taken all the philosophical and spiritual
travail of the centuries to discover that there may be a
concrete Infinite, an organic Absolute, an immanent
Reality, and that the way to share in this comprehending
Life is at least as much a way of affirmation as of negation,
a way that leads not into " the Dark " but into the
Light, and not into a " fathomless nothing," but into
an abundant and radiant life.

Mysticism, as a type of religion, has further staked its
precious realities too exclusively upon the functions of
what to-day we call the sub-conscious.   Impressed with
the divine significance of " inward bubblings," the mystic
has made too slight an account of the testimony of Reason
and the contribution of history.   The subconscious
functions are very real and very important aspects of
personal life, and can never again be ignored in any full
account of personality.   They influence every thought,
feeling, attitude, volition, opinion, mood, and insight,
and are thus operative in all the higher as well as in all
the lower phases of human life and character.   Metaphorically, but only metaphorically, we speak of the
sub-conscious as a vast zone, an indefinable margin,
surrounding the narrow focus of attention, and we may

figuratively, but only figuratively, call it the subliminal
" region " where all our life-gains, and often the gains
of the race, are garnered. The contributions from this
mental underworld are inestimable—we could not be
men without them—but this subconscious zone is a source
of things bad as well as good, things silly as well as things
wise, of rubbish as well as of treasures, and it is diabolical
as well as divine. It seems in rare moments to connect,
as though it were a hidden inland stream, with the
"immortal sea which brought us hither," and we feel at
times, through its incomes, as though we were aware of
tides from beyond our own margin. And, in fact, I
believe we are.

But obviously we cannot assume that whatever
comes spontaneously out of the subconscious is divinely
given. It mothers strange offspring—Esaus as well as
Jacobs; its openings, its inrushes, its bubblings must
be severely tested. Impulses of many sorts feel categoric-
ally imperative, but some call to deeds of light and some
to deeds of darkness. They cannot be taken at their face
value; they must be judged in some Court which is less
capricious and which is guided by a more universal
principle — something *semper et ubique*. A spiritual
religion of the full and complete type will, I believe, have
inward, mystical depth, it will keep vitalized and intensified
with its experiences of divine supplies, and of union and
unification with an environing Spirit, but it must at the
same time soundly supplement its more or less capricious
and subjective, and always fragmentary, mystical insights
with the steady and unwavering testimony of Reason,
and no less with the immense objective illumination of
History.

III

The men whom I am here calling Spiritual Reformers
are examples of this wider synthesis. They all read and
loved the mystics and they themselves enjoyed times of
direct refreshment from an inward Source of Life, but

they were, most of them, at the same time, devoted
Humanists.   They shared with enthusiasm the redis-
covery of those treasures which human Reason had produced, and they rose to a more virile confidence in the
sphere and capacity of Reason than had prevailed in Christian circles since the days of the early Greek Fathers. They
took a variety of roads to their conclusion, but in one
way or another they all proclaimed that deep in the
central nature of man—an inalienable part of Reason—
there was a Light, a Word, an Image of God, something
permanent, reliable, universal, and unsundered from God
himself.   They all knew that man is vastly more than
" mere man."   Hans Denck, one of the earliest of this
group of Spiritual Reformers, declared that there is a
witness to God in the soul of every man, and that without
this inward Word it would be as impossible to bring men
to God by outward means as it would be to show sunlight
to eyeless men.   He anticipated the great saying of
Pascal in these words, " Apart from God no one can
either seek or find God, for he who seeks God already in
truth has Him." [1]   " We are," says Jacob Boehme, who
belongs in this line of Spiritual Reformers, " of God's
substance : we have heaven and hell in ourselves." [2]
There is in us, Peter Sterry says, a *unity of spirit* which
holds all things together in an *at-once* experience, " a
spire-top of spirit where all things meet and sit recollected
and concentred in an unfathomed Depth of Life." [3]
Most of these men were in revolt against scholasticism
and all its works.   They speak often very slightingly of
" Reasoning," the attempt to find a way to ultimate
Realities by logical syllogisms, but they, nevertheless,
believed great things of man's rational and moral nature.
They are often confused and cloudy in their explicit
accounts of this ultimate moral and rational nature.
They everywhere indicate the conceptual limitations

---

[1] Denck's *Was geredet sey, dass die Schrift*, B. 2.   Pascal's saying is : " Comfort
thyself ; thou wouldst not be seeking Me hadst thou not already found Me."
—*Le Mystère de Jésus*, sec. 2.

[2] *The Threefold Life of Man*, xiv. 72.

[3] Sterry's *Rise, Race, and Royalty of the Kingdom of God in the Soul of Man*,
p. 24.

under which even those who were the most emancipated
from tradition were compelled to do their thinking in
that age. They could not break the age-long spell and
mighty fascination with which the Adam story and the
Garden of Eden picture had held the Christian world.
They were convinced, however, that the Augustinian
interpretation of the fall, with its entail of an indelible
taint upon the race forever, was an inadequate, if not an
untrue account, though they could not quite arrive at
an insight which enabled them to speak with authority
on the fundamental nature of man. But with an instinct
that pointed right, they took Adam as a type of the
unspoiled man, and they saw writ large in him the possibilities and potentialities of man. What had been
originally possible in Adam became, according to their
thought, actual realization in Jesus Christ—the form
and type of man, the true Head of the race—and in spite
of the havoc and spoiling, which sin had wrought, that
original possibility, that divine potentiality, still reappears
in every child, who comes now, as Adam did, made in
the image of God, with the breath of God in him, and
with creative freedom of will to settle his own destiny.
Some of the Reformers whom I am here studying centre
this image of God, this immense divine potentiality, in
the ideal man, in man as God conceives him in his perfect
state, or as God by His Grace intends him to be, and they
do not go the whole bold way of asserting that this man
we know, this man who lives in time and space, who
loves and sins and suffers, has and always has, in the
very structure of his inmost moral and rational being, a
divine, unlost, inalienable, soul-centre which is unsundered
from God, and bears eternal witness to our origin from
Him, our potential likeness to Him, and our capacity
to receive illumination from Him.[1] But this latter

---

[1] " The finite individual soul seems naturally to present a double aspect. It
looks like, on the one hand, a climax or concentration of the nature beneath it
and the community around it, and, on the other hand, a spark or fragment from
what is above and beyond it. It is crystallized out of the collective soul of
nature or society, or it falls down from the transcendental soul of heaven or
what is above humanity. In both cases alike it has its share of divinity."—
Bernard Bosanquet, *The Value and Destiny of the Individual* (London, 1913), p. 1.

bolder view of the inherent greatness of man's essential
nature is the prevailing tendency of these men. They
are thus the forerunners of the Quaker faith that there
is something of God in man, and they continue the direct
line, which goes back for ancestry to the Socratic movement in philosophy of those who find God involved and
implicated in the nature of normal self-consciousness and
in the idea of the Good toward which we live.[1]

Mystics and prophets, as Seely well says in *Ecce Homo*,
seem to themselves to " discover truth not so much by
a process of reasoning as by *an intense gaze,* and they
announce their conclusions with the voice of a herald,
using the name of God and giving no reasons." The
rational way of approach is different. It seeks to draw
out by a process of rational argument what is involved
in the outer or inner facts that are present to consciousness. It does not claim the power to make bricks without
clay, to construct its conclusions out of nothing. Its
only legitimate field is that of interpreting experience.
There have always been men who were religious because
they could not help being religious, because a Universe
without God seemed to them utterly irrational and un-
thinkable. Schleiermacher is only one witness in a long
and impressive succession of thinkers that have insisted
that " consciousness of God and self-consciousness are
inseparable.[2] It is obvious even to the unmetaphysical
person that self-consciousness always presupposes and
involves something prior to one's own existence and some
reality transcending the reality of one's own self. The
finite is intelligible only through the infinite, the temporal
only through the eternal. We cannot think at all without
appealing to some *permanent more of reality* than is just
now given in our particular finite experience, and no
matter how far one travels on the road of knowledge one
always finds it still necessary to make reference to *a
transcending more.* " All consciousness is," as Hegel

---

[1] The way to the world of Perfect Reality, Socrates says in the *Theaetetus,*
consists in likeness to God, nor is there, he adds, anything more like God than is
a good man.—*Theaetetus* 176 A and B.

[2] Schleiermacher's *Glaubenslehre.*

showed in 1807, in his philosophical Pilgrim's Progress, the *Phenomenology of Spirit*, " an appeal to more consciousness," and there is no rational halting-place short of a self-consistent and self-explanatory spiritual Reality, which explains the origin and furnishes the goal of all that is real.

On the other hand, there have always been men who have not granted any such compelling implications to self-consciousness. They have maintained that " finites " are forever " finites," and that there are no bridges that carry us from our finite " nows " and " heres " to an infinite Reality. The infinite Reality, they all admit, is conceivable ; it is " an idea " to which any mind can rise by normal processes of thought, " but," so they say, " an *idea* of an infinite Reality, an Infinite merely conceived in the mind, is different, by the whole width of the sky, from an actual objective infinite Reality that is *there*, and that contains inherently all that our hearts seek in God."

It is quite true, of course, that the presence of " an idea " in our mind does not of itself prove the existence of a corresponding objective reality *out there* in a world independent of our mind. There is most assuredly no way of bridging " the chasm " between mind and an objective world beyond and outside of mind, when once the " chasm " is assumed. But the fundamental error lies in the assumption of any such " chasm." The " chasm " which yawns between the inner and outer world is of our own making. Whenever we know anything, wherever there is knowledge at all, there is a synthetic indivisible whole of experience in which a subject knows an object. Subject and object cannot be really sundered without putting an instant end to knowledge— leaving " a bare grin without a face ! " The only way we know anything is that we know we know it in experience. We do not ever succeed in proving that objects exist *out there* in the world beyond us exactly correspondent to these ideas in our minds. That is a feat of mental gymnastics quite parallel to that of " finding " the self with which we do the seeking. The crucial problem of knowledge is not to discover a bridge to leap the chasm between the mind within and the world beyond. It is rather the problem of finding a basis of verifying and testing what we know, and of making knowledge a consistent rational whole.

The method of testing and verifying any fact of truth which we have on our hands, is always to organize it and link it into a larger whole of knowledge which we ourselves, or the wider group of persons in which we are organic members, have verified, and to see that it fits in consistently into this larger whole, and in this rational process we always assume, and are bound to assume, some sort of Reality that transcends the fleeting and temporal, the caprice of the moment, the will of the subject, the here and the now. The mind that knows and knows that it knows must, as Plato centuries ago declared, rise from the welter and flux of momentary seemings to true Being, to the eternally Real,[1] and the knowledge process of binding fragments of experience into larger wholes and of getting articulate insight into the significance of many facts grasped in synthetic unity—in the " spire-top of spirit," as Sterry puts it—carries the mind steadily and irresistibly on to an infinitely-inclusive and self-explanatory spiritual Whole, which is always implied in knowledge. Some reference to the *permanent* is necessary in judging even the fleetingness of the " now," some confidence in the eternally true is essential for any pronouncement upon the false, some assurance of the infinite is presupposed in the endless dissatisfaction with the finite, some appeal to a total whole of Reality is implicated in any assertion that *this fact here and now* is known as real. Any one who feels the full significance of what is involved in knowing the *truth* has a coercive feeling that Eternity has been set within us, that our finite life is deeply rooted in the all-pervading Infinite.

The great thinkers of the first rank who have undertaken to sound the significance of rational knowledge,

[1] *Republic* vii. 518 B.

and who have appreciated the meaning of the synthetic unity of the knowing mind and the world of objects that submit to its forms of thought, have recognized that there must be some deep-lying fundamental relation between the mind that knows and the world that is known, some Reality common to both outer and inner realms. They have, almost without exception, found themselves carried along irresistibly to an ultimate Reality that is the ground and explanation of all the fragmentary facts of experience, and without which nothing can be held to be permanent or rational—

> Something far more deeply interfused,
> Whose dwelling is the light of setting suns,
> And the round ocean and the living air,
> And the blue sky, and in the mind of man ;
> A motion and a Spirit, that impels
> All thinking things, all objects of all thought,
> And rolls through all things.[1]

The technical logical formulation of arguments to *prove* the existence of God as objectively real—arguments from causality, ontological arguments, and arguments from design—all of which assume a " chasm " between the knower and the object known, seem to us perhaps on critical analysis thin and insufficient. The bridge of formal logic seems too weak to carry us safely over from a finite here to an infinite yonder, from a contingent fact to an Absolute Reality, from something given *in* consciousness to Something existent outside and beyond it ; but it is an impressive and significant fact that all finite experience, both of inner and outer events, involves a More yet, that we cannot think finite and contingent things without rational appeal to Something infinite and necessary, that human experience cannot be rationally conceived except as a fragment of a vastly more inclusive Experience, always recognized within the finite spirit, that unifies and binds together into one self-explanatory whole all that is absolutely Real and True, and this is Reason's conviction of God.

[1] Wordsworth's " Tintern Abbey."

When once the conviction is *felt* and the rational postulate of God is made, it immediately verifies its practical value in the solution of our deepest problems. A happy illustration of the practical value and verifying evidence of the rational postulate of God has been given by James Ward : " Suppose," he says, " that the earth were wrapt in clouds all day while the sky was clear at night, so that we were able to see the planets and observe their movements as we do now, though the sun itself was invisible. The best account we could give of the planetary motions would still be to refer them to what for us, in accordance with our supposition, would only be an imaginary focus [or centre of physical energy], but one to which was assigned a position identical with the sun's [present] position." [1] This assumption would at once unlock the mystery and account for the varying movements of these visible bodies and the more rigorously the hypothesis were applied, the more exactly it would verify itself. So, too, with Reason's sublime venture of faith. The nature of self-consciousness demands the postulate, and once it is made it *works*.

The same result follows any attempt adequately to account for the moral imperative—the will to live the truly good life. The moral will turns out always to be imbedded in a deeper, richer, more inclusive Life than that of the fragmentary finite individual. There is a creative and autonomous central self in us which puts before us ideals of truth and beauty and goodness that are nowhere to be " found " in this world of sense-facts, and that yet are more real and august than any things our eyes see or our hands handle. Our main moral problem is not to adjust our inner ideals to our environment, but rather to compel the environment to level up to our ideals. The world that ought to be makes us forever dissatisfied with the world that is, and sets us with a fixity of purpose at the task of realizing the Kingdom which might possibly be, which we know ought to be, and which, therefore, has our loyal endeavour that it

[1] *Realm of Ends*, p. 230.

shall be, regardless of the cost in pain and sacrifice. Man, as William Wallace has put it, " projects his own self-to-be into the nature he seeks to conquer. Like an assailant who should succeed in throwing his standard into the strong central keep of the enemy's fortress, and fight his way thereto with assured victory in his eyes of hope, so man with the vision of his soul prognosticates his final triumph." [1] But if the life of moral endeavour is to be essentially consistent and reasonable there must be a world of Reality that transcends this realm of empirical, causal, and utilitarian happenings. Struggle for ends of goodness must be at least as significant in function as struggle for existence ; our passion for what ought to be must have had birth in an inner eternal environment at least as real as that which produced our instincts and appetite for the things by which we live in time. If the universe is through and through rational, there must be some personal Heart that *cares* ; some moral Will that guarantees and backs our painful strivings— our groaning and travailing—to make what ought to be come into play here in the world which is. This postulate is Reason's faith in God, and again it *works*.

The evolution of life—if it is evolving as we believe it is, and if it is to be viewed with rational insight as an upward process—irresistibly involves and implies some sort of fundamental intelligence and conscious purpose, some Logos steering the mighty movement. We have outgrown crude arguments from " design," and we cannot think of God as a foreign and external Creator, working as a Potter on his clay ; but it is irrational to " explain " a steadily unfolding movement, an ever-heightening procession of life, by " fortuitous variations," by " accidental " shifts of level, or even by a blind *élan vital*. If there is an increasing purpose and a clearly culminating drama unfolding in this moving flood of life, then there is some Mind that sees the way, and some Will that directs the march of Life. And this confidence of ours in some divine Event to which the whole creation moves,

[1] *Lectures and Addresses*, p. 193.

this insight that there must be a significant and adequate
explanation for the immanent teleology and beauty with
which our universe is crammed, is, once more, Reason's
postulate of God.   There is something in us, indissoluble
from Reason itself—a Light, a Word, a Witness as these
Spiritual Reformers insisted—which links us in all the
deeper processes of self-consciousness with *That Which Is*
and without which " knowledge " would be a mere flux
of seemings, a flight of *seriatim* items.

IV

> When this world's pleasures for my soul sufficed,
> Ere my heart's plummet sounded depths of pain,
> I called on reason to control my brain,
> And scoffed at that old story of the Christ.
>
> But when o'er burning wastes my feet had trod,
> And all my life was desolate with loss,
> With bleeding hands I clung about the cross,
> And cried aloud, " Man needs a suffering God." [1]

There can be no doubt that the compulsions and
implications of rational insight have brought multitudes
of men to God, have given them an unescapable conviction
of His reality, and have swayed their wills to live in conformity to His perfect Goodness ; and it is also true that
when for any cause this clue of rationality is missed or
lost, men flounder about in the fog and pass through
periods of inward tragedy amounting often to despair.
But the approach of Reason still leaves much to be
desired.   It points to something deeper than the transitory
flux of things, it raises our minds to some sort of ultimate
and self-explanatory Reality, it compels the conviction
that there is an all-inclusive Logos—Mind or Spirit—that
explains what is and what ought to be, and what in the
unfolding course of things is to be ; but it does not bring
us to a personal God who is our loving Friend and the

---

[1] Ella Wheeler Wilcox, *Poems of Life and Moments.*

intimate Companion of our souls, it does not help us solve the mystery of human suffering that lies heavily upon our lives, and it does not bring to our spirits *the saving reinforcement of personal Love* that must be a central feature of a spiritual and adequate religion.

There is still another way of approach to a Religion for mature minds which has been no less universally operative and no less dynamic in its transforming effects upon human lives than either of the two tendencies so far considered—I refer to the way of Faith. By Faith I mean the soul's moral or appreciative apprehension of God as *historically revealed,* particularly as revealed in the personal life of Jesus Christ. This Faith-way to God cannot be wholly separated—except by an artificial abstraction—from the inward way of mysticism, or from the implications of Reason. It is no blind acceptance of traditional opinions, no uncritical reliance on "authority," or on some mysterious infallible oracle. It is the spiritual response—or "assent," as Clement of Alexandria called it—the moral swing of our inmost self, as we catch insights of a loving Heart and holy Will revealed through the words and lives and sufferings of saints and prophets, who have lived by their vision of God, and supremely revealed in the Life and Love, the Passion and the Triumphs of that Person whose experience and character and incarnation of life's possibilities seem at last adequate for all the needs—the heights and the depths—of this complex life of ours.

It was Luther's living word which first brought the momentous significance of Faith to clear consciousness in the sixteenth century. But the new way of Faith meant many and discordant things, according to the preparation of the ears of those who heard. It spoke, as all Pentecosts do, to each man in his own tongue. To those who came to the Lutheran insight with a deep hunger of spirit for reality and with minds liberated by Humanistic studies, the Faith-message meant new heavens and a new earth. It was a new discovery of God, and a new estimate of man. They suddenly caught a vision of life as it was capable of becoming, and they committed their fortunes to the task of making that possible world real. By a shift of view, as revolutionary as that from Ptolemaic astronomy to the verifiable insight of Copernicus, they passed over from the dogma of a Christ who came to appease an angry God, and to found a Church as an ark of safety in a doomed world, to the living apprehension of a Christ—verifiable in experience —who revealed to them, in terms of His own nature, an eternally tender, loving, suffering, self-giving God, and who made them see, with the enlightened eyes of their heart, the divine possibilities of human life. Through this insight, they were the beginners of a new type of Christianity, which has become wide-spread and impressive in the modern world, a type that finds the supreme significance of Christ's Life in His double revelation of the inherent nature of God, and the immense value and potentiality of man, and that changes the emphasis from schemes of salvation to interpretations of life, from the magic significance of doctrine to the incalculable worth of the moral will.

These men were weak in historical sense, and, like everybody else in their generation, they used Scripture without much critical insight. But they hit upon a principle which saved them from slavery to texts, and which gave them a working faith in the steady moral and spiritual development of man. I mean the principle that this Christ whom they had discovered anew was an eternal manifestation of God, an immanent Word of God, a Spirit brooding over the world of men, as in the beginning over the face of the waters, present in the unfolding events of history as well as in the far-away " dispensations of Grace." As a result, they grew less interested in the problem that had fascinated so many mystics, the problem of the super-empirical evolution of the divine Conscious-ness ; the super-temporal differentiation of the unity of the Godhead into a Father and Son and self-revealing Holy Ghost ; and they tried rather to appreciate and to declare the concrete revelation through Christ, and the import of His visible and invisible presence in the world.[1]

This approach of Faith, this appreciation of the nature of God as He has been unveiled in the ethical processes of history, especially in the Person of Christ, and in His expanding conquest of the world, must always be one of the great factors of spiritual religion. The profound results of higher criticism, with its stern winnowings, have brought us face to face with problems unknown to the sixteenth and seventeenth centuries. So much of what seemed the solid continent of historical truth has weathered and crumbled away that some have wondered whether any irreducible nucleus would remain firm and permanent above the flood of the years, and whether the religion of the future must not dispense with the historical element, and the Faith-aspect that goes with it, and rest wholly upon present inward experience.

There are, however, I believe, no indications worth considering, of the disappearance of Jesus Christ from human history. On the contrary, He holds, as never before, the commanding place in history. He still dominates conscience, by the moral sway of His Life of Goodness, as does no other Person who has ever lived ; and by the attractive power of His life and love He still sets men to living counter to the strong thrust of instinct and impulse as does no one else who has ever touched the springs of conduct. The Faith-aspect is still a very live element in religion, and it is, as it has been so often before, precisely the aspect which supplies concrete body and filling and objective ethical direction to our deep sub-conscious yearnings and strivings and experiences.

Once at least there shone through the thin veil of matter a personal Life which brought another kind of world than this world of natural law and utilitarian aims full into light. There broke through here in the face of Jesus

---

[1] Jacob Boehme, however, shows this fascination for the super-empirical at its height and culmination. It was an attempt, though a bungling attempt, to pass from an abstract God to a God of *character*, and it was a circuitous way of getting round the problem of evil.

Christ a revelation of Purpose in the universe so far beyond the vague trend of purpose dimly felt in slowly evolving life that it is possible here to catch an illuminating vision of what the goal of the long drama may be— the unveiling of sons of God. Here the discovery can be made that the deepest Reality toward which Reason points, and which the mystical experience *feels*, is no vague Something Beyond, but a living, loving Some One, dealing with us as Person with person. In Him there comes to focus in a Life that we can love and appreciate a personal character which impresses us as being absolutely good, and as being in its inexhaustible depth of Love and Grace worthy to be taken as the revelation of the true nature of the God whom all human hearts long for. And finally through this personal revelation of God in Christ there has come to us a clear insight that pain and suffering and tragedy can be taken up into a self-chosen Life and absorbed without spoiling its immense joy, and that precisely through suffering-love, joyously accepted, a Person expressing in the world the heart of God may become the moral and spiritual Saviour of others. As von Hügel has finely said : " A Person came and lived and loved, and did and taught, and died and rose again, and lives on by His power and His Spirit forever within us and amongst us, so unspeakably rich and yet so simple, so sublime and yet so homely, so divinely above us precisely in being so divinely near that His character and teaching require, for an ever fuller yet never complete understanding, the varying study, and different experiments and applications, embodiments and unrollings of all the races and civilizations, of all the individual and corporate, the simultaneous and successive experiences of the human race to the end of time." [1]

The only salvation worth talking about is that which consists of an inner process of moral transformation, through which one passes over " the great divide " from a life that is self-centred and dominated by impulse and sin to a life that is assured of divine forgiveness, that has

[1] *Mystical Elements of Religion*, i. p. 26.

conceived a passion for a redeemed inward nature, that is conscious of help from beyond its own resources, and that is dedicated to the task of making moral goodness triumph over the evil of the world. Any experience which brings to the soul a clear vision of the moral significance of human life, and that engenders in us a practical certainty that God is working with us in all our deepest undertakings, tends to have saving efficacy and to bring about this inward transformation. But nowhere else in the universe—above us or within us—has the moral significance of life come so full into sight, or the reality of actual divine fellowship, whether in our aspirations or in our failures, been raised to such a pitch of practical certainty as in the personal life and death and resurrection and steady historical triumph of Jesus Christ. He exhibits in living fulness, with transforming power, a Life which consciously felt itself one with the heart and will of God. He reveals the inherent blessedness of Love—even though it may involve suffering and pain and death. He shows the moral supremacy, even in this imperfect empirical world, of the perfectly good will, and He impresses those who *see* Him—see Him, I mean, with eyes that can penetrate through the temporal to the eternal and find His real nature—as being the supreme personal unveiling of God, as worthy to be our Leader, our Ideal Life, our typical personal Character, and strong enough in His infinite Grace and divine self-giving to convince us of the eternal co-operation of God with our struggling humanity, and to settle our Faith in the essential Saviourhood of God.

He who sees *that* in Christ has found a real way to God and has discovered a genuine way of salvation. It is the way of Faith, but Faith is no airy and unsubstantial road, no capricious leap. There is no kind of aimful living conceivable that does not involve faith in something trans-subjective—faith in something not given in present empirical experience. Even in our most elementary life-adjustments there is something operative in us which far underlies our conscious perceiving and the logic of our conclusions. We are moved, not alone by what we clearly picture and coldly analyse, but by deep-lying instincts which defy analysis, by background and foreground fringes of consciousness, by immanent and penetrative intelligence which cannot be brought to definite focus, by the vast reservoirs of accumulated wisdom through which we *feel* the way to go, though we can pictorially envisage no " spotted trees " that mark the trail.

This religious and saving Faith, through which the soul discovers God and makes the supreme life-adjustment to Him, is profoundly moral and, in the best sense of the word, rational. It does not begin with an assumption, blind or otherwise, as to Christ's metaphysical nature, it does not depend upon the adoption of systematically formulated doctrines ; it becomes operative through the discovery of a personal Life, historically lived—and continued through the centuries as a transforming Spirit —rich enough in its experience to exhibit the infinite significance of life, inwardly deep enough in its spiritual resources to reveal the character of God, and strong enough in sympathy, in tenderness, in patience, and in self-giving love to beget forever trust and confidence and love on the part of all who thus find Him.

The God whom we learn to know in Christ—the God historically revealed—is no vague first Cause, no abstract Reality, no all-negating Absolute. He is a concrete Person, whose traits of character are intensely moral and spiritual. His will is no fateful swing of mechanical law ; it is a morally good will which works patiently and forever toward a harmonized world, a Kingdom of God. The central trait of His character is Love. He does not *become* Father, He is not reconciled to us by persuasive offerings and sacrifices. He is inherently and by essential disposition Father and the God of all Grace. He is not remote and absentee—making a world " in the beginning," and leaving it to run by law, or only occasionally interrupting its normal processes—He is immanent Spirit, working always, the God of beauty and organizing purpose. He is Life and Light and Truth, an Immanuel God who can and does show Himself in a personal Incarnation, and so exhibits the course and goal of the race. The way of Faith is a way to God, and the religion of this type is as properly *a first-hand religion* as that of any other type.

I have, of course, by no means exhausted the types of mature religion. There are other ways of approach to God, other roads by which the soul finds the way home—" On the East three gates ; on the North three gates ; on the South three gates ; and on the West three gates "—and they will continue to be sacred ways —*viae sacrae*—for those who travel them and thus find their heart's desire. What we should learn from this brief study is that religion is too rich and complex an experience to be squeezed down to some one isolated aspect of life or of consciousness. There are many ways to God and any way that actually brings the soul to Him is a good way, but the best way is that one which produces upon the imperfect personal life the profoundest saving effects, the most dynamic moral reinforcement, and which brings into sway over the will the goal of life most adequate for men like us in a social world like ours.

For most of us no one way of approach—no single type of religion—is quite sufficient for all the needs of our life. Most of us are fortunate enough to have at least moments when we feel in warm and intimate *contact* with a divine, enwrapping environment more real to us than things of sense and of arithmetic, and when the infinite and eternal is no less, but immeasurably more, sure than the finite and temporal. Most of us, again, succeed, at least on happy occasions of mental health, in finding rational clues which carry us through the maze of contingency and clock-time happenings, through the imperfections of our slow successive events, to the One Great Now of perfect Reality which explains the process, and we attain to an intellectual love of God. And in spite of the literary difficulties of primitive narratives and of false trails which the historical Church has again and again taken, almost any serious, earnest soul to-day may find that divine Face, that infinitely deep and luminous Personality who spoke as no man ever spake, who loved as none other ever loved, who saw more in humanity than anybody else has ever seen, and who felt as no other person ever has that He was one in heart and mind and will with God ; and having found Him, by a morally responsive Faith which dominates and transforms the inward self, one has found God as Companion, Friend, and Saviour.   Where all these ways converge, and a soul enjoys the privilege of mystical contact, the compulsion of rational insight, and the moral reinforcement of personal Faith in Christ, religion comes to its consummate flower, and may with some right be called " spiritual Religion."

V

The most radical step which these spiritual Reformers took—the step which put them most strikingly out of line with the main course of the Reformation—was their break with Protestant Theology.   They were not satisfied with a programme which limited itself to a correction of abuses, an abolition of mediaeval superstitions, and a shift of external authority.   They were determined to go the whole way to a Religion of inward life and power, to a Christianity whose only authority should be its dynamic and spiritual authority.   They placed as low an estimate on the saving value of orthodox systems of theological formulation as the Protestant Reformers did on the saving value of " works."   To the former, salvation was an affair neither of " works " nor of what they called " notions," *i.e.* views, beliefs, or creeds.   They are never weary of insisting that a person may go on endless pilgrimages to holy places, he may repeat unnumbered " paternosters," he may mortify his body to the verge of self-destruction, and still be unsaved and unspiritual ; so, too, he may " believe " all the dogma of the most orthodox system of faith, he may take on his lips the most sacred words of sound doctrine, and yet be utterly alien to the kingdom of God, a stranger and a foreigner to the spirit of Christ. They were determined, therefore, to go through to a deeper centre and to make only those things pivotal which are absolutely essential to life and salvation.

They began their reconstruction of the meaning of salvation with (1) a new and fresh interpretation of God, and (2) with a transformed eschatology. As I have already said, they re-discovered God through Christ, and in terms of His revelation ; and coming to God *this way*, they saw at once that the prevailing interpretations of the atonement were inadequate and unworthy. God, they declared, is not a Suzerain, treating men as his vassals, reckoning their sins up against them as infinite debts to be paid off at last in a vast commercial transaction only by the immeasurable price of a divine Life, given to pay the debt which had involved the entire race in hopeless bankruptcy. Nor, again, in their thought is He a mighty Sovereign, meting out to the world strict justice and holding all sin as flagrant disloyalty and appalling violation of law, never to be forgiven until the full requirements of sovereign justice are met and balanced and satisfied. All this seemed to them artificial and false. Salvation, as they understand it, cannot be conceived as escape from debt nor as the satisfaction of justice, since it is a personal life-relationship with a personal God who is and always was eternal Love. God's universe, both outer and inner, is loaded with moral significance, is meant for discipline, and therefore it has its stern aspects and drives its lessons home with the unswerving hammer of *consequences*. But in the personal Heart of the universe, Love and Tenderness and Sympathy and Forgiveness are supreme, and every process and every instrument of salvation, in the divine purpose, is vital, ethical, spiritual.

God has shown Himself as Father. He has revealed the immeasurable suffering which sin inflicts on love. To find the Father-Heart ; to cry " Abba " in filial joy ; to die to sin and to be born to love, is to be saved. Jacob Boehme gave this new conception of God, and its bearing

on the way of salvation, the most adequate expression
that was given by any of this group, but all these so-called
spiritual Reformers herein studied had reached the same
insight at different levels of adequacy.   Their return to
a more vital conception of salvation, with its emphasis
on the value of personality, brought with it, too, a new
humanitarian spirit and a truer estimate of the worth
of man.   As they re-discovered the love of God, they also
found again the gospel of love and brotherhood which
is woven into the very tissue of the original gospel of
divine Fatherhood.

Their revised eschatology was due, at least partly, to
this altered account of the character of God, but it was
also partly due to their profound tendency to deal with
all matters of the soul in terms of life and vital processes.
Heaven and Hell were no longer thought of as terminal
places, where the saved were everlastingly rewarded and
the lost forever punished.   Heaven and Hell were for
them inward conditions, states of the soul, the normal
gravitation of the Spirit toward its chosen   centre.
Heaven and Hell cease, therefore, to be eschatological
in the true sense of the word ;   they become present
realities, tendencies of life, ways of reacting toward the
things of deepest import.   Heaven, whether here or in
any other world, is the condition of complete adjustment
to the holy will of God ;   it is joy in the prevalence of His
goodness ;   peace through harmonious correspondence
with His purposes ;   the formation of a spirit of love, the
creation of an inward nature that loves what God loves
and enjoys what He enjoys.

Hell, here or elsewhere, is a disordered life, out of
adjustment with the universal will of God ;   it is concentration upon self and self-ends ;   the contraction of
love ;   the shrinking of inward resources ;   the formation
of a spirit of hate, the creation of an inward nature that
hates what God loves.   Hell is the inner condition
inherently attaching to the kind of life that displays
and exhibits the spirit and attitude which must be overcome before God with His purposes of goodness can be

ultimately triumphant and all in all. Salvation, therefore, cannot be thought of in terms of escape from a place
that is dreaded to a place that is desired as a haven. It
is through and through a spiritual process—escape from
a wrongly fashioned will to a will rightly fashioned. It
is complete spiritual health and wholeness of life, brought
into operation and function by the soul's recovery of God
and by joyous correspondence with Him.

Here is the genuine beginning in modern times of what
has come to be the deepest note of present-day Christianity,
*the appreciation of personality as the highest thing in earth
or heaven*, and the initiation of a movement to find the
vital sources and resources for the inner kindling of the
spirit, and for raising the whole personal life to higher
functions and to higher powers.

Putting the emphasis, as they did, on personal religion,
i.e. on experience, instead of on theology, they naturally
became exponents of free-will, and that, too, in a period
when fore-ordination was a central dogma of theology.
This problem of freedom, which is as deep as personality
itself, always has its answer " determined " by the point
of approach. For those who *begin* with an absolute and
omnipotent God, and work down from above, the neces-
sarian position is determined. Their answer is : " All
events are infallibly connected with God's disposal."
For those who start, however, from actual experience
and from the testimony of consciousness, freedom feels
as certain as life itself. Their answer is : " Human will
is a real factor in the direction of events and man shapes
his own destiny toward good or evil." Calvin's logic is
irresistible if his assumptions are once granted. These
spiritual Reformers, however, were untouched by it,
because they began from the interior life, with its dramatic
movements, as their basal fact, and man as they knew
him was free.

This spiritual movement involved, as a natural development, an entire shift from the historical idea of the Church
as an authoritative and supernatural instrument of salvation, to a Church whose authority was entirely vital,

ethical, spiritual, dynamic. The Church of these spiritual
Reformers was a Fellowship, a Society, a Family, rather
than a mysterious and supernatural entity. They felt
once again, as powerfully perhaps as it was possible in
their centuries to feel it, the immense significance of the
Pauline conception of the Church as the continued embodiment and revelation of Christ, the communion of saints
past and present who live or have lived by the Spirit.
Through this spiritual group, part of whom are visible
and part invisible, they held that the divine revelation
is continued and the eternal Word of God is being uttered
to the race. " The true religion of Christ," as one of
these spiritual teachers well puts it, " is written in the
soul and spirit of man by the Spirit of God ; and the
believer is the only book in which God now writes His
New Testament." [1] This Church of the Spirit is always
being built. Its power is proportional to the spiritual
vitality of the membership, to the measure of apprehension
of divine resources, to the depth of insight and grasp of
truth, to the prevalence of love and brotherhood, to the
character of service, which the members exhibit. It
possesses no other kind of power or authority than the
power and authority of personal lives formed into a community by living correspondence with God, and acting
as human channels and organs of His Life and Spirit.
Such a Church can meet new formulations of science and
history and social ideals with no authoritative and con-
clusive word of God which automatically settles the issue.
Its only weapons are truth and light, and these have to
be continually re-discovered and re-fashioned to fit the
facts which the age has found and verified. Its mission
is *prophetic*. It does not dogmatically decide what facts
must be believed, but it sees and announces the spiritual
significance of the facts that are discovered and verified.
It was, thus, in their thought a growing, changing, ever-
adjusting body—the living body of Christ in the world.
To the Protestant Reformers this spiritual ideal presented " a Church " so shorn and emasculated as to be

---

[1] William Dell's sermon on " The Trial of Spirits," *Works*, p. 438.

absolutely worthless. It seemed to them a propaganda which threatened and endangered the mighty work of reformation to which they felt themselves called, and they used all the forces available to suppress and annihilate those of this other " way."

Nearly four hundred wonderful years have passed since the issue was first drawn, since the first of these spiritual prophets uttered his modest challenge. There can be no question that the current of Christian thought has been strongly setting in the direction which these brave and sincere innovators took. I feel confident that many persons to-day will be interested in these lonely men and will follow with sympathy their valiant struggles to discover the road to a genuine spiritual religion, and their efforts to live by the eternal Word of God as it was freely revealed as the Day Star to their souls.

CHAPTER I

THE MAIN CURRENT OF THE REFORMATION

I

ONE of the greatest tragedies in Christian history is the division of forces which occurred in the Reformation movements of the sixteenth century. Division of forces in the supreme spiritual undertakings of the race is of course confined to no one century and to no one movement ; it is a very ancient tragedy. But the tragedy of division is often relieved by the fact that through the differentiation of opposing parties a vigorous emphasis is placed upon aspects of truth which might otherwise have been allowed to drop out of focus. This sixteenth-century division is peculiarly tragic, because through the split in the lines the very aspects of truth which were most needed to give the movement a steady increment of insight and power were lost in the din and confusion of party warfare.

There was a short but glorious period—the years from 1517 to 1523—during which it seemed as though the spiritual and intellectual travail of the three preceding centuries was to consummate in the birth of a movement that would draw together and unify all the liberating forces which had slowly become available. The Humanists of the Renaissance, no less than Columbus, were finding a new world.[1] They had boldly travelled out beyond the

[1] In the South the movement showed a tendency to drift back into a refined paganism. In the North, however, it was deeply Christian in interest, in feeling, and in its moral aspirations. Erasmus was by far the greatest figure and the most influential person in the group of Humanists of this latter type.

boundaries which the medieval mind had set to human
interests, and had discovered that man was more than
the abstract being whose " soul " had alone concerned
ecclesiastics and schoolmen. Man, the Humanists saw,
is possessed in his own right of great powers of reason.
He is a creative and autonomous being, he has vast
capacities for life and enjoyment to which the Church
had failed to minister. They stood amazed at the
artistic and literary culture, the political and intellectual
freedom and the great richness of life which the newly
discovered classical literature revealed as having existed
in the pre-Christian world, and at the wonderful comprehension of life revealed in the Gospels. With com-
mendable passion they proposed to refresh and reshape
the world through the new models, the new ideals, and
the new spirit which they had discovered. First of all
they would wipe out the old Augustinian cleavage which
had carried its sharp dualism wherever it ran. They
would no longer recognize the double world scheme—a
divine realm set over against an undivine realm, the
" sacred " set over against the " secular," the spiritual
set over against the natural, the Church set against the
world, faith set in contrast to reason, the spirit pitted
against the flesh, " the other world " put in such light
that " this world " by contrast lay dull in the shadow.
Those who were broadened and liberated by the new
learning found not only a new world in classical literature,
but they also found a new gospel in the Gospel. As
they studied the New Testament documents themselves
and became freed from the bondage of tradition they
discovered that the primitive message dealt with life
and action rather than with theology. They found the
key to the Gospel in the Sermon on the Mount, and in
the Parables of Jesus, and they shifted the emphasis from
doctrine to ethics. This change of emphasis quite
naturally involved another change. It brought man
into greater prominence, and the Church as an ecclesiastical system into less prominence ; for life, they discovered, was settled in the teaching of Christ by the

attitude of the will and by the formation of character,
rather than by the mediation of a priesthood external to
man. " I wish," Erasmus wrote to Capito in 1518,
" that there could be an end of scholastic subtleties, or,
if not an end, that they could be thrust into a second
place and Christ be taught plainly and simply. The
reading of the Bible and the early Fathers will have
this effect. Doctrines are taught now which have no
affinity with Christ, and only darken our eyes." [1]
Again in 1521 he wrote to a friend, words which appear
again and again in his letters : " It would be well for
us if we thought less about our dogmas and more about
the gospel," [2] or, as he often puts it, " if we made less
of dogmatic subtleties and more of Scripture." So far
as Humanism was a religious force it was pushing toward
a religion of the lay-type, with man himself—man with
his momentous will—as the centre of interest.

Another important influence was slowly but per-
vasively filtering down into the life of the people and
preparing the way for a religion of greater personal
vitality and spiritual inwardness ; I mean the testimony
of the great mystics. One has only to study the life
and writings of such a scholar as Nicolaus Chrypffs—
generally called Cusanus, or Nicholas of Cusa—who died
shortly before Luther was born,[3] to see what a live force
the mystical teaching was even in this period of Renaissance. God is for him, as for his great masters, Plotinus,
Erigena, Eckhart, and Tauler, the infinite and indescribable subsoil of the universe, in whose Reality all the roots
of life and all the reality of things are grounded. The
soul, by nature spiritual and immortal, at its apex rises
above the contradictions which lower knowledge everywhere meets and comes into possession, by a " learned
ignorance," of Truth itself and into an unspeakable
union with God. But it was not merely among scholars
like Nicholas that mysticism formed the elemental basis
of life and thought ; it had, through the circles of the

---

[1] Epistle CCVII.   [2] Epistle DLXXXVII.
[3] 1401–1464.

" Brothers of the Common Life," [1] and through such masterpieces as the *Imitation of Christ*, the *Theologia Germanica*, and the Sermons of Eckhart and of John Tauler, become a part of the spiritual atmosphere which serious-minded men breathed. Every one of the men who belong in my list of " Spiritual Reformers " read and loved " the golden book of German Theology," and most of them knew the other writings of the great fourteenth-century mystics. There are unmistakable evidences of a subtle formative influence from these rich sources, which explains the simultaneous sporadic outbreak of similar views in widely sundered places.

There was, thus, abroad at the opening of the Reformation a deep yearning among serious people for a religion of inward experience, a religion based not on proof-texts nor on external authority of any kind, but on the native capacity of the soul to seek, to find and to enjoy the living God who is the Root and Sap of every twig and branch of the great tree of life. The general trend of this mystical tendency, as also of the Humanistic movement, was in the direction of lay-religion, and both movements alike emphasized the inherent and native capacity of man, whose destiny by his free choice is in his own hands.

There were, too, at work many other deep-lying tendencies away from the bondage and traditions of the past ; aspiration for economic and social reforms to liberate the common people and give them some real chance to be persons—tendencies which all the Reformers treated in this book deeply felt and shared.

All these movements toward intellectual, spiritual, and social freedom seemed at first to find their champion in the dynamic hero, whose ninety-five theses on the door at Wittenberg shook the world awake in 1517. He was by birth and spirit a child of the people—" ein Kind des Volkes "—and he seemed to be a prophet, divinely called to voice their dumb aspirations. He possessed,

---

[1] Nicholas belonged to one of these circles. " The Brethren of the Common Life " are treated in my *Studies in Mystical Religion*, chap. xiv.

like all great prophets, a straightforward moral honesty
and sincerity, an absolute fearlessness, a magnetic and
commanding personality, an unusual mastery of the
vernacular speech, and an abundant power of pathos,
humour, and satire. All the world loves a hero who
can say in the face of real danger, " I would go forward
to Worms if there were as many devils there as there are
tiles on the roof ! " or again, " I would go to Leipzig
if it rained Duke Georges for nine days running ! " [1]

He had, too, unusual religious depth and power which
sprang, as in the case of the great mystics, from a profound inward experience. Luther, like St. Paul and
St. Augustine, and many another spiritual guide of the
race, came upon his supreme insights in sudden epoch-
making revelations or illuminations by which he found
himself on a new level, with the line of march shifted
and all values altered. His conversion and dedication
to religion was an instance of this type. So, too, was
his discovery of the way of Faith. Legend has very
likely coloured our accounts of this experience, but for
purposes of valuation it is of little moment to us whether
the dynamic flash came to him in his cell at Wittenberg
as he was studying the Epistle to the Romans, or whether
it came while he was climbing the penitential stairway
in Rome.[2] When all legendary coverings are stripped
away we have left an inner event of the first importance,
a *live idea* bursting into consciousness like a new star on
the field of vision. By processes much deeper and richer
than those of logical argument, his mind leaped to the
certainty of infinite grace and forgiving love in God as
revealed in Christ. In a word, this baffled and despairing
monk, striving in vain to heap up merits enough to win

---

[1] Letter to the Elector Frederick, March 5, 1522.
[2] The story that Luther, climbing the *Scala Santa* in 1510, suddenly was impressed by the words, " The just shall live by faith," is based on a reminiscence
of Luther's son Paul. Luther's own reference to the ascent of the *Scala Santa*
makes no allusion to any such experience. He merely says that when he reached
the top of the stairs, which he climbed in the hope of getting the soul of an ancestor
out of Purgatory, he thought to himself, " Who knows whether this prayer will
avail ? " Luther began his lectures on *Romans* in 1515, and his dynamic experience
probably belongs near this date.

divine favour, suddenly discovered a new God who filled his whole world with a new light and freedom and joy. His name for this discovery was Faith [" Glaube "], but Faith in its first intention for Luther meant a personal experience or discovery of God, brought into full view and clear apprehension in Christ. " No one can understand God or God's Word," Luther once wrote, " unless he has it revealed immediately [" on Mittel "] by the Holy Ghost, but nobody can receive anything from the Holy Ghost unless he experiences it. In experience the Holy Ghost teaches as in His own school, outside of which nothing of value can be learned." [1]

Not only was Faith for Luther thus possessed of a mystical character as an inward discovery and as a personal experience which laid hold on God immediately, but it also owed its illuminating birth in his consciousness largely to the influence of the writings and the lives of the mystics. However suddenly the " revelation " seemed to burst into his mind, there had nevertheless been a long period of psychological gestation and preparation for it before the epoch-making moment finally came. He had already in his early convent days come under the spell of St. Augustine, St. Bernard, Gerson, and many another guide into the deep regions of inward personal religion, and his intimate friend, the Vicar - general Staupitz, had been to him in some sense a personal embodiment of this type of religion. But the German mystics of the fourteenth century, with their mighty experience and their extraordinary depth, carried him still farther in this direction. He was so enthusiastic over that beautiful anonymous classic of mystical religion, the *Theologia Germanica*, that he twice edited and published it, declaring in his Preface that he had learned from it " more of what God and Christ and man and all things are " than from any other book except the Bible and St. Augustine. John Tauler, the great Dominican preacher of Strasbourg, impressed him no less profoundly. " Neither in the Latin nor the German language," he

[1] Preface to the *Magnificat* written in 1521.

wrote to Spalatin in 1516, "have I ever found purer
or more wholesome teaching, nor any that so agrees with
the Gospel." Both these great teachers of spiritual
religion helped him to see that complete confidence in
and surrender to the will of God is salvation—" Put off
thy own will and there will be no hell."

In Luther's earlier writings we come frequently
upon passages which reveal the way in which experience still saturates Faith for him, and which
exhibit the mystical depth of his Christianity at this
period. Commenting on the phrase, " Christ liveth in
me " (Gal. ii. 20), in his *Commentary on Galatians*,[1] he
says, " He [Christ] is my form, my furniture, and perfection, adorning and beautifying my faith as the colour,
the clear light, the whiteness, do garnish and beautify
the wall. Thus are we constrained grossly to set forth
this matter. For we cannot *conceive* that Christ is so
nearly joined and united unto us as the colour or whiteness is unto the wall. But Christ thus joined and united
unto me and abiding in me, liveth this life in me which
now I live ; yea, Christ Himself is this life which now I
live. Wherefore Christ and I in this behalf are both one." [2]
And in a famous passage in the tract " On Christian
Liberty," he declares that " Faith has the incomparable
grace of uniting the soul to Christ as bride to husband,
so that the soul possesses whatever Christ Himself
possesses."

Not only was this Luther of the early period the hero
of the people and the prophet of a deep and inward
religion, he seemed also to have found, even more
emphatically than had the Humanists, a far-reaching
principle of individualism which took the key from the
Church and put it into the hands of the Christian man
himself. Salvation in its essence, he sees, is conferred
upon no one from without. The soul is dependent for
it upon no organization, no traditions, no dogma, no
sacred performances. It is a transaction between the

---

[1] First given as Lectures in 1516–17, and published in 1519.
[2] *A Commentary on St. Paul's Epistle to the Galatians.*

individual soul and God, and the person who lays hold on God in living faith thereby has salvation, assurance, and joy. With this principle of individualism there came naturally to Luther a new conception of the Church altogether." [1] It was for him, in ideal at least, a community or congregation [" Gemeinde "] of believers, each member a spiritual priest, ministering to the spiritual and social life of all : ." I believe that there is on earth, wide as the world is, not more than one holy universal Christian Church, which is nothing else than the community or assembly of the saints. . . . I believe that in this community or Christendom, all things are common, and each one shares the goods of the others and none calls anything his own. Therefore all the prayers and good works of the entire community help me and every believer, and support and strengthen us at every time in life and in death." [2]

This ideal of a priesthood of believers, ministering to each other in mutual service and practising neighbourly love in daily life, would, if it had been actually carried into effect, have marked a great step in the direction in which the Humanists were going, namely, the transfer of the emphasis from dogma to life, from doctrine to ethics, from ecclesiasticism to personality. Luther's great discovery that personal faith is the only thing which counts toward God, and that love and service are the only things in the human sphere which have religious significance would have introduced, if it had been put full into play, a new era of personal freedom and a new stage in the progress of the Kingdom of God as a world-wide brotherhood of men engaged in mutual service.

[1] Dilthey says in *Archiv für Geschichte der Philosophie*, Bd. v. Heft 3, p. 358 : " The Justification of which the medieval man had inward experience was the descending stream of objective forces upon the believer from the transcendental world, through the Incarnation, in the channels of the ecclesiastical institutions, priestly consecration, sacraments, confession, and works. It was something which took place in connection with a super-sensible regime. The Justification by faith of which Luther was inwardly aware was the personal experience of the believer standing in the continuous line of Christian fellowship, by whom assurance of the Grace of God is experienced in response to personal faith, an experience derived from the appropriation of the work of Christ."

[2] *Sämmtliche Werke* (Erlangen edition), xxii. p. 20.

II

But the young Luther of these glowing ideals is not the actual Luther of the Protestant Reformation, any more than the Augustine of the mighty spiritual experiences portrayed in the *Confessions* is the St. Augustine of history. The historical Luther had the hero-spirit in him in high degree ; he had mystical depth and inward experience as we have seen, and he possessed the prophetic power of vision and forereach which makes him often seem far in advance of his time ; but these dynamic traits were more than overbalanced by his fundamentally conservative disposition and by his determination not to go faster or farther than he could carry Germany, especially the nobility, with him. He was, in a very real sense, a child of his time, a product of medieval Europe, and he never succeeded in liberating himself from the tight swaddling-bands in which his youth was wrapped. He could not comprehend, as we shall see, the bold spirits who were dedicated to the task of re-interpreting Christianity in terms of the new age ; he loved the old, in so far as it seemed to him unspoiled by apostacy and corruption, and he naturally kept reverting to the ancient dogma and the accepted theology of the old Church instead of leading the way into a fresh, vital, spiritual form of Christianity adapted to the social aspiration of the time.

In spite of the fact that Luther knew and loved the German mystics and had himself received a powerful inward experience of Christ as the bridegroom of his soul—an experience which quickened all the forces of his will and raised him to the rank of a world-hero— nevertheless his normal tendency was toward a non-mystical type of Christianity, toward a Christianity thoroughly based on Scripture, logically constructed out of concepts of the nature of God and Man, so ancient, sacred, and orthodox, that they seemed to him axioms of theology and capable of being formulated into a saving system of truth, as universal and as unalterable as the multiplication table.

However unconscious Luther himself may have been of the shift of emphasis that was taking place in him as the movement progressed, the historical observer has no difficulty in noting the change from the Luther who is endeavouring to sound the deeps of life itself, and whose religion is the creation of the inward stream of life within him ; and the Luther who wanders far afield from experience, draws curious conclusions from un- verified concepts, piles text on text as though heaven could be scaled by another Pelion on Ossa, and once more turns religion back to the cooled lava-beds of theology. He never could succeed in getting the God of his heart's glowing faith into the theologies which he laboriously builded.   As soon as he started constructing he invariably fell back upon the building-material which had already been quarried, and which lay at hand.   His experimental Faith discovered a God of all Grace, but his inherited *concept* of God, the God of the Old Testament and of theology, was vastly different, and remained to the end unrevolutionized by his heart's insight.   This background conception of God comes to extreme expression in his *De servo arbitrio* [" The Unfree Will "] of 1525 : " This is the acme of faith, to believe that God who saves so few and condemns so many is merciful ; that He is just who at His own pleasure has made us necessarily doomed to damnation, so that . . . He seems to delight in the tortures of the wretched and to be more deserving of hatred than of love. *If by any effort of reason I could conceive how God, who shows so much anger and harshness, could be merciful and just, there would be no need of faith.*"   There could, in his thought, be no salvation for man, no hope, and no joy, until some way of escape was found from the stern judgments of this angry and wrathful God.   This way of escape is found in what Luther calls " the Word of God," by which he means " the Gospel of God con- cerning His Son, incarnate, suffering, risen, and glorified."[1]

[1] On Christian Liberty, *Primary Works*, p. 106.

This Word of God is for him the sum total of " the promises that God is *for us* " ; " the pure Gospel " of a pardoning, forgiving God ; the revelation in the Cross of Christ that no self-merit counts or is needed, but that on Christ's account God forgives the sinner and bestows His Grace upon him.

Speaking theologically, Faith consists in believing in the God whom Christ has historically revealed—believing without any doubt that He will be and will do to us according to the things which are said of Him in " the Word of God." It must be said that for Luther himself, Faith was an " active, powerful thing," " a deliberate confidence in the grace of God," which made him " joyous and intrepid " and " for which he could die a thousand deaths " ; [1] but there was always an irresistible tendency in the Lutheran teaching for faith to drop to the lower level of doctrine, and to consist in the acceptance of a scheme of justification.

This tendency was, I say, easy and irresistible just because Luther did not normally and naturally think of God as being inherently and essentially loving, gracious, tender, and forgiving, that is to say, *fundamentally a Father* and in his deepest nature like the self-giving Christ. For him, as for so many other theologians, God *becomes* forgiving and gracious on account of Christ's merit and righteousness and thus no longer imputes sin to us. Because of what Christ did, God now beholds us with an attitude of mercy, grace, and forgiveness, and, on condition of our faith, imputes to us the righteousness of Christ. Salvation is, thus, a plan by which we escape from the God of justice and wrath and have our dealings with a God who has become merciful because our sin has been balanced off by somebody else's merit and righteousness.

Not only did Luther continue this medieval fiction of God's nature and character, he had also always in mind a fictitious and constructed " man." Man for him is a being devoid of " merit," a creature whose personal

---

[1] See his Preface to *The Epistle to the Romans*.

goodness in and of itself is of no value. Even Faith
itself, by which salvation is received, is not an attitude
or function of man's own will or reason. It is, like everything else connected with salvation, something divinely
given, supernaturally initiated, a work of God, an *opus
operatum*—" Mit unserer Macht ist nichts gethan "—and
therefore " faith " and " reason " belong in totally
different compartments of the human being. Nor,
furthermore, when he is absorbed with his system, is
salvation ever synonymous for him with an inwardly-
transformed and spiritually-renewed self. Salvation
means for him *certainty of divine favour*. It does not
inherently carry with it and involve in its intrinsic meaning a new life, a joyous adjustment of will to the Will of
God. If man is to attain to a moral transformation of
life, he must receive an added gift of supernatural grace,
that is, the power of sanctification through the Holy
Spirit. This conception made it impossible for him to
look for the coming of a divine kingdom by slow processes
now at work in the world.

Luther did not intend to make the " Word of God "
synonymous with the Scriptures, and in his great Prefaces
to St. Paul's *Epistles* he does not identify the two. The
Word of God is, as we have seen, the revelation, the
message, the gospel, of Grace through Christ Jesus,
wherever expressed, enunciated, or preached. But the
pledged Word of God found in the Scriptures seemed
to him the main miracle of the ages, and as, in his con-
tests with Zwickau " Prophets," " Anabaptists," and
" Spiritualists," he found himself forced to produce a
fixed touchstone of faith and a solid authority to take the
place left vacant by the Old Church, he swung naturally
toward the dogma of the absolute authority of Scripture,
and he laid, without wishing to do so, the foundation for
the view of the second generation of Protestantism, that
the infallible Scripture is God's final communication to
helpless man, and is the ultimate and only basis of
authority in religion.

His conception of the sacraments in like manner,

because of his crude supernaturalism and his inadequate intellectual and spiritual penetration, drifted to a semi-medieval view. He intended to transform these ceremonies and to have them fit " the pure Word of God." In his primary *intention* they were to be no longer objective works of grace, but were to have a subjective value only, a faith-significance. They were to be conceived as pictorial, symbolic ways of learning the one important truth of salvation—God's grace and forgiveness ; for God deigns, he said, to speak to his immature creatures by signs and pictures. But the imperial sway of the past powerfully moved him ; his own conservative disposition carried him along paths which an enlightened reason would not have taken, and the heat of the controversy often blinded him to some of the precious truths that had seemed clear to him in the creative period of Faith. In the bitter controversy with the " spiritual prophets " on the question of sacraments, he wrote words which seem strangely out of harmony with his earlier views and with his own experience : " External things in religion must precede internal experiences which come through [*i.e.* are mediated by] external things, for God has resolved to give nobody the internal gifts except through the external things. He will give nobody the Spirit and Faith without the use of external word and sign." [1] Without meaning to surrender the precious jewel of a religion spiritually grounded, he once more introduced " the awful mystery " of the sacraments, and opened the door for the conception of the rite as an *opus operatum*—a grace of God objectively real. He retained infant baptism as *an efficacious act*, and, obsessed as he was by the literal words, *Hoc est corpus*—" this is my body "—he went back into the abandoned path of scholasticism,[2] and restored the mysterious and miraculous real presence of Christ in the Eucharist.[3] It is true, as Loofs has said, that

---

[1] *Wider die himlichen Propheten vom Sacrament*, ii. Anno 1525.

[2] See F. Loofs, *Dogmengeschichte* (Vierte Auflage, 1906), pp. 752-755.

[3] In his instructions to Melanchthon for the Cassel Conference with Butzer in 1534, Luther said, " In and with the bread, the body of Christ is truly partaken

" Luther re-discovered Christianity as religion," but it is also unfortunately true as well that he lacked the insight, faith, and boldness of spirit to trust the people of his age and of the future with " Christianity as religion," and instead gave them a Christianity theologically con- structed, deeply marred with residual superstitions and mysteries, and heavily laden with the inheritances of dark and medieval ages.

III

There are two types of religious genius, both of which play great rôles in history.   There is first the genius who, inspired by the ideal of some earlier prophet, or made wise because he has himself discovered the trend of celestial currents, sees through the complex and tangle of his time, and forecasts a truth which all men in a happier coming age will recognize.   When he has once seen it, this vision transforms all his ideas and aims, and spoils forever for him all meaner gains, all half truths, all goods which must be won through surrender of a possible better.   He will be obedient to that vision regardless of all cost.   He will bear witness to the full light which he has seen even though he can compel nobody else in the heedless world of his generation to see it.   He may only cry in the wilderness, but at all events he will *cry*, and he will cry of that highest thing his heart knows.

There is, on the other hand, the genius who understands his own age like an open book.   He is almost hyper- sensitive to the movings of his time.   He feels the silent yearnings and strivings of the dumb multitudes about him ; he anticipates in his thought what the rest are incipiently thinking—he is the clear voice and oracle of the spirit of his age.   He knows to a nicety how far his contemporaries will allow themselves to be carried.

---

of, accordingly all that takes place actively and passively in the bread takes place actively and passively in the body of Christ and the latter is distributed, eaten and masticated with the teeth."

He will not over-hurry, he will not outrun their possible speed, and he will sacrifice everything to carry his epoch with him toward the goal which he sees. He is contented to keep his roots deep in the past, and he tempers all his creative insights with a judicious mixture of the experience of the past and the ideas which time has made sacred. He will not satisfy the idealist who wants leaps, and he will not please the radical in any period ; but if he is brave, wise, and sincere, and, withal, possessed of rare gifts of interpretation and unusual powers of leadership, he may be able to shape the course of history no less effectively, perhaps more surely, than the genius who insists upon an immediate march straight across country to Canaan the moment he glimpses it from his Pisgah.

Luther was a reformer of this second type. He was beset by very real limitations. Dr. McGiffert does not overstate the facts when he says: "He cared little for clearness and consistency of thought. A satisfactory and adequate world-view was not of his concern. Of intellectual curiosity he had scarcely any ; of interest in truth for truth's sake none at all. . . . He remained entirely without intellectual difficulties, finding no trouble with the most extreme supernaturalism." [1] In many respects, as Harnack has insisted, his Christianity was a " medieval phenomenon." [2] Only in one thing was he supremely the master of his age and the hero of a new time—in his discovery of a way of Faith which makes a man " intrepid " even in the wreck of worlds and " in a thousand deaths." On the lower levels of life, where most of his work was done, he was strangely under the sway of the past, a distruster of reason, a restorer of ancient doctrine, a conservative in thought and action, a friend of rulers, a guardian, as far as he could be, of the *status quo*—a leader who anathematized radicals and enthusiasts and who staved off and postponed for nearly four hundred years the truly liberating and thoroughly

---

[1] McGiffert, *Protestant Thought before Kant* (1911), p. 20. See also the same view in Troeltsch, *Protestantisches Christentum und Kirche in der Neuzeit* (2nd Auflage), p. 481.

[2] *History of Dogma*, vii. p. 169.

adequate reformation.   He was determined to be the repairer of the " Old Church," not the builder of a " New Church," and he was resolved not to travel farther nor faster than the substantial men of his time considered safe and wise.

But less was perhaps more.   There will at least always be those who think that the sinuous way of progress is the most certain way of advance.   The slow incline, the gradual spiral, each wind of the curve " ever not quite " the old level—that is the most approved method of leaving an outworn past and of moving forward into a new stage of history.   It may be so.   It certainly is true that through Luther's *insight* new reliance upon God came to men, new energy of faith was won, and by his work of repair, conservative and cautious though it was, in the long sweep of time a liberated Christianity has come, a vital social gospel has become effective, and great vistas of progress are opening out before the Church of Christ.   But it is impossible to forget that other group—those men of the other type—who even in Luther's day saw the way straight across into Canaan, the men who saw their vision fade away unrealized, and who failed to behold the fruit of their spiritual travail largely because Luther misunderstood them, refused to give them aid and comfort, and finally helped to marshal the forces which submerged them and postponed their victory.   We may not blame him, but it is not fair to these heroic souls that they should longer lie submerged in the oblivion of their defeat.   I shall try in these pages to bring up into the light the principles and ideas which they proclaimed to Europe, perhaps ahead of their time.

CHAPTER II

HANS DENCK has generally been enrolled among the Anabaptists, and it is possible to use that name of scorn with such a latitude and looseness that it includes not only Denck but all the sixteenth-century exponents of a free, inward religion. Anabaptism has often been treated as a sort of broad banyan-tree which flourished exuberantly and shot out far-reaching branches of very varied characters, but which held in one organic unity all the branches that found soil and took root. A name of such looseness and covering capacity is, however, of little worth, and it would promote historical accuracy if we should confine the term to those who opposed infant baptism and who insisted instead upon adult baptism, not as a means of Grace, but as a visible sign of the covenant of man with God. The further characteristic marks which may be selected to differentiate Anabaptism from other movements of the period are :

1. The treatment of the Gospel as a new law to be literally followed and obeyed by all who are to have the right to be called " saints."

2. The true Church is a *visible* Church, the community of the saints, founded by covenant, with adult baptism as its sign, formed exactly on the pattern of the apostolic

---

[1] The best studies on Denck are Heberle's articles in *Theol. Studien und Kritiken* (1851), Erstes Heft, and (1855) Viertes Heft. Gustave Roehrich's *Essai sur la vie, les écrits et la doctrine de Jean Denk* (Strasbourg, 1853). Ludwig Keller's *Ein Apostel der Wiedertäufer* (Leipzig, 1882). The last two books must, however, be followed with much caution.

Church and preserved in strict purity by rigorous church discipline ; and

3. The denial to magistrates of all power to persecute men for their faith and doctrine on the ground that the Gospel gives them no such authority—its great commandment being love.[1]

Hans Denck, though in his early period of activity closely identified with this movement and regarded as one of its chief leaders in Germany, does not properly belong, however, to the banyan-tree of Anabaptism. His writings reveal ideas and tendencies of such enlarged scope that it appears clear that he had discovered and was teaching another type of Christianity altogether.[2] He is the earliest exponent in the sixteenth century of a fresh and unique type of religion, deeply influenced by the mystics of a former time, but even more profoundly moulded by the new humanistic conceptions of man's real nature.

There are few biographical details of Denck's life available. He was, most probably, a native of Bavaria,[3] and he was born about the year 1495. He studied in the University of Ingolstadt, where he was admitted among the baccalaureates in 1517.[4] In the year 1520 we catch a glimpse of him in close association with the Humanists of Augsburg.[5] In 1522 he was at work in Basle as proof-reader for the famous publisher, Valentin Curio, and was living in intimate fellowship with the great scholar Œcolampadius, whose lectures on the Prophet Isaiah he heard.[6] In the autumn of the same year, on the recommendation of Œcolampadius, he was appointed Director of St. Sebald's School in Nuremberg, which was then the foremost seat of learning in that city,

---

[1] One branch of the Anabaptists held that the "saints" may, however, rightly use the sword to execute the purposes of God upon the godless, and to hasten the coming of the Thousand Years' Reign of the Kingdom.

[2] I have included him, in my *Studies in Mystical Religion* (1908), among the Anabaptists, but he can be called one only by such a loose use of the word that it ceases to have any *definite* significance.

[3] See J. Kessler's *Sabbata* (1902), p. 150.

[4] L. Keller, *Johann von Staupitz*, p. 207.

[5] *Ibid.* p. 208.

[6] Œcolampadius' Letter to Pirkheimer, April 25, 1525.

a great centre of classical humanistic studies. During
the first period of his life in Nuremberg he was closely
identified with the Lutheran movement, but he soon
shifted his sympathies, and aligned himself with the
radical tendencies which at this period were championed
in Nuremberg by Thomas Münzer, who, in spite of his
misguided leadership and fanatical traits, had discovered
a genuine religious principle that was destined to become
significant in safer hands.[1] Münzer read Tauler's sermons
from his youth up ; in his own copy of these sermons,
preserved in the library at Gera, a marginal note says
that he read them almost continually, and that here he
learned of a divine interior Teaching. It was Münzer's
teaching of the living Voice of God in the soul,
his testimony to the reality of the inner heavenly
Word, which God Himself speaks in the deeps of man's
heart, that won the Humanist and teacher of St.
Sebald's School to the new and perilous cause. He
also formed a close friendship with Ludwig Hetzer, who,
like Münzer, taught that the saving Word of God must be
inward, and that the Scriptures can be understood only by
those who belong to the School of Christ. Having once
caught the *idea* from these impassioned leaders, Denck
proceeded directly to work it out and to develop its
implications in his own fashion. He was himself sane,
clear-minded, modest, sincere, far-removed from fanaticism,
and eager only to find a form of religion which would fit
the eternal nature of things on the one hand, and the
true nature of man on the other—man, I mean, as the
Humanist conceived him.[2]

Already in this Nuremberg period, Denck became fully
convinced that Luther's doctrine of sin and justification
was an artificial construction—*Einbildung*—and that his
conception of Scripture and the Sacraments was destined
to clamp the new-found faith in iron bonds, tie it to
outworn tradition, and make it incapable of a progressive

[1] Georg Theodor Strobel, *Leben, Schriften und Lehren Münzers* (Nürnberg,
1795) ; J. R. Seidemann, *Thomas Münzer* (Dresden, 1842).
[2] A contemporary chronicle calls Denck a scholar, eloquent, modest and,
withal, learned in Hebrew.—Kessler's *Sabbata*, p. 150.

and vital unfolding. He declared in his testimony or
" confession " to the city council of Nuremberg in 1524,
that although he had not yet a full experience of the
inward, powerful Word of God, he distinctly felt its life
as an inner witness which God had planted within him,
a spark of the Divine Light breaking into his own soul,
and in the strength of this direct experience he denied
the value of external ceremonies, and declared that even
the Bible itself cannot bring men to God without the
assistance of this inner Light and Spirit.[1]

As a result of this change of attitude, the schoolmaster
of St. Sebald's was banished from the city of Nuremberg,
January 21, 1525, and from this time until his early
death he was homeless and a wanderer. He spent some
months—between September 1525 and October 1526—
in Augsburg endeavouring to organize and direct the
rapidly expanding forces of the liberal movement. He
was during these months, and especially during the period
of the great Anabaptist synod which was held at this
time in Augsburg, endeavouring to give the chaotic
movement of Anabaptism a definite direction, with the
main emphasis on the mystical aspect of religion. He
hoped to call a halt to the vague socialistic dreams and
the fanatical tendencies that put the movement in
constant jeopardy and peril, and he was striving to call
his brotherhood to an inner religion, grounded on the
inherent nature of the soul, and guided by the inner Word
rather than on " a new law " set forth in the written
word. There were, however, too many eddies and
currents to be mastered by one mind, too many varieties
of faith to be unified under one principle, and Denck's
own view was too intangible, inward, and spiritual, to
satisfy the enthusiasm either of the seething masses or of

---

[1] This " Confession " is in the archives of Nuremberg, and has been extensively
used in Keller's *Ein Apostel der Wiedertäufer*, see especially pp. 49-62. See also
Th. Kolde, *Kirchengeschichtliche Studien* (1888), p. 231 f. In this connection
much interest attaches to a passage in a letter which Luther wrote to Johann
Brismann, February 4, 1525. He says : " Satan has carried it so far that in
Nuremberg some persons are denying that Christ is anything, that the Word of
God is anything, that the Eucharist is anything, that Magistracy is anything.
They say that only God is."

the leaders who saw a new Jerusalem just ready to come down out of heaven from God.[1]

After the Augsburg period, Denck spent some time in Strasbourg, where he gained many followers. Capito bears testimony at this time to the purity of Denck's life, to his moderation and goodwill, and to the impressive effect of his preaching and teaching upon the people of the city.[2] Vadian, the Humanist and reformer of St. Gall, too, in spite of his disapproval of some of Denck's ideas, speaking of him in retrospect after his death, called him " a most gifted youth, possessed of all excellencies." But his teaching was too strange and unusual to be allowed currency even in free Strasbourg. After being granted a public discussion he was ordered to leave the city forthwith. During a short stay in Worms, following the Strasbourg period, in collaboration with Ludwig Hetzer, they brought to a successful conclusion a German translation of the Prophets from the Hebrew, a work which Hetzer had begun. This important piece of scholarly work was published under the title, *Alle Propheten nach hebräischer Sprache verteutscht*, in Worms, April 3, 1527, and had a wide circulation and use, its main demerit being that it had been done by " Anabaptists."

Pursued on every hand, hunted from place to place, he finally sought peace and shelter with his old friend, the teacher who had first inspired him in his youth, Œcolampadius, and here in Basle in a quiet retreat, he died of the plague in November 1527, hardly more than thirty-two years of age.[3]

We must now turn to the little books of this persecuted and homeless Humanist to see what his religious teaching really was, and to discover the foundation principle which lay at the root of all the endeavours of this period to launch a Christianity grounded primarily on the

---

[1] See Nicoladoni's *Johannes Bünderlin von Linz* (Berlin, 1893), p. 114.

[2] Letter of Capito to Zwingli, December 26, 1526.

[3] Kessler says that Œcolampadius in a Christian spirit was with him at his death. *Op. cit.* p. 151.

fundamental nature of man.[1] Denck writes like a man
with a message—straight to the mark, lucid, vivid, and
intense. He believes what he says and he wants others
to see it and believe it. His writings are entirely free
from the controversial temper, and they breathe throughout the spirit of tolerance and charity. He knows when
to stop, and brings his books to an end as soon as he has
made his points clear. The fundamental fact of man's
nature for Denck is personal *freedom*. Starting with no
theological presuppositions he is under no obligation to
make the primary assumption common to all Augustinian
systems that man is devoid of any native capacities
which have to do with spiritual salvation. He begins
instead with man as he knows him—a sadly marred
and hampered being, but still possessed of a potentially
Divine nature, and capable of co-operating, by inward
choices and decisions, with the ceaseless effort of God
to win him completely to Himself. His little book, *What
does it mean when the Scripture says God does and works
Good and Evil*, is throughout a protest against the idea
of " election," which, he says, involves " a limitation of
the Love of God," and it is a penetrating account of the
way in which man by his free choices makes his eternal
destiny.[2] " God compels nobody, for He will have no
one saved by compulsion." [3] " God has given freewill
to men that they may choose for themselves, either the
good or the bad. Christ said to His disciples, ' Will ye

---

[1] The little books of Denck from which I shall extract his teaching are :
(1) *Vom Gesetz Gottes* (" On the Law of God "), printed without place or date, but
probably published in 1526. I have used the copy in the Königliche Bibliothek in
Berlin. sig. Co. 2152. (2) *Was geredet sey dass die Schrift sagt Gott thue und mache
guts und böses* (" What does it mean when the Scripture says God does and works
Good and Evil "), 1526. Copies of this are to be found in the University Library
of Marburg, also in the Königliche Bibliothek of Dresden. (3) *Widerruf* (" Confession "), 1527. I have used the copy in the Königliche Bibliothek in Dresden
sig. Theol. Cathol. 817   (4) *Ordnung Gottes und der Creaturen Werck* (" The Divine
Plan and the Work of the Creature "), 1527, in the above library in Dresden.
(5) *Wer die Warheit warlich lieb hat*, etc., no date (" Whoever really loves the
Truth," etc.), and (6) *Von der wahren Liebe* (" On the True Love "), 1527. This last
tract has been republished in America by the Mennonitische Verlagshandlung,
Elkhart, Indiana, 1888.

[2] " To hear the Word of God," he elsewhere says, " means life ; to hear it
not means death."—*Ordnung Gottes*, p. 17.

[3] *Was geredet sey*, p. C. (The paging is by letters.)

go away?' as though He would say, 'You are under no compulsion.'"[1] "God," he says again in the *Widerruf*, "forces no one, for love cannot compel, and God's service is, therefore, a thing of complete freedom."[2]

It is freedom, too, which explains the fact of sin. God is in no way the author of sin; He is wholly good; He can do nothing but what is good; He ordains no one to sin; He is the instigator of no evil at all. All the sin and moral evil of the world have come from our own evil choices and purposes. "The thing which hinders and has always hindered is that our wills are different from God's will. God never seeks Himself in His willing—we do. There is no other way to blessedness than to lose one's self-will."[3] "He who surrenders his selfishness," he says in another treatise, "and uses the freedom which God has given him, and fights the spiritual battle as God wills that such battles are to be fought and as Christ fought His, can in his measure be like Christ."[4] The whole problem of salvation for him is, as we shall see, to bring about such a transformation in man that sin ceases, and the least thing thought, said, or done out of harmony with the will of God becomes bitter and painful to the soul.[5] "To be a Christian," he once wrote, "is to be in measure like Christ, and to be ready to be offered as He gave Himself to be offered. I do not say that we *are* perfect as Christ was, but I say rather that we are to seek the perfection which Christ never lost. Christ calls Himself the Light of the world, but He also tells His disciples that *they* too are the light of the world. All Christians in whom the Holy Ghost lives—that is all real Christians—are one with Christ in God and are like Christ. They will therefore have similar experiences, and what Christ did they will also do."[6]

Not only is there a power of free choice in the soul; there is as well an elemental hunger in man which pushes him Godward. "God," he often says, "can give only

---

[1] *Was geredet sey*, B. 3.
[2] *Widerruf*, sec. iv.
[3] *Was geredet sey*, B.
[4] *Ibid*. B. 5.
[5] *Vom Gesetz Gottes*, p. 15.
[6] *Was geredet sey*, B. 6.

to those who hunger." In a very great passage which
reminds one of Pascal he says : " The kingdom of God is
in you and he who searches for it outside himself will
never find it, for *apart from God no one can either seek or
find God, for he who seeks God, already in truth has Him.*" [1]
He says nearly the same thing again in the little book,
Vom Gesetz Gottes : " He who does not know God from
God Himself does not ever know Him." This central
insight of Denck's religious faith that God and man are
not completely sundered, but meet, as he says,[2] in the
deeps of ourselves, is grounded upon the fact of experience
that there is within us a supra-individual Reality which
becomes revealed to us sometimes as a Light, sometimes
as a Word, sometimes as a Presence or environing Spirit.
This testimony is Denck's main contribution, and we
must next see how he sets it forth. There is, he says, a
witness in every man. He who does not listen to it
blinds himself, although God has given him originally
a good inward eyesight. If a man will keep still and
listen he will hear what the Spirit witnesses within him.
Not only in *us* but in the heathen and in Jews this witness
is given, and men might be preached to outwardly
forever without perceiving, if they did not have
this witness in their own hearts.[3] The Light shines,
the invisible Word of God is uttered in the hearts of all
men who come into the world, and this Light gives all
men freedom and power to become children of God.[4]
There is both an inward principle of revelation which he
calls *das innere Wort*, and a principle of active power
which he calls *die Kraft des Allerhöchsten* (the power of
the Highest), not two things, but one reality under two
aspects and two names, and he insists that he who turns
to this Divine, spiritual reality, which is one with God, and
obeys it and loves its leading has already found God
and has come to himself. " Oh, who will give me a
voice," he writes, " that I may cry aloud to the whole
world that God, the all highest, is in the deepest abyss

---

[1] *Was geredet sey*, B. 2.   [2] *Ibid.* B. 5.
[3] *Ibid.* B. 1 and 2.   [4] *Ordnung Gottes*, p. 7.

within us and is waiting for us to return to Him. Oh,
my God, how does it happen in this poor old world, that
Thou art so great and yet nobody finds Thee, that Thou
callest so loudly and nobody hears Thee, that Thou art
so near and nobody feels Thee, that Thou givest Thyself
to everybody and nobody knows Thy name ! Men flee
from Thee and say they cannot find Thee ; they turn their
backs and say they cannot see Thee ; they stop their ears
and say they cannot hear Thee ! " [1]

This self-giving nature of God is everywhere taken
for granted—it is just *that* which he feels that Christ has
once for all made sun-clear, and it is because He is essentially self-giving that God pours out His life and love upon
us as He does His sunshine upon the grass and flowers.
" The Word of God is with thee before thou seekest ;
He gives before thou hast asked ; He opens to thee before
thou hast knocked." God like a Father deals with
His wayward children. " Oh, blessed is the man," he
writes, " who in his need finds the love of God and comes
to Him for forgiveness ! " [2] No one of us who has been
washed from his sins, he beautifully says, ought to eat a
piece of bread without considering how God loves him
and how he ought to love God, who in Jesus Christ His
Son laid aside His right to Divinity that His love might
appear complete.[3] " It has pleased the eternal Love,"
he writes, " that that Person in whom Love was shown
in the highest degree should be called the Saviour of His
people. Not that it would be possible for human nature
to make anybody saved, but God was so completely
identified in Love with Him that all the Will of God was
the will of this Person, and the sufferings of this Person
were and counted as the sufferings of God Himself." [4]

Christ is for him the complete manifestation of life
and the perfect exhibition or unveiling of God's love,
and he who appreciates this love, feels its attraction, and
lives a life which corresponds to his soul's insight, becomes

---

[1] *Vom Gesetz Gottes*, p. 27.   [2] *Was geredet sey*, D. 1 and 2.
[3] *Vom Gesetz Gottes*, p. 33.
[4] *Von der wahren Liebe* (Elkhart reprint), p. 7.

himself Christlike, forsakes sin and self, and enters upon
a life of salvation. " All who are saved," he says, " are
of one spirit with God, and he who is the foremost in love
is the foremost of those who are saved." [1] " He who
gets weary of God has never found Him," while the
person who has found Him in this love-way will be ready
and willing to give up even his own salvation and accept
damnation for the love of God, since he knows in his heart
that " God is so wholly good that He can give to such a
man only what is highest and best, and that is Himself ! " [2]
That is to say, he who is willing to be damned for the
love of God never will be damned !

But salvation must never be conceived as something
which is the result of a transaction. It is from beginning
to end a life-process and can in no way be separated from
character and personal attitude of will. " He who
depends on the merit of Christ," he says, " and yet continues in a fleshly, wicked life, regards Christ precisely
as in former times the heathen held their gods. He who
really believes that Christ has saved him can no longer
be a servant of sin, for no one believes rightly until he
leaves his old life." [3] " It is not enough," he elsewhere
writes, " that God is in thee ; thou must also be in God,
that is, partake of the life of God. It does not help to
have God if thou dost not honour Him. It is no avail
to call thyself His child *if thou dost not behave thyself
like a child* ! " [4] He insists that no one can be " called
righteous " or be " counted righteous " until he actually
is righteous. Nothing can be " imputed " to a man
which is not ethically and morally present as a living
feature of his character and conduct. No one, he truly
says, can know *Christ as a means of salvation* unless
he follows Him in his life. He who does not witness
to Christ in his daily walk grows into a different
person from the one he is called to be.[5] The person
who lives on in sin does not really know God, and,

---

[1] *Von der wahren Liebe* (Elkhart reprint), p. 8.
[2] *Vom Gesetz Gottes*, p. 19. [3] *Widerruf*, ii.
[4] *Was geredet sey*, B. 1. [5] *Ibid.* D.

to use his fine figure, is like a man who has lost his home and gone astray, and does not even know that he is *at home,* when his Father has found him and has welcomed him back, but still goes on hunting for home and for Father, since he does not recognize his home or his Father when he has found them ! [1]

Salvation, then, for Hans Denck is wholly an inward process, initiated from above through the Divine Word, the Christ, whom we know outwardly as the |historical Person of the Gospel, and whom we know inwardly as the Revealer of Light and Love, the Witness in us against sin, the Voice of the Father to our hearts, calling us home, the Goal of our spiritual quest, the Alpha and the Omega of all religious truth and all spiritual experience. The Way to God, he says, is Christ inwardly and spiritually known.[2] But however audible the inner Word may be ; however vivid the illumination ; however drawing the Love, there is never compulsion. The soul itself must hear and see and feel ; must say *yes* to the appeal of Love, and must co-operate by a continuous adjustment of the personal will to the Will of God and " learn to behave as a child of God."

Having reached the insight that salvation is entirely an affair of the spirit, an inward matter, Denck loosened his hold upon the external things which had through long centuries of history come to be considered essential to Christianity. Sacraments and ceremonies dropped to a lower level for him as things of no importance. With his characteristic breadth and sweetness, he does not smite them as an iconoclast would have done ; he does not cry out against those who continue to use them. He merely considered them of no spiritual significance. " Ceremonies," he writes in his dying confession, " in themselves are not sin, but whoever supposes that he can attain to life either by baptism or by partaking of bread, is still in superstition." [3] " If all ceremonies," he adds, " were lost, little harm would come of it." [4]

---

[1] *Was geredet sey,* A. 4 and 5.   [2] *Ibid.* B. 3.
[3] *Widerruf,* vii.   [4] *Ibid.* vii.

He appeals to Christians to stop quarrelling over these outward and secondary matters, and to make religion consist in love to neighbour rather than in zeal for outward ceremonies. He laid down this great principle : " All externals must yield to love, for they are for the sake of love, and not love for their sake." [1]

He was, consistently with his fundamental ideas, profoundly opposed to every tendency to make Christianity a legal religion. His friends, the Anabaptists, were inclined to turn the Gospel of Christ into " a new law," and to make religion consist largely in scrupulous obedience to this perfect law of life. To all this he was radically alien, for it was, he thought, only another road back to a religion of the letter, while Christ came to call us to a religion of the spirit. " He who has not the Spirit," he wrote, " and who fails to find Him in the Scriptures, seeks life and finds death ; seeks light and finds darkness, whether it be in the Old or in the New Testament." [2] " He who thinks that he can be *made truly righteous* by means of a Book is ascribing to the dead letter what belongs to the Spirit." [3] He does not belittle or undervalue the Scriptures—he knew them almost by heart and took the precious time out of his brief life to help to translate the Prophets into German—but he wants to make the fact forever plain that men are saved or lost as they say *yes* or *no* to a Light and Word within themselves. " The Holy Scriptures," he writes in his dying testimony, " I consider above every human treasure, but not so high as the Word of God which is living, powerful, and eternal, for it is God Himself, Spirit and no letter, written without pen or paper so that it can never be destroyed. For that reason, salvation is not bound up with the Scriptures, however necessary and good they may be for their purpose, because it is impossible for the Scriptures to make good a bad heart, even though it may be a learned one. A good heart, however, with a Divine Spark in it is improved by everything, and to such the Scriptures will bring blessed-

---

[1] *Vom Gesetz Gottes*, p. 33.   [2] *Ibid.* p. 22.
[3] *Ibid.* p. 21.

ness and goodness." [1]   The Scriptures—the external Word
—as he many times, in fact somewhat tediously, declares,
are witnesses and pointers to the real and momentous
thing, the Word which is very near to all souls and is
written in the heart, and which increases in clearness
and power as the will swings into parallelism with the
will of God, and as the life grows in likeness to the Divine
image revealed in Christ.   This inward life and spiritual
appreciation do not give any ground for relaxing the
moral obligations of life.   No fulfilling of the law by
Christ, no vanishing of the outward and temporal, furnish
any excuse to us for slacking a jot or tittle of anything
which belongs to the inherent nature of moral goodness.
" Christ," he says, " fulfilled the law, not to relieve us
of it, but to show us how to keep it in truth.   The member
must partake of what the Head partakes." [2]   *To love
God alone and to hate everything that hinders love* is a
principle which, Denck believes, will fulfil all law, ancient
or modern.[3]

Such were the ideas which this young radical reformer,
dreamer perhaps, tried to teach his age.   The time was
not ripe for him, and there was no environment ready
for his message.   He spoke to minds busy with theological systems, and to men whose battles were over the
meaning of inherited medieval dogma.   He thought and
spoke as a child of another world, and he talked in a
language which he had learned from his heart and not
from books or from the schools.   It is " the key of David,"
he says, that is, an inward experience, which unlocks
all the solid doors of truth, but there were so few about
him who really had this " key " !   His task, which was
destined to be hard and painful, which was in his lifetime
doomed to failure, was not self-chosen.   " I opened my
mouth," he says, " against my will and I am speaking
to the world because God impels me so that I cannot keep
silent.   God has called me out and stationed me at my
post, and He knows whether good will come of it or not." [4]

---

[1] *Widerruf*, i.   [2] *Vom Gesetz Gottes*, p. 9.
[3] *Ibid.* p. 12.   [4] *Was geredet sey*, Preface.

It is not often that a man living in the atmosphere of seething enthusiasm, pitilessly pricked and goaded by brutal and unfeeling persecutors, compelled to hear his precious truth persistently called error and pestilent heresy, keeps so calm and sane and sure that all will be well with him and with his truth as does Denck. " I am heartily well content," is his dying testimony, " that all shame and disgrace should fall on my face, if it is for the truth. It was when I began to love God that I got the disfavour of men." [1] He confesses that he has found it difficult to " keep a gentle and a humble heart " through all his work among men, to " temper his zeal with understanding," and to " make his lips say always what his heart meant," [2] but he did, at least, succeed in loving God and in hating everything that hindered love. In an epoch in which the doctrine was new and revolutionary, he succeeded in presenting the principle of the Inward Word as the basis of religion without giving any encouragement to libertinism or moral laxity, for he found the way of freedom to be a life of growing likeness to Christ, he held the fulfilling of the law to be possible only for those who accept the burdens and sacrifices of love, and he insisted that the privileges of blessedness belong only to those who *behave like sons*.

---

[1] *Widerruf*, Preface.   [2] *Ibid.*, Preface.

CHAPTER III

TWO PROPHETS OF THE INWARD WORD : BUNDERLIN
AND ENTFELDER

I

THE study of Denck in the previous chapter has furnished
the main outlines of the type of Christianity which a
little group of men, sometimes called " Enthusiasts,"
and sometimes called " Spirituals," but in reality
sixteenth - century Quakers, proclaimed and faithfully
practised in the opening period of the Reformation.
They differed fundamentally from Luther in their conception of salvation and in their basis of authority,
although they owed their first awakening to him ; and
they were not truly Anabaptists, though they allied
themselves at first with this movement, and earnestly
laboured to check the ominous signs of Ranterism and
Fanaticism, and the misguided " return " to millennial
hopes and expectations, to which many of the Anabaptist
leaders were prone.

The inner circle of " Spirituals " which we are now
engaged in investigating was never numerically large
or impressive, nor was it in the public mind well
differentiated within the larger circle of seething ideas
and revolutionary propaganda. The men themselves,
however, who composed it had a very sure grasp of a few
definite, central truths to which they were dedicated,
and they never lost sight, in the hurly-burly of contention
and in the storm of persecution, of the goal toward which
they were bending their steps. They did not endeavour

to found a Church, to organize a sect, or to gain a personal following, because it was a deeply settled idea with them all that the true Church is invisible. It is a communion of saints, including those of all centuries, past and present, who have heard and obeyed the divine inner Word, and through co-operation with God's inward revelation and transforming Presence have risen to a mystical union of heart and life with Him. Their apostolic mission—for they fully believed that they were " called " and " sent "— was to bear witness to this eternal Word within the soul, to extend the fellowship of this invisible Zion, and to gather out of all lands and peoples and visible folds of the Church those who were ready for membership in the one family and brotherhood of the Spirit of God. They made the mistake, which has been very often made before and since, of undervaluing external helps and of failing to appreciate how important is the visible fellowship, the social group, working at common tasks and problems, the temporal Church witnessing to its tested faith and proclaiming its message to the ears of the world ; but they did nevertheless perform a very great service in their generation, and they are the unrecognized forerunners of much which we highly prize in the spiritual heritage of the modern world.

The two men whose spiritual views we are about to study are, I am afraid, hardly even " names " to the world of to-day. They were not on the popular and winning side and they have fallen into oblivion, and the busy world has gone on and left them and their little books to lie buried in a forgotten past. They are surely worthy of a resurrection, and those who take the pains will discover that the ideas which they promulgated never really died, but were quick and powerful in the formation of the inner life of the religious societies of the English Commonwealth, and so of many things which have touched our inner world to-day.

Johann Bünderlin, like his inspirer Denck, was a scholar of no mean rank. He understood Hebrew ; he knew the Church Fathers both in Greek and Latin ; he makes frequent reference to Greek literature for illustration, and he was well versed in the dialectic of the schools, though he disapproved of it as a religious method.[1] He was enrolled as a student in the University of Vienna in 1515, under the name of Johann Wunderl aus Linz, Linz being a town of Upper Austria. After four years of study he left the University in 1519, being compelled to forgo his Bachelor's degree because he was too poor to pay the required fee.[2] The next five years of his life are submerged beyond recovery, but we hear of him in 1526 as a preacher in the service of Bartholomäus von Starhemberg, a prominent nobleman of Upper Austria, and he was at this time a devout adherent of the Lutheran faith. He was in Augsburg this same year, 1526, at the time of the great gathering of Anabaptists, and here he probably met Hans Denck, at any rate he testified in 1529 before the investigating Judge in Strasbourg that he received adult baptism in Augsburg three years before. He seems to have gone from Augsburg to Nikolsburg, where he was present at a public Discussion in which a definite differentiation appeared between the moderate and the radical, the right and left, wings of the Anabaptists. Bünderlin took part in this Discussion on the " moderate " side. He remained for some time—perhaps two years — in Nikolsburg and faced the persecution which prevailed in that city during the winter of 1527–1528. The next year he comes to notice in Strasbourg where, for a long time, a much larger freedom of thought was allowed than in any other German city of the period. The great tragedy which he had to experience was the frustration of the work of his life by the growth and spread of the Ranter influence in the Anabaptist circles, through the leadership of Melchior Hoffman and others of a similar spirit. He loved freedom, and here he saw it degenerating into license. He was devoted to a religion of experience and of inner authority, and now

---

[1] See Veesenmeyer's article on Bünderlin in *N. lit. Anzeiger* for August 1807, p. 535.
[2] The details of his life here given have been gathered mainly from the excellent monograph on *Johannes Bünderlin* by Dr. Alexander Nicoladoni. (Berlin, 1893.)

he saw the wild extremes to which such a religion was exposed. He was dedicated to a spiritual Christianity, and now he was compelled to learn the bitter lesson that there are many types and varieties of " spiritual religion," and that the masses are inclined to go with those who supply them with a variety which is spectacular and which produces emotional thrills. Our last definite information concerning Bünderlin shows him to have been in Constance in 1530, from which city he was expelled as a result of information against the " soundness " of his doctrine, furnished in a letter from Œcolampadius. From this time he drops completely out of notice, and we are left only with conjectures. One possible reference to him occurs in a letter from Julius Pflug, the Humanist, to Erasmus in 1533. Pflug says that a person has newly arrived in Litium (probably Lützen) who teaches that there are no words of Christ as a warrant for the celebration of the Sacrament of the Supper, and that it is to be partaken of only in a spiritual way. He adds that God had intervened to protect the people from such heresy and that the heretic had been imprisoned. The usual penalty for such heresy was probably imposed. This description would well fit Johann Bünderlin, but we can only guess that he was the opponent of the visible Sacrament mentioned in the letter which Erasmus received in 1533.[1]

Bünderlin's religious contribution is preserved in three little books which are now extremely rare, the central ideas of which I shall give in condensed form and largely in my own words, though I have faithfully endeavoured to render him fairly.[2] His style is difficult,

---

[1] This incident is given in Dr. Carl Hagen's *Deutschlands literarische und religiöse Verhältnisse im Reformationszeitalter*, 1868, iii. p. 310.

[2] The books are :—

(1) *Ein gemayne Berechnung über der Heiligen Schrift Inhalt*, etc. (" A General Consideration of the Contents of Holy Scripture.") Printed in Strasbourg in 1529.

(2) *Aus was Ursach sich Gott in die nyder gelassen und in Christo vermenschet ist*, etc., 1529. (" For what cause God has descended here below and has become incarnate in Christ.")

(3) *Erklärung durch Vergleichung der biblischen Geschrift, dass der Wassertauf sammt andern äusserlichen Gebräuchen in der apostolischen Kirchen geübet, on Gottes Befelch und Zeugniss der Geschrift, von etlichen dieser Zeit wider efert wird*, etc., 1530. (" Declaration by comparison of the Biblical Writings that Baptism with Water, together with other External Customs practised in the Apostolic

mainly because he abounds in repetition and has not
learned to write in an orderly way. I am inclined to
believe that he sometimes wrote, as he would no doubt
preach, in a prophetic, rapturous, spontaneous fashion,
hardly steering his train of thought by his intellect, but
letting it go along lines of least resistance and in a
rhythmic flood of words ; his central ideas of course
all the time holding the predominant place in his utterance. He is essentially a mystic both in experience and
in the ground and basis of his conception of God and
man. This mystical feature is especially prominent in
his second book on why God became incarnate in
Christ, and I shall begin my exposition with that
aspect of his thought.

God, he says, who is the eternal and only goodness,
has always been going out of Himself into forms of self-
expression. His highest expression is made in a heavenly
and purely spiritual order of angelic beings. Through
these spiritual beings He objectifies Himself, mirrors
Himself, knows Himself, and becomes revealed.[1] He
has also poured Himself out in a lower order of manifestation in the visible creation where spirit often finds
itself in opposition and contrast to that which is not
spirit. The highest being in this second order is man,
who in inward essence is made in the image and likeness
of God, but binds together in one personal life both
sensuous elements and divine and spiritual elements
which are always in collision and warfare with each other.
Man has full freedom of choice and can swing his will
over to either side—he can live upward toward the divine
goodness, or he can live downward toward the poor,
thin, limiting isolation of individual selfhood. But

Church, have been reinstated by some at this time without the Command of God
or the Witness of the Scriptures.")

These three books can be found bound in one volume, with writings of Denck
and others, in the Königliche Bibliothek in Dresden. There is also a copy of his
third book in Utrecht. Besides using the books themselves I have also used the
monograph by Nicoladoni and the study of Bünderlin in Hagen, op. cit. iii.
pp. 295-310.

[1] This idea is reproduced and greatly expanded in the writings of the famous
Silesian Mystic, Jacob Boehme.

through the shifting drama of our human destiny God never leaves us. He is always within us, as near to the heart of our being as the Light is to the eye. Conscience is the witness of His continued Presence ; the drawing which we feel toward higher things is born in the unlost image of God which is planted in our nature "like the tree of Life in Eden." He pleads in our hearts by His inner Word ; He reveals the goodness of Himself in His vocal opposition to all that would harm and spoil us, and He labours unceasingly to be born in us and to bring forth His love and His spiritual kingdom in the domain of our own spirits. The way of life is to die to the flesh and to the narrow will of the self, and to become alive to the Spirit and Word of God in the soul, to enter into and participate in that eternal love with which God loves us. This central idea of the double nature of man—an upper self indissolubly linked with God and a lower self rooted in fleshly and selfish desires—runs through all his writings, and in his view all the processes of revelation are to further the liberation and development of the higher and to weaken the gravitation of the lower self.

His first book deals with God's twofold revelation of Himself—primarily as a living Word in the soul of man, and secondarily through external signs and events, in an historical word, and in a temporal incarnation. With a wealth and variety of expression and illustration he insists and reiterates that only through the citadel—or better the sanctuary—of his inner self can man be spiritually reached, and won, and saved. Nobody can be saved until he knows himself at one with God ; until he finds his will at peace and in harmony with God's will ; until his inward spirit is conscious of unity with the eternal Spirit ; in short, until love sets him free with the freedom and joy of sons of God. Priests may absolve men if they will, and ministers may pronounce them saved, but all *that* counts for nothing until the inward transformation is a fact and the will has found its goal in the will of God : " Love must bloom and the spirit of the man must follow the will of God written in his heart." [1]

All external means in religion have one purpose and one function ; they are to awaken the mind and to direct it to the inward Word. The most startling miracle, the most momentous event in the sphere of temporal sequences, the most appealing account of historical occurrences can do nothing more than give in parable-fashion hints and suggestions of the real nature of that God who is eternally present within human spirits, and who is working endlessly to conform all lives to His perfect type and pattern. In the infant period of the race, both among the Hebrews and the Gentile peoples, God has used, like a wise Teacher, the symbol and picture-book method. He has disciplined them with external laws and with ceremonies which would move their child-minded imaginations ; but all this method was used only because they were not ripe and ready for the true and higher form of goodness. "They used the face of Moses until they could come to the full Light of the truth and righteousness of God, for which all the time their spirits really hungered and thirsted." [2] The supreme instance of the divine pictorial method was the sending of Christ to reveal God visibly. Before seeing God in Christ men falsely thought of Him as hostile, stern, and wrathful ; now they may see Him in this unveiling of Himself as He actually is, eternally loving, patiently forgiving, and seeking only to draw the world into His love and peace : "When the Abba-crying spirit of Christ awakens in our hearts we commune with God in peace and love." [3] But no one must content himself with Christ after the flesh, Christ historically known. That is to make an idol of Him. We can be saved through Him only when by His help we discover the essential nature of God and when He moves us to go to living in the spirit and power as Christ Himself lived. His death as an outward, historical fact does not save us ; it is the supreme expression of His limitless love and the complete dedication

---

[1] *Ein gemayne Berechnung*, p. 57.   [2] *Ibid.* p. 14.   [3] *Ibid.* p. 221.

of His spirit in self-giving, and it is effective for our salvation only when it draws us into a similar way of living, unites us in spirit with Him and makes us in reality partakers of His blood spiritually apprehended. Christ is our Mediator in that He reveals the love of God towards us and moves our will to appreciate it.[1]

Every step of human progress and of spiritual advance is marked by a passage from the dominion of the external to the sway and power of inward experience. God is training us for a time when images, figures, and picture-book methods will be no longer needed, but all men will live by the inward Word and have the witness—" the Abba-crying voice "—in their own hearts. But this process from outward to inward, from virtue impelled by fear and mediated by law to goodness generated by love, gives no place for license. Bünderlin has no fellow-ship with antinomianism, and is opposed to any tendency which gives rein to the flesh. The outward law, the external restraint, the discipline of fear and punishment are to be used so long as they are needed, and the written word and the pictorial image will always serve as a norm and standard, but the true spiritual goal of life is the formation of a rightly fashioned will, the creation of a controlling personal love, the experience of a guiding inward Spirit, which keep the awakened soul steadily approximating the perfect Life which Christ has revealed.

The true Church is, for Bünderlin as for Denck, the communion and fellowship of spiritual persons—an invisible congregation, ever-enlarging with the process of the ages and with the expanding light of the Spirit. He blames Luther for having stopped short of a real reforma-tion, of having " mixed with the Midianites instead of going on into the promised Canaan," and of having failed to dig down to the fundamental basis of spiritual religion.[2]

In his final treatise [3] he goes to the full length of the implication of his principle. He recounts with luminous

---

[1] *Ein gemayne Berechnung*, pp. 218-221, freely rendered.
[2] *Ibid*. pp. 30-34.   [3] *Erklärung durch Vergleichung*.

simplicity the mystical *unity* of the spiritual Universe
and tells of the divine purpose to draw all our finite and
divided wills into moral harmony with the Central Will.
Once more religion is presented as wholly a matter of
the inward spirit, a thing of insight, of obedience to a
living Word, of love for an infinite Lover, the bubbling of
living streams of water in the heart of man.   He declares
that the period of signs and symbols and of " the scholastic
way of truth " is passing away, and the religion of the
New Testament, the religion of life and spirit, is coming
in place of the old.   As fast as the new comes ceremonies
and sacraments vanish and fall away.   They do not
belong to a religion of the Spirit ; they are for the infant
race and for those who have not outgrown the picture-
book.   Christ's baptism is with power from above, and He
cleanses from sin not with water but with the Holy Ghost
and the burning fire of love.   As soon as the spiritual
man possesses " the key of David," and has entered
upon " the true Sabbath of his soul," he holds lightly
all forms and ceremonies which are outward and which
can be gone through with in a mechanical fashion
without creating the essential attitude of worship and
of inner harmony of will with God :   " When the
Kingdom of God with its joy and love has come in us
we do not much care for those things which can only
happen outside us." [1]

II

Christian Entfelder held almost precisely the same
views as those which we have found in the teaching of
Bünderlin.   He has become even more submerged than has
Bünderlin, and one hunts almost in vain for the events
of his life.   Hagen does not mention him.   Grützmacher
in his *Wort und Geist* never refers to him.   The great
Realencyklopädie für protestantische Theologie und Kirche
has no article on him.   Gottfried Arnold in his *Kirchen-*

---

[1] *Aus was Ursach*, p. 33.   These phrases, " Key of David " and " Sabbath
Rest for the Soul," occur in the writings of all the spiritual reformers.

und Ketzer-Historien merely mentions him in his list of
" Witnesses to the Truth." The only article I have
ever found on him is one by Professor Veesenmeyer in
Gabler's *N. theol. Journal* (1800), iv. 4, pp. 309-334.

He first appears in the group of Balthasar Hübmaier's
followers and at this period he had evidently allied himself
with the Anabaptist movement, which gathered into
itself many young men of the time who were eager for
a new and more spiritual type of Christianity. Hübmaier
mentions Entfelder in 1527 as pastor at Ewanzig, a small
town in Moravia, where, as he himself later says, he
diligently taught his little flock the things which concerned their inner life. In the eventful years of 1529–
1530 he was in Strasbourg in company with Bünderlin,[1]
and in this latter year he published his first book, with
the title : *Von den manigfaltigen in Glauben Zerspaltungen
dise jar erstanden.* (" On the many Separations which
have this year arisen in Belief.") A second book,
which is also dated 1530, bears the title : *Von waren
Gotseligkayt,*etc. (" On true Salvation.") He wrote also a
third book, which appeared in 1533 under the title : *Von
Gottes und Christi Jesu unseres Herren Erkandtnuss,* etc.
(" On the Knowledge of God and Jesus Christ our Lord.")

His style is simpler than that of Bünderlin. He
appears more as a man of the people ; he is fond of
vigorous, graphic figures of speech taken from the life
of the common people, much in the manner of Luther,
and he breathes forth in all three books a spirit of deep
and saintly life. His fundamental idea of the Universe
is like that of Bünderlin. The visible and invisible
creation, in all its degrees and stages, is the outgoing
and unfolding of God, who in His Essence and Godhead
is one, indivisible and incomprehensible. But as He
is essentially and eternally Good, He *expresses* Himself
in revelation, and goes out of Unity into differentiation
and multiplicity ; but the entire spiritual movement of
the universe is back again toward the fundamental Unity,
for Divine Unity is both the Alpha and the Omega of the

[1] See *N. lit. Anzeiger* (1807), p. 515.

deeper inner world. His main interest is, however, not philosophical and speculative ; his mind focuses always on the practical matters of a true and saintly life. Like his teacher, Bünderlin, his whole view of life and salvation is mystical; everything which concerns religion occurs in the realm of the soul and is the outcome of direct relations between the human spirit and the Divine Spirit. In every age, and in every land, the inner Word of God, the Voice of the Spirit speaking within, clarifying the mind and training the spiritual perceptions by a progressive experience, has made for itself a chosen people and has gathered out of the world a little inner circle of those who know the Truth because it was formed within themselves. This " inner circle of those who know " is the true Church : " The Church is a chosen, saved, purified, sanctified group in whom God dwells, upon whom the Holy Ghost has poured out His gifts and with whom Christ the Lord shares His offices and His mission."[1]

There is, however, through the ages a steady ripening of the Divine Harvest, a gradual and progressive onward movement of the spiritual process, ever within the lives of men : " Time brings roses. He who thinks that he has all the fruit when strawberries are ripe forgets that grapes are still to come. We should always be eagerly looking for something better." [2] There are, he says, three well-marked stages of revelation : (1) The stage of the law, when God, the Father, was making Himself known through His external creation and by outward forms of training and discipline ; (2) the stage of self-revelation through the Son, that men might see in Him and His personal activity the actual character and heart of God ; and (3) the stage of the Holy Spirit which fills all deeps and heights, flows into all lives, and is the One God revealed in His essential nature of active Goodness— Goodness at work in the world. Externals of every type—law, ceremonies, rewards and punishments, his-

---

[1] Entfelder to his brethren at the end of his first book : *Von Zerspaltungen.*
[2] Vorrede to *Von Zerspaltungen.*

torical happenings, written Scriptures, even the historical doings and sufferings of Christ—are only pointers and suggestion-material to bring the soul to the living Word within, " to the Lord Himself who is never absent," and who will be spiritually born within man. " God," he says, " has once become flesh in Christ and has revealed thus the hidden God and, as happened in a fleshly way in Mary, even so Christ must be spiritually born in us." So, too, everything which Christ experienced and endured in His earthly mission must be re-lived and reproduced in the life of His true disciples. There is no salvation possible without the new birth of Christ in us, without self-surrender and the losing of oneself, without being buried with Christ in a death to self-will and without rising with Him in joy and peace and victory.[1] He who rightly loves his Christ will speak no word, will eat no bit of bread, nor taste of water, nor put a stitch of clothes upon his body without thinking of the Beloved of his soul. . . . In this state he can rid himself of all pictures and symbols, renounce everything which he possesses, take up his cross with Christ, join Him in an inward, dying life, allow himself, like grain, to be threshed, winnowed, ground, bolted, and baked that he may become spiritual food as Christ has done for us. Then there comes a state in which poverty and riches, pain and joy, life and death are alike, when the soul has found its sabbath-peace in the Origin and Fount of all Love.[2] His first book closes with a beautiful account of the return of the prodigal to His Father and to His Father's love, and then he breaks into a joyous cry, as if it all came out of his own experience : " Who then can separate us from the Love of God ? "

Those who rightly understand religion and have had this birth and this Sabbath-peace within themselves will stop contending over outward, external things, which make separations but do not minister to the spirit ; they will give up the Babel-habit of constructing theological

[1] *Von waren Gotseligkayt*, pp. 18-21.
[2] See especially *Von Zerspaltungen*, pp. 6-8.

systems,[1] they will pass upward from elements to the essence, they will stop building the city-walls of the Church out of baptism and the supper, which furnish " only clay-plastered walls " at best, and they will found the Church instead upon the true sacramental power of the inward Spirit of God.[2] The true goal of the spiritual life is such a oneness with God that He is in us and we in Him, so that the inner joy and power take our outer life captive and draw us away from the world and its " pictures," and make it a heartfelt delight to do all His commandments and to suffer anything for Him.[3]

Here, then, in the third decade of the sixteenth century, when the leaders of the Reformation were using all their powers of dialectic to formulate in new scholastic phrase the sound creed for Protestant Christendom, and while the fierce and decisive battle was being waged over the new form in which the Eucharist must be celebrated, there appeared a little group of men who proposed that Christianity should be conceived and practised as *a way of living*—nothing more nor less. They rejected theological language and terminology root and branch. They are as innocent of scholastic subtlety and forensic conceptions as though they had been born in this generation. They seem to have wiped their slate clean of the long line of Augustinian contributions, and to have begun afresh with the life and message of Jesus Christ, coloured, if at all, by local and temporal backgrounds, by the experience of the earlier German mystics who helped them to interpret their own simple and sincere experiences. They are as naïve and artless as little children, and they expect, as all enthusiasts do in their youth, that they have only to announce their wonderful truths and to proclaim their " openings " in order to bring the world to the light ! They go to the full length of the implications of their

---

[1] This " Babel-habit of constructing theological systems " is constantly referred to by Jacob Boehme, as we shall see. I believe that Boehme had read both Bünderlin and Entfelder.

[2] See *Von Zerspaltungen*, passim, especially p. 17.

[3] *Von waren Gotseligkayt*, p. 13.

fresh insight without ever dreaming that all the theological world will unite, across the yawning chasms of difference, to stamp out their " pestilent heresy," and to rid the earth of persons who dare to question the traditions and the practices of the centuries.

Instead of beginning with the presupposition of original sin, they quietly assert that the soul of man is inherently bound up in the Life and Nature of God, and that goodness is at least as " original " as badness. They fly in the face of the age-long view that the doctrine of Grace makes freewill impossible and reduces salvation wholly to a work of God, and they assert as the ineradicable testimony of their own consciousness that human choices between Light and Darkness, the personal response to the character of God as He reveals Himself, the co-operation of the will of man with the processes of a living and spiritual God are the things which save a man—and this salvation is possible in a pagan, in a Jew, in a Turk even, as well as in a man who ranges himself under Christian rubrics and who says paternosters. They reject all the scholastic accounts of Christ's metaphysical nature, they will not use the term Trinity, nor will they admit that it is right to employ any words which imply that God is divided into multiform personalities; but nevertheless they hold, with all the fervour of their earnest spirits, that Christ is God historically and humanly revealed, and that to see Christ is to see the true and only God, and to love Christ is to love the Eternal Love.

In an age which settled back upon the Scriptures as the only basis of authority in religious faith and practice, they boldly challenged that course as a dangerous return to a lower form of religion than that to which Christ had called men and as only legalism and scribism in a new dress. They insisted that the Eternal Spirit, who had been educating the race from its birth, bringing all things up to better, and who had used now one symbol and now another to fit the growing spiritual perception of men, is a real Presence in the deeps of men's consciousness, and is ceaselessly voicing Himself there as a living Word whom it is life to obey and death to disregard and slight. Having found this present, immanent Spirit and being deeply convinced that all that really matters happens in the dread region of the human heart, they turned away from all ceremonies and sacraments and tried to form a Church which should be purely and simply a Communion of saints — a brotherhood of believers living in the joy of an inward experience of God, and bound together in common love to Christ and in common service to all who are potential sons of God.

CHAPTER IV

SEBASTIAN FRANCK is one of the most interesting figures
in the group of German Reformers, a man of heroic spirit
and a path-breaking genius, though for many reasons
his influence upon his epoch was in no degree com-
parable with that of many of his great contemporaries.
No person, however great a genius he may be, can get
wholly free from the intellectual climate and the social
ideals of his period, but occasionally a man appears who
has the skill and vision to hit upon nascent aspirations
and tendencies which are big with futurity, and who
thereby seems to be far ahead of his age and not explic-
able by any lineage or pedigree. Sebastian Franck was
a man of this sort. He was extraordinarily unfettered
by medieval inheritance, and he would be able to adjust
himself with perfect ease to the spirit and ideas of the
modern world if he could be dropped forward into it.

He is especially interesting and important as an
exponent and interpreter of a religion based on inward
authority because he unites, in an unusual manner, the
intellectual ideals of the Humanist with the experience
and attitude of the Mystic. In him we have a Christian
thinker who is able to detach himself from the theological
formulations of his own and of earlier times, and who
could draw, with breadth of mind and depth of insight,
from the wells of the great original thinkers of all ages,
and who, besides, in his own deep and serious soul could
feel the inner flow of central realities. He was no doubt

too much detached to be a successful Reformer of the
historical Church, and he was too little interested in
external organisations to be the leader of a new sect;
but he was, what he aspired to be, a sincere and unselfish
contributor to the spread of the Kingdom of God, and a
significant apostle of the invisible Church.[1]

Sebastian Franck was born in 1499 at Donauwörth
in Schwabia. He began his higher education in the
University of Ingolstadt, which he entered March 26,
1515. He went from Ingolstadt to Heidelberg, where
he continued his studies in the Dominican College which
was incorporated with the University. Here he was
associated in the friendly fellowship of student life with
two of his later opponents, Martin Frecht and Martin
Bucer, and here he came under the influence of Humanism
which in the scholarly circles in Heidelberg was beginning
to take a place along with the current Scholasticism of the
period. While a student in Heidelberg he first heard
Martin Luther speak on the insufficiency of works and
on faith as the way of salvation, and though he must
have felt the power of this great personality and the
freshness of the message, he was not yet ripe for a radical
change of front.[2] He seems to have felt through these
student years that a new age was in process of birth, but
though he was following the great events he remained
to the end of his University period an adherent of the
ancient Church and was ordained a priest about the year
1524; but very soon after he went over to the party
of Reform, and was settled as a reforming preacher
in the little church at Gustenfelden near Nuremberg.
During this period he came into close and intimate
relation with the powerful humanistic spirit of that
important city. Hans Sachs was already a person of
fame and influence in Nuremberg, and here he became
acquainted with the writings of the most famous humanists
of the day — Erasmus, Hutten, Reuchlin, Pirkheimer,

---

[1] Troeltsch calls him a " literarischer Prophet der alleinigen Erlösungskraft
des Geistes und des inneren Wortes," *Die Soziallehren*, p. 886.

[2] See article by M. Cunitz in *Nouvelle Revue de Théologie*, vol. v. p. 361.

Althamer and others. In 1528 he married Ottilie Behaim, a woman of rare gifts, whose brothers were pupils of Albrecht Dürer, and who were themselves in sympathy with the freer tendencies of the time as expressed by the Anabaptists. Franck, however, though sympathizing with the aspirations of the Anabaptists for a new age, did not feel confidence in their views or their methods. His first literary work was a translation into German of Althamer's *Diallage*, which contained an attack from the Lutheran point of view upon the various Enthusiasts of the period, especially the Anabaptists. In his original preface to this work Franck, though still in most respects a Lutheran, already reveals unmistakable signs of variation from the Wittenberg type, and he is plainly moving in the direction of a religion of the spiritual and mystical type freed from the limitations of sect and party. Even in this formative stage he insists that the Spirit, and not commentaries, is the true guide for the interpretation of Scripture ; he already contrasts Spirit and letter, outer man and inner man, and he here lays down the radical principle, which he himself soon put into practice, that a minister of the Gospel should resign his charge as soon as he discovers that his preaching is not bearing spiritual fruit in the transformation of the lives of his congregation.[1]

Sometime before 1530 Franck had come into intimate connection with Denck, Bünderlin, Schwenckfeld, and other contemporary leaders of the " Spiritual " movement, and their influence upon him was profound and lasting, because their message fitted the aspirations which, though not yet well defined, were surging subconsciously in him.[2] There are throughout his writings very clear marks of Schwenckfeld's influence upon him, but Bünderlin especially spoke to his condition and helped him discover the road which his feet were seeking. In an important letter which Franck wrote to Johann Campanus in 1531, he calls Bünderlin a scholar, a wonder-

---

[1] See Alfred Hegler's *Geist und Schrift bei Sebastian Franck* (Freiburg), 1892, pp. 28-48.   [2] See next chapter for an account of Caspar Schwenckfeld.

fully reverent man, dead to the world, powerful in the Scriptures, and mightily gifted with an enlightened reason ; and this letter shows that he himself has been moving rapidly in the direction in which Bünderlin and Denck were travelling, though neither now nor at any time was Franck a mere copier of other men's ideas.[1] " We must unlearn," he writes, " all that we have learned from our youth up from the papists, and we must change everything we have got from the Pope or from Luther and Zwingli." He predicts that the external Church will never be set up again, " for the inward enlightenment by the Spirit of God is sufficient."

In his *Türkenchronik*, or " Chronicle and Description of Turkey," published in 1530, he had already declared his dissatisfaction with ceremonies and outward forms of any sort, his refusal to be identified with any existing, empirical Church, his solemn dedication to the invisible Church, and his determination to be an apostle of the Spirit. " There already are in our times," he writes, " three distinct Faiths, which have a large following, the Lutheran, Zwinglian and Anabaptist ; and a *fourth* is well on the way to birth, which will dispense with external preaching, ceremonies, sacraments, bann and office as unnecessary, and which seeks solely to gather among all peoples an invisible, spiritual Church in the unity of the Spirit and of faith, to be governed wholly by the eternal, invisible Word of God, without external means, as the apostolic Church was governed before its apostasy, which occurred after the death of the apostles." [2]

The year that dates his autobiographical letter to Campanus saw the publication in Strasbourg of Franck's best - known literary work : *Chronica, Zeitbuch und Geschichtsbibel* (" A Universal Chronicle of the World's History from the Earliest Times to the Present ").[3] It has

---

[1] This Letter to Campanus, written originally in Latin, is extant in a Dutch translation, " Eyn Brieff van Sebastiaen Franck van Weirdt, geschreven over etlicken jaren in Latijn, tho synen vriendt Johan Campaen." See Hegler, *op. cit.* pp. 50-53.

[2] *Chronica und Beschreibung der Türkey* (Nürnberg, 1530), K. 3 b.

[3] My copy is the first edition, printed in Strasbourg by Balthasser Beck, 1531.

often been pointed out that much of the material of this great Chronicle is taken over from earlier Chroniclers, especially from the Nuremberger Schedel, and it is furthermore true that Franck's *Book of the Ages* contains large tracts of unhistorical narrative, set forth after the manner of Chroniclers without much critical insight, but the book, nevertheless, has a unique value. It abounds in Franck's peculiar irony and paradox, and it unfolds his conception of the spiritual history of the race, under the tuition of the Divine Word. At the beginning are patriarchs living in the dawn of the world under the guidance of inward vision, and at the end are saints and heretics, whom Franck finds among all races, bravely following the same inward Light, now after the ages grown clearer and more luminous, and sufficient for those who will patiently and faithfully heed it, while the real " heretics " for him are " heretics of the letter." " We ought to act carefully before God "—this is Franck's constant testimony—" hold to God alone and look upon Him as the cause of all things, and we ought always in all matters to notice what God says *in us*, to pay attention to the witness of our hearts, and never to think, or act, against our conscience. For everything does not hang upon the bare letter of Scripture ; everything hangs, rather, on the spirit of Scripture and on a spiritual under-standing of the inner meaning of what God has said. If we weigh every matter carefully we shall find its true meaning in the depth of our spiritual understanding and by the mind of Christ. Otherwise, the dead letter of Scripture would make us all heretics and fools, for every-thing can be bedecked and defended with texts, therefore let nobody confound himself and confuse himself with Scripture, but let every one weigh and test Scripture to see how it fits his own heart. If it is against his conscience and the Word within his own soul, then be sure he has not reached the right meaning, according to the mind of the Spirit, for the Scriptures must give witness *to* the Spirit, never against it." [1]

[1] *Chronica*, p. 452 b.

The *Chronica* naturally aroused a storm of opposition against this bold advocate of the inner Way. Even Erasmus, who had been canonized in Franck's list of heretics, joined in the outcry against the chronicler of the world's spiritual development. His book was confiscated, he was temporarily imprisoned, and for the years immediately following he was never secure in any city where he endeavoured to pursue his labours. He supported himself and his family, now by the humble occupation of a soap-boiler, now by working in a printing-house, sometimes in Strasbourg, sometimes in Esslingen, and sometimes in Ulm, only asking that he " might not be forced to bury the talent which God had given him, but might be allowed to use it for the good of the people of God."

In 1534 his *Weltbuch* appeared from a press in Tübingen, and the same year he published his famous *Paradoxa*, which contains the most clear and consistent exposition of his mystical and spiritual religion. Other significant books from his pen are his translation of Erasmus' *Moriae Encomion* ("Praise of Folly"), with very important additions ; *Von der Eitelkeit aller menschlichen Kunst und Weisheit* ("The Vanity of Arts and Sciences"), following the treatise by Agrippa von Nettesheim ; *Von dem Baum des Wissens Gutes und Böses* ("Of the Tree of the Knowledge of Good and Evil") ;[1] the *Germaniae Chronicon* ("Chronicle of Germany"), 1538 ; *Die guldin Arch* ("Golden Arch"), 1538 ; and *Das verbütschiert mit 7 Siegeln verschlossene Buch* ("The Seven-sealed Book"), 1539.

The closing years of his life were passed in Basle, where he peacefully worked at his books and at type-setting, while the theologians fired their paper guns against him, and here in Basle he "went forth with God" on his last journey to find a safe and quiet "city with foundations," probably about the end of the year 1542. Three years before his

---

[1] These three books were included in a volume entitled *Die vier kron-büchlein* (1534).

death he had written in his " Seven-sealed Book "
of the soul's journey toward God in these words :
" The longer one travels toward the city he seeks the
nearer and nearer he comes to the goal of his journey ;
exactly so is it with the soul that is seeking God. If he
will travel away from himself and away from the world
and seek only God as the precious pearl of his soul, he
will come steadily nearer to God, until he becomes one
spirit with God the Spirit ; but let him not be afraid of
mountains and valleys on the way, and let him not give
up because he is tired and weary, *for he who seeks finds.*" [1]
" The Sealed Book " contains an " apology " by Franck
which is one of the most touching and one of the most
noble documents from any opponent of the course which
the German Reformation was taking. " I want my
writings accepted," he declares, " only in so far as they
fit the spirit of Scripture, the teaching of the prophets,
and only so far as the anointing of the Word of God,
Christ the inward Life and Light of men, gives witness
to them. . . . Nobody is the master of my faith, and
I desire to be the master of the faith of no one. I love
any man whom I can help, and I call him brother whether
he be Jew or Samaritan. . . . I cannot belong to any
separate sect, but I believe in a holy, Christlike Church,
a fellowship of saints, and I hold as my brother, my
neighbour, my flesh and blood, all men who belong to
Christ among all sects, faiths, and peoples scattered
throughout the whole world—only I allow nobody to
have dominion over the one place which I am pledged to
the Lord to keep as pure virgin, namely my heart and
my conscience. If you try to bind my conscience, to
rule over my faith, or to be master of my heart, then I
must leave you. Except *that*, everything I am or have
is thine, whoever thou art or whatever thou mayest
believe." [2]

It was Franck's primary idea—the principle to which
he was dedicated and for which he was content to suffer,

---

[1] *Das verbütschierte Buch*, p. 5.
[2] Pp. 5-8 of the Apologia to *Das verbütschierte Buch*.

in the faith that men in future times would come to see
as he did [1]—that man's soul possesses a native capacity
to hear the inward Word of God. He often calls Plato
and Plotinus and " Hermes Trismegistus " his teachers,
who " had spoken to him more clearly than Moses did," [2]
and, like these Greek teachers of the nature of the
soul's furnishings, he insisted that we come " not in
entire forgetfulness and not in utter nakedness," but
that there is a divine element, an innermost essence in
us, in the very structure of the soul, which is the starting-
point of all spiritual progress, the mark of man's dignity,
the real source of all religious experience, and the eternal
basis of the soul's salvation and joy. He names this
inward endowment by many names. It is the Word of
God ("Wort Gottes"), the Power of God ("Kraft Gottes"),
Spirit (" Geist "), Mind of Christ (" Sinn Christi "), Divine
Activity ("göttliche Wirkung"), Divine Origin ("göttlicher
Ursprung "), the inward Light (" das innere Licht "), the
true Light (" das wahre Licht "), the Lamp of the soul
("das innere Ampellicht").   " The inward Light," Franck
says in the *Paradoxa*, " is nothing else than the Word of
God, God Himself, by whom all things were made and by
whom all men are enlightened." It is, in Franck's thought,
not a capricious, subjective impulse or vision, and it is
not to be discovered in sudden ecstatic experiences ; nor,
on the other hand, is the divine Word, for Franck, something purely objective and transcendent. It is rather a
common ground and essence for God and man. It is
God in His self-revealing activity ; God in His self-
giving grace ; God as the immanent ground of all that
is permanently real, and at the same time this divine
endowment forms the fundamental nature of man's
soul—" Gottes Wort ist in der menschlichen Natur
angelegt " [3]—and is the original substance of our being.
Consciousness of God and consciousness of self have one
fundamental source in this deep where God and man
are unsundered. " No man can see or know himself
unless he sees and knows, by the Light and Life that is

[1] See *Apologia*, p. 2.   [2] *Ibid.* p. 3.   [3] Hegler, *op. cit.* p. 98.

in him, God the eternally true Light and Life ; wherefore nobody can ever know God outside of himself, outside that region where he knows himself in the ground of himself. . . . Man must seek, find, and know God through an interrelation—he must find God in himself and himself in God." [1] This deep ground of inner reality is in every person, so far as he is a person ; it shines forth as a steady illumination in the soul, and, while everything else is transitory, this Word is eternal and has been the moral and spiritual guide of all peoples in all ages.

Franck thus differs in a vital point from Schwenckfeld. The latter starts with man as utterly lost and devoid of any inherent goodness. By a sudden, supernatural event, at a temporal moment, divine forces break into the soul from without and supply it with a revitalizing energy. Man—lost, fallen, sin-blasted and utterly helpless—is by a divine and heavenly creative movement *made* a new Adam. For Franck, the soul has never lost the divine Image, the pearl of supreme price, the original element which is God Himself in the soul. We are all, in the deepest centre of our being, like Adam, possessed of a substantial essence, not of earth, not of time and space, not of the shadow but of the eternal, spiritual, and heavenly type. It may become overlaid with the rubbish of earth, it may long lie buried in the field of the human heart, it may remain concealed, like the grain of radium in a mass of dark pitchblende, and be forgotten, but we have only to return home within ourselves to find the God who has never been sundered from us and who could not leave us without leaving Himself. We do not need to cross the sea to find Him, we do not need to climb the heavens to reach Him—the Word is nigh thee, the Image is in thy heart, turn home and thou shalt find Him.[2]

The bottomless and abysmal nature of the human soul comes first into clear revelation in the Person of Christ, who is, Franck declares, truly and essentially both God and Man. In Christ the invisible, eternal,

---

[1] *Die guldin Arch*, Preface 3b-4a.   [2] *Paradoxa*, sec. 101.

self-existent God has clothed Himself with flesh and become Man, has made Himself visible and vocal to our spiritual eyes and ears, and in Christ God has given us an adequate goal and norm of life, a perfect pattern (" Muster ") to walk by and to live by. Here we can see both the character of God and the measure of His expectation for us. But we must not stop with the Christ after the flesh, the Christ without. He first becomes our life and salvation when He is born within us and is revealed in our hearts, and has become the Life of our lives. We must eat His body, drink His blood until our nature is one with His nature and our spirit one in will and purpose with His spirit.[1]

Franck belongs in many respects among the mystics, but with peculiar variations of his own from the prevailing historical type of mysticism. He is without question saturated with the spirit of the great mystics ; he approves their inner way to God and he has learned from them to view this world of time and space as shadow and not as reality. No mystic, further, could say harsher things than he does of " Reason." [2] Human reason—or more properly " reasoning "—has for him, as for them, a very limited area for its demesne. It is a good guide in the realm of earthly affairs. It can deal wisely with matters that affect our bodily comfort and our social welfare, but it is " barren " in the sphere of eternal issues. It has no eye for realities beyond the world of three dimensions. It goes blind as soon as it tries to speculate about God. He looks for no final results in spiritual matters from intellectual dialectics, whether they be of the old scholastic type, or of the new type of speculations, formulations and subtleties of the Protestant theologians.

Franck always comes back to *experience* as his basis of religion, as his way to truth and to divine things. " Many," he says, " know and teach only what they have picked up and gathered in, without having experienced it

---

[1] *Paradoxa*, sec. 99 and 138.
[2] Franck translated both Erasmus' *Praise of Folly* and Agrippa's *Vanity of Arts and Sciences.*

in the deeps of themselves." [1] " He who wishes to know
what is in the Temple must not stand outside, merely
hearing people read and talk about God. *That* is all a
dead thing. He must go inside and have the experience
for himself (" selbst erfahren "). Then first everything
springs into life." [2] But " experience " with him does
not mean enthusiastic visions and raptures. He puts as
little value on ecstasies and emotional vapourings as he
does on dialectic. Ecstasies lead men as often on false
trails as on right tracks. They supply no criterion of
certitude ; they furnish no concrete ideas or ideals to
live by ; but still further, they do not bring all the
deep-lying powers of the soul into play as any true source
of religion must do. *He* is striving to find a foundation-
principle for the spiritual life which shall not be
capricious or sporadic, and which shall not be confined
to one aspect of the inner self, but which shall burn on as
a steady illumination in the soul and be the basis of all
moral activity and all spiritual development. He finds
this principle, as we have seen, in the Word of God,
which is a divine reality, an eternal and self-existent
activity, opening upward into all the resources of God,
and at the same time forming the fundamental nature
and ground-structure of the soul. A person may live—
many persons do—in the outer region of the self, using
the natural instincts with which he is supplied, pursuing
the goals of life which appeal to common sense and
steering the earthly course by custom and by reason, but
it is always possible to have a wider range of experience,
to live in deeper currents, and to draw upon a *profounder
source of insight*. This deeper experience—which is the
basis of Franck's mysticism and, for him, the very heart
of any genuine religion—consists of a personal discovery
of this eternal Word of God within and an irradiation of the
whole being through the co-operation of the will with it.
The will is king in man,[3] and can open or shut the gate
which leads to life. It can make its world good or it

can make it evil ; just as out of one and the same flower
the bee gets honey and the spider poison.[1]   It can swing
over its allegiance to God the Spirit of truth, or to the
god of the world who is anti-Christ.

This experience of the Word of God which is thus
brought about by the will of man—by an innermost
personal choice—affects, Franck insists, all the faculties
of the inner life.   Reason now becomes illumined with
a Light which it never had until the gate into its deeper
region was opened.   Now, through co-operation with the
Spirit of God, reason becomes capable of higher processes,
and can deal with divine things because it has actual
data to work upon.   The emotions, too, are no longer
blind and instinctive, they no longer carry the will whither
it would not.   They are now the overflow of an inner
experience which is too rich and full for expression,[2]
which transcends the intellectual apprehension of it,
but they are spiritualized and controlled from within.
The moral life is especially heightened, and this is for
Franck one of the main evidences that a divine source has
been tapped.   The discovery of the Word of God creates
and constructs an autonomous " kingdom of the conscience " (" Reich des Gewissens "), gives us " a thousand-
fold witness of God," and becomes to us the tree of life
and the tree of knowledge.[3]

In his little book on " the Tree of the Knowledge of
Good and Evil "—a book which was destined to have a far-
reaching influence—he declares that the Garden-of-Eden
story is a mighty parable of the human soul.   All that is
told in the Genesis account is told of what goes on in the
mysterious realm within us.   It is told as though it were
an external happening, it is in reality an internal affair.
The Paradise and the Fall, the Voice of God and the
tempting voice of the serpent, the Tree of Life and the
Tree of the knowledge of Good and Evil, are all in our
own hearts as they were in the heart of Adam.   Heaven
and Hell are there.   The one stands fully revealed in
the triumphant Adam, who is Christ ;   the other is ex-

[1] *Paradoxa*, sec. 29.   [2] *Moriae Enc.* p. 93a.   [3] *Paradoxa*, sec. 63.

hibited in its awfulness in the disobedient Adam of the Fall.

As fast as the life comes under the sway of the " kingdom of conscience " and a solid moral character is formed, the inner guidance of the Word of God becomes more certain and more reliable. Only the good person has a sure and unerring perception of the truth, just as only the scientist sees the laws of the world, and as only the musician perceives the harmony of sounds. Not only must all spiritual experience be subject to the moral test, it must further be tested by the Light of God in other men and in history, and by the *spirit of Scripture*, which is the noblest permanent fruit of the Eternal Word. Every person must *prove* the authority of his religion. He must have his heart conquered and his mind taken captive and his will directed by his truth so that he would be ready to face a thousand deaths for it,[1] and he must, through his truth and insight, come into spiritual unity and co-operation with all who form the invisible Church.

The invisible Church forms the central loyalty of Franck's fervent soul. " The true Church," he writes, " is not a separate mass of people, not a particular sect to be pointed out with the finger, not confined to one time or one place ; it is rather a spiritual and invisible body of all the members of Christ, born of God, of one mind, spirit, and faith, but not gathered in any one external city or place. It is a Fellowship, seen with the spiritual eye and by the inner man. It is the assembly and communion of all truly God-fearing, good-hearted, new-born persons in all the world, bound together by the Holy Spirit in the peace of God and the bonds of love—a Communion outside of which there is no salvation, no Christ, no God, no comprehension of Scripture, no Holy Spirit, and no Gospel. I belong to this Fellowship. I believe in the Communion of saints, and I am in this Church, let me be where I may ; and therefore I no

---

[1] *Moriae Enc.* p. 110. For the testing of the Word, see Hegler, *op. cit.* pp. 117-119.

longer look for Christ in lo heres or lo theres."[1] This Church, which the Spirit is building through the ages and in all lands, is, once more, like the experience of the individual Christian, entirely an inward affair. " Love is the one mark and badge of Fellowship in it."[2] No outward forms of any sort seem to him necessary for membership in this true Church. " External gifts and offices make no Christian, and just as little does the standing of the person, or locality, or time, or dress, or food, or anything external. The kingdom of God is neither prince nor peasant, food nor drink, hat nor coat, here nor there, yesterday nor to-morrow, baptism nor circumcision, nor anything whatever that is external, but peace and joy in the Holy Spirit, unalloyed love out of a pure heart and good conscience, and an unfeigned faith."[3]

In his Apology he says that he has withdrawn " from all theological disputations, from all sectarian statements of creed, from baptism and all ceremonies," and " I stand now," he adds, " only for what is fundamental and essential for salvation "—that is, vital participation in the Life of God revealed in the soul.[4] " I am looking," he writes in the opening of the *Paradoxa*, " for no new and separate Church, no new commission, no new baptism, no new dispensation. The Church has already been founded on Christ the Rock, and since the outward keys and sacraments have been misused and have gone by, He now administers the sacraments inwardly in spirit and in truth. He baptizes His own, even in the midst of Babylon, and feeds them with His own body, and will do so unto the end of the world."[5]

In a letter to Campanus he says, " I am fully convinced [by a study of the early Church Fathers] that, after the death of the apostles, the external Church of Christ, with its gifts and sacraments, vanished from the earth and withdrew into heaven, and is now hidden in spirit and in truth, and for these past fourteen hundred years

---

[1] *Paradoxa*, Vorrede, sec. 8.   [2] *Paradoxa*, sec. 9.   [3] *Ibid.* sec. 45.
[4] *Das verbütschierte Buch*, Apology, p. 11.   [5] *Paradoxa*, Vorrede, sec. 8.

there has existed no true external Church and no efficacious sacraments." [1]

His valuation of Scripture fits perfectly into this
religion of the inward life and the invisible Church.   The
true and essential Word of God is the divine revelation
in the soul of man.   It is the *prius* of all Scripture and
it is the key to the spiritual meaning of all Scripture.
To substitute Scripture for the self-revealing Spirit is
to put the dead letter in the place of the living Word,
the outer Ark in place of the inner sanctuary, the sheath
in place of the sword, the horn-pane Lantern in place of
the Light.[2]   This letter killed Christ in Judea ; it is
killing Him now.   It has split the Church into fragments
and sects and is splitting it now.[3]   It always makes a
" Babel " instead of a Church.   It kept the Pharisees
from seeing Moses face to face ; it keeps men now from
seeing the Lord face to face.[4]   Franck insists that, from
its inherent nature, a written Scripture cannot be the
final authority in religion : (*a*) It is outward, external,
while the seat of religion is in the soul of man.   (*b*) It is
transitory and shifting, for language is always in process
of change, and written words have different meanings to
different ages and in different countries, while for a permanent religion there must be a living, eternal Word that
fits all ages, lands, and conditions.   (*c*) Scripture is full
of mystery, contradiction, and paradox which only " The
key of David "—the inner experience of the heart—can
unlock.   Scripture is the Manger, but, unless the Holy
Spirit comes as the day star in the heart, the Wise man
will not find the Christ.[5]   (*d*) Scripture at best brings only
knowledge.   It lacks the power to deliver from the sin
which it describes.   It cannot create the faith, the desire,
the love, the will purpose which are necessary to win that
which the Scriptures portray.   No book—no amount of
" ink, paper, and letters "—can make a man good, since
religion is not knowledge, but a way of living, a trans-

---

[1] This Letter is preserved in J. G. Schellhorn's *Amoenitates literariae* (1729),
xi. pp. 59-61.

[2] *Paradoxa*, Vorrede, sec. 4.   [3] *Ibid.* sec. 6.   [4] *Ibid.* sec. 2.

[5] See *Das verbütschierte Buch, passim.*

formed life, and *that* involves an inward life-process, a
resident creative power. " In Pentecost all books are
transcended." [1]

As Franck pushes back through " the ink, paper, and
letters of Scripture " to the Spirit and Truth which these
great writings reveal, when they are read and apprehended in the light of an inward spiritual experience,
so, too, he is always seeking, *through* the historical Christ,
to find the Eternal Christ—the ever-living, ever-present,
personal Self-Revelation of God. He says, in his " Seven-
Sealed Book," " I esteem Christ the Word of God above
all else, for without Him there is no salvation, and without
Him no one can enjoy God." [2] " Christ," he says in the
Paradoxa, " has been called the Image, the Character,
the Expression of God, yes, the Glory and Effulgence of
His Splendour, the very Impression of His Substance,
so that in Him God Himself is seen and heard and known.
For it is God Himself whom we see and hear and perceive
in Christ. In Him God becomes visible and His nature is
revealed. Everything that God is, or knows, or wills,
or possesses, or can do, is incarnated in Christ and put
before our eyes. Everything that can be said of God
can as truly be said of Christ." [3]

But this Christ, who is the very Nature and Character
of God made visible and vocal, is, as we have seen,
not limited to the historical Person who lived in Galilee
and Judea. He is an eternal Logos, a living Word,
coming to expression, in some degree, in all times and
lands, revealing His Light through the dim lantern of
many human lives—a Christ reborn in many souls, raised
again in many victorious lives, and endlessly spreading
His Kingdom through the ever-widening membership
of the invisible Church.[4] Without this eternal revelation
of Himself in a spiritual Fellowship of many members,
God would not be God, as a Vine would not be a Vine
without branches ; and contrariwise there could be no
spiritual humanity without the inward immanent pres-

---

[1] Quoted from Hegler, *op. cit.* p. 104.   [2] *Das verbütschierte Buch*, p. 3.
[3] *Paradoxa*, sec. 101.   [4] *Ibid.* sec. 101.

ence of this Self-Revealing God in Christ.[1] As in Pales-
tine, so everywhere, Christ—not only Christ after the
flesh, but after the Spirit—is a crucified Christ. Only
those can open the Sealed Book—can penetrate the divine
Revelation—who bear the mark of the Cross on their
forehead, who have eaten the flesh and drunk the blood
of the suffering and crucified Christ, who have discovered
that the Word of God is eternally a Word of the Cross.[2]
God is nearest to us when He seems farthest away. He
was nearest to Christ when He was crying : " My God,
why hast Thou forsaken me ? " So, too, now he who is
nearest to the cross is nearest to God, and where the flesh
is being crucified and the end of all outward things is
reached, *there God is found*.[3]

Sin means, for Franck, as for all mystics of his type,
the *free choice* of something for one's private and particular
self in place of life-aims that fulfil the good of the whole
and realize the universal Will of God. To live for the
flesh instead of for the spirit, to pursue the aims of a
narrow private self where they conflict with the spirit
of universal love, to turn from the Word of God in the
soul to follow the idle voices of the moment—that is the
very essence of sin. It is not inherited, it is self-chosen,
and yet there is something in our disposition which sets
itself in array against the divine revelation within us.
The Adam-story is a genuine life-picture. It is a chapter
out of the book of the ages, the life of humanity. We do
not sin and fall because he did ; we sin and fall because
we are human and finite, as he was, and choose the darkness instead of the Light, prefer Satan to God, pursue the
way of death instead of the way of Life, as he did.[4]

This will be sufficient to show the essential character
of the religion of this lonely man and to present the main
tendencies of his bold and independent thought. He had
no desire to be the head of a party ; he was too remote

[1] *Paradoxa*, sec. 8.
[2] *Das verbütschierte Buch*, pp. 6-9, and *Paradoxa*, sec. 41.
[3] *Paradoxa*, sec. 41 and 42.
[4] *Moriae Enc.* p. 111. *Paradoxa, passim*, especially sec. 28-32. See also
Hegler *op. cit.* pp. 127-136.

from the currents of evangelical Christianity to impress the common people whom he loved, and he was too radical a thinker to lead even the scholars who had become liberated from tradition by their humanistic studies and by historical insight. He was a kind of sixteenth-century Heraclitus, seeing the flow and flux of all things temporal, finding paradox and contradiction everywhere, discovering life to be a clash of opposites, with its " way up " and its " way down," on the surface a pessimist, but at the heart of himself an optimist ; and finally, beneath all the folly of history and all the sin and stupidity of human life, seeing with the eye of his spirit One Eternal Logos who steers all things toward purpose, who suffers as a Lamb slain for the flock, who reveals His Truth and Life in the sanctuary of the soul, and who through the ages is building an invisible Church, a divine Kingdom of many members, in whom He lives as the Life of their lives.

CHAPTER V

CASPAR SCHWENCKFELD AND THE REFORMATION OF THE " MIDDLE WAY " [1]

AMONG all the Reformers of the sixteenth century who worked at the immense task of recovering, purifying, and restating the Christian Faith, no one was nobler in life and personality, and no one was more uncompromisingly dedicated to the mission of bringing into the life of the people a type of Christianity winnowed clean from the husks of superstition and tradition and grounded in ethical and spiritual reality, than was Caspar Schwenckfeld, the Silesian noble. No one, to a greater degree than he, succeeded in going behind, not only Scholastic formulations but even behind Pauline interpretations of Christ, to Christ Himself. The aspects of the Christ-life which powerfully moved him were very different from

[1] The most important material for a study of Schwenckfeld is the following :—

Corpus Schwenckfeldianorum, edited by C. D. Hartranft. Published Leipzig, vol. i. (1907) ; vol. ii. (1911) ; vol. iii. (1913). Other volumes to follow.

Schriften von Kaspar Schwenckfeld, in 4 folio volumes. Published between the years 1564–1570. Indicated in my notes as vol. i., vol. ii., vol. iii. A, vol. iii. B. There are, too, many uncollected books and tracts, to some of which I refer in footnotes.

Karl Ecke, *Schwenckfeld, Luther, und der Gedanke einer apostolischen Reformation* (Berlin, 1911). Important book, but to be followed with caution.

R. H. Grützmacher, *Wort und Geist* (Leipzig, 1902).

Gottfried Arnold, *Kirchen- und Ketzer-Historien*, i. pp. 1246-1299. (Edition of 1740.)

H. W. Erbkam, *Geschichte der protestantischen Sekten im Zeitalter der Reformation* (Hamburg und Gotha, 1848), pp. 357-475.

Döllinger, *Die Reformation*, i. pp. 257-280.

Ernst Troeltsch, *Die Soziallehren der christlichen Kirchen und Gruppen* (Tübingen, 1912), pp. 881-886.

those which moved Francis of Assisi three centuries earlier, but the two men had this much in common—they both went to Jesus Christ for the source and inspiration of their religion, they both lived under the spell of that dominating Personality of the Gospels, they both felt the power of the Cross and saw with their inner spirits that the real healing of the human soul and the eternal destiny of man were indissolubly bound up with the Person of Christ.[1] Here again, as in the early years of the thirteenth century, there came a gentle Reformer of religion, who would use no compulsion but love, who knew how to suffer patiently with his Lord, and whose entire programme was the restoration of primitive Christianity, though of necessity it would be restored, if at all, in terms of the spiritual ideals of the sixteenth century, as the Christianity of St. Francis had been in terms of thirteenth-century ideals.

Caspar Schwenckfeld was born of a noble family in the duchy of Liegnitz, in Lower Silesia, in 1489. He studied in Cologne, in Frankfurt-on-the-Oder, and probably also in the University of Erfurt, though he attained no University degree. His period of systematic study being over, about 1511 he threw himself into the life of a courtier, with the prospect of a successful worldly career before him. Luther's heroic contest against the evils and corruptions of the Church and his proclamation of a Reforming faith shook the prosperous courtier wide awake and turned the currents of his life powerfully toward religion. He deeply felt at this time, what he expressed a few years later, that a new world was coming to birth and the old one dying away. To the end of his days, and in spite of the harsh treatment which he later received from the Wittenberg Reformer, Schwenckfeld always remembered that it was the prophetic trumpet-call of Luther which had summoned him to a new life, and he always carried about with him in his long exile—an exile for which Luther was largely responsible—a beautiful respect and apprecia-

---

[1] Christ, Schwenckfeld insisted, is the sum of the whole Bible, and to learn to know Christ fundamentally is to grasp the substance of the entire Scripture.

tion for the man who had first turned him to a knowledge of the truth.[1]

From the very beginning of his awakening he shows the moral earnestness of a prophet, and even in his earliest writings he emphasizes the inwardness of true religion and the importance of a personal experience of the living, creative Divine Word.[2] As a result of this passion of his for the formation of moral and spiritual character in the lives of the people, he was very acute and sensitive to note the condition which actually existed around him, and he was not long in detecting, much to his sorrow, aspects of weakness in the new type of Christianity which was spreading over Germany. Even as early as 1524, in *An Admonition to all the Brethren of Silesia*,[3] he called attention to the superficiality of the change which was taking place in men's lives as a result of the Reformation—" the lack of inward grasp " as he calls it—and to the externality of the new Reform, the tendency to stop at " alphabetical promises of salvation." He gives a searching examination to the central principles of Luther's teachings and approves of them all, but at the same time he points out that little will be gained if they be adopted only as intellectual statements and formulated views. He pleads for a faith in Christ and an appreciation of Him that shall " reach the deep regions of the spirit," renew the heart, and produce a new man in the believer—" the atoning work of Christ must be vital "—and for a type of religion that will involve suffering with Christ, real conformity of will to His will, dying to self and rising again with Him, which means that we cannot " take the

---

[1] He wrote in 1543 to Luther : " I owe to you in God and the truth all honour, love, and goodwill, because from the first I have reaped much fruit from your service, and I have not ceased to pray for you according to my poor powers." —*Schriften*, ii. p. 701 d.

[2] In *An Epistle to the Sisters in the Cloister at Naumberg*, written probably in the autumn of 1523, he says : " A true Christian life in its essential require- ments does not consist in external appearance . . . but quite the contrary, it does consist in personal trust in God through an experience of Jesus Christ, which the Holy Ghost brings forth in the heart by the hearing of the Divine Word."—*Corpus Schwenckfeldianorum*, i. p. 118.

[3] *Ermahnung dess Missbrauchs etlicher fürnemsten Artikel des Evangelii* (1524). *Corpus Schw.* ii. pp. 26-105.

cross at its softest spot." [1]   He calls with glowing passion
for a radical transformation of personal and social life,
and for a serious attempt to revive primitive Christianity
with its conquering power.

Luther himself was always impressed with the lack of
real, intense, personal religion which resulted from the
Reformation movement, and he often bewailed this lack.
He said once to Schwenckfeld in this early period, " Dear
Caspar, genuine Christians are none too common.   I wish
I could see two together in a place ! "   But with all his
titanic power to shake the old Church, Luther was not
able to sift away the accumulated chaff of the ages and
to seize upon the inward, living kernel of Christ's Gospel
in such a real and vivid presentation that men were once
again able to find the entire Christ, and were once again
lifted into apostolic power through the discovery of Him.
This was the task to which Schwenckfeld now felt himself
summoned.   It seemed to him that the entire basis of
salvation should be grasped in a way quite different from
Luther's way of formulation, and this called for a restate-
ment of the whole revelation of God in Christ and of the
work of Christ in the soul of man. [2]

Luther's final break with the spiritual Reformer of
Silesia, which occurred in 1527, was primarily occasioned
by Schwenckfeld's teaching on the meaning and value of
the Lord's Supper, though their difference was by no
means confined to that point.   Schwenckfeld's position
had culminated in 1526 in a suspension of the celebration
of the Lord's Supper—the so-called *Stillstand*—until a
right understanding and true practice of it according to
the will of the Lord should be revealed. [3]   " We know at
present of no apostolic commission," he wrote, " nor

[1] " Wir greyffen das Creutz noch am waichsten Ort an."—*Ermahnung dess
Missbrauchs.   Corpus Schw.* ii. p. 89.
[2] " There are now in general two parties that make wrong use of the Gospel
of Christ, one of which turns to the right and the other to the left of the only
true and straight way.   The first party is that of the Papacy . . . the other
party consists of those to whom God has now granted a gracious light—But ! "
—*Ermahnung dess Missbrauchs.*
[3] The *Stillstand* was proposed in a *Circular Letter* written by Schwenckfeld,
Valentine Crautwald, and the Liegnitz Pastors, April 21, 1526.—*Corpus Schwenckfeld.* i. pp. 325-333.

again do we make any claim to be regarded as apostles, for we have neither received the fulness of the Holy Spirit nor the apostolic seal for such an office. We dwell in humility and ascribe nothing to ourselves, except that we bear witness to Christ, invite men to Christ, preach Christ and His infinite work of salvation, and labour as much as we can that Christ may be truly known." [1]

Into the bitter controversy over the Sacrament—a controversy between noble and sincere Reformers, which forms the supreme internal tragedy of the Reformation—we need not now enter. We shall in the proper place give Schwenckfeld's position upon it, though only in so far as it belongs in an exposition of his type of spiritual Christianity ; but the immediate effect of his position and practices was such a collision with Luther, and the arousal of such hostility on the part of the Lutherans of Silesia, that the continued pursuit of Schwenckfeld's mission in that country became impossible. He was, however, not expelled by edict, but under compulsion of the existing situation ; and in order not to be a trouble to his friend, the Duke of Liegnitz, he went in 1529 into voluntary exile, never to return. For thirty years he was a wanderer without a permanent home on the earth, but he could thank his Lord Christ, as he did, for granting him through all these years an inward freedom, and for bringing him into " His castle of Peace." He once wrote : " If I had wanted a good place on earth, if I had cared more for temporal than for eternal things, and if I would have deserted my Christ, then I might have stayed in my fatherland and in my own house, and I might have had the powerful of this world for my friends." [2]

He sojourned for longer or shorter periods in Strasbourg, Augsburg, Ulm, and other cities, but nowhere was he safe from his enemies, and he always faced the prospect of banishment even from his place of temporary sojourn.

---

[1] The revival of this idea of a *Stillstand*, that is, of a suspension of certain time-honoured practices of the Church until a further revelation and new enduement should be granted, will be referred to in later chapters, especially in connection with the *Collegiants* of Holland and the English *Seekers*.

[2] Ecke, *op. cit.* p. 217.

Furious declarations were passed against him by the
Schmalkald League in 1540, for to his anti-Lutheran
views on the sacraments he had now added teachings on
the nature of Christ which the theologians pronounced
unorthodox. Three years later he sent a messenger to
Luther in hope of a friendly understanding. Luther's
answer was brief and final : " The stupid fool, possessed
by the devil, understands nothing. He does not know
what he is babbling. But if he won't stop his drivel,
let him at least not bother me with the booklets which
the devil spues out of him." [1] At the ministerial Council
of Protestant States in 1556 Schwenckfeld was denounced
in the most vituperous language of the period, and the
civil authorities were urged to proceed against him as a
dangerous heretic. He always had, notwithstanding
this pursuit of theological hate, many powerful friends,
and a large number of brave and devoted followers who
were glad to risk goods, home, and life for the sake of
what was to them the living Word of God. He died—or
as his friends preferred to say, he had a quiet and peaceful
" home passage "—at Ulm in 1561. Of the purity, the
brave sincerity, the nobility, the outward and inward
consistency of his life there is no question. His enemies
had no word to say which reflected upon the motives of
his heart or upon the genuine piety of his life. His
religion cost him all that he held dear in the outer world—
he had not taken " the cross at the softest spot "—and he
practised his faith as the most precious thing a man could
possess in this world or in any other.

We must now turn to a study of his type of Christianity, which will be presented here not in the order of
its historical development, but as it appears in perspective
in his life and writings. He does not ground his conception of salvation, his idea of religion *überhaupt*, as
the humanistic Reformers, Denck, Bünderlin, Entfelder,
and Franck, do, on the essentially divine nature of the

---

[1] Arnold, *op. cit.* ii. p. 251. There are many similar references to Schwenckfeld
in Luther's *Table Talk*, and he usually calls him by the opprobrious name of
" Stenkfeld."

soul in its deepest reality,[1] nor again as the medieval
mystics do, on the substantial presence within the soul
of a divine soul-centre, an unlost and inalienable Spark
or Image of God which can turn back home and unite
itself with its Source, the Godhead.   He begins, as Luther
does, with man " fallen," " dead in sin," by nature
" blind and deaf " to divine realities.   For him, as for
Luther, there exists no *natural* freedom of the will, by
which a person can spontaneously and of his own initiative
rise up, shake off the shackles of sin, and go to living as a
son of God.   This stupendous event, this absolute shift
of the life-level, comes, and can come, he thinks, only
through an act of God, directly, immediately wrought
upon the soul.   Salvation must be a supernatural event.
Through this act of God from above there results within
the soul an experience which in every respect is a new
creation.   It is a cataclysmic event of the same order as
the *fiat lux* of cosmic creation, a rebirth through which
the man who has it once again comes into the condition
Adam was in before he fell.

Everything which has to do with salvation in Schwenckfeld's Christianity goes back to the historical Christ.[2]
Christ is the first-born of this new creation.   He is the
first " new Adam," who by His triumphant life and
victorious resurrection has become for ever " a life-giving
Spirit," the creative Principle of a new humanity.   In
Christ the Word of God, the actual Divine Seed of God,
became flesh, entered into our human nature and penetrated it with Spirit and with Life, conquered its stubborn
bent toward sin, and transfigured and transformed this
human flesh into a divine and heavenly substance.   By
obedience to the complete will of God, even to the extreme
depths of suffering, sacrifice, and death on the Cross for

---

[1] " Ein natürliches Licht kennt Schwenckfeld nicht."—Grützmacher, *Wort
und Geist* (Leipzig, 1902), p. 168.

[2] The important data for Schwenckfeld's doctrine of Christ and the way of
salvation will be found in the following writings by him :—

Von der göttlichen Kindschaft und Herrlichkeit des ganzen Sones Gottes (1538).

Ermanunge zum wahren und selig machende Erkänntnis Christi (1539).

*Konfession und Erklärung von Erkänntnus Christi und seiner göttlichen
Herrlichkeit* (1540).

the love of men, Christ glorified human flesh, exalted it
from flesh to spirit, and in His resurrected heavenly life
He is able to unite Himself inwardly with the souls of
believers, so that His spiritual resurrected flesh and blood
can be their food and drink, and He can become the
life-giving source of a new order of humanity, the spiritual
Head of a new race. " If the soul of man," he wrote,
" is to be truly nourished, vitally fed and watered, so
that it comes into possession of Eternal Life, it must
die to its fleshly life and *receive into itself a divine and
spiritual Life, having its source in the Being of God and
mediated to the soul by the living, inward-working Flesh
and Blood of Jesus Christ,"* through which mediation
we come into spiritual union and vital fellowship with
God who is Spirit.[1]

Salvation for Schwenckfeld, therefore, is participation
in the life of this new creation, this new world-order.
To become a Christian, in his sense of the word, is to pass
over one of the most decisive watersheds in the universe,
to go from one kingdom to another kingdom of a higher
rank. The *process*—for it is a vital process—is from
beginning to end in the realm of experience. By the
exercise of faith in the crucified, risen, and glorified God-
Man, as the life-giving Spirit, real power from a higher
world streams into the soul. Something " pneumatic,"
something which belongs ontologically to a higher spiritual
world-order, comes into the person as a divinely bestowed
germ-plasm, with living, renewing, organizing power.
As with Irenaeus, so with Schwenckfeld, salvation is
" real redemption," the " deification " of mortal man,
the actual formation of an immortal nature, the restoration of humanity to what it originally was, through the
in-streaming life-energy of a mystical Adam-Christ, the
Founder and Head of a new spiritual race.[2]

By this incoming spiritual power and life-substance
the entire personality of the recipient is affected. The

---

[1] *Schriften*, i. p. 664. See also p. 662.
[2] For the doctrine of deification in Irenaeus see Harnack, *Hist. of Dogma*,
ii. pp. 230-318.

recreative energy which pours in transforms both soul and body. The inner eternal Word of God, who became flesh, acts upon the inner nature of man, so that the believing man is changed into something spiritual, divine and heavenly, and like Jesus Christ, the incarnated Word of God.[1] There comes, with this epoch-making experience, a sense of freedom not known before, a power of control over the body and its appetites, an illumination of the intellect, a new sensitiveness of conscience to the meaning of sin, an extraordinary expansion of the vision of the goal of life—which is a full-grown man in Christ,— and an apprehension of the gift of the Spirit sufficient for the achievement of that goal. Not least among the *signs* of transfiguration and of heightened life is the attainment of a joy which spreads through the inward spirit and shines on the face—a joy which can turn hard exile into a *Ruheschloss*, " a castle of peace."

Those who have experienced this dynamic transfiguration gain thereby gifts, capacities, and powers to hear the Word of God within their own souls, and thus this Word, which is the same life-giving Spirit that became flesh in Christ and that produces the new creation in man, becomes a perpetual inward Teacher in those who are reborn. " Precious gifts of the Holy Ghost flow from the essential Being of God into the heart of the believer." There is, Schwenckfeld holds, a double revelation of God. The primary Word of God is eternal, spiritual, inward. " The Word, when spiritual messengers preach or teach, is of two kinds with a decided difference in their manner of working. One is of God, even is God, and lives and works in the heart of the messenger. This is the inner Word, and is in reality nothing else than the continued manifestation of Christ. He is inwardly revealed, and heard with the inward ears of the heart." [2] It is, in fact, God Himself *operating* as Life and Spirit and Light upon the spiritual substance of the human soul, first as the Life-Seed which forms the new creation in man, and afterwards as the permanent

[1] See *Schriften*, i. p. 768. [2] *Ibid.* i. p. 767 a.

nourishing and tutoring Spirit who leads the obedient soul on into all the Truth, and perfects it into the likeness and stature of Christ. " There is a living, inner Scripture, written in the believer's heart by the finger of God." " This inner Scripture has an active creative power of holiness, and makes holy, living, righteous and saved all those in whose hearts it is written."

The *divine word* in the secondary sense is the outward word—the word of Scripture. " The other word which serves the inner Word with voice, sound, and expression is the external word, and is heard by the external man with his ears of sense, and is written and read in letters. He who has read and heard only that, and not the inner Word, has not heard the Gospel of Christ, the Gospel of Grace, nor has he received or understood it." [1] It is at best only the witness or testimony which assists the soul to find the real life-giving Word. Cut apart from the inner spiritual Word, the word of the letter is " dead," as the body would be if sundered from the spirit. " It paints truth powerfully for the eye, but it cannot bring it into the heart." [2] " The Scriptures cannot bring to the soul that of which they speak. This must be sought directly from God Himself." [3] In his practical use of Scripture and in his estimate of its importance he is hardly behind Luther himself. " There is," he says, " no writing on earth like the Holy Scriptures." [4] His Christianity is penetrated and illuminated at every point by the profound spiritual experiences of the saints of the Bible, and still more by the vivid portraits of Christ in the Gospels, by the words from His lips recorded there, and by the experiences of the apostles and the development of the primitive Church. He never doubts or questions the inspiration of the Scriptures ; quite the contrary, he holds that Scripture is " given by God " and is an inexhaustible well of inspired truth from which the soul can endlessly draw. The actual content of Christian faith is supplied by the historical revelation ;

[1] *Schriften*, i. p. 767 a. [2] *Die heilige Schrift*. x. d.
[3] *Ibid*. cviii. c. [4] *Ibid*. ii. b.

but Schwenckfeld always insists that written words, however inspired, are still external to the soul, and merely record historical events which have happened to others in other ages. " If man," he writes, " is to understand spiritual things and is to know and judge rightly, he must bring the divine Light to the Scriptures, the Spirit to the letter, the Truth to the picture, and the Master to His created work. . . . In a word, to understand the Scriptures a man must become a new man, a man of God ; he must be in Christ who gave forth the Scriptures." [1] That which is to change the inner nature of a man must be something personally experienced and not external to him ; must be in its own nature as spiritual as the soul itself is and not material, as written words are. " The pen cannot completely bring the heart to the paper, nor can the mouth entirely express the well of living water within itself." [2] The Bible leads to Christ and bears witness of Him as no other book does, but it is not Christ. And even the Bible remains a closed book until Christ opens it.[3] The Scriptures tell, as no other writings do, of the Word of God and its life-operations in the world, but they are still not the Word of God. The spiritual realities of life cannot be settled by laboriously piling up texts of Scripture, by subtle theological dialectic, or by learned exegesis of sacred words. If these spiritual realities are to become real and effective to us, it must be through the direct relation of the human spirit with the divine Spirit—the inward spiritual Word of God.[4] " He who will see the truth must have God for eyes." [5]

Schwenckfeld's view of the process of salvation and the permanent illumination of the reborn soul by a real incoming divine substance—whether called Word or Seed—is the *dynamic* feature of his Christianity. He is endeavouring to find a foundation for a religious energism that will avoid the dangers which beset Luther's principle

---

[1] *Die heilige Schrift.* vi. and vii.   [2] *Vom Worte Gottes*, xxii. c.
[3] *Die heilige Schrift.* iv. b.
[4] *Catechismus vom Wort des Creützes, vom Wort Gottes, und vom Underscheide des Worts des Geists und Buchstabens.*
[5] *Die heilige Schrift.* iv. c.

of " justification by faith." From the inception of the
Reformation movement there had appeared a tendency
to regard the exercise of " faith " as all that was required
for human salvation. Luther did not mean it so, but it
was the easy line of least resistance to hold that " faith "
had a magic effect in the invisible realm, that is to say :
As soon as a person exercised " faith," God counted the
" faith " for righteousness, and regarded that person as
" justified." The important operation was thus in a
region outside the soul. The momentous shift was not
in the personal character of the individual, but in the
way the individual was regarded and valued in the
heavenly estimates. It was the discovery of the prevalence of this crude and magical reliance on " faith "
which first drove Schwenckfeld to a deeper study of the
problems of religion. It was the necessity that he felt
to discover some way by which man himself could be
actually renewed, transformed, recreated, and *made*
righteous—rather than merely counted or reckoned
righteous by some magical transaction—that made him
an independent reformer and set him on his solitary way.

To this deep and central question of religion, How is
a human soul saved ? there were in Schwenckfeld's day
four well-known answers :

(1) There was the answer of the Church in which he
was born. Salvation is by Grace, mediated through the
sacramental channels of the mysterious and divinely
founded Church. Man's part consists in the performance
of the " works " which the Church requires of him and
the proper use of the sacramental means of Grace.
Through these sacramental channels actual Grace, substantial divine help, comes into man and works the
miracle of salvation in him.

(2) There was the answer of the great mystics, not
always clear and simple, but very profound and significant.
The Ground and the Abyss of the soul is one substance
with the eternal and absolute Godhead. Finite strivings,
isolated purposes, selfish aims, centrifugal pursuits are
vain and illusory. We lose our lives in so far as we live

in self-will and in self-centred joys. The way home, the way of salvation, is a return to that Ground-Reality from which we have gone out—a return to union and oneness of Life with the infinite Godhead.

(3) The third answer is that of Luther : "Salvation is by faith." This seems at first to be a dynamic answer. It breaks in on the distracted world like a new moral trumpet-call to the soul. It comes to men like a fresh Copernican insight which discovers a new religious world-centre. The soul by its own inward vision, by its moral attitude, by the swing of the will, can initiate a new relation with God, and so produce a new inward kingdom. That, however, is not Luther's message. He could not take that optimistic view of life because it implied that man has within himself a native capacity for God, and can rise to the vision and attitude which lead to a moral renewal of the self. Luther never succeeded in clearing his principle from scholastic complications. He never put it upon a moral and dynamic foundation. It remains to the last a mysterious principle, and was easily open to the antinomian interpretation, that upon the exercise of faith God for Christ's merits " counts man justified "— an interpretation dear to those who are slack-minded and prone to forensic schemes of salvation.

(4) The fourth view was that of the humanist-spiritual Reformers, men of the type of Denck and Bünderlin, who are the precursors of what we to-day call the ethical way of salvation. They assume that salvation is from beginning to end a moral process. God is in essence and nature a loving, self-revealing, self-giving God, who has in all ages unveiled Himself in revelations suited to the spiritual stature of man, has in the fulness of time become incarnate in Christ, and forever pleads with men through His Spirit to come to Him. Those who see and hear, those who respond and co-operate, i.e. those who exercise faith, are thereby morally transformed into an inward likeness to Him, and so enter upon a life which prefers light to darkness, goodness to sin, love to hate.

Schwenckfeld was not satisfied with any of these views. He knew and loved the mystics, but he was too much impressed with the mighty Life and message of the historical Christ to adopt the mystic's way. He felt that Lutheran Christianity was too scholastic, too dependent on externals, too inclined to an antinomian use of " faith." He could not go along the path of the Humanist-Spirituals, for he believed that man had been ruined in the Fall, was too deeply scarred with sin to help himself, was without freewill, was devoid of native capacity for spiritual vision and saving faith. Salvation, if it is to be effected at all, must be initiated by Divine Grace and must be accomplished *for man* by God. But it could be for Schwenckfeld no forensic adjustment, no change of reckoning in the heavenly ledgers. " Justification," he once wrote, " is not only forgiveness of sins, but it is more, it is the actual healing and renewing of the inward man." [1] It must involve a real and radical transformation of man's nature—man must cease from sin and the love of it, he must receive from beyond himself a passion for goodness and a power to enable him to achieve it. The *passion* for goodness, in Schwenckfeld's view, is created through the vision of the God-Man who has suffered and died on the Cross for us, and has been glorified in absolute newness of life ; and the *power* for moral holiness is supplied to the soul by the direct inflowing of divine Life-streams from this new Adam, who is henceforth the Head of the spiritual order of humanity, the Life-giving Spirit who renews all who receive Him in faith. " Faith," he says, " is a penetrating stream of light flowing out from the central divine Light and Fire, which is God Himself, into our hearts, by which we are inflamed with love for God and for our neighbour, and by which we see both what we lack in ourselves and what can abundantly supply our lack, so that we may be made ready for the Kingdom of God and be prepared to become children of God." [2] " Real faith," he elsewhere says, " that is to say, justifying faith, can come from nothing

---

[1] *Schriften*, i. p. 725.   [2] *Ibid.* i. p. 634.

external. It is a gracious and gratuitous gift of God through the Holy Spirit. It is an emanation ["Tröpflein"] from the eternal Life of God, and is of the same essence and substance as God Himself." [1] It is, in fact, the Eternal Word of God become vocal and vital within the inner region of our own lives.[2]

The Church, in Schwenckfeld's conception, is this complete spiritual community of which Christ is the Head. " We maintain," he wrote in the early period of his mission, and it remained the settled view of his life, " that the Christian Church according to the usage of the Scripture is the congregation or assembly of all or of many who with heart and soul are believers in Christ, whose Head is Christ our Lord, as St. Paul writes to the Ephesians and elsewhere, and who are born of God's Word alone, and are nourished and ruled by God's Word."[3] " The Christian Church," he elsewhere says, " is the entire community of the children of God. It is the actual Body of Christ, the Seed of Abraham, the House of the living God, the Temple of the Holy Spirit. It has its life and power through the obedience of faith, it manifests to the world the Name of the Lord, the goodness and the glory of Him who called its members from darkness into His marvellous Light. Wherever such a Church is gathered, there also is Christ, its Head, who governs it, teaches it, guards and defends it, works in it and pours His Life into its members, to each according to the measure of his living faith. This inward invisible Christ belongs to all ages and all times and lands." [4] The Church, in its true life and power, is thus for him a continuation of the apostolic type. He had no interest in the formation of a sectarian denomination, and he was fundamentally averse to a State-Church system. The true Church community can be identified with no temporal, empirical organization—whether established or separatist. It is a spiritual, invisible community as wide as the world, including all persons in all regions of

[1] *Schriften*, i. p. 380.   [2] See *ibid*. ii. p. 421.
[3] *Corpus Schwenck.* i. p. 295.   [4] *Schriften*, iii. A.

the earth and in all religious communions who are joined
in life and spirit to the Divine Head. It expands and
is enlarged by a process of organic growth under the
organizing direction of the Holy Spirit. " As often," he
writes, " as a new warrior comes to the heavenly army,
as often as a poor sinner repents, the body of Christ
becomes larger, the King more splendid, His Kingdom
stronger, His might more perfect. Not that God becomes
greater or more perfect in His essence, but that flesh
becomes more perfect in God, and God dwells in all His
fulness in the flesh into which in Jesus Christ He ever
more pours Himself." [1] Each soul that enters the
kingdom of experience through the work of the Life-giving
Spirit is builded into this invisible expanding Church of
the ages, and is endowed with some " gift " to become an
organ of the Divine Head. All spiritual service arises
through the definite call and commission of God, and the
persons so called and commissioned are rightly prepared
for their service, not by election and ordination, but by
inward compulsion and illumination through the Word of
God. The preacher possesses no magical efficacy. His
only power lies in his spiritual experience, his clarified
vision, and his organic connection with Christ the Head
of the Church and the source of its energy. If his life is
spiritually poor and weak and thin, if it lacks moral
passion and insight, his ministry will be correspondingly
ineffective and futile, for the dynamic spiritual impact
of a life is in proportion to its personal experience and its
moral capacity to transmit divine power. Here again
the emphasis is on the moral aspect of religion as contrasted with the magical. There can be no severing of
the ecclesiastical office or function from the moral character of the person himself. Schwenckfeld has cut away
completely from sacerdotalism and has returned, as far
as with his limited historical insight he knew how to do it,
to the ideal of the primitive Apostolic Church. The true
mark and sign of membership in the community of saints
—the invisible Church—is, for him as for St. Paul,

[1] *Schriften*, ii. p. 290.

possession of the mind of Christ, faith, patience, integrity, peace, unity of spirit, the power of God, joy in the Holy Ghost, and the abounding gifts and fruits of the Spirit. " No outward unity or uniformity, either in doctrine or ceremonies, or rules or sacraments, can make a Christian Church; but inner unity of spirit, of heart, soul and conscience in Christ and in the knowledge of Him, a unity in love and faith, does make a Church of Christ." [1] The Church is in a very true sense bone of Christ's bone and flesh of His flesh, vitalized by His blood, empowered by His real presence, and formed into an organism which reveals and exhibits the divine and heavenly Life—a world-order as far above the natural human life as that is above the plant.

Quite consistently with this spiritual view of religion— this view that the true Church is an invisible Church— Schwenckfeld taught that the true sacrament is an inner and spiritual sacrament, and not legal and external like those of the Old Testament. " God must Himself, apart from all external means, through Christ touch the soul, speak in it, work in it, if we are to experience salvation and eternal life." [2] The direct incoming of the Divine Spirit, producing a rebirth and a new creation in the man himself, is the only baptism which avails with God or which makes any difference in the actual condition of man. Baptism in its true significance is the reception of cleansing power, it is an inward process which purifies the heart, illuminates the conscience, and is not only necessary for salvation but in fact *is* salvation. Christian baptism is therefore not with water, but with Christ : it is the immersion of the soul in the life-giving streams of Christ's spiritual presence.

Schwenckfeld was always kindly disposed toward the Anabaptists, but he was not of them. He presented a very different type of Christianity to their type, which he penetratingly criticized, though in a kindly spirit. He did not approve of rebaptism, for he insisted that the all-important matter was not how or when water was applied,

---

[1] *Schriften*, ii. p. 785.   [2] *Ibid.* i. p. 768 b.

but the reception of *Christ's real baptism*, an inner baptism, a baptism of spirit and power, by which the believing soul, the inner man, is clarified, strengthened, and made pure.[1]

His view of the Lord's Supper in the same way fits his entire conception of Christianity as an inward religion. It was through his study of the meaning and significance of the Supper that he arrived at his peculiar and unique type of religion. He began his meditation with the practical test—the case of Judas. If the bread and wine of the Last Supper were identical with the body and blood of Christ, then Judas must have eaten of Christ as the other disciples did, and, notwithstanding his evil spirit, he must have received the divine nature into himself— but that is impossible.

In his intellectual difficulty he turned to the great mystical discourse in the sixth chapter of John, in the final interpretation of which he received important suggestion and help from Valentine Crautwald, Lector of the Dom in Liegnitz. In this remarkable discourse Christ promises to feed His disciples, His followers, with His own flesh and blood, by which they will partake of the eternal nature and enter with Him into a resurrection life. The " flesh and blood " here offered to men cannot refer to an outward sacrament which is eaten in a physical way, because in the very same discourse Christ says that outward, physical flesh profits nothing. It is the Spirit that gives life, and, therefore, the " flesh and blood " of Christ must be synonymous with the Word if they are actually to recreate and nourish the soul and to renew and vitalize the spirit of man.

This feeding and renewing of the soul through Christ's " flesh and blood," Schwenckfeld treats, as we have seen, not as a figure or symbol, but as a literal fact of Christian experience. Through the exercise of faith in the person of the crucified, risen, and glorified Christ—the creative Adam—incorruptible, life-giving substance comes into the soul and transfigures it. Something from the divine

---

[1] *Schriften*, i. p. 513. For a criticism of the legalism of the Anabaptists see *ibid*. i. pp. 801-808.

and heavenly world, something from that spiritualized
and glorified nature of Christ, becomes the actual food
of man's spirit, so that through it he partakes of the same
nature as that of the God-Man. Not once or twice, but
as a continuous experience, the soul may share this
glorious meal of spiritual renewal—this eating and drinking of Christ.

The external supper—and for that matter the external
baptism too—may have a place in the Church of Christ as
a pictorial symbol of the actual experience, or as a visible
profession of faith, but this outward sign is, in his view,
of little moment, and must not occupy the foreground of
attention, nor be made a subject of polemic or of insistence.
The new Creation, the response of faith to the living Word,
the transfiguration of life into the likeness of Christ, are
the momentous facts of a Christian experience, and none
of these things is *mediated* by external ceremonies.

It was his ideal purpose to promote the formation of
little groups of spiritual Christians which should live in
the land in quietness, and spread by an inward power and
inspiration received from above. He saw clearly that
no true Reformation could be carried through by edicts
or by the proclamations of rulers, or by the decision of
councils. A permanent work, from his point of view,
could be accomplished only by the slow and patient
development of the religious life and spiritual experience
of the people, since the goal which he sought was the
formation, not of state-made Churches, but of renewed
personal lives, awakened consciences, burning moral
passion, and first-hand conviction of immediate relation
with the World of Divine Reality. To this work of
arousing individual souls to these deeper issues of life,
and of building up little scattered societies under the
headship of Christ, which should be, as it were, oases of
the Kingdom of God in the world, he dedicated his years
of exile. All such quiet inward movements progress, as
Christ foresaw, too slowly and gradually " for observation " ; but this method of reforming the Church through
rebirth and the creation of Christ-guided societies accom-

plished, even during Schwenckfeld's life, impressive results. There were many, not only in Silesia but in all regions which the missionary-reformer was able to reach, who " preferred salt and bread in the school of Christ " to ease and plenty elsewhere, and they formed their little groups in the midst of a hostile world. The public records of Augsburg reveal the existence, during Schwenckfeld's life, of a remarkable group of these quiet, spiritual worshippers in that city. Their leaders were men of menial occupations—men who would have attracted no notice from the officials of city or Church if they had been contented to conform to any prevailing or recognized type of religion. Under the inspiration which they received from the writings of Schwenckfeld they formed " a little meeting "—in every respect like a seventeenth-century Quaker meeting—in their own homes, meeting about in turn, discarding all use of sacraments, and waiting on God for edification rather than on public preaching. They read the books and epistles of Schwenckfeld in their gatherings, they wrote epistles to other groups of Schwenckfeldians, and received epistles in turn and read them in their gatherings. They objected to any form of religious exercise which seemed to them incomprehensible to their spirits and which did not spring directly out of the inward ministry of the Word of God. They were eventually discovered, their leaders banished, their books burned, and their little meeting of " quiet spirituals " (" stillen Frommen ") as they called themselves was ruthlessly stamped out.[1] Societies something like this were formed in scores of places, and continued to cultivate their inward piety in the Fatherland, until harried by persecution they migrated in 1734 to Pennsylvania, where they have continued to maintain their community life until the present day.

But the most important effect of Schwenckfeld's life and work must not be sought in the history of these

[1] The details are given in Friederich Roth's *Augsburgs Reformations-Geschichte* (München, 1907), iii. p. 245 ff.

visible societies which owed their origin to his apostolic activity. His first concern was always for the building of the invisible community of God throughout the whole world—not for the promotion of a sect—and his greatest contribution will be found in the silent, often unnoticed, propagation of his spirit, the contagious dissemination of his ideas, the gradual influence of his truth and insight upon Christian communions and upon individual believers that hardly knew his name. His correspondence was extraordinarily extensive ; his books and tracts, which were legion, found eager readers and transmitters, and slowly—too slowly for observation—the spiritual message of the homeless reformer made its way into the inner life of faithful souls, who in all lands were praying for the consolation of God's new Israel. Even so early as 1551, an English writer, Wyllyam Turner, in a book written as " a preservative and treacle against the poyson of Pelagius," especially as " renewed " in the " furious secte of the Annabaptistes," mentions the " Swengfeldianes " as one of the heads of " this monstre in many poyntes lyke unto the watersnake with seven heads." [1] There is, however, slight evidence of the spread of Schwenckfeld's views, whether they be called " poyson " or " treacle," in England during the sixteenth century, though they are clearly in evidence in the seventeenth century. One of the most obvious signs of his influence in the seventeenth century, both in England and in Holland, appears in the spread of principles which were embodied in the " Collegiants " of Holland and the corresponding societies of " Seekers " in England.[2] The cardinal principle of these groups in both countries was the belief that the visible Church had become apostate and had lost its divine authoritative power, that it now lacked apostolic ministry and efficacious sacraments and " the gifts of the Spirit " which demonstrate the true apostolic succession. Therefore those who held this view, " like doves without their mates," were *waiting* and *seeking* for the appearing of a

[1] *A Preservative or Treacle against the Poyson of Pelagius, etc.* (1551), A iii.
[2] For a fuller account of the Collegiants see Chap. VII.

new apostolic commission, for the fresh outpouring of God's Spirit on men, and for the refounding of the Church, as originally, in actual demonstration and power.

It was a settled view of Schwenckfeld's that the visible Church had lost its original power and authority, and he cherished, too, a persistent faith and hope that in God's good time it would again be restored to its pristine vitality and its original conquering power. " We ask," he writes, " where in the world to-day there is gathered together an external Church of the apostolic form and type, and according to the will of Christ." [1] And yet scattered everywhere throughout the world—even in Turkey and Calcutta [2]— God has, he says, His own faithful people, known only to Him, who live Christlike and holy lives, whom Christ the living Word, that became flesh, baptizes inwardly with the Holy Spirit and inwardly feeds without external preaching or sacrament, writes His law in their hearts and guides into Eternal Life.[3] But the time is coming when once more there will be in the world an apostolic and completely reformed Church of Christ, His living body and the organ of the Spirit, with divine gifts and powers and commission. In the interim let the chosen children of God, he writes, rejoice and comfort themselves in this, that their salvation rests neither in an external Church, nor in the external use of sacraments, nor in any external thing, but that it rests alone in Jesus Christ our Lord, and is received through true and living faith.[4]

For Schwenckfeld himself the important matter was the increase of this inward life, the silent growth of this kingdom of God in the hearts of men, the spread of this invisible Church, but his writings plainly suggest that God will eventually restore the former glory to His visible Church. " You are," he says, in one of his epistles, " to pray earnestly that God will raise up true apostles and preachers and evangelists, so that His Church may

---

[1] *Schriften*, iii. B, p. 572.   [2] *Ibid.* ii. p. 783.
[3] *Ibid.* ii. p. 784.   [4] *Ibid.* iii. A, p. 146.

be reformed in Christ, edified in the Holy Ghost, and unified into one, and so that our boasting of the pure preaching of the Gospel and the right understanding and use of the sacraments may be true before God," [1] and the time is coming, we may in good faith believe, when the sacraments will be used according to the will of Christ, and then there will be a true Christian Church, taught outwardly by apostolic ministers and taught inwardly by the Lord Himself.[2]   Fortunately, however, salvation does not depend upon anything outward, and during the *Stillstand* or interim there is no danger to be feared from the intermission of outward ceremonies.[3]

Sebastian Franck graphically describes this waiting, seeking attitude as well known in his time.   He wrote in his "Chronicle" (1531): "Some are ready to allow Baptism and other ceremonies to remain in abeyance [" stilston," evidently Schwenckfeld's *Stillstand*] until God gives a further command and sends true labourers into His harvest-field.   For this some have great longings and yearnings and wish nothing else." [4]   The intense *expectation* which the Seekers, both in Holland and England, exhibit was, of course, a much later development, was due to many influences, and is connected only indirectly with the reforming work and the Gospel message of Schwenckfeld.   It indicates, in the exaggerated emphasis of the Seekers, a failure to grasp the deeper significance of spiritual Christianity as a present reality, and it misses the truth, which the world has so painfully slowly grasped, that the only way to form an apostolic and efficacious visible Church is not through sudden miracles and cataclysmic " restorations " and " commissions," but by the slow contagion and conquering power of this inward kingdom, of this invisible Church, as it becomes the spirit and life of the outward and visible Church. This truth the Silesian reformer knew full well, and for this reason he was ready at all costs to be a quiet apostle of the invisible Community of God and let the outward

[1] *Schriften*, ii. p. 785.   [2] *Ibid*. ii. p. 783.
[3] *Ibid*. iii. A, p. 74.   [4] Franck's *Chronica* (1531), p. ccccli.

organism and organ of its ministry come in God's own way. The nobler men among the English Seekers, as also among the Dutch Societies, rose gradually to this larger view of spiritual religion, and came to realize, as Schwenckfeld did, that the real processes of salvation are inward and dynamic. Samuel Rutherford is not a very safe witness in matters which involve impartial judgment, or which concern types of spiritual experience foreign to his own type, but he is following a real clew when he connects, as he does, the leaders of spiritual, inward religion in his day, especially those who had shared the seeker aspirations, with Schwenckfeld.[1] Rutherford's account is thoroughly unfair and full of inaccuracies, but it suffices at least to reveal the fact that Schwenckfeld was a living force in the period of the English Commonwealth, and that, though almost a hundred years had passed since his " home-passage " from Ulm was accomplished, he was still making disciples for the ever-enlarging community and household of God.

[1] Rutherford, *A Survey of the Spiritual Antichrist* (1648), chap. v.

CHAPTER VI

REFORMATION history has been far too closely confined to a few main highways of thought, and few persons therefore realize how rich in ideas and how complex in typical religious conceptions this spiritual upheaval really was. The types that prevailed and won their way to wide favour have naturally compelled attention and are adequately known. There were, however, very serious and impressive attempts made to give the Reformation a totally different course from the one it finally took in history, and these attempts, defeated by the sweep of the main current, became submerged, and their dedicated and heroic leaders became forgotten. Many of these spiritual ventures which for the moment failed and were submerged are in striking parallelism with currents of thought to-day, and our generation can perhaps appreciate at their real worth these solitary souls who were destined to see their cause defeated, to hear their names defamed, and to live in jeopardy among the very people whom they most longed to help.

Sebastian Castellio is one of these submerged venturers. While he lived he was so absolutely absorbed in the battle for truth that he took no pains at all to acquaint posterity with the details of his life, or to make his name quick and powerful in the ears of men. When he died

---

[1] F. Buisson, *Sébastien Castellion, sa vie et son œuvre* (Paris, 1892), 2 vols. ; Charles Jarrin, *Deux Oubliés* (Bourg, 1889) ; Émile Broussoux, *Sébastien Castellion, sa vie, ses œuvres, et sa théologie* (Strasbourg, 1867) ; A. Schweizer, *Die protestantischen Centraldogmen* (Zürich, 1854), pp. 311-373.

and laid down the weapons of his spiritual warfare his pious opponents thanked God for the relief and did what they could to consign him to oblivion. But after the long and silent flow of years the world has come up to his position and can appreciate a spirit who was too far in advance of the line of march to be comprehended in his lifetime. He was born in the little French village of St. Martin du Fresne—not many miles west of Lake Geneva—in the year 1515. The home was pinched with poverty, but somebody in the home or in the village discovered that little Bastian was endowed with unusual gifts and must be given the chance to realize the life which his youth forecast ; and that ancient family sacrifice, which has glorified so many homes of poverty, was made here in St. Martin, and the boy, possessed with his eager passion for knowledge, was started on his course in the Collège de la Trinité in Lyons. He soon found himself bursting into a new world, the world of classic antiquity, which the Humanists were restoring to the youth of that period, and he experienced that emancipating leap of soul and thrill of joy which such a world of beauty can produce upon a lofty spirit that sees and appreciates it. Some time during the Lyons period he came also under a still greater and more emancipating influence, the divine and simple Christ of the Gospels, whom the most serious of the Humanists had rediscovered, and to whom Castellio now dedicated the central loyalty of his soul.

At twenty-five years of age, now a splendid classical scholar, radiant with faith and hope and the vision of a new age for humanity which the recovered gospel was to bring in, Castellio went to Strasbourg to share the task of the Reformers and to put his life into the new movement. Calvin, then living in Strasbourg, received the brilliant recruit with joy and took him into his own home. When the great Reformer returned to Geneva in 1541 to take up the mighty task of his life he summoned Castellio to help him, and made him Principal of the College of Geneva, which Calvin planned to make one of the fore-

most seats of Greek learning and one of the most illuminating centres for the study of the Scriptures. The young
scholar's career seemed assured. He had the friendship
of Calvin, he was head of an important institution of
learning, the opportunity for creative literary work was
opening before him, and he was aspiring soon to fulfil
the clearest call of his life—to become a minister of the
new gospel. His first contribution to religious literature
was his volume of " Sacred Dialogues," a series of vivid
scenes out of the Old and New Testaments, told in dialogue
fashion, both in Latin and French.[1]　They were to serve
a double purpose : first, to teach French boys to read
Latin, and secondly, to form in them a love for the great
characters of the Bible and an appreciation of its lofty
message of life. The stories were really good stories,
simple enough for children, and yet freighted with a
depth of meaning which made them suitable for mature
minds. Their success was extraordinary, and their fine
quality was almost universally recognized. They went
through twenty-eight editions in their author's lifetime,
and they were translated into many languages.[2]　His
bent toward a religion of a deeply ethical and spiritual
type already appears in this early work, and here he
announces a principle that was to rule his later life and
was to cost him much suffering : " The friend of Truth
obeys not the multitude *but the Truth*."

At the very time this book was appearing, an opportunity offered for testing the mettle of his courage. One
of those ever-recurrent plagues that harassed former
ages, before microbes were discovered, fell upon Geneva.
The minister, who had volunteered to give spiritual
comfort to those who were suffering with the plague in
the hospital, was stricken with the dread disease, and a
new volunteer was asked for. The records of the city
show that Castellio, though not yet ordained, and under
no obligation to take such risk, offered himself for the

---

[1] *Dialogi sacri, latino-gallici, ad linguas moresque puerorum formandos.* Liber
primus. Genève, 1543.

[2] There were at least three English translations—1610, 1715, and 1743.

hazardous service when the ministers of the city declined
it. The ordination through human hands was, however,
never to come to him, and a harder test of courage than
the plague was before him. In the course of his studies
he found himself compelled to take the position that the
" Song of Solomon " was an ancient love poem, and that
the traditional interpretation of it as a revelation of the
true relation between Christ and the Church was a
strained and unnatural interpretation. He also felt
that as a scholar he could not with intellectual honesty
agree with the statement in the Catechism that " Christ
descended into Hell." Calvin challenged both these
positions of Castellio, but his opposition to him was
clearly far deeper than a difference of opinion on these
two points. Calvin instinctively felt that the bold and
independent spirit of this young scholar, his qualities of
leadership, and his literary genius marked him out as a
man who could not long be an easy-minded and supple
subordinate. A letter which Calvin wrote at this time
to his friend Viret shows where the real tension lay.
" Castellio has got it into his head," he writes, " that I
want to rule ! " The great Reformer may not have
been conscious yet of such a purpose, but there can be
no question that Castellio read the signs correctly, and
he was to be the first, as Buisson has said, to discover that
" to resist Calvin was, in the mind of the latter, to resist
the Holy Ghost." [1] Calvin successfully opposed his
ordination, and made it impossible for him to continue
in Geneva his work as an honest scholar. To remain
meant that he must surrender his right of independent
judgment, he must cease to follow the line of emancipated
scholarship, he must adjust his conscience to fit the ideas
that were coming to be counted orthodox in the circle
of the Reformed faith. *That* surrender he could no more
make than Luther could surrender to the demands of his
opponents at Worms. He quietly closed up his work in
the College of Geneva and went into voluntary exile, to
seek a sphere of life where he might think and speak as

[1] Buisson, *op. cit.* i. p. 205.

he saw the truth and where he could keep his conscience
a pure virgin.

He settled in Basle, where Erasmus had found a
refuge, and where, two years before, the exiled and
hunted Sebastian Franck, the spiritual forerunner of
Castellio, had died in peace. For ten years (1545–1555)
he lived with his large family in pitiable poverty. He
read proof for the Humanist printer Oporin, he fished
with a boat-hook for drift-wood along the shores of the
Rhine,—" rude labour no doubt," he says, " but honest,
and I do not blush for having done it,"—and he did
whatever honest work he could find that would help
keep body and soul together. Through all these years,
every moment of the day that could be saved from
bread-winning toil, and much of his night-time, went into
the herculean task to which he had dedicated himself—
the complete translation of the Bible from its original
languages into both Latin and French.[1] Being himself
one of the common people he always had the interests
and needs of the common people in view, and he put the
Bible into current sixteenth-century speech. His French
translation has the marked characteristics of the Renaissance period. He makes patriarchs, prophets, and the
persons of the New Testament live again in his vivid
word-pictures, as the great contemporary painters were
making them live on their canvases. But that which
gave his translation its great human merit and popular
interest was a serious defect in the eyes of the theologians.
It was vivid, full of the native Oriental colour, true in
the main to the original, and strong in its appeal to
religious imagination, but painfully weak in its support
of the dogmas and doctrines around which the theological
battles of the Reformation were centring. Still less
were the theologians pleased with the Preface of his
Latin Bible, dedicated to the boy-king of England,
Edward VI. Here he boldly insists that the Reformation,

---

[1] His Latin Bible appeared in 1551 and the French Bible in 1555. During
this period he also brought out a new edition of his " Sacred Dialogues," an edition
of Xenophon, a translation of the Sibylline Oracles, a Latin poem on Jonah, and
a Greek poem on John the Baptist, the Forerunner.

wherever it spreads, shall champion the principle of *free conscience*, and shall wage its battles with spiritual weapons alone. The only enemies of our faith, he says, are vices, and vices can be conquered only by virtues. The Christ who said if they strike you on one cheek turn the other, has called us to the spiritual task of instructing men in the truth, and that work can never be put into the hands of an executioner! " I address you, O king," he concludes, " not as a prophet sent from God, but as a man of the people who abhors quarrels and hatred, and who wishes to see religion spread by love rather than by fierce controversy, by purity of heart rather than by external methods. . . . Read these sacred writings with a pious and religious heart, and prepare yourself to reign as a mortal man who must give an account to immortal God. I desire that you may have the meekness of Moses, the piety of David, and the wisdom of Solomon." [1]

Two years after this appeal to the new Protestantism to make the great venture of spreading its truth by love and persuasion, there came from Geneva the decisive answer in the burning of Servetus, followed by the famous *Defence* before the world, written mainly by Calvin, of the course that had been taken. One month later, a brief Latin work appeared from the press with the title, *De haereticis, an sint persequendi, etc.* (Magdeburgi, 1554), followed in very short time by a French edition (Rouen, 1554). The body of the work contained impressive passages in favour of toleration from Church Fathers, from Luther, Erasmus, Sebastian Franck, and others, concluding with a passage from " Basil Montfort," a name which thinly veils Bastian Castellio himself. The Preface was addressed to the Duke of Wurtemberg, bore the name of " Martinus Bellius," and was beyond doubt written by Castellio, who inspired and directed the entire work, in which he was assisted by a very small group of refugees in Basle of similar ideas on this subject to his

---

[1] Calvin, in striking contrast, had written to the same boy-king in 1548 : " Under the cover of the Gospel, foolish people would throw everything into confusion. Others cling to the superstitions of the Antichrist at Rome. *They all deserve to be repressed by the sword which is committed to you.*"

own. This Preface is one of the mother documents on freedom of conscience, from which in time came a large offspring, and it is, furthermore, an interesting interpretation of a type of Christianity then somewhat new in the world. Its simplicity, its human appeal, its restrained emotional power, its prophetic tone, its sincerity and depth of earnestness mark it as a distinct work of genius, almost in the class with Pascal's *Provincial Letters*.

" If thou, illustrious Prince, had informed thy subjects that thou wert coming to visit them at an unnamed time and had requested them to be prepared in white garments to meet thee on thy coming ; what wouldst thou do, if, on arrival, thou shouldst find that instead of robing themselves in white they had occupied themselves in violent debate about thy person—some insisting that thou wert in France, others that thou wert in Spain ; some declaring that thou would come on horseback, others that thou would come by chariot ; some holding that thou would come with great pomp, others that thou would come without train or following ? And what especially wouldst thou say if they debated not only with words but with blows of fist and strokes of sword, and if some succeeded in killing and destroying others who differed from them ? ' He will come on horseback.' ' No, he won't ; he will come by chariot.' ' You lie.' ' No, I do not ; *you* are the liar.' ' Take *that* '—a blow with the fist. ' You take *that* '—a sword-thrust through the body. O Prince, what would you think of such citizens ? Christ asked *us* to put on the white robes of a pure and holy life, but what occupies our thought ? We dispute not only of the way to Christ, but of His relation to God the Father, of the Trinity, of predestination, of free will, of the nature of God, of angels, of the condition of the soul after death,— of a multitude of matters that are not essential for salvation, and *matters, in fact, which never can be known until our hearts are pure, for they are things which must be spiritually perceived*."

With a striking boldness, but with beautiful simplicity of spirit, he describes " an honest follower of Christ "—

and it is himself whom he is describing—" who believes in God the Father and in His Son Jesus Christ, and who wants to do His will, but cannot see that will just as others about him see it, in matters of intellectual formulation and in matters of external practice." " I cannot," he adds, " do violence to my conscience for fear of disobeying Christ. I must be saved or lost by my own personal faith, not by that of another. I ask you, whether Christ, who forgave those who went astray, and commanded His followers to forgive until seventy times seven, Christ who is the final Judge of us all, if He were here, would command a person like that to be killed ! . . . O Christ, Creator and King of the world," he cries out, " dost Thou see and approve these things ? Hast Thou become a totally different person from what Thou wert ? When Thou wert on earth, nothing could be more gentle and kind, more ready to suffer injuries. Thou wert like a sheep dumb before the shearers. Beaten, spit upon, mocked, crowned with thorns, crucified between thieves, Thou didst pray for those who injured Thee. Hast Thou changed to this ? Art Thou now so cruel and contrary to Thyself ? Dost Thou command that those who do not understand Thy ordinances and commandments as those over us require, should be drowned, or drawn and quartered, and burned at the stake ! "

The Christian world holds this view now. It is a part of the necessary air we breathe. But at this crisis in modern history it was unforgivably *new*.[1] One man's soul had the vision, one man's entire moral fibre throbbed with passion for it, and his rich intellectual nature pleaded for it as the only course of reason : " To burn a man is not to defend a doctrine, it is to *burn a man* ! " But it was a voice crying in a wilderness, and from henceforth Castellio was a marked and dangerous man in the eyes of all who were opposed to " Bellianism "—as the principle of toleration was nicknamed in honour of Martinus Bellius —and that included almost all the world. But to the end of his life, and in almost every one of his multitudinous

[1] Beza called it " diabolical doctrine."

tracts he continued to announce the principle of religious liberty, and to work for a type of Christianity which depended for its conquering power solely on its inherent truth and on its moral dynamic.

Calvin, who recognized the hand of Castellio in this powerful defence of freedom of thought, called his opponent " a monster full of poison and madness," and proceeded to demolish him in a Reply. In his *Contra libellum Calvini*, which is an answer to this Reply, Castellio declares that Calvin's act in burning Servetus was a bloody act, and that now his book is a direct menace to honest, pious people. " I," he adds, " who have a horror of blood, propose to examine the book. I do not defend Servetus. I have never read his books. Calvin burned them together with their author. I do not want to burn Calvin or to burn his book. I am only going to *answer* it." He notes that Calvin complains of " novelties and innovations," a strange complaint, he thinks, from a man who " has introduced more innovations in ten years than the entire Church had introduced in six centuries ! " All the sects, he reminds the great Reformer, claim to be founded on the Word of God. They all believe that their religion is true. Calvin says that his is *the only true one*. Each of the others says that his is the only true one. Calvin says that they are wrong. He makes himself (by what right I do not know) the judge and sovereign arbiter. He claims that he has on his side the sure evidence of the Word of God. Then why does he write so many books to prove what is evident ? The truth is surely not evident to those who die denying that it is truth ! Calvin asks how doctrine is to be guarded if heretics are not to be punished. " Doctrine," cries Castellio, " Christ's doctrine means loving one's enemies, returning good for evil, having a pure heart and a hunger and thirst for righteousness. *You* may return to Moses if you will, but for us others Christ has come."

Love, he constantly insists, is the supreme badge of any true Christianity, and the traits of the beatitudes in a person's life are a surer evidence that he belongs in

Christ's family, than is the fact that he holds current opinions on obscure questions of belief. " Before God," he writes in his *Defensio*, a work of the year 1562, to those who wish to hunt him off the face of the earth, " and from the bottom of my heart, I call you to the spirit of love." " By the bowels of Christ, I ask and implore you to leave me in peace, to stop persecuting me. Let me have the liberty of my faith as you have of yours. At the heart of religion I am one with you. It is in reality the same religion ; only on certain points of interpretation I see differently from you. But however we differ in opinion, why cannot we love one another ? "

He was, however, never to have the peace for which he pleaded, and he was never to experience the love and brotherly kindness for which he longed. Whole sheaves of fiery arrows were shot at him, and in tract after tract he had to see himself called " monster," " wretch," " dog," " pest," " fog-bank," and finally to see himself proclaimed to the world as a petty thief " who was supporting himself by stealing wood from his neighbours " ! With beautiful dignity Castellio tells the story of how he fished for public drift-wood on the shores of the Rhine, and how he kept his family alive by honest toil, when he was living in pitiable poverty, " to which," he says to Calvin, " everybody knows that thy attacks had brought me." " I cannot conceive how thou of all persons, thou who knowest me, can have believed a tale of theft about me, and in any case have told it to others." [1]

Compelled, as he was, to see the Reformation take what seemed to him the false course—the course of defending itself by persecution, of buttressing itself on election, of elevating, through a new scholasticism, doctrine above life,—he turned more and more, as time went on, toward interior religion, the cultivation of an inner sanctuary, the deepening of the mystical roots of his life, and the perfection of a religion of inner and spiritual life. " I have never taken holy things lightly,"

[1] He selected as the title of this book the opprobrious word which Calvin had used in the charge—*Harpago, i.e.* " Boat-hook."

he once wrote, and in the later years of what proved to be his brief as well as stormy life, he drew nearer to Christ as the Life of his life, and laboured with deepening passion to practise and present a religion of veracity, of reality and of transforming power. " It is certain," he says in his *Contra libellum Calvini*, " that Jesus is the Christ, the Son of God, and there is furthermore no doubt about the worth of love—love to God and love to man. There is no doubt, again, of the worth of forgiveness, of patience, of pity, of kindness, and of obedience to duty. Why leave these sure things and quarrel over inscrutable mysteries ? "

This point that the things which are essential to salvation are clear and luminous is a frequently occurring one in his writings. Impenetrable mysteries do not interest him, and he declares with reiteration that controversies and divisions are occasioned mainly by the proclamation of dogma on these inscrutable things. In a remarkable work, which remains still in manuscript—his *De arte dubitandi et confidendi, sciendi et ignorandi,*—he pleads for a religion that fits the facts of life and for the use of intelligence even in these lofty matters of spiritual experience where most astonishing miracles occur. He returns, in this writing, to his old position that the truths which concern salvation are clear and appeal powerfully to human reason. " There are, I know," he says, " persons who insist that we should believe even against reason. It is, however, the worst of all errors, and it is laid upon me to fight it. I may not be able to exterminate the monster, but I hope to give it such a blow that it will know that it has been hit. Let no one think that he is doing wrong in using his mental faculties. It is our proper way of arriving at the truth." [1]

Without entering in detail into the bottomless controversy of those times, let us endeavour to get an adequate view of Castellio's type of Christianity, and then we shall be able to form an estimate of the man who in the

---

[1] This MS. is in the Bibliothèque de l'Église des Remontrants in Rotterdam. I have used only the extracts given from it in Buisson and Jarrin.

strong power of his faith stood almost alone as the great battle of words raged around him.[1]

Those on the other side of the controversy began always from the opposite end of the spiritual universe to his point of departure. *They* were fascinated with the mysteries of the Eternal Will, and used all the keys of their logic to unlock the mysteries of foreknowledge, predestination, and grace which has wrought the *miracle* of salvation for the elect. Castellio, on the other hand, in true modern fashion, starts always with the concrete, the near and the known, to work upward to the nature of the unknown. We must, he says, try to discover the Divine attributes and the Divine Character by first finding out what our own deepest nature implies. If God is to speak to us it must be in terms of our nature. Before undertaking to fathom with the plummet of logic the unsoundable mystery of foreknowledge, let us see what we can know through a return to the real nature of man as he is, and especially to the real nature of the new Adam who is Christ, the Son of God. Man, as both Scripture and his own inner self testify, is made *in the image of God*, is dowered with freedom to determine his own destiny, may go upward into light, or downward into darkness. Man thus made, when put to trial, *failed*, followed lower instincts instead of higher, and experienced the awful penalty of sin, namely its cumulative power, the tendency of sin to beget sin, and to make higher choices ever more difficult. Christ, however, the new Adam, has *succeeded*. He has completely revealed the way of obedience, the way in which spirit conquers flesh. He is the new kind of Person who lives from above and who exhibits the cumulative power of goodness. His victory, which was won by His own free choice, inspires all men who see it with faith and hope in man's spiritual possibilities. Castellio declines to discuss Christ's metaphysical nature, except in so far as His life has revealed

[1] The main lines of Castellio's Christianity can be found in his *Dialogi quatuor* : (i.) De praedestinatione, (ii.) De electione, (iii.) De libero arbitrio, (iv.) De fide (Gouda, 1613) and in his *Scripta selecta* (1596).

it to us. He sees in Him the Heart and Character of God, the certainty of Divine love and forgiveness, and the way of life for all who desire to be spiritually saved, which means, for him, the formation of a new inward self, a purified nature, a morally transformed man, a will which no longer loves or wills sin. " Christ alone," he says, " can heal the malady of the soul, but He can heal it." " There is," he says again, " no other way of salvation for any man than the way of self-denial. He must put off his old man and put on Christ—however much blood and sweat the struggle may cost." Man, he insists, is always wrong when he represents God as angry. Christ showed that God needed no appeasing, but rather that man needed to be brought back to God by the drawing of Love, and be reconciled to Him.

Faith—which for every prophet of human redemption is the key that unlocks all doors for the soul—is for Castellio the supreme moral force by which man turns God's revelations of Himself into spiritual victories and into personal conquests of character. It is never something forensic, something magical. It is, as little, mere belief of historical facts and events. It is, on the contrary, a moral power that moves mountains of difficulty, works miracles of transformation, and enables the person who has it to participate in the life of God. It is a passionate leap (" élan ") of the soul of the creature toward the Creator ; it is a way of renewing strength in Him and of becoming a participator in His divine nature. It is a return of the soul to its source. It is a *persistent will*, which multiplies one's strength a hundredfold, makes Pentecost possible again, and enables us to achieve the goal which the vision of our heart sees. The only obstacle to this all-conquering faith is selfishness, the only mortal enemy is self-will.[1]

There have been, Castellio holds, progressive stages in the Divine education of the race, and in man's apprehension of God. The mark of advance is always found in the progress from law and letter to spirit, and from

[1] For Faith see *De fide* and *De arte dub.* ii. 212.

outward practices and ceremonies to inward experience. Divine revelations can always be taken at different levels. They can be seen in a literal, pictorial, temporal way, or they can be read deeper—by those who are purified by faith and love, and made partakers of the self-giving Life of God—as eternal and spiritual realities. The written word of God is the garment of the Divine Thought which is the real Word of God. It takes more than eyes of flesh to see through the temporal garment to the inner Life and Spirit beneath. Only the person who has in himself the illumination of the same Spirit that gave the original revelation can see through the garment of the letter to the eternal message, the ever-living Word hidden within.[1] In the Christianity of the full-grown spiritual man, sacraments and everything external must be used only as pictorial helps and symbolic suggestions for the furtherance of spiritual life. Within us, as direct offspring of God, as image of God, there is a Divine Reason, which existed before books, before rites, before the foundation of the world, and will exist after books and rites have vanished, and the world has gone to wreck. It can no more be abolished than God Himself can be. It was by this that Jesus Christ, the Son of God—called, in fact, Logos of God—lived and taught us how to live. It was in the Light of this that He transcended books and rites and declared, without quoting text, " God is Spirit and thou shalt worship God in spirit and in truth." This Reason is in all ages the right investigator and interpreter of Truth, even though time changes outward things and written texts grow corrupt.[2]

As his life was drawing to a close, he sent forth anonymously another powerful prophet-call for the complete liberation of mind and conscience. Ten years before the awful deeds of St. Bartholomew's Day, he issued his little French book with the title *Conseil à la France désolée*—

---

[1] This idea comes out in his Preface to the Bible, in his *Moses latinus*, and in his manuscript work, *De arte dubitandi*.

[2] *De arte dubitandi.*

Counsel to France in her Distress. It is a calm and penetrating diagnosis of the evils which are destroying the life of France and working her desolation. It throbs with noble patriotism and is full of real prophetic insight, though he spoke to deaf ears and wrote for blind eyes. The woes of France—her torn and distracted condition—are mainly due to the blind and foolish method of attempting to force intelligent men to accept a form of religion which in their hearts they do not believe is true. There can be no united people, strong and happy, until the blunder of compelling conscience entirely ceases. He pleads in tenderness and love with both religious parties, Catholics and Evangelicals, to leave the outgrown legalism of Moses and go to the Gospels for a religion which leads into truth and freedom. "O France, France," he cries—as formerly a greater One had said, "O Jerusalem, Jerusalem "—" my counsel is that thou cease to compel men's consciences, that thou cease to kill and to persecute, that thou grant to men who believe in Jesus Christ the privilege of serving God according to their own innermost faith and not according to some one else's faith. And you, that are private people, do not be so ready to follow those who lead you astray and push you to take up arms and kill your brothers. And Thou, O Lord our Saviour, wilt Thou give to us all grace to awake and come to our senses before it is forever too late. I, at least, have now done my duty and spoken my word of truth." St. Bartholomew's Day was the answer to this searching appeal, and the land, deaf to the call of its prophet, was to become more " desolate " still.

Just as the storm of persecution that had been gathering around him for years was about to burst pitilessly upon him in 1563, he quietly died, worn out in body, and " passed to where beyond these voices there is peace." His students in the University of Basle, where, in spite of the opposition from Geneva, he had been Professor of Greek for ten years, bore his coffin in honour on their shoulders to his grave, and his little band of disciples devoted themselves to spreading, in Holland and wherever they could find soil for it, the precious seed of his truth, which had in later years a very wide harvest.[1]

He was not a theologian of the Reformation type. He did not think the thoughts nor speak the dialect of his contemporaries. They need not be blamed for thanking God at his death nor for seeing in him an arch-enemy of their work. They were honestly working for one goal, and he was as honestly living by the light of a far different ideal. The spiritual discipline of the modern world was to come through their laborious systems, but he, anticipating the results of the travail and the slow spiral progress, and seeing in clear vision the triumph of man's liberated spirit, with exuberant optimism believed that the religion of the Spirit could be had for the taking—and he stretched out his hand for it !

" I am," he cried out beneath the bludgeons, " a poor little man, more than simple, humble and peaceable, with no desire for glory, only affirming what in my heart I believe ; why cannot I live and say my honest word and have your love ? " The time was not ready for him, but he did his day's work with loyalty, sincerity, and bravery, and seen in perspective is worthy to be honoured as a hero and a saint.[2]

---

[1] Under the nom-de-plume of John Theophilus, Castellio translated the *Theologia Germanica* into Latin, and published it with an Introduction. His translation carried this " golden book " of mystical religion into very wide circulation, and became a powerful influence, especially in England, as we shall see, in reproducing a similar type of religious thought.

The Quaker William Caton, who spent the latter part of his life in Holland, cites Castellio seven times in his Tract, *The Testimony of a Cloud of Witnesses, who in their Generation have testified against that horrible Evil of Forcing of Conscience and Persecution about Matters of Religion* (1662), and he seems very familiar with his writings. He also cites Schwenckfeld and Franck on pp. 37 and 17 respectively.

[2] Castellio's plea for toleration, *Traité des Hérétiques a savoir, si on les doit persécuter* (Rouen, 1554), has just been reissued in attractive form in Geneva, edited by Olivet and Choisy.

CHAPTER VII

COORNHERT AND THE COLLEGIANTS—A MOVEMENT
FOR SPIRITUAL RELIGION IN HOLLAND

I

THE struggle for political liberty in the Netherlands forms one of the most dramatic and impressive chapters in modern history, but the story of the long struggle in these same Provinces for the right to believe and to think according to the dictates of conscience is hardly less dramatic and impressive. Everybody knows that during the early years of the seventeenth century Holland was the one country in Europe which furnished cities of refuge for the persecuted and hunted exponents of unpopular faiths, and that the little band of Pilgrims who brought their precious seed to the new world had first preserved and nurtured it in a safe asylum among the Dutch ; but the slow spiritual travail that won this soul freedom, and the brave work of spreading, on that soil, a religion of personal insight and individual experience are not so well known.[1] The growth and development of this great movement, with its numerous ramifications and differentiations, obviously cannot be told here, but one or two specimen lines of the movement will be briefly studied for the light they throw upon this general type of religion under consideration, and for their specific influence

[1] Three important books on this subject are C. B. Hylkema, *Réformateurs* (Haarlem, 1902) ; Dr. Heinrich Heppe, *Geschichte des Pietismus und der Mystik in der reformirten Kirche, namentlich der Niederlande* (Leiden, 1879) ; and Wilhelm Goeters, *Die Vorbereitung des Pietismus in der reformierten Kirche der Niederlande* (Leipzig, 1911).

upon corresponding spiritual movements in England and America.

The silent propagation and germination of religious ideas in lands far away from their original habitat, their sudden appearance in a new spot like an outbreak of contagion, are always mysterious and fascinating subjects of research. Some chance talk with a disciple plants the seed, or some stray book comes to the hand of a baffled seeker at the moment when his soul is in a suggestible state, and lo ! a new vision is created and a new apostle of the movement is prepared, often so inwardly and mysteriously that to himself he seems to be " an apostle not of men nor by man." One of the earliest Dutch exponents and interpreters of this type of spiritual religion which we have been studying as a by-product of the Reformation in Germany, and one who became an apostle of it because at a critical period of his life the seeds of it had fallen into his awakened mind, was Dirck Volckertsz Coornhert.[1]

He was born in Amsterdam in 1522. He perfected himself as expert in copper-plate engraving and etching, and intended to pursue a quiet career in his adopted city of Haarlem, but he found himself disturbed with " intimations clear of wider scope." A keen desire to go back to the original sources of religious truth and to read the New Testament and the Fathers in their own tongue induced him to learn Greek and Latin after he was thirty years of age. He possessed excellent gifts and natural abilities of mind, and he soon had an enviable reputation for skill and learning. Like Sebastian Franck, whom he resembled in many points, he was profoundly interested in history and in the stages of man's historical development, and, like the former, he undertook the translation of great masterpieces which expressed the ideas that peculiarly suited his own temper of mind, such as Boethius' *Consolation of Philosophy* ; Cicero, *On Duties* ; and Erasmus' *Paraphrases of the New Testament*. He was throughout

---

[1] The biographical details of his life are given in a Preface to the three-volume edition of his collected works, published in Amsterdam in 1631.

his life deeply influenced by Erasmus, and his writings show everywhere a very strong humanistic colouring. It was no accident that one of his most important literary works was on Ethics (" Sittenkunst "), for his primary interest centred in man and in the art of living well (" Die Kunst wohl zu leben ").[1]

As he developed into independent manhood, he threw himself with great zeal into the cause of political freedom for the city of Haarlem, on account of which he suffered a severe imprisonment in the Hague in 1560, and at a later time was compelled to flee into temporary exile. He attracted the attention of William of Orange, who discovered his abilities and made him Secretary to the States-General in 1572, prized him highly for his character and abilities, commissioned him to write important state papers, and intrusted very weighty affairs to him.

In his youth he had been an extensive traveller and had seen with his own eyes the methods which the Spanish Inquisition employed to compel uniformity of faith and, with his whole moral being revolting from these un-spiritual methods, he dedicated himself to the cause of liberty of religious thought, and for this he wrote and spoke and wrought with a fearlessness and bravery not often surpassed.[2] With this passion of his for intellectual and spiritual freedom was joined a deeply grounded disapproval of the fundamental ideas of Calvinism, as he found it expounded by the preachers and theologians of the Reformed Church in Holland. As a Humanist, he was convinced of man's freedom of will, and he was equally convinced that however man had been marred by a *fall* from his highest possibilities, he was still possessed of native gifts and graces, and bore deep within himself an unlost central being, which in all his wanderings joined him indissolubly to God. On the great theological

---

[1] The title of this work is *Zedekunst, dat is, Wellevens Kunst, vermits waar-heydts kennisse vanden Mensche, vande Zonden ende vande Deughden. Nu alder-eerst beschreven in't Neerlandtsch.* Coornhert's *Wercken* (1631), i. fol. 268-335a.

[2] Two of his powerful pleas for the freedom of the mind are, *Epitome processus de occidendis haereticis et vi conscientiis inferenda* (Gouda, 1591), and *Defensio processus de non occidendis haereticis* (Hannover, 1593).

issues of the day he " disputed," with penetrating insight, against the leading theologians of the Netherlands, and he always proved to be a formidable antagonist who could not be put down or kept refuted. Jacobus Arminius, at the turning of his career, was selected by the Consistory to make once for all a refutation of Coornhert's dangerous writings. He, however, became so impressed, as he studied the works which he was to refute, that he shifted his own fundamental points of belief, accepted many of Coornhert's views, and became himself a greater " heretic " and a more dangerous opponent of Calvinism than the man whom he was chosen to annihilate.[1]

Sometime in his religious development—it is impossible to settle precisely when or where—he read the writings of the spiritual Reformers, and received from them formative influences which turned him powerfully to the cultivation of inward religion for his own soul and to the expression and interpretation of a universal Christianity— a Christianity of the inward Word and of an invisible Church. The lines of similarity between many of his views and those of Franck are so marked that no one can doubt that he read the books and meditated upon the bold teachings of this solitary apostle of the invisible Church. In fact he frequently mentions Franck by name in his writings and quotes his views. It is certain, too, that he admired, loved, and translated the writings of Sebastian Castellio, the French Humanist, first an admirer and then opponent of Calvin, pioneer defender of freedom of thought, and exponent of inward and spiritual religion of the type of the German Spiritual Reformers,[2] and it is unmistakable that we have, in this Dutch self-taught scholar, a virile interpreter of this same type of Christianity, marked with his own peculiar variation, and penetrated with the living convictions of his personal faith and first-hand experience. While putting emphasis on personal experience and on inward insight he nevertheless, like Franck, was suspicious

<hr>

[1] Gottfried Arnold, *Kirchen- und Ketzer-Historien*, ii. p. 378, sec. 3.
[2] See Chap. VI.

and wary of mystical " enthusiasm " and of " private openings." He criticized the " revelations " of David Joris and Henry Nicholas, and in place of their caprice he endeavoured to find the way to a religion grounded in the nature of things and of universal value. He was deeply read in the Mystics and constantly used their terminology, but he often gave new meaning to their words and pursued quite a different goal from that which absorbs the true mystic.

Coornhert makes a sharp distinction between lower knowledge and higher knowledge—knowledge proper. Lower knowledge does not get beyond images and copies of true reality. It is sufficient for man's practical guidance in the affairs of this world of space and time, but it becomes only a " dead knowledge " when it is applied to matters of eternal moment. The higher knowledge, on the other hand, is knowledge won through direct experience and practice of the will. This higher knowledge is possible for man because through Reason he partakes of the Word of God which is Reason itself revealed and uttered, and therefore he may know God and know of his own salvation with a certainty that far transcends the lower knowledge which he possesses of external things, or of mere historical happenings.[1]

This Word of God is eternal, and is the source of all spiritual light and truth that have come to the race in all ages. Through it the patriarchs discovered how to live well, even in a world of sin, and through this same Word the prophets saw the line of march for their people, and by the power and inspiration of this Word the written word was given as a temporary guidance, as a pedagogical help, as a lantern on men's paths, until the morning Star, Jesus Christ, the living Word, should rise and shine in men's hearts. The living Word is, thus, vastly different from the written word. One is essence, the other only image or shadow ; one is eternal, the other is temporal ; one is uncreated, the other is made ; one is the Light itself, the other is the lantern through which the

[1] *Zedekunst*, chaps. i. and ii.

Light shines ; one is Life itself, the other is only the witness of this Life—the finger which points toward it.[1]

True religion is distinguished from all false or lower forms of religion in this, that true religion is always inward and spiritual, is directly initiated within the soul, is independent of form and letter, is concerned solely with the eternal and invisible, and verifies itself by producing within man a nature like that of God as He is seen in Christ. The " law " of true religion is a new and divinely formed disposition toward goodness—a law written in the heart ; its temple is not of stone or wood, but is a living and spiritual temple, its worship consists entirely of spiritual activities, *i.e.* the offering of genuine praise from appreciative hearts, the sacrifice of the self to God, and the partaking of divine food and drink through living communion with Christ the Life. Religion, of this true and saving sort, never comes through hearsay knowledge, or along the channels of tradition, or by a head knowledge of texts of the written word. It comes only with inward experience of the Word of God, and it grows and deepens as the will of man lives by the Will of God, and as the kingdom of God comes, not in some far-away Jerusalem, or in some remote realm above the sky, but *in a man's own heart.*

This true and saving religion is begun, and completed, within the soul by a process which Coornhert names by the great historic word, *faith*. Faith is the soul's free assent to the living Word of God as, through amazing grace, it offers itself to man in the desperate straits of his life. Man is so made that he perpetually seeks some desired satisfaction and, in his restless search for this unattained good, he tries many false and specious trails, is endlessly baffled and deceived, and finally discovers, if he is fortunate enough to come to himself, that he is like a shipwrecked man on a single plank with sea everywhere about him and no haven in sight. In this strait the Light, which he has not noted before, breaks in on his darkness, and the way of Grace is presented to him in

[1] *Zedekunst*, chaps. iv. and v.

Christ. He feels himself called to a strange way of finding his desired satisfaction—no longer the way of flesh and worldly wisdom, but the way of the cross, of suffering, and of sacrifice. Reason, enlightened by the Word of God, prompts him to assent; the Scriptures, laden with promises, bear their affirmative testimony, and thus he makes his venture of faith, takes the risk of the voluntary sacrifice of his own pleasant desires, his preference for ways of ease and comfort, his self-will, and makes the bold experiment of trusting the Word of God, as it reveals itself to him, and of following Christ. He finds that his faith verifies itself at every step, his experiment carries him on into an experience, his venture brings him to the reality he is seeking. Every stage of this pragmatic faith, which in a word is *obedience to the Light*, makes the fact and the meaning of sin clearer, at the same time makes the knowledge of God more real and the nature of goodness more plain, and it leads away from a superstition of fear to a religion of love and of joy.[1]

All other religions, besides this true and inward religion of the spirit, called by Coornhert " outer or external religions," are considered of value only as preparatory stages toward the one true religion which establishes the kingdom of God in man's heart. With this fundamental view, he quite naturally regards all external forms and ceremonies as temporary, and he holds that all of them, even the highest of them, are nothing else than visible signs, figures, shadows, symbols, pointing to invisible, spiritual, eternal realities, which in their nature are far different from the signs and symbols. The signs and symbols can in no way effect salvation; they can at best only suggest to the quickened soul the true realities, to know which *is* salvation. The real and availing circumcision, as the spiritual prophets and apostles always knew, was a circumcision of the heart, and not of the flesh, and so, too, the true and availing baptism is a baptism into the life, death, and resurrection of Christ.

---

[1] *Wercken*, iii. fol. 413-427. See also " Hert-Spiegel godlycker Schrifturen," *Wercken*, i. fol. 1-44.

and cleanses the soul of its sins and produces " a good conscience toward God "—the old sinful man is buried and a new and Christlike man is raised. The same transforming effects attach to the real communion in which the finite human spirit feeds upon its true divine food and drink—the Life of Christ given for us. The real Sabbath is not a sacred day, kept in a ceremonial and legal sense, but rather an inward quiet, a prevailing peace of soul, a rest in the life of God from stress and strain and passion. The Church has been pitiably torn and mutilated by disputes over the genuine form of administering these outer ceremonies, supposing them to be in themselves sacraments of life. As soon as they are recognized to be what they really are, only temporary signs and symbols, then the main emphasis can be put where it properly belongs, and where Christ himself always put it, on love and on the practice of love. No ceremony, even though instituted by Christ himself and practised with absolute correctness, can make a bad heart good, but love—love which suffers long and is kind—flows only from a renewed and transformed heart which already partakes of the same nature as that which was incarnate in Christ. Imprisonment, isolation, exile, excommunication may deprive one of the outward ceremonies, but neither death nor life, nor any outward circumstance in the universe, need separate the soul from the love of God in Christ, or deprive it of the privilege of loving ! [1]

Coornhert criticizes the great Reformers for having put far too weighty emphasis on externals, and he especially criticizes Calvin for having given undue prominence to " pure doctrine " and to the right use of sacraments. It is impossible, he insists, to establish authoritatively from Scripture this so-called " pure doctrine." In fact, many parts of Scripture are against the doctrine of predestination, and Scripture is always against the doctrine of perseverance in sin. All speculations about the Trinity, or about the dual nature of Christ, transcend our knowledge and should be rejected. Furthermore

[1] *Wercken*, iii. fol. 413-427.

there is no authoritative Scripture or revelation for the new forms of the sacrament that have been introduced by the Reformers and are being made essential to salvation. The true Reformation, he thinks, should be devoted to the construction of the invisible Church, which has existed in all ages of the world, but which is kept from realizing its full scope and power because the attention of men is too greatly absorbed with signs and symbols and outward things.[1]

For similar reasons he disapproved of the Anabaptists, even in their purified form as worked out under the guidance of Menno Simons. They still held, as did the reformed churches, that the true Church is a visible church which every one to be a Christian must join, though this true Church, as they conceive it, consists only of " saints." They claim the authoritative right to ban all persons who, according to their opinion, are not " saints." This right Coornhert denies. He further disapproves of their literal interpretations of the Sermon on the Mount, and of the obstacles which they put in the way of the free exercise of prophecy on the part of the members of the community. He insists that a person may be a Christian and yet belong to no visible church, if meantime he is a true member of the invisible Communion. He himself refrained from taking the communion supper, either with Papists, Lutherans, or Calvinists, because he said they all set the sacrament above the real characteristic mark of Christian membership, which is love, and because there is no divine command, with distinct and unambiguous authority, for the efficacious celebration of the sacrament, which in any case could not be rightly kept so long as sectarian hostility and lack of love prevail in the contending visible churches.[2] Under these circumstances, Coornhert, who was intensely concerned for the sincere, simpleminded souls, perplexed by the maze of varying sects and parties, refused to found a new sect or to head a new schismatic movement. On behalf of those who could not

---

[1] See Arnold, *op. cit.* ii. p. 380, sec. 8.
[2] His views in this particular are very similar to those of Schwenckfeld.

conform, he pleaded for freedom of conscience and for
the right to live in the world undisturbed as members of
the invisible Church, using or omitting outward ceremonies as conscience might direct, waiting meantime
and seeking in quiet faith for the coming of new and
divinely commissioned apostles who would *really reform*
the apostate Churches, unite all divided sects, and gather
in the world a true Church of Christ.[1]

Meantime, while waiting for this true apostolic Church
to appear, Coornhert approved of the formation of an
interim-Church. This Church, according to his programme,
would accept as truth, and as true practice, anything
plainly and clearly taught in the canonical Scripture,
but he advised against using glosses and commentaries
made by men, since that is to turn from the sun to the
stars and from the spring to the cistern. This interim-
Church was to have no authoritative teachers or preachers.
In place of official ministry, the members were to edify
one another in Christian love, with the reservation that
they would welcome further illumination out of the
Scriptures wherever they have made a mistake or gone
wrong. All persons who confess God as Father, and
Jesus Christ as sent by God, and who in the power of
faith abstain from sins, may belong to this interim-
Church. For the sake of those who are still weak
and spiritually immature, he allowed the use of ceremonies
in the interim-Church, but all ceremonies are held as
having no essential function for salvation, and the
believer is at liberty to make use of them or to abstain
from using them as he prefers.[2]

II

Coornhert's proposed interim-Church, which at best
was conceived as only a temporary substitute for the
true apostolic Church, for which every spiritual Christian
is a " waiter " or " seeker," found actual embodiment in
a very interesting movement of the early seventeenth

---

[1] Arnold, *op. cit.* pp. 381-382.   [2] *Wercken*, i. fol. 554 ff.

century, known in Dutch history as the " Collegiants "
or " Rynsburgers," which we shall now proceed to
study.[1] The Collegiants had their origin in one of
the stormiest of the many theological controversies
which swept over the Netherlands in this critical period
of religious history, a controversy arising over the views
taught by Jacobus Arminius (1560–1609). The Dutch
Protestants who accepted his views presented a " Remonstrance " to the States of Holland and Friesland in
1610, in which they formulated their departure from
strict, orthodox Calvinism. The " Remonstrance " contained five main Articles : (1) that the divine decrees
of predestination are conditioned and not absolute ;
(2) that the atonement is in intention universal ; (3) that
a man cannot of himself do anything good without regeneration ; (4) that though the Grace of God is a necessary
condition of human effort it does not act irresistibly in
man ; (5) that believers are able to resist sin, but are not
beyond the possibility of falling from Grace. The
opponents to these views, often called " Gomarists,"
issued a counter-blast from which they received the
name " counter-Remonstrants." The States-General
passed an edict tolerating both parties and forbidding
further dispute, but the conflict of views would not
down. It spread like a prairie fire, became complicated
with political issues, had its martyrdoms, and produced
far-reaching results and consequences.[2] At the Synod
of Dort, on April 24, 1619, the Remonstrants were
declared guilty of falsifying religion and of destroying
the unity of the Church, and were deposed from all their
ecclesiastical and academic offices and positions. Two
hundred were deposed from the ministerial office for life,
and one hundred were banished.

Among the number of deposed ministers was Christian

---

[1] The best history of the Collegiants is J. C. Van Slee's *De Rijnsburger Collegianten* (Haarlem, 1895).

[2] One of the most tragic consequences of the controversy was the
martyrdom of John of Barneveldt, the political head of the Remonstrants.
Hugo Grotius was thrown into prison, but escaped through the bold ingenuity
of his wife.

Sopingius, the pastor of Warmund, and the "Remon-strants," who formed an important part of his congrega-tion, were left without the opportunity of hearing any ministry of which they approved.   In this strait Giesbert Van der Kodde, an Elder in the Warmund church, took a bold step.   He was the son of a prosperous farmer who had given his children, John, William, Adrian, and Giesbert, an unusually extended education.   All the sons learned Latin, Italian, French, and English, while William (known in the scholarly world as Gulielmus Coddaeus) was a Hebrew and Oriental scholar of note, and at the age of twenty-six was made Professor of Hebrew in the University of Leyden.   They owed the course of their religious development and their particular bent of mind to the writings of men like Sebastian Castellio; Coorn-hert, whose views have been given above; and Jacobus Acontius, the Italian humanist, who laid down the principles that no majority can make a binding law in matters of faith, that only God's Spirit in the hearts of men can certify what is the truth, and that "Confessions of Faith" have been the ruinous source of endless divisions in the Church.   Deeply imbued with the ideas of these spiritual reformers, and in sympathy as they were with many of the views and practices of the Mennonites about them, the Van der Kodde brothers decided, under the leadership of the boldest and most conscientious of them, Giesbert, to come together without any minister and hold a meeting of a free congregational type.   At first the meeting was probably held in Giesbert's house, and consisted of readings from the Scripture, prayers, and the public utterance of messages of edification by those who formed the group.   A little later a "Remonstrant" preacher was sent to care for the orphaned Church in Warmund, but Giesbert had become satisfied with the new type of meeting, and now expressed himself emphatic-ally against listening to preachers who lived without working and at the expense of the community, and who hindered the free exercise of "prophecy."   Many of the members of the Church did not share these views, but much preferred to have the comfort of a minister, so that a " separation " occurred, and Giesbert, with his brothers and fellow-believers, rented a house and perfected their new type of congregational meeting. They soon moved their meeting (called a " Collegium," *i.e.* gathering) to the neighbouring town of Rynsburg, where it received additions to its adherents, largely drawn from the Mennonites, many of whose ideas were strongly impressed upon the little " Society,"—for example, opposition to taking oaths, refusal to fight, or even to take measures of self-defence, and rejection of the right of magistrates and other political officers to inflict punishment. They also adopted, as the Mennonites did, the Sermon on the Mount as the basis of their ethical standard, which they applied with literalness and rigour. They insisted on simplicity of life, the denial of " worldly " occupations or professions, plainness of garb, rejection of the world's etiquette, absence of titles in addressing persons, and equality of men and women, even in public ministry. They introduced the practice of immersion ("Dompeldoop") as a mark of initiation into the Society, but they considered true Christian baptism to be with the Spirit and not with water, and they allowed their members a large range of liberty in the use or disuse of water baptism, as well as in the form of receiving it. They rejected the Supper as an ecclesiastical ceremony, but they highly prized it as an occasion of fellowship and of group worship. Every person might share the supper with them if he confessed his faith in Christ and were not living in unrepented sin, though they were inclined to exclude persons occupying offices which involved the violation of the Sermon on the Mount. The one essential mark of fellowship was brother-love, which was not to be confined to the narrow limits of the Society, but that person was regarded the truest disciple of Christ who practised the neighbour-spirit in the broadest and most effective manner. They cared for their own sick and poor, and they had a wide sympathy for all oppressed and suffering people. They pushed to the farthest limit their opposition to war and all other forms of destroying human life.

From the first there was a decided strain of " Enthusiasm " evident in the movement, and a pronounced tendency to encourage a ministry of " prophetic openings." One of the original members, John Van der Kodde, declared that he should fear the loss of his salvation if he failed in a meeting to give utterance to the Word of God revealed to him in his inner being. They encouraged the custom of silent waiting in their gatherings as a preparation for " openings." They proved from the fourteenth chapter of 1 Corinthians that free prophecy is the highest form of ministry, and they held that God by His grace could pour out His Spirit upon men in the seventeenth century as well as in the days of the Apostles and Evangelists, who did their mighty work, not as Church officials, but as recipients of gifts from God. They felt that prayer accompanied by *tears* was true prayer, " moved " from above. They, however, were persons of scholarship and refinement, and not tumultuous or strongly emotional, but, on the contrary, they highly valued dignity and propriety of behaviour.

As the movement spread, *Collegia*, or societies, were formed in Leyden, Rotterdam, Amsterdam, and in other localities, essentially like the mother-society in Rynsburg, but with characteristic variations and with particular lines of local developments. Once every year they had a large yearly meeting in Rynsburg, to which the scattered members came from all parts of Holland where there were societies. As time went on, two marked lines of differentiation appeared in the movement, due to the trend of the influence of important leaders, one group emphasizing especially the *seeker-attitude*, and the other group receiving its formative influence from Cartesian philosophy. Daniel Van Breen, Adam Boreel, and Michael Comans were the early leaders and pillars of the Amsterdam *Collegium*, which was begun in 1645, and some years later the group was greatly strengthened by the " convincement " of the young Mennonite doctor and teacher, Galenus Abrahams, who soon became the most prominent Collegiant leader in Holland.

Adam Boreel gave the movement a strong impetus and did much toward putting the teachings of Coornhert into practice. He was born at Middleburg in 1603. He was a man of good scholarship, being especially learned in Hebrew, and he was thoroughly impregnated with the views of the spiritualistic Humanists of the former century, Franck, Castellio, and Coornhert, as well as with the views of the mystics, and he was himself a champion of individual religious freedom. He held that the visible Church since the apostolic age has been astray and apostate, that Confessions of faith, Church officers, and sacraments are without " authority," that the uncontaminated teaching of the Holy Scripture is the only safe norm of faith, and that until a true apostolic Church is again established in the world by divine commission, each faithful, believing Christian should maintain meantime the worship of God in his own way and *wait* in faith for a fuller revelation.[1] His mystical piety appears strongly in his hymns, which are preserved in his complete works. One of these hymns of Boreel has been very freely translated into English " by a Lover of the Life of our Lord Jesus," probably Henry More, the Platonist. More says that he finds the hymn " running much upon the mortification of our own wills and of our union and communion with God," and he loves it as a deep expression of his own faith that " no man can really adhere to Christ, and unwaveringly, but by union to Him by His Spirit." I give a few extracts from More's free Translation :

1. O Heavenly Light ! my spirit to Thee draw,
   With powerful touch my senses smite,
   Thine arrows of Love into me throw
      With flaming dart
      Deep wound my heart,
   And wounded seize for ever, as thy right.

---

[1] Adam Boreel's teaching is set forth in his treatise, *Ad legem et testimonium* (Amsterdam, 1645). Information upon his life and teaching is given in Arnold, *op. cit.* ii. 386-387 ; in Hylkema, *Reformateurs* ; and in Walter Schneider, *Adam Boreel* (Giessen, 1911).

3. Do thou my faculties all captivate
Unto thyself with strongest tye ;
My will entirely regulate :
　　Make me thy slave,
　　Nought else I crave
For this I know is perfect Liberty.

5. 　　O endless good !
　　Break like a flood
Into my soul, and water my dry earth,

6. That by this mighty power I being reft
Of everything that is not One,
To Thee alone I may be left
　　By a firm will
　　Fixt to Thee still
And inwardly united into one.

11. So that at last, I being quite released
From this strait-laced Egoity
My soul will vastly be increased
　　Into that All
　　Which One we call,
And One in itself alone doth All imply.

12. Here's Rest, here's Peace, here's Joy and Holy Love,
The heaven is here of true Content,
For those that seek the things above,
　　Here's the true light
　　Of Wisdom bright
And Prudence pure with no self-seeking blent.

15. Thus shall you be united with that One,
That One where's no Duality,
For from that perfect Good alone
　　Ever doth spring
　　Each pleasant thing
The hungry soul to feed and satisfy.[1]

Stoupe, in his *Religion of the Dutch*,[2] gives some interesting contemporary light on this branch of Collegiants whom he calls " Borellists," as follows : " The Borellists had their name from one Borrell, the Ringleader of their

---

[1] Henry More's *Annotations upon the Discourse of Truth* (London, 1682), pp. 271-276.

[2] Stoupe, *La Réligion des Hollandois* (Paris, 1673), translated into English under the title *The Religion of the Dutch* (London, 1680). The extract is from p. 82 of the French edition and pp. 26-28 of the English edition.

sect, a man very learned, especially in the Hebrew, Greek, and Latine tongues. He was brother to Monsieur Borrell, ambassador from the States-General to his most Christian Majesty. These Borrellists do for the most part maintain the opinions of the Mennonites though they come not to their assemblies. They have made choice of a most austere kind of life, spending a considerable part of their Estates in almsgiving and a careful discharge of all the duties incumbent on a Christian. They have an aversion for all Churches, as also for the use of the Sacraments, publick prayers, and all other external functions of God's Service. They maintain that all Churches which are in the world and have been since the death of the apostles and their first subsequent successors have degenerated from the pure doctrine which they preached to the world ; for this reason, that they have suffered the infallible Word of God contained in the Old and New Testaments to be expounded and corrupted by Doctors who are not infallible and would have their own confessions, their catechisms, and their Liturgies and their sermons, which are the works of men, to pass for what they really are not, to wit, for the pure Word of God. They hold also that men are not to read anything but the Word of God alone without any additional application of men."

Abrahams (*b.* 1622) intensified the *seeker* aspect of the Amsterdam group, emphasizing the view that the existing Church, even in its best form, is only an interim-Church with no saving sacraments and no compelling authority. His position is expressed in the highly important " Nineteen Articles " which he, and his fellow-believer, David Spruyt, drew up in 1658, and in the further Exposition *Nader Verklaringe* of 1659. These documents present the apostolic pattern or model as the ideal of the visible Church for all ages. There neither is nor can be any other true Church. It is essentially a Church managed, maintained, and governed through " gifts " bestowed by the Holy Spirit, and in this Church each spiritual member takes his part according to the measure of his special " gift." This pattern Church, however, *fell away* and became corrupted after the death of the apostles, and instead of this glorious Church an external Church was established, claiming to possess authoritative officials, saving sacraments, and infallible doctrines, but really lacking the inward power of the apostolic Church, no longer following and imitating Christ, on the contrary adopting the world's way and the world's type of authority, and destitute of the very mark and essence of real Christianity, *the spirit of love.* Through all the apostasy of the visible Church, however, an invisible Church has survived and preserved the eternal ideal. It consists of all those, in whatever ages and lands, who have lived by their faith in Christ, have kept themselves pure and stainless in the midst of a sinful world, have practised love, even when they have received the buffets of hate, have lived above division and schism and sect, and have steadily believed that their names were written in heaven and that their Church was visible to God, even though none on earth called them brother, or recognized their membership in the body of Christ. Some time, in God's good time, that invisible Church, which no apostasy has annulled or destroyed, will become once again a visible Church, equipped with " gifted " teachers and with apostolic leaders as at the first, beautiful once more as a bride adorned for her husband, and powerful again as the irresistible sword of the Spirit.

But the Reformers — Luther, Calvin, Zwingli, and even Menno Simons—have taken an unwarranted course toward the reform and restoration of the Church. It was within their right and power to *improve* the unbearable condition of the outward Church, by faithfully following the plain teaching of the New Testament, and without usurping authority. They, however, have not been satisfied to do what lay within the narrow limits of their commission. They have ambitiously undertaken to set up again an authoritative visible Church, even though they lacked the gifts of the Spirit for it, and were without the necessary apostolic commission. They insisted on their form of sacraments as essential to salvation ; they drew up their infallible creeds ; they set up Church officials who were to rule over other men's faith, and they assumed a certain divine right to compel the consciences of their members. Most of the Reformers have even sanctioned the use of bonds and prisons to secure uniformity of faith ! The primitive apostles claimed no such right and made use of no such unspiritual methods. Order is a good thing and is everywhere to be sought, but God nowhere has conferred upon the heads of His Church the authority to compel conscience or to force tender souls to submit to a system which reveals in itself no inherent evidences of divine origin.

The writers of these Nineteen Articles fail to see anywhere in the world a divinely established and spiritually endowed Church of Jesus Christ. They are determined to live in purity and love, to avoid dissension and strife, to guard their membership in the invisible Church, and to *wait* in faith for the outpouring of the Spirit and the bestowal of miraculous gifts for the restoration of the Church in its pristine apostolic purity and power. We have thus, here in Holland, an almost exact parallel to the " Seekers " who were very numerous in England in the middle decades of the seventeenth century.

We get a very interesting side - light on Galenus Abrahams in the *Journal* of George Fox. William Penn and George Keith held a " discussion " with this famous Collegiant leader in 1677, at which time the latter " asserted that nobody nowadays could be accepted as a messenger of God unless he confirmed his doctrine by miracle," [1] and Fox says that Abrahams was " much confounded and truth gained ground." [2] Fox himself was not present at the " discussion," but he had a personal interview with Abrahams at about the same time as the " discussion." The interview was not very satisfactory. Fox says that he found this " notable teacher " " very high and shy, so that he would not let me touch him nor look upon him, but he bid me keep my eyes off him, for

---

[1] Sewel, *History of the People called Quakers* (Phila. edition, 1823), ii. p. 368.
[2] *Journal*, (ed. 1901), ii. p. 310.

he said they pierced him!"[1] But at a later visit, in
1684, Fox found the Collegiant doctor, now venerable
with years, "very loving and tender." "He confessed
in some measure to truth," Fox says, "and we parted
very lovingly." At a meeting, held in Amsterdam a
few weeks later, Abrahams was among the large group
of attenders, and "was very attentive to the testimony of
the truth," and, when the meeting was over, Fox says,
"he came and got me by the hand very lovingly,"[2] and
seemed no longer afraid of the Quaker's "piercing eyes."
In spirit they were very near together, and with a little
more insight on both sides the two movements might have
joined in one single stream. For many years afterwards
the common people, not given to nice distinctions, called
the annual gathering of the Collegiants at Rynsburg
"the meeting of the Quakers."[3]

The other tendency in the movement, which received
its fullest expression in the group of Collegiants at
Rynsburg and their friends in Amsterdam, had a still
greater parallelism with Quakerism, in fact, the most
important book which came from a member of this group
—*The Light on the Candlestick*—is indistinguishable in its
body of ideas from Quaker teaching, and differs only in
one point, that it reveals a more philosophically trained
mind in the writer than does any early Quaker book with
the single exception of Barclay's *Apology*. The author
of *The Light on the Candlestick*—written originally in
Dutch and published in 1662 under the title *Lucerna
super candelabro*—was probably Peter Balling, though
the book, with characteristic Collegiant modesty, was
published anonymously. Peter Balling was one of an
interesting group of scholarly Collegiants who became
very intimate friends of Baruch Spinoza, and who received
from the Jewish philosopher a strong impulse toward
mystical religion. Before they became acquainted with
the young Spinoza, however, they had already received
through Descartes a powerful intellectual awakening,

---

[1] *Journal*, ii. p. 401. [2] *Ibid.* ii. pp. 401-402.
[3] Simeon Friderich Rues, *Mennoniten und Collegianten* (Jena, 1743), p. 244.

and had discovered that consciousness itself, when fully sounded, has its own unescapable evidence of God. It is not possible here to turn aside and study adequately this extraordinary philosophical movement known as Cartesianism, beginning in Descartes (1596–1650) and culminating in Spinoza (1632–1677), but the distinct religious influence of it is so profoundly apparent, both in Peter Balling and in the Quaker apologist Robert Barclay (1648–1690), that a very brief review of the contribution from this source seems necessary.

René Descartes, like almost every other supreme genius who has discovered a new way and has forever shifted the line of march for the race, passed through a momentous inward upheaval, amounting to a conversion experience, and emerged into a new moral and intellectual world.[1] It was on November 10, 1619, in the midst of a great campaign during the opening stages of the Thirty Years' War, in which at this time the young Frenchman was a soldier on the Roman Catholic side, that Descartes, sitting alone all day in a heated room of some German house, resolved to have done with outworn systems of thought and with tradition, and determined to make the search for truth the object of his life.[2] The new scientific method, which was the fruit of his reflections and experiments, and which has since been carried into every field of human research, does not now concern us. The feature of his philosophy which impressed these serious seekers after God was his fresh discovery of what is involved in the nature of self-consciousness. Beginning with the bold resolution to accept nothing untested, to doubt everything in the universe that can be doubted, and to receive as truth only that which successfully resists every attempt to doubt it, he found one absolutely solid point with which to start, in the self-existence of self-consciousness—" At least I who am doubting am thinking, and to think is to exist."

---

[1] See E. S. Haldane, *Descartes, His Life and Times* (1905), pp. 51-53.

[2] The autobiographical account of this experience is given in the opening of part ii. of the *Discourse on Method*.

Pushing his search deeper down to see what is further involved in the constitution of this self-consciousness, he discovered a consciousness of God—the idea of an infinitely perfect Being—within himself, and this consciousness of God seemed to him to be the underlying condition of every kind of knowledge whatever. It turns out to be impossible, he believes, to think of the " finite " without contrasting it, in implication at least, with the " infinite " which is therefore in consciousness, just as it is impossible to talk of " spaces " without presupposing the one space of which given " spaces " are parts. That we are oppressed with our own littleness, that we " look before and after and sigh for what is not," that we are conscious of finiteness, means that we partake in some way of an infinite which reveals itself in us by an inherent necessity of self-consciousness. There are, then, some ideas within us—at least there is this one idea of an infinitely perfect reality—*implanted* in the very structure of our thinking self, which could have come from no other source but from God, who is that infinitely perfect Reality. Other things may still be doubtful, and a tinge of uncertainty may rest upon everything external to the mind that perceives them, but *the soul and God are sure*, and, of these two certainties, God is as sure as the soul itself, because an idea of Him is native to the soul as a necessary part of its " furnishings," and is the condition of thinking anything at all.[1]

Spinoza, though bringing to his philosophy elements which are foreign to Descartes, and though fusing his otherwise mathematical and logical system with the warmth and fervour of mystical experience that is wholly lacking in the French philosopher, carried Cartesianism to its logical culmination, and has given the world one of the most impressive presentations that ever has been given of the view that all things centre in God and are involved in His existence, that it belongs to the very nature of the

[1] Descartes' famous argument is found in Meditations III. and IV. of his *Meditations on First Philosophy*, first published in 1641. For an illuminating interpretation of the entire movement, see Edward Caird's Essay on Cartesianism in *Essays on Literature and Philosophy* (1892), ii. pp. 267-383.

human mind to know God, and that all peace and felicity come from " the love of an infinite and eternal object which feeds the soul with changeless and unmingled joy." He, too, had his conversion-awakening which took him above the love of earthly things, and through it he found an unvarying centre for his heart's devotion, which made his life, outwardly extremely humble, inwardly one of the noblest and most saintly in the history of philosophy. " After experience had taught me," he writes in the opening of his early *Treatise on the Improvement of the Understanding*, " that all things which are ordinarily encountered in common life are vain and futile . . . I at length determined to inquire if there were anything which was a TRUE GOOD, capable of imparting itself, and by which alone the mind could be affected to the exclusion of all else ; whether, indeed, anything existed by the discovery and acquisition of which I might have continuous and supreme joy to all eternity," and the remainder of his life was penetrated by a noble passion for the Eternal, and dedicated to the interpretation of the Highest Good which he had discovered, and which henceforth no rival good was ever to eclipse. Dr. A. Wolf well says of him : " His moral ardour seems almost aglow with mystic fire, and if we may not call him a priest of the most high God, yet he was certainly a prophet of the power which makes for righteousness." [1] He is giving his own experience in the spiritual principle which he laid down early in his life : " So long as we have not such a clear idea of God as shall unite us with Him in such a way that it will not let us love anything beside Him, we cannot truly say that we are united with God, so as to depend immediately on Him." [2]

It is Spinoza's primary principle that the only Reality in the universe is an all-inclusive Reality which is the origin, source, and explanation of all that is. All human experience, either of an inward or outward world, if it is to have any meaning and reality at all, involves the

---

[1] Spinoza, *Short Treatise on God, Man, and his Well-Being*, Wolf's edition (London, 1910), p. 102.   [2] *Ibid.* p. 40.

existence of this inclusive Whole of Reality, that is of God. It belongs, thus, fundamentally to the nature of human consciousness to know God, for if we did not know Him we should not know anything else. The moment a " finite thing " or a " finite idea " is severed from the Whole in which it has its ground and meaning, it becomes *nothing* ; it is " real " only so long as it is a part of a larger Reality, and so every attempt to understand a " flower in a crannied wall," or any other object in the universe, drives us higher up until we come at last to that which is the *prius* of all being and knowledge, the explanation of all that is.

But this ultimate Reality up to which all our experience carries us—if we take the pains to think out what is involved in the experience—is no mere sum of " finites," no bare aggregation of " parts," no heaped-up totality of separate " units." It is an Absolute Unity which binds all that is into one living, organic Whole, a Divine Nature,—*natura naturans* Spinoza calls it,—and which lives and is manifested in all the finite " parts," in so far as they are real at all. And as soon as the mind finds itself in living unity with the eternal Nature of things, and views all things from their centre in God, and sees how all objects and events flow from the eternal Being of God, it is " led as by the hand to its highest blessedness." [1] The complications of Spinoza's system, and the difficulty of finding a " way down " from the Absolute Unity of God to the differentiation of the modes of a world—*natura naturata*—here, in space and time, do not now concern us.

The point of contact between Spinoza and the spiritual movement which we are studying is found in his central principles that God is the *prius* of all finite reality, that to know things or to know one's own mind truly is to know God, and that a man who has formed a pure love for the eternal is above the variations of temporal fortune, is not disturbed in spirit by changes in the object of his love, but loves with a love which eternally feeds the soul with joy.

[1] *Ethics*, part ii. Preface.

During the most important period of his intellectual and spiritual development, Spinoza spent three years (1660–1663) in the quiet village of Rynsburg, living in close and intimate contact with his Collegiant friends. It was here during these happiest years of his life, in this quiet retreat and surrounded with spiritually - minded men with whom he had much in common, that he wrote his *Short Treatise on God, Man and his Well-Being*, as well as his *Treatise on the Improvement of the Under-standing*, which opens with his account of the birth of his own spiritual passion. These intellectual and high-minded Collegiants had their influence upon the philosopher, and he in turn had a deep influence upon them. Peter Balling translated into Dutch in 1664 Spinoza's version of Descartes' *Principia*, and Balling turned to his friend Spinoza for consolation in his great loss occasioned by the death of his child that same year,[1] while the philosopher at his death left all his unpublished manuscripts to another life-long intimate Collegiant friend of his, John Rieuwertsz.

The Light on the Candlestick, to which we shall now turn for the ripest ideas of the little sect, was written while Spinoza was living among the Collegiants in Rynsburg. It was very quickly discovered by the Quakers, who immediately recognized it as " bone of their bone," and circulated it as a Quaker Tract. It was translated into English in 1663 by B. F.,[2] who published it with this curious title-page : " The Light upon the Candlestick. Serving for Observation of the Principal things in the Book called, *The Mystery of the Kingdom of God, &c. Against several Professors, Treated of, and written by Will Ames.* Printed in Low Dutch for the Author, 1662, and translated into English by B. F."

The Collegiant author, quite in the spirit and style of Spinoza, urges the importance of discovering a central love for " things which are durable and incorruptible," " knowing thereby better things than those to which the

---

[1] See Spinoza's *Correspondence*, Letter No. XXX.

[2] Benjamin Furley, a Quaker merchant of Colchester, then living in Rotterdam.

multitude are link't so fast with love." We have outgrown the " toyes with which we played as children,"
there is now " no desire or moving thereunto, because we
have found better things for our minds " ; so, too, " all
those things in which men, even to old age, so much
delight " would seem like " toyes " if they once discovered the true Light " which abides forever unchange-
able," and if through it they got a sight of " those things
which are alone worthy to be known." This " true and
lasting change," from " toyes " to " the things which are
durable and eternal," can come only through an inward
conversion. When a new vision begins from within,
then the outward action follows of itself, but no man will
part with what he judges best till he sees something better,
and then the weaker yields to the stronger without any
forcing.[1] This whole work of conversion, of transformation, of " lasting change," must have its origin in something within ourselves. We cannot turn from baubles
and " toyes " and our " desire for that which is high in
the world " until a Light from some source plainly shows
us an eternal reality for which we may " highly adventure
the tryal." There is, our author insists, only one place
where such a guiding Light could arise, and that is within
the soul itself, as an inward and immediate knowledge :
" 'Tis not far to seek. We direct thee to within thyself.
Thou oughtest to turn into, to mind and have regard
unto, that which is within thee, to wit, the Light of Truth,
the true Light which enlighteneth every man that cometh
into the world. Here 'tis that thou must be and not
without thee. Here thou shalt find a Principle certain
and infallible, through which increasing and going on
into, thou mayest at length arrive unto a happy condition.
Of this thou mayest highly adventure the tryal. And if
thou happenest to be one of those that would know all
things before thou dost begin . . . know this, Thou dost
therein just as those that would learn to read without
knowing the Letters. He that will not adventure till
he be fully satisfied, shall never begin, much less finish

[1] *The Light upon the Candlestick*, p. 8, freely rendered.

his own salvation. We say then, that we exhort every one to turn unto the Light that's in him." [1]

In true Cartesian fashion, he demonstrates why this Light must have its *locus* within the soul and not in some external means or medium. All knowledge that God is being revealed in external signs, or through external means, already presupposes a prior knowledge of God. We can judge no doctrine, no Book to be Divine except by some inward and immediate knowledge of what really is Divine. Without this Light the Scriptures are only Words and Letters. But " if we experience that the Book called the Bible in regard to the Divine doctrine therein comprised hath such a harmony with That [in us] by which God is known, that He must needs have been the Author of it, there cannot rationally be any more powerful demonstration." [2]

The same principle is true with regard to every conceivable form of revelation which could be made to our outward senses, whether by words, or by miracles, or by any other visible " operations." No finite thing can bring us a knowledge of God unless we already have within us a sufficient knowledge of Him to make us able to appreciate and judge the Divine character of the particular revelation ; that is to say, we must already have God in order either to seek Him or to find Him ; or, as Balling puts it, " Unless the knowledge of God precedes, no man can discern Him." God is, therefore, the *prius* of all knowledge : " The knowledge of God must first be, before there can be knowledge of any particular things," [3] and God must be assumed as present in the soul before any basis of truth or of religion can be found. " The Light is the first Principle of Religion ; for, seeing there can be no true Religion without the knowledge of God, and no knowledge of God without this Light, Religion must necessarily have this Light for its first Principle." [4] " Without thyself, O Man," he concludes, " thou hast no

---

[1] *The Light upon the Candlestick*, pp. 3-4.

[2] *Op. cit.* p. 10. He uses also the Cartesian argument that there must at least be as much reality in the cause as there is in the effect, p. 12.

[3] *Op. cit.* p. 12.   [4] *Ibid.* p. 6.

means to look for, by which thou mayest know God. Thou must abide within thyself ; to the Light that is in thee thou must turn thee ; there thou wilt find it and nowhere else. God is nearest unto thee and to every man. He that goes forth of himself to any creature, thereby to know God, departs from God. God is nearer unto every man than himself, because He penetrates the most inward and intimate parts of man and is the Life of the inmost spirit. Mind, therefore, the Light that is in thee." [1]

This Light—the first Principle of all Religion—is also called in this little Book by many other names. It is " the living Word," " the Truth of God," " the Light of Truth "; it is " Christ "; it is the " Spirit." [2] As a Divine Light, it reproves man of sin, shows him that he has strayed from God, accuses him of the evil he commits. It leads man into Truth, " even though he has never heard or read of Scripture "; it shows him the way to God; it gives him peace of conscience in well-doing; and, if followed and obeyed, it brings him into union with God, " wherein all happiness and salvation doth consist." [3] It operates in all men, though in many men there are serious " impediments " which hinder its operations— " the lets to it are manifold "—but as soon as a man turns to it and cleanses his inner eye—removes the " lets "—he discovers " a firm foundation upon which he may build stable and enduring things : A Principle whereby he may, without ever erring, guide the whole course of his life, how he is to carry himself toward God, his Neighbour and himself." [4]   The writer, having thus delivered his message, wishes to have it distinctly understood that he is not trying to draw his readers to any new sect, or to any outward and visible church. " Go to, then, O Man," he says, " whoever thou art, we will not draw thee off from one heap of men to carry thee over unto another, 'tis somewhat else we invite thee to ! We invite thee to Something which may be a means to attain thy own

[1] *The Light upon the Candlestick*, pp. 12-13.   [2] *Ibid.* pp. 4 and 9.
[3] *Ibid.* p. 5.   [4] *Ibid.* p. 6.

salvation and well-being "—a membership in the invisible Church.

Such is the teaching of this strange little book, written by the friend of Spinoza, and revealing the maturest expression of this slowly developing spiritual movement, which began with Hans Denck and flowed uninterruptedly through many lives and along many channels and burst out full flood in England in " the Children of the Light," who were known to the world as Quakers.

CHAPTER VIII

VALENTINE WEIGEL AND NATURE MYSTICISM

It is a central idea of mysticism that there is a way to God through the human soul. The gate to Heaven is thus kept, not by St.Peter or by any other saint of the calendar ; it is kept by each individual person himself as he opens or closes within himself the spiritual circuit of connection with God. The door into the Eternal swings within the circle of our own inner life, and all things are ours if we learn how to use the key that opens, for " to open " and " to find God " are one and the same thing. The emphasis in " Nature Mysticism " lies not so much on this direct pathway to God through the soul as upon the symbolic character of the world of Nature as a visible revelation of an invisible Universe, and upon the idea that man is a microcosm, a little world, reproducing in epitome, point for point, though in miniature, the great world, or macrocosm. On this line of thought, *everything is double*. The things that are seen are parables of other things which are not seen. They are like printed words which *mean* something vastly more and deeper than what the eye sees as it scans mere letters. One indwelling Life, one animating Soul, lives in and moves through the whole mighty frame of things and expresses its Life through visible things in manifold ways, as the invisible human soul expresses itself through the visible body. Everything is thus, in a fragmentary way, a focus of revelation for the Divine Spirit, whose garment is this vast web of the visible world. But man in a very special way, as a complete microcosm, is a concentrated extract, a comprehensive quintessence of the whole cosmos, visible and invisible—an image of God and a mirror of the Universe.

These views have a very ancient history and unite many strands of historic thought. They came to light in the sixteenth century with the revival through Greek literature of Stoic, Neo-Platonic, and Neo-Pythagorean ideas. But the Greek stream of thought as it now re-appeared was fused with streams of thought from many other sources—medieval mysticism, Persian astrology, Arabian philosophy, and the Jewish Cabala, which, in turn, was a fusing of many elements—and the mixture was honestly believed to be genuine, revived Christianity, and Christ, as the new Adam, is throughout the central Figure of these systems.

Marsilius Ficino, the Italian Humanist, who translated Plato and the writings of the Neo-Platonists into Latin and so made them current for the readers of the sixteenth century, gave a profoundly mystical colouring to the re-vived classical philosophy and identified it with pure and unadulterated Christianity.[1] His contemporary, Pico of Mirandola (1463–94), joined the teachings of the Cabala with his Neo-Platonized Christianity and so produced a new blend. Johann Reuchlin (1455–1522), great German classical and Hebrew scholar, brave opponent of obscurantism, forerunner of the Reformation, introduced the Neo-Platonic and Cabalistic blend of ideas into German thought.

The Cabala, it may be said briefly, in the primary meaning of the word, is the doctrine received by oral tradition as an important supplement to the written Jewish Scriptures, but the Cabala as we know it is an esoteric system which was formed under the influence of many streams of ancient thought-systems, and which came into vogue about the thirteenth century, though its devout adherents claimed that it had been orally trans-mitted through the intervening ages from Adam in Paradise. According to the teaching of the Cabala, the original Godhead, called *En-Soph*, the Infinite, is in essence

---

[1] Ficino is dealt with at greater length in Chapter XIII.

incomprehensible and immutable, and capable of description only in negations. God, the En-Soph, is above and beyond contact with anything finite, material, or imperfect. It would be blasphemous to suppose that God the infinitely perfect, God the absolutely immutable One, by direct act made a world of matter or created a realm of existence marked with evil as this lower realm of ours is. Instead of supposing a creative act, therefore, the Cabala supposes a series of emanations, or overflows of divine splendour, arranged in three groups of threes, called *Sephiroth*, which reveal all that is revealable in God, and by means of which invisible and visible worlds come into being. These *Sephiroth*, or orders of emanation, are *thoughts* of the Wisdom of God become objectively and permanently real, just because He thought them ; and though He is vastly, inexhaustibly more than they, yet He is actually immanent in them and the ground of their being. They are (1) the intelligible world, or world of creative ideas ; (2) the world of spiritual forms, such as the hierarchies of angels, souls, and the entire universe of immaterial beings, the world of astral substance or of creative soul-matter ; and (3) the natural world, in which the divine plan of Wisdom, the creative ideas, and the astral soul become visibly and concretely revealed. Man unites all the worlds in himself, and in his unfallen state as Adam-Cadmon combined all men in one ideal, undifferentiated Man. The visible world is full of hints and symbols of the invisible, and the initiated learn to read the *signs* of things seen, the meanings of sacred letters, and so to discover the secrets and mysteries of the inner world. The Cabala is full of unrestrained oriental imagination, of fancies run riot, and of symbolisms ridden to death. Its confusion of style and thought and its predilection for magic unfortunately proved contagious, and played havoc with the productions of those who came under its spell. Its marvels, however, powerfully impressed the minds of its German readers. Through it they believed they were privileged to share in mysteries which had been hid from the creation of the world, and they conceived the idea that they had at last discovered a clue that would eventually lead them into all the secrets of the universe.[1]

Cornelius Agrippa of Nettesheim (1487–1535) by his writings increased the prevailing fascination for occult knowledge and pushed this particular line of speculation into an acute stage. He was a man of large learning and of heroic temper, and, possessed as he was of undoubted gifts, in a different period and in a different environment he would, no doubt, have played a notable part in the development of human thought. But he became enamoured in his youth with the adventurous quest for the discovery of Nature's stupendous secrets, and under the spell of the Cabala, and under the influence of eager expectations entertained in his day by men of rank and learning, that fresh light was about to dawn upon the ancient mysteries of the world, he took the false path of magic as the way to the conquest of the great secret. It was, however, not the crude, cheap magic of popular fancy, a magic of mad and lawless caprice, to which he was devoted ; it was a magic grounded in the nature of the deeper inner world which he believed was the Soul of the world we see and touch. The English translator of Agrippa's *Occult Philosophy* in 1651 very clearly apprehended and stated in his quaint " Preface to the Judicious Reader," the foundation idea of Agrippa's magic : " This is," he says, " true and sublime Occult Philosophy—to understand the mysterious influence of the intellectual world upon the celestial world, and of both upon the terrestrial world, and to know how to dispose and fit ourselves so as to be capable of receiving the *superior operations of these worlds, whereby we may be enabled to operate wonderful things by a natural power*." [2] That saying precisely defines Agrippa's faith. There are, he thinks,

---

[1] The Cabala was, as I have tried to make clear, only one of the influences which produced this new intellectual climate. The rediscovered " Hermes Trismegistus," the mystically coloured Platonism, as it came from Italy, the awakened interest in Nature and in man, and the powerful message of the German Mystics all played an important part toward the formation of the new *Weltanschauung*.

[2] *Three Books of Occult Philosophy*, translated by J. F. (London, 1651).

three worlds : (1) the Intellectual world ; (2) the Celestial, or Astral, world ; and (3) the Terrestrial world ; and man, who is a microcosm embodying in himself all these worlds, may, in the innermost ground of his being, come upon a divine knowledge which will enable him to unlock the mysteries of all worlds and to " operate wonderful things." In quite other ways than Agrippa dreamed, science has found the keys to many of these mysteries, and has learned how to " operate wonderful things by a natural power." His enthusiasm and passion were right, but he had not learned the slow and patient and laborious way.

A still greater figure in this field of occult knowledge and of nature mysticism was the far-travelled man and medical genius, Aureolus Theophrastus Bombast, of Hohenheim, generally known as Paracelsus. He was born in 1493 in the neighbourhood of Einsiedeln, not far from Zurich, the son of a physician of repute. He studied in the University of Basle, and later was instructed by Trithemius, Abbot of St. Jacobs at Wurtzburg, an adept in magic, alchemy, and astrology. He passed a long period—probably ten years—of his later youth in travel, studying humanity at close range, gathering all sorts of information, forming his theories of diseases and their cure, and learning to know Nature " by treading her Books, through land after land, with his feet," which, he once testified, is the only way of knowing her truly.[1]

In 1525 he settled in Basle, and, on the recommendation of Œcolampadius, was appointed professor of physic, medicine, and surgery in 1527, but his revolutionary teaching and practice, his scorn for traditional methods, his attacks on the ignorance and greed of apothecaries raised a storm which he could not weather, and he secretly left the city in 1528. Again he became a wanderer, having extraordinary experiences of success and defeat, treating all manner of diseases, writing books on medicine and on the fundamental nature of things, and finally died at Salzburg in Bavaria in 1541.

Paracelsus is a strange and baffling character. He had

---

[1] Stoddart's *Life of Paracelsus* (London, 1911), p. 76.

much of the spirit of the new age, tangled with many of the ideas and fancies of his time. His aspirations were lofty, his medical skill was unique for his day, he was in large measure liberated from tradition, and he was dedicated, as Browning truly represents him, to his mission, but he was still under the spell of " mystic " categories, and he still held the faith that Nature's secrets were to be suddenly surprised by an inward way and by an inward Light :

> Truth is within ourselves ; it takes no rise
> From outward things, whate'er you may believe.
> There is an inmost centre in us all,
> Where truth abides in fulness ; and around,
> Wall upon wall, the gross flesh hems it in,
> This perfect, clear perception—which is truth,
> A baffling and perverting carnal mesh
> Binds it, and makes all error : and, to KNOW,
> Rather consists in opening out a way
> Whence the imprisoned splendour may escape,
> Than in effecting entry for a light
> Supposed to be without.[1]

There are, again, in his Universe, as in the other occult systems, three elemental worlds—the spiritual or intellectual world, the astral world or universal Soul, and the terrestrial world ; and all three worlds are man's " mothers." Man is a quintessence of all the elements, visible and invisible. He has a spiritual essence within him which is an emanation of God ; he has an astral-soul essence, from the Soul of the world ; and he partakes, too, of the material and earthly world. His supreme aim in life should be to establish, or rather re-establish, a harmony between his own little world and the great Universe, so that all the worlds have their right proportions in him, and so that through his highest essence he can win the secrets of the lower worlds—the astral and the material. To accomplish *that* is to be spiritual, to become like Adam,

---

[1] Browning, *Paracelsus*, B. i. This passage fairly represents Paracelsus' general position. " There is," he says in his *Philosophia sagax*, " a Light in the spirit of man which illuminates everything. . . . The quality of each thing created by God, whether it be visible or invisible to the senses, may be perceived and known. If man knows the essence of things, their attributes, their attractions, and the elements of which they consist, he will be a Master of nature, of the elements, and of the spirits."

a paradisaical Man, or like Christ the new Adam. Even the lowest world is penetrated with the spiritual " seed " or " element." The very basic substances of which it is composed—sulphur, mercury, and salt—are in essence spiritual principles, elemental forces, rather than crude matter, and the lower world is written over, like a palimpsest, with " signatures " of the divine world to which it belongs. All doors into all the worlds of God open to faith and prayer, and he who subordinates lower elements in himself to higher has power and potency in all realms.

But far more important for the development of spiritual religion, and far more important as a living link between Reformers like Denck, Schwenckfeld, and Franck of the sixteenth century, and Jacob Boehme and the spiritual interpreters of the English Commonwealth, was Valentine Weigel, Pastor of Zschopau. Like so many of the men who figure in these chapters, he is little known, seldom read, not a quick and powerful name in the world, but he is worth knowing, and he was the bearer of a burning and kindling torch of truth. He was born at Naundorf, a suburb of Grossenhain, District of Meissen, in 1533. He received the Bachelor's and Master's degree of the University of Leipzig, and he pursued his studies still further in the University of Wittenberg, his study-period having continued until 1567. In the autumn of that year he was ordained and called to be Pastor of Zschopau, where he passed as a minister his entire public life, which came to a peaceful end in 1588. He was an ideal pastor and true shepherd of his flock—loving them and being beloved by them. His ministry was fresh and vital, and made his hearers *feel* the presence and the power of the Spirit of God.

There was, so far as I can discover the facts, only one blemish on his really beautiful character. He lacked that robust, unswerving conscience which compels a man who sees a new vision of the truth to proclaim it, to champion it, and to suffer and even die for it when it comes into collision with views which his own soul has outgrown.

Weigel was resolved not to have his heart's deepest faith, his mind's most certain truth, known, at least during his lifetime, by the persons who were the guardians of orthodoxy. He signed the " Confessions " of his time as though they expressed his own convictions ; he counted it a duty of the first importance to guard his pastoral flock from the distractions and assaults of heresy-hunters, and he left his matured and deeply meditated views for posterity to discover. How far he was personally timid cannot now be determined. It would seem, however, from his own words,[1] that he was especially concerned for the safety and welfare of his own flock, who would suffer if he were cried down as an enthusiast or a spiritual prophet. But even so, it is very doubtful if any man can rightly permit anything on earth to take precedence to his own loyalty to the vision of truth which his soul sees. As a result, however, of the course he took, he died in good odour of sanctity, and the epigones of that day had no suspicion of the ideas that were swarming in the mind of the quiet Pastor of Zschopau, or of the mass of manuscripts proclaiming his faith in the inner Word which he was leaving behind him, to fly over the world like the loose leaves of the Sibyl.

His writings were not printed until 1609 and onwards, and as his disciples went on producing writings, somewhat in the style and spirit of the master who inspired them, the list of books in Weigel's name is considerably larger than the actual number of manuscripts extant at his death in 1588. It is not always easy to distinguish the pseudo-writings from the genuine ones, but there is a vividness and pregnancy of style, a spiritual depth and power in the earlier writings which are lacking in the later group, and there is an emphasis on the magical and occult in the secondary writings that is largely absent in the primary ones.[2] The most important of his books will be referred to and quoted from as I present his type of religion and his message, but I shall draw especially upon his little

---

[1] *Christliches Gespräch*, chap. iii.

[2] There is an excellent critical study of Weigel's writings by A. Israel, entitled, *Weigels Leben und Schriften nach den Quellen dargestellt* (Zschopau, 1888).

book, *Von dem Leben Christi, das ist, vom wahren Glauben*
(" On the Life of Christ, or True Faith "), as it is the one
of Weigel's writings which, in English translation, most
deeply influenced kindred spirits in the English Commonwealth.[1]

His spiritual conception of Christianity was formed
and fed by the sermons of Tauler, and by that little book
which was " the hidden Manna " for all the spiritual
leaders of these two centuries—the *German Theology.*
Weigel edited it with an introduction. He calls it " a
precious little book," " a noble book "; but he tells
his readers that they can understand it and find it fruitful
only if they read it " with a pure eye " and with " the
key of David," *i.e.* with a personal experience. But
while he loved the golden book of mysticism and the
sermons of the great Strasbourg preacher, and was led
by the hand of these guides, he drew also from many other
sources and finally arrived at a type of religion, still interior
and personal, but less negative and abstract than that
of the fourteenth-century mystics, and more penetrated
and informed with the presence of the Christ of the Gospels.
He insists always that in the last analysis it is Christ in us
that saves us, but it was Christ in the flesh, the Christ of
Galilee and Golgotha, that revealed to men the way to
apprehend the inward and eternal Christ of God. " The
indwelling Christ," he wrote, " is all in all. He saves thee.
He is thy peace and thy comfort. The outward Christ,
the Christ in the flesh, and according to the flesh, cannot
save thee in an external way. He must be in thee and
thou must abide in Him. Why then did He become man
and suffer on the Cross ? There are many reasons why,
but it was especially that God by the death and suffering
of Christ might take the wrath and hostility out of *our*
hearts, on account of which we falsely conceive of God
as a wrathful enemy to us. He had to deal that way with
poor blind men like us and so reconcile us with Himself.

---

[1] " Of the Life of Christ, That is, Of True Faith which is the Rule, Square,
Levell or Measuring Line of the Holy City of God and of the Inhabitants thereof
here on Earth. Written in the German Language by Valentine Weigelus."
(London, Giles Calvert, 1648.)

There was no need of it on His part. He was always Love and He always loved us, even when we were enemies to Him, but we should never have known it if God had not condescended to show Himself to us in His Son and had not suffered for us." [1]

Weigel everywhere maintains Christ's double identity —an identity with God, so that in Christ we see God ; and an equal identity with man, so that Christ is man revealed in his fulfilled possibilities. In Him God and man are *one*. In this deep-lying and fundamental idea of his entire Christianity he was undoubtedly influenced, profoundly influenced, by Schwenckfeld. He presents in chapter i. of his *Life of Christ* the Schwenckfeldian view that Christ is God and Man in *one*. But He is Man not in the crass, crude and earthly form : He is not composed of mortal and earthly substance as our " Adamical bodies " are. He is wholly and absolutely composed of heavenly, spiritual, divine substance. His flesh and blood are as divine and spiritual in origin as is His spirit, so that His resurrection and ascension are the normal outcome of His nature. It was as natural for Him to rise into life and to ascend into glory as it is for heavy things to fall. But that divine, spiritual, heavenly nature, which appeared in Him, is the true, original, consummate nature of Man. Man, as we know him, is cloudy, or even muddy, with a vesture of decay, but that is not a feature of his *real* nature—either in its original or its potential form—and all who " put on Christ," all who have " Christ in them," become one flesh with Him and gain an indestructible and permanent inward substance like His.

Consistently with this view, Weigel declares that here lies the significance of Christ's saying, " I am Bread " ; " I am Meat and Drink." The only adequate Supper of the Lord, he says, is real feeding upon His spiritual, life-giving flesh and blood, so that Salvation is not tied to external sacraments, but stands only in the faith that Christ feeds us with Himself.[2] There are, he proceeds to show, two radically diverse natures, the traits and char-

---

[1] Quoted from Israel, *op. cit.* p. 107.   [2] *On the Life of Christ*, part i. chap. ii.

acteristics of which he arranges in opposing pairs, in two
parallel columns as follows :

A. The Nature of Christ and
   of those who live in Him
   and by Him.

B. The nature of Adam and
   those who live by him,
   i.e. those who live the
   natural, earthly life.

1. This Nature turns from
   creatures to God.

1. This nature turns from God
   to creatures.

2. This Nature hates itself and
   loves others.

2. This nature loves itself more
   than it loves God or
   others.

3. This Nature abhors all it
   itself does or omits.

3. This nature delights only
   in itself and in things of
   self.

4. This Nature seeks to lose
   self.

4. This nature seeks itself in
   everything.

5. This Nature denies self.

5. This nature cleaves to self.

6. This Nature patiently bears
   the Cross.

6. This nature thrusts the
   Cross away.

.   .   .   .   .

15. This Nature desires to be
    conformed to Christ and
    His Cross in all things.

.   .   .   .   .

15. This nature desires to be
    equal with God without
    any humility at all.[1]

Christ is thus for Weigel entirely a new order of Being
—the Beginner of a new race. Adam had in himself all
the possibilities which Christ realized, but the former
failed and the latter succeeded and so has become the
Head of a divine and heavenly type of humanity. By
" a new nativity," a rebirth from above, any man in
the world who wills it in living faith may be a
recipient of the divine-principle, the Christ-Life, and
may thereby be raised to membership in the Kingdom
of the Christ-Humanity, which is as far above the Adam-
Humanity as the flower is above the soil from which it
first sprang. When Christ is formed within and the
Humanity which He produces appears in the world, then
a new way of living comes into operation. Love is the
supreme " sign " of the new type or order. " The man
who has the Christ-Life in him does not quarrel ; he does
not go to law for temporall goods ; he does not kill ; he
lets his coat and cloke go rather than oppose another." [2]
" If Christ were of the seed of Adam, He would have the

---

[1] *On the Life of Christ*, part i. chap. iii.   [2] *Ibid.* part i. chap. viii.

nature and inclinations of Adam. He would hang thieves, behead adulterers, rack murderers with the wheel, kill hereticks, and put corporeally to death all manner of sinners ; but now He is tender, kind, loving. He kills no one. The Lamb kills no woolf." [1] Weigel goes the whole bold way in his revolt from legalism, and he accepts the principle of love as a structural principle of the society which Christ is forming in the world : " Where the Life of Christ is, there is no warre made with corporall weapons." " The world wars but Christ doth not so. His warfare is spiritual." " He that maketh warre is no Christian but a woolf, and belongs not to the sheepfold nor hath he anything to expect of the Kingdom of God, nor may the warrs of the Old Testament, of the time of darknesse serve his turne, for Christians deal not after a Mosaicall, earthly fashion, but they walke in the Life of Christ, without all revenge." " We walk no longer under Moses but under Christ." [2]

The Christian man, however, even with his new " nativity " and with his re-created spirit of love, differs in one respect from Christ. Christ is wholly heavenly, His Nature is woven throughout of spiritual and divine substance. There is no rent nor seam in it. Man, on the other hand, is double, and throughout his temporal period he remains double. By his new " nativity " man can become inwardly spirit though he remains outwardly composed of flesh. [3]

Before the " fall " Adam was unsundered from God. It was sin which made the cleft or rent which separated God and man. Through Christ, the new and heavenly Adam, the *junction* may be formed again in man's inner self, and once again God and man in us may be unsundered. The flesh is not destroyed, but it ceases to be the dominating factor. It serves now merely as the " habitation " of an invisible spirit, and it exists for the spirit, not the spirit for it. [4] Not only is the body a

---

[1] *On the Life of Christ*, part i. chap. ix.
[2] *Ibid.* part ii. chap. ix.; part i. chap. x.; part ii. chap. x.; and part. i. chap. xiv.
[3] *Ibid.* part ii. chaps. iii. and iv.
[4] This is the view set forth in his Γνῶθι Σεαυτόν [Know Thyself].

" habitation " for the Christ-formed soul, but the world now becomes to the enlightened soul an Inn for a transient guest rather than a permanent abiding-place : " like as in an Inne there is meat set before the guest and bedding is allowed to him, even so Christians are in this world guests and their country is above." " It is not fitting for a guest that comes into an Inne, where nothing is his own, that he should appropriate things to himself and quarrel about them ! "[1]

As fast as Christ is formed within, as the Life of one's life, the believer attains thereby a peace and a power which make the " rent " between flesh and spirit ever less disturbing, though it still remains until the fleshly taber- nacle dissolves. The goal of the spiritual life here on earth is the attainment of " the silent Sabbath of the soul," in which God becomes so completely the soul's sufficiency that the flesh has little scope or sway any more, and there is no longer need of furious struggle against it, " like a serpent between two rocks, trying to pull off his old skin ! "[2] In his *Heavenly Jerusalem in Us*, he says : " It is an attribute of God that He is the Eternal Peace which is longed for by us men, but found by few because they do not *mind Christ*, who is the Way. God has not grounded either thy Peace or thy Salvation on thy running hither and yon, nor on thy works and thy creaturely activities, but on an inner calm and quiet, on a Sabbath of the soul, in which thou canst hear, with the simple and the tender-minded, what the Lord is saying and doing."[3]

In close conformity to the teaching of Sebastian Franck,[4] Weigel thinks of the Church of God as an in- visible Assembly of all true Believers in the entire world, united, not outwardly but inwardly, in the unity of the Spirit and by the bond of Love and Peace. There are for him, as for Franck and other " Spirituals," two kinds of churches : (1) The church composed of a visible group,

---

[1] *On the Life of Christ*, part ii. chaps. v. and vii.
[2] *Ibid.* part i. chap. viii.
[3] *Vom himmlischen Jerusalem in uns*, chap. viii.
[4] Weigel enjoins his readers to read Franck's book on " the Tree of the Know- ledge of Good and Evil." See *On the Life of Christ*, part ii. p. 57.

" to be pointed out with the finger," located in a definite country, allied with a temporal government, held together by a body of doctrine, " tied to " certain sacraments and possessed of force to constrain men, by " carnall perswasions," to conform.[1]   Then there is (2) the real Church of God, " the upper Jerusalem," a body visible in no one locality, but dispersed over the earth like wheat in chaff, held together by no declarations of doctrine, tied to no sacraments, dependent on no earthly Lieutenant or Vice-gerent, and on no university-trained Doctors, which recognizes Prince and Ploughman alike, and secures its unity through Christ and through the invisible cement of Love.   " To this Assembly," writes Weigel, " doe I stick ; in this holy Church doe I rejoice to be. . . . Jesus Christ is my Head, my Teacher.   He is everywhere with me and in me, and I in Him.   Although the Protestants should chase me amongst Papists or Atheists, yet I should still be in the holy Church and should have all the heavenly Gifts common to all Believers, and although the Papists should banish me into Turkey, yet even there should I be in the holy Church." [2]

No book appeared in England before 1648—the date of the translation of Weigel's *Life of Christ*—which more closely approached the Quaker position.   That religion must have an inward seat and origin ; that divine things must be learned of God, are taken as axiomatic truths throughout this book.   If a man is to *see*, he must have eyes of his own ; if he is to teach, he must have the Word of God within him.   People say that " there can be no true Faith without outward preaching ministry."   That is not so, Weigel declares.   The way to heaven is open to hungry penitent souls everywhere, although, as is the case with infants, they may hear no sermons at all : " Faith comes by inward hearing.   Good books, outward verbal ministry have their place, they testify to the real Treasure, they are witnesses to the inner Word within us, but Faith is not tied to books ; it is a new nativity which

---

[1] " Faith," he says, " cannot be forced into any person by gallows or pillory." *On the Life of Christ*, part i. chap. xv.
[2] *Ibid.* part ii. chap. xiv.   This is built on a passage in Franck's *Apologia*.

cannot be found in a book. He who hath the inward Schoolmaster loseth nothing of his Salvation although all preachers should be dead and all books burned." [1]   Many take great pains to be baptized, and " to hear sermons of their hired priests," and to use the Lord's Supper, and to read theological books, who, nevertheless, show no "spiritual profit " therefrom.   The reason is that " Truth runs into no one by a pipe ! " [2]   " In the Church of men—the man-made Church—the measuring-line," or standard, he says, is the written Scripture, according to one's own interpreta-tion, or according to books, or according to University men ; but in the true Church the measuring-reed is the inward Word, the Spirit of Christ, within the believer. Those who are in the Universities and Churches of men have Christ in their mouths, and they have a measuring-reed by their side—the inhabitants of God's Church on the other hand have the Life of Christ and the testing-standard within themselves.[3]   Those who are " nominal professors " hang salvation on a literal knowledge of the merit secured by Christ's death ; the true believer knows that salvation is never a purchase, is never outwardly effected, but is a new self, a new spirit, a new relation to God : " Man must cease to be what he is before he can come to be another kind of person." [4]   Outward baptism and external supper may, if one wishes, be used as symbols of the soul's supreme events, but they cannot rightly be thought of as effecting any change of themselves in the real nature of the man ; only Christ the Life-bringer, only the resident work of God within the soul, can produce the transformation from old self to new self.   " Salvation is not tyed to sacraments." [5]

It is a well-settled view of Weigel's that Heaven and Hell are primarily in the soul of man.   He says, in *Know Thyself*, that both the Trees of Paradise are in us ; and in his *Ort der Welt* he declares that " the Eternal Hell of the lost will be their own Hell." [6]   And in his *Christliches*

[1] *On the Life of Christ*, part i. chaps. iv. and v.
[2] *Ibid*. part i. chap. vi.   [3] *Ibid*. part i. chaps. xii. and xiii.
[4] Quoted from Tauler by Weigel, *ibid*. chap. vii.   See also part iii. chap. i.
[5] *Ibid*. part ii. chap. ii.   [6] *Op. cit*. chap. xx.

Gespräch he insists that the holy Spirit, the present Christ, does not need to *come down* from Heaven to meet with us, for when He is in our hearts there then is Heaven.[1] No person can ever be in Heaven until Heaven is in him.

In *Der güldene Griff* and elsewhere Weigel works out a very interesting theory of knowledge, which fits well with the inwardness of his religious views. He holds that in sense perception the percipient brings forth his real *knowledge* from within. The external " object," or the outward stimulus, is the soliciting occasion, or suggestion, or the sign for the experience, but what we see is determined from within rather than from without. All real knowledge is in the knower. Both external world and written scriptures are in themselves *shadows* until the inward spirit interprets them, and through them comes to the Word of God which they suggest and symbolize.

Weigel plainly arrived at his ground ideas under the formative influence of Schwenckfeld and Franck, but he also reveals, especially in his conception of the deeper inner world and of the microcosmic character of man, the influence of Paracelsus and of the nature mystics of his time. He was himself, in turn, a most important influence in the development of the religious ideas of Jacob Boehme, and he is historically one of the most significant men of the entire spiritual group before the great Silesian mystic.[2]

This chapter cannot come to a proper close without some consideration of a Weigelean book which was translated into English in 1649, under the title, "*Astrologie Theologized* : That the Inward man by the Light of Grace, through possession and practice of a holy life, is to be acknowledged and live in us : which is the only means to keep the true Sabbath in inward holinesse."

---

[1] *Christ. Gespräch*, chap. ii.

[2] In his *Der güldene Griff*, he tells of a personal spiritual " opening " which is very similar to the one which occurred later in the life of Boehme. He found himself astray in " a wilderness of darkness " and he cried to God for Light to enlighten his soul. " *Suddenly*," he says, " *the Light came and my eyes were opened so that I saw more clearly than all the teachers in all the world with all their books could teach me.*" Chap. xxiv.

The anonymous translator ascribes the book to Weigel. It is, in fact, Part Two of Γνῶθι Σεαυτόν, but it is uncertain whether it was written by Weigel himself. But whether written by Weigel or later by one of his school, it is a good illustration of the way in which mystically inclined Christians of that period endeavoured to make spiritual conquest of the prevailing Astrology and, through its help, to discover the nature of the inner, hidden universe. Astrology, this little book declares, is " conversant with the secrets of God which are hidden in the natural things of creation." It is the science of reading the unseen through the seen, for, according to the teaching of this book, everything visible is an unveiling of something invisible. Man—who is a centre of the whole universe, who has in himself elements of all the worlds, inner and outer—" is created to be a visible Paradise, Garden, Tabernacle, Mansion, House, Temple and Jerusalem of God." All the wisdom, power, virtue, and glory of God are hidden and are slumbering in man. There is nothing so near to man as God is—" He is nearer to us than we are to ourselves " [1]—and the only reason we do not find Him and know Him and open out our life *interiorly*, so that the true Sabbath comes to the soul, is due to our " vagabond and unquiet ways of keeping busy with our own will, outside our internal country." If I could desist from the things with which I vex and worry myself, and study to be at rest in my God who dwells with me ; if I could accustom my mind to spiritual tranquillity and cease to wander in a maze of thoughts, cares, and affections ; if I could be at leisure from the external things and creatures of this world, and chiefly from myself ; if, in short, I might " come into a plenary dereliction of myself," I should at once " begin to see and know of the most present habitation of God in me and so I should eat of the Tree of Life in the midst of the Paradise, *which Paradise I myself am*, and be a Guest of God." [2] Adam, who was " the Protoplast " and begetter of all men, and who, like everything else in the universe, was " double,"

---

[1] *Astrologie Theologized*, p. 8. [2] *Ibid.* pp. 16-17.

allowed himself to live toward the outward instead of toward the inward, permitted the seed of the serpent to grow in him instead of the divine seed, and so came under the dominance of the natural, elemental world, with its " lesser light " of knowledge and with its " tree of death." But the Paradise, with its greater Light of Wisdom and with its Tree of Life, is always near to man and can be repossessed and regained by him. The outer elements, and the astral world with its visible stars, *rule* no one, determine no one. Each man's " star " is in his own breast. It lies in his own power to " theologize his astrologie," to turn his universe into spiritual forces. By " a new nativity," initiated by obedient response to the inward Light—the spiritual Star, not of earth and not of the astral universe, but of God the indwelling Spirit— he may put on the new man, created after the likeness of God, and become the recipient of heavenly Wisdom springing up within him from the Life of the Spirit.[1]

There can be no question in the mind of any one who is familiar with the literature and religious thought of seventeenth-century England, that the ideas set forth in this chapter exerted a wide and profound influence, and were a part of the psychological climate of the middle decades of that century. The channel here indicated was only one of the ways through which these ideas came in. In due time we shall discover other channels of this spiritual message.

---

[1] This little book refers with much appreciation to Theophrastus Paracelsus. It uses his theory of " first matter " and his doctrine of " the seven governours of the world," which we shall meet in a new form in Boehme. Another book which carried astrological ideas into religious thought in a much cruder way was Andreas Tentzel's *De ratione naturali arboris vitae et scientiae boni et mali*, etc., which was Pars Secunda of his *Medicina diastatica* (Jena, 1629). It was translated into English in 1657 by N. Turner with the title : " The Mumial Treatise of Tentzelius, being a natural account of the Tree of Life and of the Tree of Knowledge of Good and Evil, with a mystical interpretation of that great Secret, to wit, the Cabalistical Concordance of the Tree of Life and Death, of Christ and Adam." Tentzel was a famous doctor and disciple of Paracelsus and " flourished " in Germany during the first half of the seventeenth century.

CHAPTER IX

JACOB BOEHME: HIS LIFE AND SPIRIT [1]

FEW men have ever made greater claim to be the bearer of a new revelation than did the humble shoemaker-prophet of Silesia, Jacob Boehme. " I am," he wrote in his earliest book, " only a very little spark of God's Light, but He is now pleased in this last time to reveal through me what has been partly concealed from the beginning of the World," [2] and he admonished the reader, if he would understand what is written, to let go opinion

---

[1] I have used as primary source the German edition of Boehme's Works—*Theosophia revelata*—published in 1730 in 8 vols. All my references are to the English translations made by Sparrow, Ellistone, and Blunden, 1647-61. These translations were republished, 1764, in 4 vols. in an edition which has incorrectly been called William Law's edition. Four volumes have been republished by John M. Watkins of London, as follows : *The Threefold Life of Man*, 1909 ; *The Three Principles*, 1910 ; The *Forty Questions* and *The Clavis*, 1911 ; and *The Way to Christ*, 1911. The *Signatura rerum*, in English, has been published in " Everyman's Library." A valuable volume of selections from " Jacob Behmen's Theosophic Philosophy " was made by Edward Taylor, London, 1691. Many volumes of selections have been published in recent years. The books on Boehme which I have found most suggestive and helpful are the following : Franz von Baader's " Vorlesungen und Erläuterungen über J. Böhme's Lehre," *Werke* (Leipzig, 1852), vol. iii. [edition of 1855, vol. xiii.]; Emile Boutroux, *Le Philosophe allemand* (Paris, 1888): translated into English by Rothwell in Boutroux's *Historical Studies in Philosophy* (London, 1912), pp. 169-233 ; Hans Lassen Martensen's *Jacob Boehme* (translated from the Danish by T. Rhys Evans, London, 1885) ; Franz Hartmann's *Life and Doctrine of Jacob Boehme* (London, 1891) ; Von Harless' *Jacob Boehme und die Alchymisten* (Leipzig, 1882) ; Eder-heimer's *Jakob Boehme und die Romantiker* (Heidelberg, 1904) ; Paul Deussen's *Jacob Boehme*—an Address delivered at Kiel, May 8, 1897—translated from the German by Mrs. D. S. Hehner and printed as Introduction to Watkin's edition of *The Three Principles* (1910) ; Christopher Walton's *Notes and Materials for a Biography of William Law* (London, 1854)—a volume of great value to the student of Boehme; Rudolph Steiner's *Mystics of the Renaissance* (translated, London, 1911), pp. 223-245 ; A. J. Penny's *Studies in Jacob Boehme* (London, 1912), uncritical and written from the theosophical point of view ; Hegel's *History of Philosophy* (translated by Haldane and Simson, London, 1895), iii. pp. 188-216.

[2] *Aurora*, John Sparrow's translation (London, 1656), ii. 79-80.

and conceit and heathenish wisdom, and read with the Light and Power of the Holy Spirit, " for this book comes not forth from Reason, but by the impulse of the Spirit." [1] " I have not dared," he wrote to a friend in 1620, " to write otherwise than was given and indited to me. I have continually written as the Spirit dictated and have not given place to Reason." [2]   Again and again he warns the reader to let his book alone unless he is ready for a new dawning of divine Truth, for a fresh Light to break : " If thou art not a spiritual overcomer, then let my book alone.   Do not meddle with it, but *stick to thy old matters* ! " [3]

Before the Spirit came upon him, he felt himself to be a " little stammering child," and he always declared that without this Spirit he could not comprehend even his own writings—" when He parteth from me, I know nothing but the elementary and earthly things of this world " [4]—but with this divine Spirit unfolding within him " the profoundest depth " of mysteries, he believed, though with much simplicity and generally with humility, that the true ground of things had " not been so fully revealed to any man from the beginning of the world "— " but," he adds, " seeing God will have it so, I submit to His will." [5]   Nobody before him, he declares, no matter how learned he was, " has had the ax by the handle," but, with a sudden change of figure, he proclaims that now the Morning Glow is breaking and the Day Dawn is rising.[6]   In his *Epistles* he says : " I am only a layman, I have not studied, yet I bring to light things which all the High Schools and Universities have been unable to do. . . . The language of Nature is made known to me so that I can understand the greatest mysteries, in my own mother-tongue.   Though I cannot say I have *learned or comprehended* these things, yet so long as the hand of God stayeth upon me I understand." [7]

We shall be able to estimate the value of these lofty

---

[1] *Aurora*, iii. 1-3.   [2] *Third Epistle*, 15.   [3] *Aurora*, xiii. 27.
[4] *Ibid*. viii. 19.   [5] *Ibid*. ix. 90.
[6] *Ibid*. xiii. 2-4.   [7] *Third Epistle*, 22.

claims after we have gathered up the substance of his teaching, but it may be well to say at the opening of this Study of Boehme that in my opinion no more remarkable religious message has come in modern centuries from an untrained and undisciplined mind than that which lies scattered through the voluminous and somewhat chaotic writings of this seventeenth-century prophet of the common people.[1]

He frequently speaks of himself as " unlearned," and in the technical sense of the word he was unlearned. He had only a simple schooling, but he possessed extraordinary native capacity and he was well and widely read in the books which fitted the frame and temper of his mind, and he had very unusual powers of meditation and recollection, so that he thought over and over again in his quiet hours of labour the ideas which he seized upon in the books he read.

There are many strands of thought woven together in his writings, and everything he dealt with is given a

[1] Many thinkers of prominent rank have borne testimony to the greatness of Boehme's genius. I shall mention only a few of these estimates :

" I would recommend you to procure the writings of Boehme and diligently read them. For though I have studied philosophy and theology from my youth . . . yet I must acknowledge that the above writings have been to me of more service for the understanding of the Bible than all my University learning."— J. G. Gichtel, 1698.

" Jacob Boehme, as a religious and philosophical genius, has not often had his equal in the world's history."—" Jacob Boehme : His Life and Philosophy." An Address by Dr. Paul Deussen.

" Jacob Boehme est le seul, au moins dont on ait eu les écrits jusqu'à lui, auquel Dieu ait découvert le fond de la nature, tant des choses spirituelles, que des corporelles."—Peter Poiret, in a note at the end of his *Théologie germanique*, 1700.

" As a chosen servant of God, Jacob Boehme must be placed among those who have received the highest measures of light, wisdom, and knowledge from above. . . . All that lay in religion and nature as a mystery unsearchable was in its deepest ground opened to this instrument of God."—William Law, *Works* (ed. 1893), vi. p. 205.

" To Jacob Boehme belongs the merit of having taught more profoundly than any one else before or after him the truth that back of and behind all that has come to appear of good and evil there is an immaterial World which is the essence and reality of all that is."—Franz von Baader, *Werke* (Leipzig, 1852), iii. p. 382.

Novalis wrote in a letter to Ludwig Tieck in 1800 : " Man sieht durchaus in ihm [Jakob Böhme] den gewaltigen Frühling mit seinen quellenden, treibenden, bildenden, und mischenden Kräften, die von innen heraus die Welt gebären. Ein echtes Chaos voll dunkler Begier und wunderbarem Leben—einen wahren auseinandergehenden Mikrokosmos."—Quoted from Edgar Ederheimer's *Jakob Boehme und die Romantiker* (1904), p. 57.

new aspect through the vivid insights which he always brings into play, the amazing visual power which he displays, and his profoundly penetrating moral and intellectual grasp. But, nevertheless, he plainly belongs in the direct line of these spiritual reformers whom we have been studying. He was deeply influenced, first of all, by Luther, especially in two directions. He got primarily from the great reformer his transforming insight of the immense importance of personal faith for salvation, and secondly he was impressed—almost over-whelmingly impressed in his early years—with the awful reality and range of the principle of positive evil in the universe, upon which Luther had insisted with intensity of emphasis. His feet, however, were set upon the track which seemed to him to lead to light by the help which he got from the other line of reformers. Schwenckfeld made him feel the impossibility of any scheme of salvation that rested on transactions and operations external to the human soul itself, and through that same noble Silesian reformer he discovered the central significance of the new birth through a creative work of Grace within. Sebastian Franck was clearly one of his spiritual masters. From him, directly or indirectly, he learned that the spirit must be freed from the letter, that external revelations are symbols which remain dead and inert until they are vivified and vitalized by the inwardly illuminated spirit. He was still more directly influenced by Valentine Weigel, the pastor of Zschopau, who united the spiritual-mystical views of Schwenckfeld, Franck, and the other teachers of his type with a nature mysticism or theosophy which had become, as we have seen, a powerful interest in the sixteenth century when a real science was struggling to be born, but had not yet seen the light. This nature mysticism came to him also in a crude and indigestible form through the writings of Paracelsus. Through him Boehme acquired a vocabulary of alchemistical terms which he was always labouring to turn to spiritual meaning, but which always baffled him. It has been customary to treat Boehme as a mystic, and he has not

usually been brought into this line of spiritual development where I am placing him, but his entire outlook
and body of ideas are different from those of the great
Roman Catholic mystics.   He has read neither the
classical nor the scholastic interpreters of mysticism.
In so far as he knows of historical mysticism he knows
it through Franck and Weigel and others, where it
is profoundly transformed and subordinated to other
aspects of religion and thought.   Unlike the great mystics,
he does not treat the visible and the finite as unreal and
to be negated.   The world is a positive reality and a
divine revelation.   Nor, again, are sin and evil negative
in character for him.   Evil is tremendously real and
positive, in grim conflict with the good and to be conquered
only through stern battle.   A mystic, an illuminate, he
undoubtedly was in his first-hand experience, but his
message of salvation and his interpretation of life are
of the wider, distinctively " spiritual " type.

Jacob Boehme [1] was born in November 1575 in the
little market-town of Alt Seidenberg, a few miles from
Görlitz.   His father's name was Jacob and his mother's
Ursula, both persons of good old German peasant stock,
possessed of a strong strain of simple piety.   The family
religion was Lutheran, and Jacob the son was brought
up both at home and at church in the Lutheran faith as
it had shaped itself into definite form at the end of the
sixteenth century.   His early education was very limited,
but he was possessed of unusual fundamental capacity
and always exhibited a native mental power of very high
order.   He was always a keen observer ; he looked
through things, and whether he was in the fields, where
much of his early life was spent as a watcher of cattle,
or reading the Bible, which he knew as few persons have
known it, he saw everything with a vivid and quickened
imagination.   He plainly began, while still very young,
to revolt from the orthodox theology of his time, and his

[1] His English translators in the seventeenth century variously spelled his
name Behm, Behme, and Behmen.   This latter spelling was adopted in the so-
called Law Edition of 1764, and has thus come into common use in England and
America.

years of reading and of silent meditation and reflection were the actual preparation for what seemed finally to come to him like a sudden revelation or, to use his own common figure, as " a flash." [1]

His external appearance has been quaintly portrayed by his admiring friend and biographer, Abraham von Franckenberg, who, like a good portrait-painter, strives to let the body reveal the soul. " The external form of Jacob's body," he says, " was worn and very plain ; his stature was small, his forehead low, his temples broad and prominent, his nose somewhat crooked, his eyes grey and rather of an azure-cast, lighting up like the windows of Solomon's Temple ; his beard was short and thin ; his voice was feeble, yet his conversation was mild and pleasant. He was gentle in manner, modest in his words, humble in conduct, patient in suffering and meek of heart. His spirit was highly illuminated of God beyond anything Nature could produce." [2]

This youth, with " azure-grey eyes that lighted up like the windows of Solomon's Temple," was from his childhood possessed of a most acutely sensitive and suggestible psychical disposition. He always felt that the real world was deeper than the one which he saw with his senses, and he was frequently swept from within by mighty currents which he could not trace to any well-mapped region of the domain of Nature. His vivid and pictorial imagination, his consciousness of inrushes from the unplumbed deeps within, and his inclination to solitude and meditation are well in evidence at an early age, and we have no difficulty at all in seeing that his psychological equilibrium was unstable, and that he was capable of sudden shifts of inward level.

The first sign of his psychical peculiarity comes to light in an incident of his early childhood. While he was tending cattle in the fields one day he climbed alone a neighbouring

---

[1] Boehme refers frequently to " the writings of high masters," whom he says he read (*Aurora*, x. 45), and he often names Schwenckfeld and Weigel in particular. See especially *The Second Epistle*, sec. 54-62.

[2] *Memoirs of the Life, Death and Burial, and Wonderful Writings of Jacob Behmen*, translated by Francis Okeley (1780), p. 22.

mountain-peak, and on the summit he espied among the
great red sandstones a kind of aperture overgrown with
bushes. Boy-like he entered the opening, and there
within, in a strange vault, he descried a large portable
vessel full of money. The sight of it made him shudder,
and, without touching the treasure, he made his way out
to the world again. To his surprise he was never able
to find the aperture again, though, in company with the
other less imaginative cowboys, he often hunted for it.
His friend, von Franckenberg, who relates the story and
says that he had it from Boehme's mouth, thinks that the
experience was " a sort of emblematic omen or presage
of his future spiritual admission to the sight of the hidden
treasury of the wisdom and mysteries of God and Nature,"[1]
but we are more interested in it as a revelation of the
extraordinary psychical nature of the boy, with his
tendency to hallucination.

When he was in his fourteenth year he was apprenticed
to a shoemaker in Seidenberg, and devoted himself diligently to the mastery of his trade. It was during this
period of apprenticeship, which lasted three years, that
there was granted to him " a kind of secret tinder and
glimmer " of coming fame. One day a stranger, plain
and mean in dress, but otherwise of good presence, came
to the shop and asked to buy a pair of shoes. As the
master shoemaker was absent, the uninitiated prentice-
boy did not feel competent to sell the shoes, but the buyer
would not be put off. Thereupon young Jacob set an
enormous price upon them, hoping to stave off the trade.
The man, however, without any demur paid the price,
took the shoes, and went out. Just outside the door the
stranger stopped, and in a serious tone called out, " Jacob,
come hither to me ! " The man, with shining eyes looking
him full in the face, took his hand and said, " Jacob,
thou art little but thou shalt become great—a man very
different from the common cast, so that thou shalt be
a wonder to the world. Be a good lad ; fear God and
reverence His Word." With a little more counsel, the

---

[1] *Memoirs*, p. 2.

stranger pressed his hand and went his way, leaving the boy amazed.[1]

He had, his intimate biographer tells us, lived from his very youth up in the fear of God, in all humility and simplicity, and had taken peculiar pleasure in hearing sermons, but from the opening of his apprenticeship he began to revolt from the endless controversies and " scholastic wranglings about religion," and he withdrew into himself, fervently and incessantly praying and seeking and knocking, until one day " he was translated into the holy Sabbath and glorious Day of Rest to the soul," and, according to his own words, was " enwrapt with the Divine Light for the space of seven days and stood possessed of the highest beatific wisdom of God, in the ecstatic joy of the Kingdom." [2] Boehme looked upon this " Sabbatic " experience as his spiritual call, and from this time on he increased his endeavours to live a pure life of godliness and virtue, refusing to listen to frivolous talk, reproving his fellows and even his shop-master when they indulged in light and wanton conversation, until finally the master discharged him with the remark that he did not care to keep " a house-prophet " any longer.[3] Hereupon he went forth as a travelling cobbler, spending some years in his wanderings, discovering more and more, as he passed from place to place, how religion was being lost in the Babel of theological wrangling, and seeing, with those penetrating eyes of his, deeper into the meaning of life and the world.   Near the end of the century—probably about 1599—he gave up his wanderings, married Catherine Kunchman, " a young woman of virtuous disposition," and opened a shoemaker's shop for himself in the town of Görlitz, where he soon established a reputation for honest, faithful work, and where he modestly prospered and was able to buy a home of his own, and where he reared the four sons and two daughters who came to the happy home.

[1] *Memoirs*, p. 6.   Von Franckenberg says that Boehme himself told him this incident.
[2] *Ibid.* pp. 4-5.   The reader will have noted the long history of this phrase, " Sabbath of the soul."   [3] *Ibid.* p. 7.

The supreme experience of his life—and one of the most remarkable instances of " illumination " in the large literature of mystical experiences—occurred when Boehme was twenty-five years of age, some time in the year 1600. His eye fell by chance upon the surface of a polished pewter dish which reflected the bright sunlight, when suddenly he felt himself environed and penetrated by the Light of God, and admitted into the innermost ground and centre of the universe. His experience, instead of waning as he came back to normal consciousness, on the contrary deepened. He went to the public green in Görlitz, near his house, and there it seemed to him that he could see into the very heart and secret of Nature, and that he could behold the innermost properties of things.[1] In his own account of his experience, Boehme plainly indicates that he had been going through a long and earnest travail of soul as a Seeker,[2] " striving to find the heart of Jesus Christ and to be freed and delivered from everything that turned him away from Christ." At last, he says, he resolved to " put his life to the utmost hazard " rather than miss his life-quest, when suddenly the " gate was opened." He continues his account as follows : " In one quarter of an hour I saw and knew more than if I had been many years together in a University. . . . I saw and knew the Being of Beings, the Byss and Abyss, the eternal generation of the Trinity, the origin and descent of this world, and of all creatures through Divine Wisdom. I knew and saw in myself all the three worlds—(1) the Divine, Angelical, or Paradisaical World ; (2) the dark world, the origin of fire ; and (3) the external, visible world as an outbreathing or expression of the internal and spiritual worlds. I saw, too, the essential nature of evil and of good, and how the

---

[1] *Memoirs*, p. 8. Paracelsus taught that the inner nature of things might be seen by one who has become an organ of the Universal Mind. He says : " Hidden things which cannot be perceived by the physical senses may be found through the sidereal body, through whose organism we may look into nature in the same way as the sun shines through a glass. The inner nature of everything may be known through Magic [The Divine Magia] and the power of inner sight." —Hartmann's *Life of Paracelsus* (1896), p. 53.

[2] He uses this word *Seeker* hundreds of times in his writings.

pregnant Mother—the eternal genetrix—brought them forth." [1]

He has also vividly told his experience in the *Aurora* : " While I was in affliction and trouble, I elevated my spirit, and earnestly raised it up unto God, as with a great stress and onset, lifting up my whole heart and mind and will and resolution to wrestle with the love and mercy of God and not to give over unless He blessed me—then the Spirit did break through. When in my resolved zeal I made such an assault, storm, and onset upon God, as if I had more reserves of virtue and power ready, with a resolution to hazard my life upon it, suddenly my spirit did break through the Gate, not without the assistance of the Holy Spirit, and I reached to the innermost Birth of the Deity and there I was embraced with love as a bridegroom embraces his bride. My triumphing can be compared to nothing but the experience in which life is generated in the midst of death or like the resurrection from the dead. In this Light my spirit suddenly saw through all, and in all created things, even in herbs and grass, I knew God—who He is, how He is, and what His will is—and suddenly in that Light my will was set upon by a mighty impulse to describe the being of God." [2]

This experience was the momentous watershed of his life. He is constantly referring to it either directly or indirectly. " I teach, write, and speak," is his frequent testimony, " of what has been wrought in me. I have not scraped my teaching together out of histories and so made *opinions*. I have by God's grace obtained eyes of my own." [3] " There come moments," he writes, " when the soul sees God as in a flash of lightning," [4] and he tells his readers that " when the Gate is opened " to them, they also " will understand." [5] " In my own faculties," he writes again, " I am as blind a man as

---

[1] *Second Epistle*, sec. 6-8.
[2] *Aurora*, xix. 10-13. He goes on in the following sections to describe how for twelve years this insight " grew in his soul like a young tree before the exact understanding of it all " was arrived at.
[3] *The Fifth Epistle*, 50.   [4] *Aurora*, xi. 146.   [5] *Ibid.* xi. 6.

ever was, but in the Spirit of God my spirit sees through all." [1]

During the ten quiet years which followed "the opening of the Gate" to him, Boehme meditated on what he had seen, and, though he does not say so, he almost certainly read much in the works of "the great masters," as he calls them, who were trying to tell, often in confused language, the central secret of the universe. Instead of fading out, his "flash" of insight grew steadily clearer to him as he read and pondered, and little by little, as one comes to see in the dark, certain great ideas became defined.   With his third "flash," [2] which came to him in 1610, when he felt once more "overshadowed by the Holy Spirit and touched by God," [3] he was moved to write down for his own use what he had seen.   "It was," he says, "powerfully borne in upon my mind to write down these things for a memorial, however difficult they might be of apprehension to my outer self [intellect] and of expression through my pen.   I felt compelled to begin at once, like a child going to school, to work upon this very great Mystery.   Inwardly [in spirit] I saw it all well enough, as in a great depth ; for I looked through as into a chaos where all things lie [undifferentiated] but the unravelling thereof seemed impossible.   From time to time an opening took place within me, *as of a growth*.[4] I kept this to myself for twelve years [1600–12], being full of it and I experienced a vehement impulse before I could bring it out into expression ; but at last it overwhelmed me like a cloud-burst which hits whatever it lights upon.   And so it went with me : whatsoever [7] could grasp sufficiently to bring it out, that I wrote down." [5]

This first book which thus grew out of his spiritual travails and "openings" Boehme called *Morning Glow*, to which later, through the suggestion of a friend, he gave

[1] *Aurora*, xxii. 47.

[2] In the *Aurora* Boehme speaks of the Flash as an experience : "As the lightning flash appears and disappears again in a moment, so it is also with the soul.   In its battle the soul suddenly penetrates through the clouds and sees God like a flash of Light."—*Ibid.* xi. 76.   [3] *Memoirs*, p. 8.

[4] Evidently the "flash" of the year 1610 was not the last one.   In fact, he seems to have had frequent ecstasies.   [5] *The Second Epistle*, 9-10.

the title *Aurora*. It is a strange *mélange* of chaos where all things lie undifferentiated and of insight ; dreary wastes of words that elude comprehension, with beautiful patches of spiritual oasis. He himself always felt that the book was dictated to him, and that he only passively held the pen which wrote it. " Art," he says, speaking of his writing, " has not written here, neither was there any time to consider how to set it down punctually, according to the understanding of the letters, but all was ordered according to the direction of the Spirit, which often went in haste, so that in many words letters may be wanting, and in some places a capital letter for a word ; so that *the Penman's hand*, by reason that he was not accustomed to it, did often shake. And though I could have wrote in a more accurate, fair, and plain manner, yet the reason was this, that the burning fire often forced forward with speed, and the hand and pen must hasten directly after it ; for it goes and comes like a sudden shower." [1] This is obviously an inside account of the production of inspirational script, amounting almost to automatic impulsion. Throughout his voluminous writings he often speaks of " this hand," or " this pen " as though they were owned and moved by a will far deeper than his own individual consciousness,[2] and his writings themselves frequently bear the marks of automatisms.

His manuscript copy of *Morning Glow* was freely lent to readers and circulated widely. Boehme himself kept no copy by him, but he tells us that during its wanderings the manuscript was copied out in full four times by strangers and brought to him.[3] One of the copies fell into the hands of Gregorius Richter, pastor primarius of Görlitz, a violent guardian of orthodoxy and a man extremely jealous of any infringement of the dignity of his official position. He proceeded at once— " without sufficient examination or knowledge "—to

---

[1] *Third Epistle*, 35.

[2] See especially *Signatura rerum*, ix. 63, and *Forty Questions*, xxvi. 2-3 and xxx. 3 and 5.

[3] *Third Epistle*, 32. The *Memoirs* describe how it was copied by " a Gentleman of some rank " [Carl von Endern].

" vilify and condemn " the writing, and in a sermon on
" False Prophets " he vigorously attacked the local
prophet of Görlitz, who meekly sat in Church and listened
to the " fulminations " against him.[1] After the sermon,
Boehme modestly asked the preacher to show him what
was wrong with his teaching, but the only answer he
received was that if he did not instantly leave the town
the pastor would have him arrested ; and the following
day Richter had Boehme summoned before the magistrates, and succeeded by his influence and authority in
overawing them so that they ordered the harmless prophet
to leave the town forthwith without any time given him
to see his family or to close up his affairs. Boehme
quietly replied, " Yes, dear Sirs, it shall be done ; since
it cannot be otherwise I am content." The next day,
however, the magistrates of Görlitz held a meeting and
recalled the banished prophet and offered him the privilege
of remaining in his home and occupation on condition
that he would cease from writing on theological matters.
On this latter point we have Boehme's own testimony,
though he does not refer the condition to the magistrates.
" When I appeared before him " [Pastor Richter], Boehme
says, " to defend myself and indicate my standpoint,
the Rev. Primarius [Richter] exacted from me a promise
to give up writing and to this I assented, since I did not
then see clearly the divine way, nor did I understand what
God would later do with me. . . . By his order I gave up
for many years [1613-18] all writing or speaking about
my knowledge of divine things, hoping vainly that the
evil reports would at last come to an end, instead of which
they only grew worse and more malignant." [2]

Boehme's friend, Doctor Cornelius Weissner, in his
account, which is none too accurate, endeavours to find an
explanation of Richter's persistent hate and persecution

---

[1] *Memoirs*, p. 9.

[2] Preserved in the Diary of Bartholomew Scultetus, then Mayor of Görlitz
(Ueberfeld's edition, 1730). This Diary does not record any actual banishment
of Boehme. The data for our knowledge of the persecutions of Boehme are
found in a personal narrative written by his friend Cornelius Weissner, M.D.
—*Memoirs*, pp, 39-50.

of the shoemaker-prophet in a gentle reproof which the latter administered to the former for having meanly treated a poor kinsman of Boehme in a small commercial transaction, but it is by no means necessary to bring up incidents of this sort to discover an adequate ground for Richter's fury. The *Aurora* itself furnishes plenty of passages which would, if read, throw a jealous guardian of orthodoxy into fierce activity. One passage in which Boehme boldly attacks the popular doctrine of pre-destination and asserts that the writers and scribes who teach it are " masterbuilders of Lies " will be sufficient illustration of the theological provocation : " This present world doth dare to say that God hath decreed or concluded it so in His predestinate purpose and counsel that some men should be saved and some should be damned, as if hell and malice and evil had been from eternity and that it was in God's predestinate purpose that men should be and must be therein. Such persons pull and hale the Scriptures to prove it, though, indeed, they neither have the knowledge of the true God nor the understanding of Scripture. These justifiers and disputers assist the Devil steadfastly and pervert God's truth and change it into lies." [1] He closed his book with these daring words : " Should Peter or Paul seem to have written otherwise, then look to the essence, look to the heart [*i.e.* to interior meaning]. If you lay hold of the heart of God you have ground enough." [2] His entire conception of salvation was, too, as we shall see, vastly different from the pre-vailing orthodox conception, and furthermore he was only a layman, innocent of the schools, and yet he was claiming to speak as an almost infallible instrument of a fresh revelation of God. Theologians of the type of the Primarius Richter need no other provocation to account for their relentless pursuit of local prophets that appear in the domain of their authority.

Meantime Boehme's fame was slowly spreading, and he was drawing into sympathetic fellowship with himself a number of high-minded and serious men who were

---

[1] *Aurora,* xiii. 7-10.   [2] *Ibid.* xxxvi. 152.

dissatisfied with the current orthodox teaching. In this group of friends who found comfort in the fresh message of Boehme were Dr. Balthazar Walther, director of the Chemical Laboratory of Dresden, Dr. Tobias Kober, physician at Görlitz, a disciple of Paracelsus, Abraham von Franckenberg, who calls Jacob " our God-taught man," Doctor Cornelius Weissner, who became intimate with him in 1618, and the nobleman Carl von Endern, who copied out the entire manuscript of the *Aurora*. These friends frequently encouraged Boehme to break his enforced silence, and he himself was restless and melancholy, feeling that he was " entrusted with a talent which he ought to put to usury and not return to God singly and without improvement, like the lazy servant." " It was with me," he writes, describing his years of silence, " as when a seed is hidden in the earth. It grows up in storm and rough weather, against all reason. In winter time, all is dead, and reason says : ' It is all over with it.' But the precious seed within me sprouted and grew green, oblivious of all storms, and amid disgrace and ridicule it has blossomed forth into a lily ! " [1]

Under the pressure, from without and from within, he resolved after five years of repression to break the seal of silence and give the world his message. Writing to a dear friend, whom he called " a plant of God," he says : " My very dear brother in the life of God, you are more acceptable to me in that it was you who awaked me out of my sleep, that I might go on to bring forth fruit in the life of God—and I want you to know that after I was awakened *a strong smell was given to me in the* life of God." [2] During the next six years (1618–24) he wrote almost incessantly, producing, from 1620 on, book after book in rapid succession.[3] In 1622, he informs a friend that he

---

[1] *Third Epistle, 7.*

[2] *Fifteenth Epistle,* 18. This " new smell in the life of God " often occurs in Boehme's writings. Compare George Fox's testimony, " The whole creation had a new smell." For further comparisons see pp. 221-227.

[3] The following is a complete list of his writings :

1612. *The Aurora.*

1619. *The Three Principles of the Divine Essence.*

1620. *The Threefold Life of Man* ; *Forty Questions* ; *The Incarnation of Jesus*

has " laid aside his trade to serve God and his brothers," [1] and in 1623, he says that he has written without ceasing during the autumn and winter. He felt throughout his life that the " illumination," which broke upon him in the year 1600, steadily increased with the years, and he came to look upon his first book as only the crude attempt of a child as compared with his later works. " The Day," he writes in 1620, " has now overtaken the *Aurora* [the morning glow]; it has grown full daylight and the morning is extinguished." [2] He says, with artlessness, that when he wrote the *Aurora*, he was not yet accustomed to the Spirit. The heavenly joy, indeed, met him and he followed the Spirit's guidance, but much of his own wild and untamed nature still remained to mar his work. Each successive book marks a growth of " the spiritual lily " in him, he thinks : " Each book from the first is ten times deeper ! " [3]

Once again, the zeal of a friend brought Boehme into the storm-centre of persecution. Until 1623, his works circulated only in manuscript and were kept from the eye of his ecclesiastical enemy, but toward the end of that year, an admirer, Sigismund von Schweinitz, printed three of his little books—*True Repentance* ; *True Resignation* ; and *The Supersensual Life*—in one volume under the title *The Way to Christ*. Richter was immediately aroused and poured forth his feelings in some desperately bad verses :

> Quot continentur lineae, blasphemiae
> Tot continentur in libro sutorio,
> Qui nil nisi picem redolet sutoriam,

Christ ; *The Suffering, Death and Resurrection of Christ* ; *The Tree of Faith* ; *Six Points* ; *Heavenly and Earthly Mysterium* ; *The Last Times.*

1621. *De signatura rerum* ; *The Four Complexions* ; *Apology to Balthazar Tilken* in 2 parts ; *Consideration on Esaias Stiefel's Book.*

1622. Sec. *Apology to Stiefel* ; *Repentance* ; *Resignation* ; *Regeneration.*

1623. *Predestination and Election of God* ; *A Short Compendium of Repentance* ; *The Mysterium magnum.*

1624. *The Clavis* ; *The Supersensual Life* ; *Divine Contemplation* ; *Baptism and the Supper* ; *A Dialogue Between the Enlightened and Unenlightened Soul* ; *An Apology on the Book of Repentance* ; *177 Theosophic Questions* ; *An Epitome of the Mysterium magnum* ; *The Holy Week* ; *An Exposition of the Threefold World.*

Undated. *An Apology to Esaias Stiefel* ; *The Last Judgment* ; *Epistles.*

[1] *Thirty-first Epistle*, 10.   [2] *The Third Epistle*, 30.   [3] *Ibid.* 29.

Atrum et colorem, quem vocant sutorium.
Pfuy ! pfuy ! teter sit fetor a nobis procul ! ! [1]

But the Primarius was not content with this harmless weapon of ridicule. He stirred up the neighbouring clergymen to join him in the attack, and a complaint was lodged in Town Council against Boehme as a " rabid enthusiast," and he was warned to leave the town. Boehme was as sweet and gentle in spirit now as he had been ten years before. He wrote in 1624 : " I pray for those who have reviled and condemned me. They curse me and I bless. I am standing the test ["Proba"] and have the mark of Christ on my forehead." [2]   But he thought that it did not befit him as an instrument of God's revelation to let the false charges against him go unanswered. He accordingly replied to the accusations in an *Apology*, in which the whole depth and beauty of his spiritual nature breathes forth. His appeal was in vain and he was forced to leave Görlitz. He went forth, however, in no discouraged mood. He saw that his message was " being sounded through Europe," and he predicts that " the nations will take up what his own native town is casting away." Already, he hears, his book has been read with interest in the Court of the Elector of Saxony, and he writes, March 15, 1624 : " I am invited there to a conference with high people and I have consented to go at the end of the Leipzig fair. Soon the revelation of Jesus Christ shall break forth and destroy the works of the Devil." [3]   The real trouble with the world, he thinks, is that the Christians in it are " titular and verbal "— they are only " opinion-peddlers," [4] and that is why a man who insists upon a reproduction of the life of Christ is persecuted. The visit to the Elector's Court in Dresden came off well for the simple shoemaker. He spent two months in the home of the Court physician, Dr. Hinkelmann, where many of the nobility and clergy came to see

---

[1] There are as many blasphemies in the shoemaker's book as there are lines. It smells of shoemaker's wax and filthy blacking. May this intolerable stench be far from us.   [2] *Thirty-fourth Epistle*, 5.
[3] *Thirty-third Epistle*.   [4] *Thirty-fourth Epistle*, 16 and 21.

him and to talk with him.   Three professors of theology
and other learned doctors were asked by the Elector to
examine him.   They reported that they did not yet quite
succeed in understanding him, and that therefore they
could not pronounce judgment.   They hoped " His
Highness would please to have patience and allow the
man sufficient time to expound his ideas "—which were,
in fact, already " expounded " in more than a score of
volumes !   One of the professors is reported to have said :
" I would not for the world be a party to this man's
condemnation," and another declared :   " Nor would I,
for who knows what lies at the bottom of it all ! " [1]

The end of the good man's life, however, was near.
He was taken ill in November 1624, while staying with
his old friend, von Schweinitz, and he hurried home to
Görlitz, where his family had remained during his absence,
to die in the quiet of his own house.   The night before
he died, he spoke of hearing beautiful music, and asked to
have the door opened that he might hear it better.   In
the morning—as the Aurora appeared—he bade farewell
to his wife and children, committed his soul to the crucified
Lord Jesus Christ, arranged a few simple matters, and,
with a smile on his face, said, " Now I go to Paradise."

His old enemy, Richter, had died a few months before
him, but the new pastor was of the same temper and
refused to preach his funeral sermon.   The second pastor
of the city was finally ordered by the Governor of Lausitz
to preach the sermon, which he began with the words,
" I had rather have walked a hundred and twenty miles
than preach this sermon ! " [2]   The common people,
however,—the shoemakers, tanners and a " great con-
course of us his fast friends," as one of them writes,—were
at the funeral, and a band of young shoemakers carried
his body to its last resting-place, where a block of porphyry
now informs the visitor that " Jacob Boehme, *philosophus
Teutonicus* " sleeps beneath.

Grützmacher holds that Boehme is an " isolated
thinker," having little, if any, historical connection with

---

[1] Weissner's Narrative, *Memoirs*, p. 49.   [2] *Ibid.* p. 58.

the past.[1] I do not agree with this view. I find in him
rather the ripe fulfilment of the powerful protest against
the dead letter, against a formal religion, and equally a
fulfilment of a Christianity of inward life, which was
voiced so vigorously in the writings of Denck, Bünderlin
Entfelder, Franck, and Weigel, neglecting for the moment
another side of Boehme and another set of influences
which appeared in him. The central note of his life-long
prophet-cry was against a form of religion built upon the
letter of Scripture and consisting of external ceremonies
and practices, and this is the ground of Richter's bitter
hostility and stubborn opposition.[2]

The Church of his day seems to him a veritable Babel—
" full of pride and wrangling, and jangling, and snarling
about the letter of the written Word," lacking in true,
real, effectual knowledge and power ; a pitiably poor
" substitute for the Temple of the holy Spirit where God's
living Word is taught." [3] Through each of his books
we hear of " verbal Christendom " ; of " titular Christians " ; of " historical feigned faith " ; of " history
religion " ; of " an external forgiveness of sins " ; of
" the work of outward letters." " The builders of Babel,"
he says, " cannot endure that one should teach that Christ
Himself must be the teacher in the human heart "—" they
jangle instead about the mere husk, about the written
word and letter while they miss the living Word." [4]

The divisions of Christendom are due to the fact that
its " master-builders " are of the Babel-type. They
always follow the line of *opinion* ; their basis is " the
letter " ; their method of approach is *external*. They
build " stone houses in which they read the writings
which the Apostles left behind them," while they themselves dispute and contend about " mental idols and

---

[1] *Wort und Geist*, p. 196 *seq.*

[2] What could be a bolder criticism of the existing Church of his day than this :
" In place of the wolf [the Roman Church] there has grown up the fox [the
Lutheran Church] another anti-Christ, never a whit better than the first. If he
should come to be old enough how he would devour the poor people's hens ! "
—*The Three Principles of the Divine Essence*, xviii. 102.

[3] *Mysterium magnum*, xxvii. 47.

[4] *Ibid.* xxviii. 49-51.

opinions."[1] **The** true Church of Christ, on the contrary, is the living **Temple** of the Spirit. It is built up of men made wholly new by the inward power of the Divine Spirit and made *one* by an inward unity of heart and life with Christ—as " a living Twig of our Life-Tree Jesus Christ." Nobody can belong to this Church unless " he puts on the shirt of a little child," dies to selfishness and hypocrisy, rises again in a new will and obedience, and forms his life in its inmost ground according to Christ, the Life.[2] " The wise world," he declares, " will not believe in the true inward work of Christ in the heart ; it will have " only an external washing away of sins in Grace," but the ABC of true religion is far different.[3] He only is a Christian in fact in whom Christ dwelleth, liveth and hath His being, in whom Christ hath arisen as the eternal ground of the soul. He only is a Christian who has this high title in himself, and has entered with mind and soul into that Eternal Word which has manifested itself as the life of our humanity.[4] He wrote near the end of his life to Balthazar Tilken : " If I had no other book except the book which I myself am, I should have books enough. The entire Bible lies in me if I have Christ's Spirit in me. What do I need of more books ? Shall I quarrel over what is outside me before I have learned what is within me ? "[5] " What would it profit me if I were continually quoting the Bible and knew the whole book by heart but did not know the Spirit that inspired the holy men who wrote that book, nor the source from which they received their knowledge ? How can I expect to understand them in truth, if I have not the same Spirit they had ? "[6]

This insistence on personal, first-hand experience and practice of the Christ-Life, as the ground of true religion,

---

[1] *Mysterium magnum*, xxxvi. 34 ; xl. 98.
[2] *Ibid.* lxiii. 47-51 ; *Twenty-first Epistle*, 1.
[3] *Myst. mag.* xxv. 13.   [4] *The First Epistle*, 3-5.
[5] *Apology to Tilken*, ii. 298.
[6] *Ibid.* 72. Compare George Fox's testimony : " All must come to that Spirit, if they would know God or Christ or the Scriptures aright, which they that gave them forth were led and taught by."—*Journal* (ed. 1901), i. 35 and *passim*.

is the fundamental feature of Boehme's Christianity. He travels, as we shall see, through immense heights and deeps. Like Dante, who immeasurably surpasses him in power of expression, but not in prophetic power of vision, he saw the eternal realities of heaven and hell and the world between, and he told as well as he could what he *saw*, but his practical message which runs like a thread through all his writings is always simple—almost childlike in its simplicity—" Thou must thyself be the way. The spiritual understanding must be born in thee." [1] " A Christian is a new creature in the ground of the heart." [2] " The Kingdom of God is not from without, but it is a new man, who lives in love, in patience, in hope, in faith and in the Cross of Jesus Christ." [3]

And this simple shoemaker of Görlitz, with his amazing range of thought and depth of experience, practised and embodied the way of life which he recommended. He was a good man, and his life touches us even now with a kind of awe. " Life," he once said, " is a strange bath of thorns and thistles," [4] and he himself experienced that " bath," but he went through the world hearing everywhere a divine music and " having a joy in his heart which made his whole being tremble and his soul triumph as if it were in God." [5]

[1] *Sig. re.* xiv. 1.
[2] *Myst. mag.* lxx. 40.
[3] *Fourth Epistle*, 27 and 32.
[4] *The Three Princ.* xxii. 2.
[5] *Aurora*, iii. 39.

CHAPTER X

"If thou wilt be a philosopher or naturalist and search into God's being in Nature and discern how it all came to pass, then pray to God for the Holy Spirit to enlighten thee. In thy flesh and blood thou art not able to apprehend it, but dost read it as if a mist were before thy eyes. In the Holy Spirit alone, and in the whole Nature out of which all things were made, canst thou search into Nature."—*Aurora*, ii. 15-17.

ONE idea underlies everything which Boehme has written, namely, that nobody can successfully " search into visible Nature," or can say anything true about Man or about the problem of good and evil, until he has " apprehended *the whole Nature out of which all things were made.*" It will not do, he thinks, to make the easy assumption that in the beginning the world was made out of nothing. " If God made all things out of nothing," he says, " then the visible world would be no revelation of Him, for it would have nothing of Him in it. He would still be off beyond and outside, and would not be known in this world. Persons however learned they may be, who hold such ' opinions ' have never opened the Gates of God." [1]

Behind the visible universe and in it there is an invisible universe ; behind the material universe and in it there is an immaterial universe ; behind the temporal universe and in it there is an eternal universe, and the first business of the philosopher or naturalist, as Boehme conceives it, is to discover the essential Nature of this invisible, immaterial, eternal universe out of which this fragment of a visible world has come forth.

[1] *Aurora*, xxi. 60-62.

> Need have we,
> Sore need, of stars that set not in mid storm,
> Lights that outlast the lightnings.[1]

The visible fragment is never self-explanatory; all attempts to account for what occurs in it drive the serious observer deeper for his answer, and with a breathless boldness this meditative shoemaker of Görlitz undertakes to tell of the nature of this deeper World within the world. As a boy he saw a vast treasury of wealth hidden in the inside of a mountain, though he could never make anybody else see it. As a man he believed that he saw an immeasurable wealth of reality hidden within the world of sense, and he tried, often with poor enough success, to make others see the inside world which he found. We must now endeavour to grasp what it was that he saw. There is no doubt at all that this inside world which he discovered within and behind visible Nature, within and behind man, is really there, nor is there any doubt in my mind that he, Jacob Boehme, got an insight into its nature and significance which is of real worth to the modern world, but he is seriously hampered by the poverty of his categories, by the difficulties of his symbolism and by his literary limitations, when he comes to the almost insuperable task of expressing what he has seen. He is himself perfectly conscious of his limitations. He is constantly amazed that God uses such " a mean instrument," he regrets again and again that he is " so difficult to be understood," and he often wishes that he could " impart his own soul " to his readers that they " might grasp his meaning," [2] for he never for a moment doubts that " by God's grace he has eyes of his own." [3] He lived in an unscientific age, before our present exact terminology was coined. He was the inheritor of the vocabulary and symbolism of alchemy and astrology, and he was obliged to force his spiritual insight into a language which for us has become largely an antique rubbish heap.[4] If he

---

[1] Swinburne, *Erechtheus.*   [2] See *Fifteenth Epistle*, 25.
[3] *Fifth Epistle*, 50.
[4] Like Paracelsus, he uses " sulphur " in a symbolic way to represent an active energy of the universe and a form of will in man. In a similar way,

had possessed the marvellous power that Dante had to compel words to express what his soul saw, he might have fused these artificial symbolisms with the fire of his spirit, and given them an eternal value as the Florentine did with the equally dry and stubborn terminology of scholasticism, but that gift he did not have.[1] We must not blame him too much for his obscurities and for his large regions of rubbish and confusion, but be thankful for the luminous patches, and try to seize the meaning and the message where it breaks through and gets revealed.

The outward, visible, temporal world, he declares, is " a spiration, or outbreathing, or egress " of an eternal spiritual World and this inner, spiritual World " couches within " our visible world and is its ground and mother, and the outward world is from husk to core a parable or figure of the inward and eternal World. " The whole outward visible world, with all its being, is a ' signature ' or figure of the inward, spiritual World, and everything has a character that fits an internal reality and process, and the internal is in the external." [2] As he expresses the same idea in another book : " The visible world is a manifestation of the inward spiritual World, and it is an image or figure of eternity, whereby eternity has made itself visible." [3]

But there is a still deeper Source of things than this inward spiritual World, which is after all a manifested and organized World, and Boehme begins his account with That which is before beginnings—the unoriginated Mother of all Worlds and of All that is, visible and invisible. This infinite Mother of all births, this eternal Matrix, he calls the *Ungrund*, " Abyss," or the " Great

---

" mercury " stands for intelligence and spirit, and " salt " is the symbol for substance. No one could find in a chemist's shop the salt or sulphur that Boehme talks about !

[1] There is a fine saying about Dante in the *Ottimo Commento* : " I, the writer, heard Dante say that never a rhyme had led him to say other than he would, but that many a time and oft he had made words say for him what they were not wont to say for other poets."

[2] *Sig. re.* ix. 1-3. Paracelsus said, " Everything is the product of one creative effort," and, " There is nothing corporeal that does not possess a soul."

[3] *The Supersensual Life*, p. 44.

Mystery," [1] or the " Eternal Stillness." Here we are
beyond beginnings, beyond time, beyond " nature," and
we can say nothing in the language of reason that is true
or adequate. The eternal divine Abyss is its own origin
and explanation ; it presupposes nothing but itself ;
there is nothing beyond it, nothing outside it—there is,
in fact, no " beyond " and " outside "—it is " neither
near nor far off." [2] It is an absolute Peace, an indivisible
Unity, an undifferentiated One—an Abysmal Deep,
which no Name can adequately name and which can be
described in no words of time and space, of here and now.

But we must not make the common blunder of supposing that Boehme means that *before* God expressed
Himself and unfolded Himself in the infinite processes of
revelation and creation, He existed apart, as this undifferentiated One, this unknowable Abyss, this incomprehensible Matrix. There is no " before." Creation,
revelation, manifestation is a dateless and eternal fact.
God to be a personal God must go out of Himself and
find Himself in something that mirrors Him. He must
have a Son. He must pour His Life and Love through
a universe. What Boehme means, then, is that no
manifestation, no created universe, no expression, is the
ultimate Reality itself. The manifested universe has
come out of More than itself. The Abyss is more than
anything, or all, that comes out of it, or can come out
of it, and it lies with its infinite depth beneath everything
which appears, as a man's entire life, conscious and
unconscious, is in and yet lies behind every act of will,
though we can " talk about " only what is voiced or
expressed.

Even within this Abysmal Depth, that underlies all
that comes to being, there is eternal process—eternal
movement toward Personality and Character : " God is
the eternal Seeker and Finder of Himself." [3] " In the

---

[1] Paracelsus and others used the term *Mysterium magnum* to denote the
original, but unoriginated, matter out of which all things were made. " Mysterium " is anything out of which something germinally contained in it can be
developed.

[2] *Mysterium magnum*, xxix. 1-2.   [3] *Forty Questions*, i. 57.

Stillness an eternal Will arises, a longing desire for manifestation, the eye of eternity turns upon itself and discovers
itself " [1]—in a word there is within the infinite Divine
Deep an eternal process of self-consciousness and personality, which Boehme expresses in the words, " The Father
eternally generates the Son." " God hath no beginning
and there is nothing sooner than He, but His Word hath
a bottomless, unfathomable origin in Him and an eternal
end : which is not rightly called *end*, but Person, *i.e.* the
Heart of the Father, for it is generated in the eternal
Centre." [2] This inner process toward Personality is
often called by Boehme " the eternal Virgin " who brings
to birth God as Person, or sometimes " the Mirror," in
which God sees Himself revealed as will and wisdom and
goodness.

In the greatest artistic creation of the modern world
—" The Sistine Madonna "—Raphael has with almost
infinite pictorial power of genius tried to express in visible
form this Birth of God. Behind curtains which hang
suspended from nowhere and stretch across the universe,
dividing the visible from the invisible, the world of Nature
from the world of holy mystery, the infinite, immeasurable
and abysmal God is pictured as defined and personal in
the face and figure of a little Child, in which the artist
suggests in symbolism the infinite depth and joy and
potency of Divinity breaking forth out of mystery into
form. It is precisely this birth of God into visibility
that Boehme is endeavouring to tell. " The Son,"
however, Boehme says, " is not divided or sundered from
the Father, as two persons side by side—there are not
two Gods. The Son is the heart of the Father—God as
Person—the outspringing Joy of the total triumphing
Reality,[3] and through this eternal movement toward
self-consciousness and Personality, God becomes Spirit,
an out-going energy of purpose, a dynamic activity,
bursting forth into infinite manifestation and differentiation—a forth-breathed or expressed Word.[4] Through

[1] *Sig. re.* ii. 4-15, and iii. 1-10.   [2] *The Threefold Life of Man*, iii. 2.
[3] *Aurora*, iii. 35-39.   [4] *Ibid.* vi. 6-8 ; *Clavis*, 18-29.

this eternal process of self-differentiation and outgoing activity, the inner spiritual universe comes into being—as an intermediate Nature or world, between the ineffable Abyss of God on the one hand, and our world of material, visible things on the other hand. "The process of the whole creation," he says, "is nothing else but a manifestation of the deep and unsearchable God, and yet creation is not God but rather like an apple which springs from the power of the tree and grows upon the tree, and yet is not the tree—even so all things have sprung forth out of the central divine Desire." [1]

This entire manifested or out-breathed universe is, he says, the expression of the divine desire for holy sport and play. The Heart of God enjoys this myriad play of created beings, all tuned as the infinite strings of a harp for contributing to one mighty harmony, and all together uttering and voicing the infinite variety of the divine purpose. Each differentiated spirit or light or property or atom of creation has a part to play in the infinite sport or game or harmony, "so that in God there might be a holy play through the universe as a child plays with his mother, and that so the joy in the Heart of God might be increased," [2] or again, "so that each being may be a true sounding string in God's harmonious concert." [3]

This eternal, interior World—the Mirror in which the Spirit manifests Himself—is a double world of darkness and light, for there can be no manifestation except through opposites.[4] There must be yes and no. In order to have a play there must be opposing players. In order to have life and reality there must be conflict and conquest. As soon as the forth-going Word of God is differentiated into many concrete expressions and the fundamental Unity of the Abyss is broken up into particular desires and wills, there is bound to be a clash of opposites—will and contra-will, strain and tension, light and joy and beauty, and over against them pain and sorrow and evil. Evil must appear as soon as there is

---

[1] *Sig. re.* xvi. i.
[2] *Aurora,* xiii. 48-57 ; *Myst. mag.* viii. 31 ; *The Three Principles,* iv. 66.
[3] *Sig. re.* xv. 38. [4] *Myst. mag.* viii. 27.

process of separation, differentiation, variety, specializa-
tion and particularity.[1] Darkness appears as soon as
there is a contraction or narrowing into concrete desire
and will.

Both worlds—the light world and the dark world—
are made by desire and will. Narrowing desires for
individual and particular aims, which sever a being from
the total whole of divine goodness, make the kingdom of
darkness, while death to self-will and a yearning desire
and will for all that is expressed in the Heart and Light
of God, in the Person of His Son, make the kingdom of
Light. Lucifer—the awful example of the dark World—
fell because he stood in pride and despised the Birth of
the Heart of God and its gentle, universalizing love-spirit ;
and so his light went out into darkness. His climbing
up into a severed will was his fall. The more he climbed
toward the sundered aim of his own will and turned away
from the Heart of God, the greater was his fall, for to
turn away from the Heart of God is always to fall.[2] There
is no darkness, no evil, in angel or devil or man, except
the nature of that particular being's own will and desire—
both darkness and light are born of desire. The origin
of the fall of any creature, therefore, is not outside that
creature, but within it.[3]

The evil in the world is only a possible good spoiled.
Beings created for a holy sport and play, for an ordered
harmony, as infinite harp-strings for a celestial music,
set their wilful desires upon sundered ends, broke the
intended harmony, or " temperature," as Boehme calls
it, introduced strife—the *turba magna*—and darkness,
and so spoiled the actual material out of which the
kingdoms of nature are made, for the attitude of will
moulds the permanent structure of the being. Through
the whole universe, visible and invisible, as a result, the
dark lines run, and the drama of the whole process of the
universe is the mighty issue between light and darkness,
good and evil : Two universal qualities persist from

---

[1] *Myst. mag.* xxix. 1-10.
[2] *The Three Principles*, iv. 68-74 ; *The Threefold Life*, iv. 33.
[3] *Myst. mag.* ix. 3-8.

beginning to end and produce two kingdoms arrayed against each other—each within the other—one love, the other wrath ; one light, the other darkness ; one heavenly, the other hellish.[1]

Now out of this inner spiritual universe—a double universe of light and darkness—this temporal, visible, more or less material, world has come forth, as an outer sheath of an inner world, and, like its Mother, it, too, is a double world of good and evil. " There is not," as William Law, interpreting Boehme, once said, " the smallest thing or the smallest quality of a thing in this world, but is a quality of heaven or hell discovered [*i.e. revealed*] under a temporal form. Every thing that is disagreeable to taste, to the sight, to our hearing, smelling or feeling has its root and ground and cause in and from hell [the dark kingdom], and is as surely in its degree the working and manifestation of hell in this world, as the most diabolical malice and wickedness is ; the stink of weeds, of mire, of all poisonous, corrupted things ; shrieks, horrible sounds ; wrathful fire, rage of tempests and thick darkness, are all of them things that had no possibility of existence, till the fallen angels disordered their kingdom [*i.e.* until the inner universe was spoiled by narrow, sundered desires]. Therefore everything that is disagreeable and horrible in this life, everything that can afflict and terrify our senses, all the kinds of natural and moral evil, are only so much of the nature, effects and manifestation of hell, for hell and evil are only two words for one and the same thing. . . . On the other hand, all that is sweet, delightful and amiable in the world, in the serenity of air, the fineness of seasons, the joy of light, the melody of sounds, the beauty of colours, the fragrance of smells, the splendour of precious stones, is nothing else but heaven breaking through the veil of this world, manifesting itself in such a degree and darting forth in such variety so much of its own nature." [2]

I have spoken so far as though Boehme traced the

[1] *Aurora*, Preface 84.
[2] Christopher Walton, *Notes and Materials for a Biography of Wm. Law* (London, 1854), 55.

source of every thing to *will and desire*, as though, in fact, the visible universe were the manifold outer expression of some deep-lying personal will, and in the last analysis that is true, but his more usual form of interpretation is that of the working of great structural *tendencies*, or *energies*, or " *qualities*," as he calls them, which are common both to the inner and the outer universe. There are, he declares again and again with painful reiteration, but with little advance of lucidity, seven of these fundamental laws or energies or qualities, like the sevenfold colour-band of the rainbow, though they can never be untangled or sundered or thought of as standing side by side, for *together* in their unity and interprocesses they form the universe, with its warp and woof of light and darkness.[1]

The first " quality " is a contracting, compacting tendency which runs through the entire universe, outer and inner. It is in its inmost essence *desire*, the egoistic tendency, the focusing of will upon a definite aim so that consciousness contracts from its universal and absolute possibilities to a definite, limited, concrete *something in particular*, and thus negates everything else. Desire always disturbs the " Quiet " and brings contraction, negation and darkness. In the outer world it appears as the property of cohesion which makes the particles of a particular thing hold and cling together and form one self-contained and separate thing. It is the individualizing tendency which permeates the universe and which may be expressed either as a material law in the outer world, or as personal will-tendency in the inner world.

The second " quality " is the attractive, gravitating tendency which binds whole with whole as an organizing, universalizing energy. This, again, is both spiritual and physical—it has an outer and an inner aspect. It is a fundamental love-principle in the inner world—the

---

[1] The great passages in which Boehme expounds the seven qualities are found in the *Aurora*, chaps. viii.-xi. ; *Sig. re.* chap. xiv. ; *The Clavis*, 54-132 ; though they are more or less definitely stated or implied in nearly everything he wrote. Seven " qualities " or " principles " or " sources " appear and reappear in ever shifting forms throughout the entire literature of Gnosticism, alchemy, and nature-mysticism.

foundation, as Boehme says, of sweetness and warmth and mercy [1]—and at the same time is a structural, organizing law of nature, which tends out of many parts to make one universe.[2]

These two diverse tendencies at work eternally in the same world produce strain and tension and *anguish*. The tension occasioned by these opposite forces gives rise to the third " quality," which is a tendency toward movement, oscillation, rotation—what Boehme often calls *the wheel of nature*, or the wheel of motion, or the wheel of life.[3]   This, too, is both outer and inner ; a law of the physical world and a tendency of spirit.   There is nothing in nature that is not ceaselessly moved, and there is no life without its restlessness and anguish, its inward strain and stress, its tension and its problem, its dizzy wheel of life—the perpetual pursuit of a goal which ends at the starting-point as an endless circular process.

The fourth " quality " is the *flash*, or ignition, due to collision between nature and spirit, in which a new principle of activity breaks through what before was mere play of *forces*, and reveals something that has activity in itself, the kindling, burning power of fire, though not yet fire which gives *light*.   In the outer world it is the bursting forth of the elemental, fusing, consuming powers of Nature which may either construct or destroy. In the inner world it is the birth of self-consciousness on its lower levels, the awaking of the soul, the kindling of passion, and desire, and purpose.   Any one of these four lower " qualities " may stay at its own level, remain in itself out of " temperature " or balance with the rest, and so be only a " dark principle " ; or it may go on and fulfil itself in one of the higher " qualities " next to be described, and so become a part of the triumphing " light principle."   Fire may be only a " fire of anguish " or it may go up into a " fire of love " ; it may be a harsh,

---

[1] *Aurora*, viii. 32-35.

[2] Some of Boehme's enthusiastic friends insist that Sir Isaac Newton, who was an admirer of Boehme, "ploughed with Boehme's heifer," *i.e.* got his suggestion of the law of universal gravitation from the philosopher of Görlitz.   See Walton, *Notes*, p. 46 and *passim*.   [3] *Sig. re.* iv. *passim*.

self-tormenting fire, or it may be a soft, light-bringing, purifying fire. Suffering may harden the spirit, or it may be the condition of joy. Crucifixion may be mere torture, or it may be the way of salvation. It is then here at the *great divide* between the " qualities " that the universe reveals its differentiation into two kingdoms —" the dark " and " the light."

The fifth " quality " is Light, springing out of the " flash " of fire and rising to the level of illumination and the revelation of beauty. It is at this stage of Light that the lower force-forms and fire-forms first stand revealed in their full meaning and come to their real fulfilment. On its inner or spiritual side this Light-quality is an " amiable and blessed Love." It is the dawn and beginning of the triumphing spirit of freedom which wills to draw all things back to one centre, one harmony, one unity, in which wild will and selfish passion and isolating pride, and all that springs from the dark fire-root are quenched, and instead the central principle of the spiritual world—Love—comes into play.

Boehme calls his sixth " quality " voice or sound, but he means by it the entire range of intelligent expression through tone and melody, music and speech, everything in the world, in fact, that gives joy and beauty through purposeful utterance. He even widens his category of " sound " to include colours and smells and tastes, in short, all the sense-qualities by which the world gets revealed in its richness of beauty and harmony to our perception. He widens it, too, to include deeper and subtler tones than those of our earth-born sense—the heavenly sports and melodies and harmonies which the rightly attuned spirit may hear with a finer organ than the ear.

The seventh, and final, " quality " is body or figure, by which he means the fundamental tendency or energy toward expression in actuality and concrete form. The final goal of intelligent purpose is the realization of wisdom, of idea, in actual Nature-forms and life-forms—the *incarnation of the spirit*. There is nothing real in the universe but has its form, its "signature," its figure, its body-aspect: "There is not anything but has its soul *and* its body, and each soul is as it were an inner kernel, or seed, to a visible and comprehensible body," [1] and, as we shall see, the supreme achievement of the universe is the visible appearance of the Word of God, the eternal Son, in flesh like ours—a visible realization in time of the eternal Heart of God. The glory of God appears in a kingdom of God, a visible vesture of the Spirit.

All these seven qualities, or "fountain-spirits," or fundamental tendencies, are in every part and parcel of the universe, and each particular thing or being finds his true place in the vast drama or play of the universe, according to which "quality" is prepotent, and marks the thing or being with its "signature." They constitute in their eternal nature what Boehme calls *The Three Principles* that underlie all reality of every order. The first principle is the substratum or essence of these first three "qualities," the nature - tendencies at the level of forces, which he generally calls the *fire-principle*, *i.e.* the dark fire, before the "flash" has come. The second principle is the substratum or essence of the last three "qualities"—the tendencies toward unity, harmony, order, love, which he calls the *light-principle*. The third principle produces the union or synthesis of the other two—the principle of realization in body and form, the triumph over opposition of these two opposing principles in the exhibition of the real, the actual, the living, the conscious, where dark and light are both joined, but are dominated by another irreducible principle. To these three fundamental principles correspond the three supreme divine aspects: Father, Son, and Holy Ghost.[2]

We are here, of course, far from a scientific account of the processes and evolution of the universe. Boehme

---

[1] *Sig. re.* xiii.
[2] For fuller treatment of this point see Boutroux, *Historical Studies in Philosophy*, chapter on "Jacob Boehme, the German Philosopher," pp. 199-201.

is no scientific genius and he did not dream that every item and event of the world of phenomena could be causally explained, without reference to any deeper abysmal world of Spirit. His mission is rather that of the prophet who " has eyes of his own." He is endeavouring to tell us, often no doubt in very laborious fashion, sometimes as " one who is tunnelling through long tracts of darkness," that this outside world which we see and describe is a parable, a pictorial drama, suggesting, hinting, revealing an inside world of Spirit and Will; that every slightest fragment of the seen is big with significance as a revelation of an unseen realm, which again is an egress from the unimaginable Splendour of God. He believes, like Paracelsus, that everything in Nature— plants, metals, and stars—" can be fundamentally searched out and comprehended " by the inward way of approach, can be read like an open book by the children of the Spirit who have caught the secret clue that leads in, and who have the key that unlocks the inner realm.[1]

Obviously his " inner way of approach " works more successfully when applied to *man* than when applied to plants and metals and stars, and when he writes of man, whether in the first or in the third person, he does often seem to have " eyes of his own," and to " hold the key that unlocks."

It is an elemental idea with him that man is " a little world "—a microcosm—and expresses in himself all the properties of the great world—the macrocosm.[2] " As you find man to be," he writes, " just so is eternity. Consider man in body and soul, in good and evil, in light and darkness, in joy and sorrow, in power and weakness, in life and death—all is in man, both heaven and earth, stars and elements. Nothing can be named that is not in man." [3] Every man's life is inwardly bottomless and opens from within into all the immeasurable depth of God. Eternity springs through time and reveals itself in every person, for the foundation property of the soul

---

[1] *Third Epistle*, 33.   [2] *Twenty-fourth Epistle*, 7 ; *Sig. re.* i.
[3] *The Threefold Life*, vi. 47.

of every man is essentially eternal, spiritual, and abysmal
—it is a little drop out of the Fountain of the Life of God,
it is a little sparkle of the Divine Splendour.[1] God is
spoken of again and again as " man's native country,"
his true " origin and home "—" The soul of man is always
seeking after its native country, out of which it has
wandered, seeking to return home again to its rest in
God." [2] " The soul of man," he says again, " has come
out from the eternal Father, out from the Divine Centre,
but this soul—with this high origin and this noble mark—
stands always at the opening of two gates." [3] Two worlds,
two mighty cosmic principles, make their appeal to his
will. Two kingdoms wrestle in him, two natures strive
for the mastery in his life, and he makes his world, his
nature, his life, his eternal destiny by his choices : " Whatsoever thou buildest and sowest here in thy spirit, be it
words, works, or thought, that will be thy eternal house." [4]
" The good or evil that men do, by acts of will, enters into
and forms the soul and so moulds its permanent habitation." [5] Adam once, and every man after him also once,
has belonged, in the centre of the soul, to God, and whether
it be Adam or some far-off descendant of him, each is the
creator of his own real world, and settles for himself the
atmosphere in which he shall live and the inner " tincture "
of his abiding nature. " Adam fell "—and any man's
name can here be substituted for " Adam "—" because,
though he was a spark of God's eternal essence, he broke
himself off and sundered himself from the universal Will
—by contraction—and withdrew into self-seeking, and
centred himself in selfishness. He broke the perfect
temperature—or harmonious balance of qualities—and
turned his will toward the dark world and the light in
him grew dim." [6] To follow the dark world is to be
Lucifer or fallen Adam, to follow the light world completely is to be Christ [7]—and before every soul the two

---

[1] *The Three Princ.* xiv. 89 ; *First Epistle,* 42.
[2] *The Three Princ.* x. 26 ; xvi. 50.
[3] *Ibid.* x. 13.   [4] *Aurora,* xviii. 49.
[5] *Myst. mag.* xxii. 41.   [6] *Ibid.* xviii. 31-43, given in substance.
[7] *Ibid.* xxvi. 19. The place of Christ in Boehme's system will be given in
the next chapter.

gates stand open.[1] In a powerful and penetrating passage he says : " We should take heed and beget that which is good out of ourselves. If we make an angel of ourselves we are that ; if we make a devil of ourselves, we are that." [2]

This last sentence is a good introduction to Boehme's conception of " the next world "—" the great beyond." He was as completely free of the crude idea that heaven is a shining locality in the sky, and hell a yawning pit of fire below the earth, as the most exact scientific scholar of the modern world is likely to be. He had grasped the essential and enduring character of man's spiritual nature so firmly that he ceased to have any further interest in the mythological aspects in which vivid and pictorial imagination has invested the unseen world. " God's presence itself," he says, " is heaven, and if God did but put away the veiling shadows, which now curtain thy sight, thou wouldst see, even where thou now art, the Face of God and the heavenly gate. God is so near that at any moment a holy Birth [a Birth into the Life of God] may be accomplished in thy heart," [3] and, again, in the same book he writes : " If man's eyes were opened he would see God everywhere, for heaven is everywhere for those who are in the innermost Birth. When Stephen saw heaven opened and Jesus at the right hand of God, his spirit did not swing itself aloft into some heaven in the sky, but it rather penetrated into the innermost Birth where heaven always is. Thou must not think that God is a Being who is off in an upper heaven, or that when the soul departs it goes many hundred thousands of miles aloft. It does not need to do that, for as soon as it has entered the innermost Birth it is in heaven already with God— *near and far in God is one thing.*" [4]

The " next world "—" the beyond "—therefore, must not be thought of in terms of space and time, of here and there, of now and then, as a place to which we shall journey at the momentous moment of death : " the soul

[1] *Myst. mag.* xxvi. 5.
[2] *Incarnation*, part ii. ix. 12-14.
[3] *Aurora*, x. 100-103.
[4] *Ibid.* xix. 56-59.

needeth no going forth." [1] As soon as the external veil of flesh dissolves, each person is in his own country and has all the time been in it. There is nothing nearer to you than heaven and hell. To whichever of them you *incline* and toward whichever of them you tend—that is most near you, and every man has in himself the key.[2] Heaven and hell are everywhere throughout the whole world. You need not seek them far off.

It is always the nature of " Anti-Christ " and " Babel " and " opinion-peddlers " to seek God and heaven and hell above the stars or under the deep. There is only one " place " to look for God and that is in one's own soul, there is only one " region " in which to find heaven or hell, and that is in the nature and character of the person's own desire and will : " Even though the devil should go many millions of miles, desiring to see heaven and enter into it, yet he would still be in hell and could not see heaven at all." [3] The soul, Boehme says in substance, hath heaven or hell in itself. Heaven is the turning of the will into God's love ; hell is the turning of the will into hate. Now when the body falls away the heavenly soul is thoroughly penetrated with the Love and Light of God, even as fire penetrates and enlightens white-hot iron, whereby it loses its darkness—this is heaven and this is the right hand of God. The soul that dwells in falsehood, lust, pride, envy, and anger carries hell in itself and cannot reach the Light and Love of God. Though it should go a thousand miles or a thousand times ten thousand miles—even climb beyond the spaces of the stars and the bounds of the universe—it would still remain in the same property and source of darkness as before.[4] The " next world "—" the world beyond "—is

---

[1] *The Supersensual Life,* 36.

[2] *The Three Princ.* ix. 25-27 and xix. 33.   [3] *Myst. mag.* viii. 28.

[4] *The Supersensual Life,* 38. Every reader will naturally be reminded of Milton's great lines :

> " The mind is its own place, and in itself
> Can make a heaven of hell, a hell of heaven."

There were no doubt many *sources* in Milton's time for such a conception, but the poet surely would read the translations of Boehme which were coming from the press all through the period of his literary activity.

just *this* world, as it is in each one of us, with its essential spirit and nature and character clearly revealed and fulfilled. God creates and maintains no hell of ever-lasting torture ; He builds and supports no heaven of endless glory. They are both formed out of the soul's own substance as it turns toward light or darkness, toward love or hate—in short, as " it keeps house," to use one of his vivid words, with the eternal nature of things.

Something like this, then, was the universe which Boehme—with those " azure-grey eyes that lighted up like the windows of Solomon's Temple "—saw there in Görlitz, as he pegged his shoes. " Open your eyes," he once said, " and the whole world is full of God." [1] But he is not a pantheist, in the usual sense of that word, blurring away the lines between good and evil, or the boundaries which mark off self from self, and self from God. There is forever, to be sure, a hidden essence or sub-stance in the soul which is from God, and which remains to the end unlost and unspoiled—something to which God can speak and to which His Light and Grace can make appeal ; but I am indestructibly a real I, and God is in His true nature no vague Abyss—He eternally utters Himself as Person : " The first Abysmal God without beginning begets a comprehensible will which is Son. Thus the Abyss which in itself is an indescribable Nothing [nothing in particular] forms itself into Some-thing [definite] through the Birth of a Son, and so is Spirit." [2] In God Himself there is only Good, only triumphing eternal Joy,[3] but as soon as finite processes appear, as soon as anything is differentiated into actuality, the potentialities of darkness and light appear, the possibilities of good and evil are there : " *All things consist in Yes or No. In order to have anything definite made manifest there must be a contrary therein—a Yes and a No."* [4] The universe, therefore, though it came forth out of the eternal Mother and remains still, in its deepest origin and being, rooted in the substance of God, is a

---

[1] *The Threefold Life*, xi. 106.   [2] *Election*, i. 10-17.
[3] *Aurora*, ii. 63.   [4] *Theosoph. Quest.* iii. 2-4.

battleground of strife, an endless Armageddon. Both within and without the world is woven of mixed strands, a warp of darkness and a woof of light, and all beings possessed of will are thus actors in a mighty drama of eternal significance, with exits, not only at the end of the Fifth Act but throughout the play, through two gates into two worlds which are both all the time present here and now.

CHAPTER XI

" I WILL write a Process or Way which I myself have gone."[1] Most writers who have treated of Boehme have mainly dealt with his *Weltanschauung*—his theosophical view of the Abyss and the worlds of time and eternity, —or they have devoted themselves to descriptions of his type of mysticism.[2] His important permanent contribution to Christianity is, however, to be found in his interpretation of the way, or, as he calls it, the process of salvation. Very much that he wrote about the procession of the universe is capricious and subjective. His interpretations of Genesis, and of Old Testament Scripture in general, are thoroughly uncritical and of value only as they reveal his own mind and his occasional flashes of insight. But his accounts of his own *experience* and his message of the way to God possess an elemental and universal value, and belong among the precious words of the prophets of the race. His Way of Salvation is in direct line with the central ideas of Denck, Bünderlin, Entfelder, Franck, Schwenckfeld, and Weigel ; that is, his emphasis is always, as was theirs, upon the native divine possibilities of the soul, upon the fact of a spiritual environment in immediate correspondence and co-operation with the soul, and upon the necessity of personal and inward experience as the key to every gate of life ; but he puts more stress even than Schwenckfeld did

---

[1] *True Repentance*, i.
[2] I have given his *Weltanschauung* in the previous chapter, and I shall discuss his *mysticism* at the end of this chapter.

upon the epoch-making new birth, and he sees more in the Person of Christ as the way of salvation than any of the spiritual Reformers of the sixteenth century had seen, while his own personal experience was so unique and illuminating, so profound and transforming, that he was able to speak on divine things with a grasp and insight and with a spiritual authority beyond that attained by any of the reformers in this group. He has given, I think, as profound and as simple, and at the same time as vital an interpretation of salvation through Christ as the Reformation movement produced before the nineteenth century, and much that he said touches the very core of what seems to us to-day to be the heart of the Gospel, the central fact of mature religion.[1]

As we have seen, Boehme does not in the least blink the tragic depth of sin, while he goes as far as anybody in holding that " the centre of man's soul came out of eternity," [2] that " as a mother bringeth forth a child out of her own substance and nourisheth it therewith, so doth God with man his child," [3] and that the inward ground and centre of the soul, with its divine capacity of response to Grace and Light, is an inalienable possession of every man.[4] Yet, at the same time, he insists that there is in every soul " both a yes and a no," a vision of the good and a *contrarium*, a hunger for the universal will of God and a hunger for the particular will of self.[5] The form of hunger, the inclination of desire, the attitude of will shapes the destiny, forms the fundamental disposition, and builds the life of every man into heaven or into hell— " a man puts on a garment of light or a garment of wrath as he puts on clothes." [6] To consent to false desire, to turn toward objects that feed only the particular selfish will, to live in the lower " qualities " of dark-fire is to

---

[1] Hegel says that Boehme's piety is " in the highest degree deep and inward." —*History of Philos.* iii. p. 216.

[2] *True Resignation*, iii. 20.   [3] *The Three Princ.*, Preface, 4.

[4] " There is in every man an incorporate ground of Grace, an inner Temple of Christ, the soul's immortal Dowry. No man can sell or pawn this ground of Grace, this habitation and dwelling-place of Christ. It remains unlost as the possession of God—an inward Ground and spiritual substance."—*Myst. mag.* lxxiv. 20-33, freely rendered.

[5] *Sig. re.* xv. 45.   [6] *Aurora*, xviii. 43.

form a soul *tinctured* with darkness and sundered from the eternal root of Life. Lucifer went the whole way in his consent to false and evil desire. He said, " Evil be thou my good ! " and formed his entire nature out of the dark-principle, and " his Light went out." Adam and his offspring after him, however, only dimmed the native Light and deadened the original power that belongs to one who comes from God, to live in heavenly harmony and joy. Man has fallen indeed, but he is not hopelessly lost, he is " forever seeking his native country," and he forever bears within himself an immortal seed which may burst into Life—into a " Lily-blossom." [1] The way of salvation for Boehme is the *process* by which this original Light and power, dimmed and deadened by sin, are restored to the soul.

He never tires of insisting that the restoration can come only by a *process of Life*, not by a " scheme " of theology. Like the early prophets of Israel, in their sweeping attacks on the ritual and sacrificial systems that were being substituted for moral and spiritual life, Boehme flings himself with holy passion against the substitution of doctrines of salvation for a real life-process of salvation, personally experienced in the soul. " Cain " and " Babel " are his two favourite types of the prevailing substitute-religion which he calls " verbal," or " historical," or " titular " Christianity.[2] " Whatever Babel teaches," he says, " of external imputed righteousness, or of external assumed adoption is without foundation or footing." [3] He is still only a follower of " Cain " who tries to cover his old, evil, unchanged self " with the purple mantle of Christ's death." [4] The " opinion " that the old man of evil-will can be " covered " with Christ's merit, the " faith " that His death pays off for us the debt of our sin is only " a supposed religion." [5] " Christianity," he says again, " does not consist in the mere knowing of history and applying the history-knowledge to ourselves,

---

[1] *The Three Princ.* xiv. 3 and 12 ; also *ibid.* 85 and 88.
[2] *Myst. mag.* xxvii. 41.   [3] *Ninth Epistle*, 16.
[4] *Myst. mag.* xxvii. *passim ;* also *Seventh Epistle*, 11-14.
[5] *Tenth Epistle*, 13-14.

saying : ' Christ died for us ; He hath paid the ransom for us, so that we need do nothing but comfort ourselves therewith and steadfastly believe that it is so.' " [1] The " doctors " and " the wise world " and " the makers of opinion " will have it that Christ has suffered on the Cross for all our sins, and that we can be justified and acquitted of all our transgressions by what He did for us, but it is no true, safe way for the soul. To stake faith upon a history that once was, to look for " satisfaction " through the sufferings which Christ endured before we were born is to be " the child of an assumed grace," is to possess a mere external and historical faith that leaves the dim, weak soul where it was before. All such " invented works " and " supposed schemes " are of Anti-Christ, they " avail nothing " whatever toward the real process of salvation.[2]

The gravamen of his charge is not that the " opinions " are false, or that the " history " is unimportant, but that " opinions " and " history " are taken as substitutes for religion itself, which is and must always be an actual inward process constructing a new and victorious life in the person himself. " All fictions, I say, and devices which men contrive to come to God by are lost labour and vain endeavour *without a new mind*. Verbal forgiveness and outward imputation of righteousness are false and vain comforts—soft cushions for the evil soul—without the creation of a will wholly new, which loveth and willeth evil no more." [3] The whole problem, then, is the problem of the formation of a new vision, a new desire, a new will, and Boehme finds the solution of this deepest human problem in Christ. Christ is the Light-revelation of God—the shining forth of the Light and Love nature of the Eternal God. It must not be supposed for a moment that once—before satisfaction was made to Him —God was an angry God who had to be " reconciled " by a transaction, or that there was *a time in history* when God began to reveal His Heart in a Christ-revelation, or

---

[1] *Regeneration*, 6.   [2] For a sample passage see *Sig. re.* xv. 22-47.
[3] *True Resignation*, 30-41.   Freely rendered.

that when Christ became man, Deity divided itself into sundered Persons.[1] " No. You ought not to have such thoughts," Boehme says. The Heart and Light and Love of God are from eternity. Christ has never sundered or broken Himself away from God ; they are not two but forever One. All the Light and Love and Joy of God have blossomed into the Christ-manifestation and become revealed in Him. Like everything else in the universe, Christ is both outward and inward. He belongs in the eternal inward world and He also has had His temporal manifestation in the visible world. The Heart of God became a human soul, brought the fulness of the Deity into humanity, and slew the spirit of the world.[2] The inward penetrated the outward and illuminated it with Light.[3] Christ entered into humanity and tinctured it with Deity.[4] In Him the Heart of God became man, and in the power of the heavenly Light He wrestled with our wild human nature and conquered it.[5] Eternity and time are united in Him.[6] He is the wedding chamber of God and man.[7] He is God and man in one undivided Person.[8] He is actual God ; He is essential man—the God-man, the man-God, in whom the arms of everlasting Love are outstretched and through whom humanity is brought into the power of the Eternal God.[9] It was in this " dear Emmanuel," as he often calls Christ, that " Love became man and put on our human flesh and our human soul," [10] and the full power of Eternal Love stood revealed in time, for " One who is Love itself was born of our own very birth." [11] The Cross was not a transaction. It was the culmination of this mighty Love, for " here on the cross hung God and man "—God's Love springing forth in a soul strong enough to show it in its full scope.[12]

But let no person think that he can " cover himself with the purple mantle of Christ's sufferings and death,"

---

[1] *The Three Princ.* xxxiii. 8-17.　　[2] *Ibid.* xix. 6.
[3] *Sig. re.* ix. 67.　　[4] *Ibid.* xi. 88.
[5] *Aurora*, Preface, 27.　　[6] *Sig. re.* xi. 80.
[7] Prayer in *True Repentance.*　　[8] *Three Princ.* xxii. 81.
[9] *Myst. mag.* lxx. 7-10 ; *Three Princ.* xviii. 80 ; and *Supersensual Life*, 27.
[10] *Three Princ.* xxv. 43.　　[11] *Ibid.* xxv. 6.
[12] Read *Ibid.* xxv. 7-41.

and so win his salvation : " Thou thyself," he says,
" must go through Christ's whole journey, and enter
wholly into His process." [1]   " We become children of
God in Christ," he wrote in one of his Epistles, " not by
an outward, adventitious show of appropriating Grace,
not through some merit of Grace appropriated from
without, or received in an historical apprehension of
being justified by another, but through an inward,
resident Grace, which regenerates us into childlikeness,
so that Christ the conqueror of death arises in us and
becomes a dominating operation in us." [2]   This is the
heart of his entire message.   Every step must be experimental.   Salvation is an inward process, and Christ is
efficacious and effective because *He lives and operates
in us.*   " The suffering and death of Christ," he says,
" avail only for those who die to their own will in and
with Christ, and are buried with Him to a new will and
obedience, and hate sin ; who put on Christ in His
suffering, reproach, and persecution, take His cross upon
them and follow Him under His red banner ; to those
who put on Christ in His process and now become in the
inward spiritual man Christ's members and the Temple
of God who dwells in us.   No one has a right to comfort
himself with Christ's merits unless he desires wholly to
put on Christ in himself.   He is not a Christian until he
has put Him on by true repentance and conversion to
Him with absolute resignation and self-denial, so that
Christ espouseth and betrotheth Himself with him. . . .
For a Christian must be born of Christ and must die to
the will of Adam.   He must have Christ in him and be a
member of His Life according to the spiritual man." [3]

Faith, which is always the key-word in any person's
interpretation of Christianity, is for Boehme a dynamic
process of appropriating Christ, and of re-living Him.
" Faith," he writes in his treatise on *The Incarnation,*

---

[1] *True Repentance.*
[2] *First Epistle,* 6.   Hegel well says of Boehme : " What marks him out and
makes him noteworthy is the Protestant principle of placing the intellectual
world within one's own mind and heart, and of experiencing and knowing and
feeling in one's own self-consciousness all that was formerly conceived as a Beyond."—*History of Philos.* iii. p. 191.   [3] *Tenth Epistle,* 16-19.

" is not historical knowledge for a man to make articles of it and to depend on them, but faith is one spirit with God, it is the activity of God ; it is free, but only for the right and for pure Love, in which it draws the breath of its power and strength. It is, finally, itself the substance."[1] Faith is, thus, not knowledge, it is not believing facts of history, it is not accepting metaphysical dogma. It is, as he is never weary of saying, " strong earnestness of spirit," the earnest will to live in the inward and eternal, passionate hunger and thirst for God, and finally the *act* of receiving Christ into the soul as a present power and spirit to live by. " I must die," he wrote, " with my outward man [the man of self-centred will] in Christ's death and arise and live anew in Him. Therefore I live now by the will of faith in the spirit of Christ and receive Christ with His humanity into my will. He makes through me a manifestation of the spiritual world and introduces the true Love-sound into the harp-strings of my life. He became that which I am, and now He has made me that which He is ! "[2]

Another word for this efficacious and dynamic Faith is " Birth " or " innermost Birth," by which Boehme means the act of discovering the Gate to the Heart and Love and Light of God, and of entering it. " The Son of God, the Eternal Word of the Father, the Glance and Brightness and Power of Eternal Light must become man and *be born in you* ; otherwise you are in the dark stable and go about groping."[3] " If thou art born of God, then within the circle of thy own life is the whole undivided Heart of God."[4] It is a transforming event by which one swings over from life in the outer to life in the inner world, from life in the dark world to life in the light world, and is born into the kingdom, or principle, which Christ revealed in His triumphant spiritual Life. The human spirit, by this innermost Birth, reaches the principle of Life by which Christ lived, and the gate into heaven is opened and paradise is in the soul. In a

[1] *Incarnation*, part iii. chap. i. 5-15.　　[2] *Sig. re.* xii. 10-13.
[3] *The Threefold Life*, iii. 31.　　[4] *Ibid.* vi. 71.

beautiful passage he says : " This birth must be wrought
within you.   The Heart, or the Son of God must arise in
the birth of your life, and then you are in Christ and He
is in you, and all that He and the Father have is yours ;
and as the Son is one with the Father, so also the new
man is one with the Father and with the Son, one virtue,
one power, one light, one life, one eternal paradise, one
enduring substance, one Father, Son, and Holy Ghost,
and thou His child ! " [1]   God is no longer conceived as
far away.   He is now with His Love and Light as near
as the soul is to itself, and the joy of being born in Christ
is like the joy of parents when a little child is born to
them.[2]   God's will now becomes the man's will, he turns
back into the unity from which he broke away, he sees
now in one moment what all the doctors in the schools,
on the mere level of reason, have never seen, and his
inward eye is so opened that he knows God as soon as his
eye turns toward Him.[3]

This Faith-process, or innermost life-birth, is not the
act of a moment that is over and done with.   It means
the progressive formation of a new man within the man,
so that the real Christian becomes a living branch in a
mighty Christ-Tree.   Just as Adam was the trunk of a
great race-tree of fallen humanity, Christ is to be the
Eternal Life-Tree of the universe in whom all the new-
born souls of men shall live as springing, flowering branches
or twigs :   God created only one Man ; all other men are
twigs of the One Stem.[4]   " In Christ," he says, " we are
all only one, as a tree in many boughs and branches,"
and, with a return to autobiography, Boehme adds, " His
Life has been brought into mine, so that I am atoned
with Him in His Love.   The will of Christ has entered
into humanity again in me, and now my will in me enters
into His humanity.[5]   He writes to one of his Silesian
friends : " You are a growing branch in the Life-Tree of
God in Christ, in whom all the children of God are also
branches," and he adds that there is " no other faith

---

[1] *The Three Princ.* iv. 9.   [2] *Aurora*, xix. 52-66.   [3] *Myst. mag.* lxxii. 7-10.
[4] *Ibid.* xxiv. 17.   [5] *Sig. re.* ix. 63.

which saves except Christ in us," the Life of our lives.[1]
Sometimes he calls this triumphant experience the birth
of a new branch in Christ's Life-Tree, sometimes the
birth of the Lily in Christ's garden of flowers, sometimes
it is the birth of the immortal seed. Sometimes it is
uniting in life and spirit with Him who is " the Treader on
the Serpent," sometimes it is finding the noble Virgin,
sometimes it is discovering the Philosopher's Stone,
sometimes it is winning the precious Diadem, sometimes
it is possessing the key which unlocks the Door, sometimes
it is arriving at the Sabbath Quiet of the soul. These
are only a variety of ways, many of them forgotten
inheritances from alchemy and astrology, of saying that
the soul finds its goal in an experience which binds it
into one common corporate life with Christ and so into
an elemental Love-Unity with God : whoever is born of
Christ liveth and walketh in Him, puts Him on in His
suffering, death, and resurrection, becomes a member of
Christ's body, is " tinctured " with His spirit, and has
his own human life rooted in the Love of God.[2] Here,
then, in the creation and formation of this organic Life-
Tree the universe attains its ultimate goal. It is wholly
an achievement of free will, of holy choice. The dark
Principle is not annihilated, is not suppressed, but the
Heart of God moves ever on in a steadily growing triumph,
binding soul after soul into the divine Igdrasil Tree of the
Light Universe, in a unity that is not now the unity of
negation and undifferentiation—an Abyss that swallows
up all that is in it,—but a unity of many wills united in
a spirit of concord and love, many persons formed by
holy desire into one unbroken symphony as harps of God.

With the change of *centre* in the inner man corresponds
also the outer life of word and deed, for the outer, here as
everywhere, is only the " signature " of an inner which
fits it : " A man must show the root of the tree out of
which spirit and flesh have their origin." [3] When the
will becomes new-born and the soul unites itself as a twig

---

[1] *Seventh Epistle*, 1.   [2] *Ibid.*, 6 and 12.
[3] *Apology to Stiefel*, 23.

in Christ's Life-Tree, then it ceases to love sin and will it.
When God brings His will into birth in us, He gives us
virtue and power to will what He wills, and to leave our
sins behind.[1]   The attitude of hate, the spirit of war are
marks of the old unchanged nature, and are heathenish
and not Christian.   When Christ is formed in the inner
ground of the soul, a man leaves the sword in the sheath
and lives in the virtue and power of peace and love. " What
will Christ say," he asks the ministers of the Church
of his day, " when He sees your apostolic hearts covered
with armor ?   When He gave you the sword of the
Spirit, did He command you to fight and make war, or
to instigate kings and princes to put on the sword and
kill ? " [2]

Like the prophets of Israel, he feels intensely the
sufferings of the poor and the oppressed, and he breaks
out frequently into a biting satire on a kind of Christianity
which not only neglects the true *cure* of soul and body,
but " consumes the sweat and blood of the needy," and
feeds upon " the sighs and groans and tears of the poor." [3]
The true idea of a *real* Christianity is " fraternity in the
Life of Christ "—" thy brother's soul," he says, " is a
fellow-member with thy soul," [4] and he insists, as though
it were the mighty burden of his spirit, that all possessions,
goods, and talents shall contribute to the common life of
humanity and to the benefit of the social group.[5]   It is
much better for parents to labour to form good souls in
their children than to strive to gather and to leave behind
for them great riches and abundance of goods ! [6]   Self-
desire is a ground not only of personal disquiet but also
of social disturbance, and Boehme feels that the way to
spread peace and joy through the world is to cultivate
the Love-spirit of Christ and to practice it in fellowship
with men.

Like his German predecessor, Sebastian Franck, he is

---

[1] *True Resignation*, iii. 21.   [2] *Myst. mag.* lxii. 25.
[3] *The Three Principles*, xix. 47 ; xxi. 32. ; *Sig. re.* viii. 27.
[4] *Forty Questions*, xii. 39.
[5] For an example of it, see *Myst. mag.* lxxiv. 46.
[6] *Forty Questions*, x. 9.

primarily concerned with the invisible Church, and he holds lightly to the empirical Church as he knows it. The Church to which his spirit is dedicated is the organic Life-Tree of which Christ is the living Stem. The holy Zion is not from without, he says, it is built up of those who are joined to Christ and who all live together in one city which is Christ in us.[1] A Christian in the life belongs to no sect, he ceases to wrangle over opinions and words, he dwells in the midst of sects and Babel-churches, but he keeps above the controversies and contentions, and " puts his knowing and willing into the Life of Christ," and works quietly on toward the formation and triumph of the one true Christian Church,[2] which will be, when its glory is complete, the visible expression of the Divine Life-Tree.

He dislikes, as much as did the English Quaker, George Fox, the custom of calling " stone houses " churches, and he will not admit that a building is anything but a building : " Stone houses, called churches, have no greater holiness than other houses, for they are built of stone and other such material, as other houses are, and God is no more powerful in them than He is in other houses, but the Church [i.e. the Congregation] which meets there, if the members of it bind themselves by prayer into one body in Christ, is a holy Temple of Jesus Christ." [3]

His attitude toward outward sacraments consistently fits in with all his central teachings. The outward, for Boehme, is never unimportant. It is always significant and can always be used as a parable or symbol of something inner and eternal. But the outward is at best only temporal, only symbolic, and it becomes a hindrance if it is taken for the real substance of which it is only the outward " signature " : " The form shall be destroyed and shall cease with time, but the spirit remains forever." [4] The sacraments, he declares, do not take away sin, for men go to church all their lives and receive the sacraments

---

[1] *Fourth Epistle*, 32, and *True Repentance*.
[2] *Regeneration*, 161-162.
[3] *Myst. mag.* lxiii. 47.   This theme constantly reappears.
[4] *Sig. re.* xv. 37.

and remain as wicked and beastly as ever—while a holy
man always has a Church within himself and an inward
ministry.[1] Blessedness, therefore, lies not in the outward, but in the life and power of the inward spirit, and
it is only a Babel-Church that claims the right to cast
out those who have the real substance and neglect only
the outward form.[2] In his *Treatise on the Holy Supper*,
he wrote : " It is not enough for a man to hear sermons
preached, and to be baptised in the name of Christ, and
to go to the Supper. This maketh no Christian. For
that, there must be *earnestness*. No person is a Christian
unless Christ live and work in him." [3]

The pith and heart of Christianity, the consummate
goal of the way of Salvation, for Boehme is, as we have
seen, not " history " and not any kind of outward " form "
or " letter "—*buchstäbliches Wort*,—it is an experience
in which the soul finds itself " at the top of Jacob's
ladder," and feels its life in God and God's Life in it in
an ineffable Love-union. He has himself given a very
simple and penetrating account of this type of experience
drawn from what he calls his own book of life : " Finding
within myself a powerful *contrarium*, namely, the desires
that belong to flesh and blood, I began to fight a hard
battle against my corrupted nature, and with the aid of
God I made up my mind to overcome the inherited evil
will, to break it, and to enter wholly into the Love of
God. . . . This, however, was not possible for me to
accomplish, but I stood firmly by my *earnest resolution*,
and fought a hard battle with myself. Now while I was
wrestling and battling, being aided by God, a wonderful
light arose within my soul. It was a light entirely foreign
to my unruly nature, but in it I recognized the true
nature of God and man, and the relation existing between
them, a thing which heretofore I had never understood." [4]
In one of his other autobiographical passages, he says
that after much earnest seeking and desire and many a
hard repulse, " the Gate was opened ! " These are char-

[1] *Resignation*, vi. 134-151.
[2] *Forty Questions*, xiv. 17-19.   [3] *Op. cit.* iv. 16.
[4] Von Hartmann's *Life and Doctrines of Jacob Boehme*, p. 50.

acteristic accounts of a profound mystical experience. There had been long stress and inward battle, the tension of a divided self, and then a great ground swell of earnest will—a resolve, he says, to put my life in hazard rather than give over, when " a wonderful light arose within the soul " and " the Gate was opened." And " when this mighty light fell upon me, I saw," he says, in still another description, " in an effectual peculiar manner, and I knew in the spirit." [1]

The central aspect of his experience was plainly an overmastering *conviction* of contact with, an immersion into, a deeper world of spirit and of inner unity of life and spirit with this deeper world. His own personal spirit united, as he once put it, " with the innermost Birth in God and stood in the Light." [2] He discovered that " God goes clean another way to work " than by the way of reasoning or of sense experience [3]—instead of waiting for man to climb up to Him, He climbs up into man's soul. [4] By a new and inner way, to change the figure, the tides of the shoreless Divine Sea break in upon the life of a man and bathe his entire being. It seems to Boehme, at one time, like the rising of a mid-noon Sun, with illuminating rays, and he describes the experience in terms of Light and enlarged Vision, or, again, it appears like the bursting open of a secret door into a world of new dimensions, and he calls it the opening of the Gate, or now again he feels as though the elemental creative power of God had burst into operation within him and that a mighty birth-process had lifted him to a new kingdom, or to a new order of nature, or, finally, hushed and soothed and healed as though he had suddenly found the breast of an infinite Mother, he describes his state as " the innermost Quiet "—the return to " the soul's eternal native country and abiding Home." Descriptions here all fail and are only " stammering words of a child," as Boehme himself says. But, as a matter of fact, descriptions fail and fall short in the case of all genuine life-experiences,

---

[1] *Twenty-fifth Epistle*, 2.   [2] *Aurora*, xix. 95.
[3] *Twenty-sixth Epistle*, 7.   [4] *Aurora*, xviii. 9.

even those that are most universal and common to the
race.   How one feels when after nights of agony from
watching over a child that is hovering between life and
death, and seemingly certain to slip away from human
reach, the doctor says, " He has passed the crisis and the
danger is over ! " one cannot describe.   Whenever it is
a matter that concerns the inner *quick* of the soul, all
words are the stammerings of a child.

The true mystical experience is not primarily a know-
ledge-experience, it is not the apprehension of one more
describable fact to be added to our total stock of information—what Boehme so often calls " opinions " and
" history,"—it is a sudden plunge or immersion into the
stream of Life itself, it is an interior appreciation of the
higher meaning of life by the discovery of a way of entering the Life-process, or, better, of letting the Life-process
enter you, on a higher level than is usual.   Life always
advances by a kind of leap, an *élan*, which would not have
been predicted or anticipated, but which, now it is here
revealed in a being with a novel function and a higher
capacity of survival, will lift the whole scale of life henceforth to a new level.   So, in some way which must for
the present at least remain mysterious, the eternal Source
of Life, when it finds a human door ready for its entrance,
breaks in—or shall we say that the *earnest will* climbs up
and pushes open the door into new regions in this eternal
Life Source ?—and it seems then, as Boehme says, as
though " the true nature of God and man and the true
relation between God and man " had been found.   The
mystical experience is, thus, one way, perhaps the
highest we have yet discovered, of entering the Life-
process itself and of gaining an interior appreciation of
Reality by living in the central stream and flow of it,
so that the Spirit can " break through " and can " see
into the Depth of Deity."

Boehme appears to hold two inconsistent and seemingly contradictory views about the human attitude
which is the psychological pre-condition for this epoch-
making experience.   In his own autobiographical ac-

counts, he always refers to the part that *earnest resolution* has played in bringing success to his momentous quest. No great mystic since St. Augustine has made more of the will in spiritual matters than he does. We have seen how the doors to both world-kingdoms stand before the soul, and how " free-will," " earnest purpose," " decisive endeavour " settle for each soul which door shall open and which shall shut, and so determine its eternal destiny. " Election " is, for Boehme, a fiction of the false imagination, a " Babel-opinion," a perverse invention of " the Church of Cain." Christ never says " thou couldst not," but rather " thou wouldst not." [1]

Not only does he, in a general way, thus make the will the decisive element in human destiny, he also implies that the creative " flash " of spiritual insight, " the innermost birth " which brings the soul into living union with its source is due, on the human side, to " resolution," to " earnestness," to " valiant wrestling," to a brave venture of faith that risks everything. It requires "mighty endurance," " hard labour," " stoutness of spirit," and " a great storm, assault, and onset " to open the Gate. In a word, the key to any important spiritual experience is *intention*, inward pre-perception, that holds the mind intently focussed in expectation, without which the " flash " of spiritual vision is not likely to come.

But on the other hand Boehme is a powerful exponent of the idea that desire and will must utterly, absolutely die before God can come to birth in the soul—" Christ is born and lives in our Nothingness." [2] A man, he says, must die wholly to self-hood, forsake it and enter again into the original Nothing,—the eternal Unity in which nothing is willed in particular,—before God can have His way with him ; all sin arises from self-hood, from desire.[3] " How," asks a disciple in one of Boehme's imaginary dialogues, " shall I come to the hidden centre where God dwelleth and not man ? Tell me plainly, loving sir, how it is to be found and entered into ? "

---

[1] *Sig. re.* xvi. 38.   [2] *Ibid.* ix. 65.
[3] *Ibid.* xiii. 27 and xv. 9.

The Master : " There where the soul hath slain its own will and willeth no more anything of itself." . . .

The Disciple : " But how shall I comprehend it ? "

The Master : " If thou goest about to comprehend in thy own will, it flieth from thee, but if thou dost surrender thyself wholly, then thou art dead to thy own will, and Love will be the Life of thy nature." [1]   He seems to go as far in this direction toward the annihilation of desire, negation of the finite, and loss of self-hood as any of the pantheistic mystics.   This sample passage will indicate his teaching : " When thou art wholly gone forth from the creature and become nothing to all that is nature and creature, then thou art in that Eternal One which is God Himself, and then thou shalt experience the supreme virtue of Love." [2]

These two diverse statements are, however, not as inconsistent as they at first seem.   The *will,* the *intention* that is a psychological preparation for this mystical experience is a will washed and purged of selfish impulse and self-seeking aims.   It is an *intention* that cannot be described in terms of any finite " content."   It is the intense heave of the whole undivided being toward God with no reservation, no calculation of return profits, no thought even of isolated and independent personality. A true account of consciousness, preceding the moment of bursting through the Gate, might emphasize with equal accuracy either the " earnest resolution," " the storm and onset of will," or " the annihilation of particular desire," " the surrender of individualistic self-hood," " death to own will in the Life and Virtue of Love."

The effects of such an experience as that which came to Boehme, if we may take his case as typical, are (1) the birth of an inner conviction of God's immediate and environing Presence amounting to axiomatic certainty— faith through experience has become " the substance," and " is now one spirit with God " ; (2) The radiation of the whole being with " a joy like that which parents have at the birth of their first-born child "—the joy now of the

---

[1] *The Supersensual Life,* 29 and 30.   [2] *Ibid.* 27.

soul crying, " Abba " ; (3) A vastly heightened perception
of what is involved in the eternal nature of the religious
life and in the spiritual relation between the soul and
God, *i.e.* increased ability to see what promotes and
furthers the soul's health and development; (4) A unification, co-ordination, and centralizing of the inner
faculties, so that there is an increment of power revealed
in the entire personality; and (5) An increase of clarity
and a sharpening of focus in the perception of moral
distinctions together with a distinctly heightened moral
and social passion.

Boehme himself always believed, further, that his
entire system of ideas, his philosophy of the universe,
and his way of salvation were a " revelation " of the
Spirit to him,—in a word, that his wisdom was " theosophy," a God - communicated knowledge. I have no
desire to mark off dogmatically the scope and possible
limits of " revelation," nor is it necessary here to discuss
the abstract question whether " ideas " are ever " communicated " to a mind *ab extra*, and without the mediation
of subjective processes, or not. In the concrete case of
Jacob Boehme, I do not find any compelling evidence of
the unmediated communication of ideas. He was a man
of unusual native capacity, and, though untrained, his
mind possessed a high order of range and quality, and
swept, as he was, by a mighty transforming experience,
he *found himself* in novel fashion, and was the recipient
of inspirations, which fired and fused his soul, gave him
heightened insight into the significance of things old and
new, and often enabled him to build better than he knew.
He is, however, obviously using the stock of ideas which
his generation, and those early and late before it, had
made " part of the necessary air men breathed." His
terminology and symbolism were as old as mythology,
and were the warp and woof of the nature philosophies
and the alchemy of his day. His impressive and spiritual
interpretation of Christianity is always deep and vital,
and freighted with the weight of his own inward direct
appreciation of God's revelation of Himself in Christ,

but even here he is walking on a road which many brave
souls before him had helped to build, and we cannot with
truth say that he supplies us with a new gospel which
had been privately " communicated " to him. In fact,
the portions of his voluminous writings which bear the
mark of having been written as automatic script—by
" this hand," as he often says—are the chaotic and
confused portions, full of monotonous repetitions, of
undigested and indigestible phrases and the dreary
re-shufflings of sub-conscious wreckage. Boehme used
to say that " in the time of the lily " his writings would
be " much sought after." But I doubt if, even " in the
time of the lily," most persons will have the patience to
read this shoemaker - prophet's books in their present
form, that is, if " in the time of the lily " men still enjoy
and prize intelligence and lucidity ; but there already is
enough of " the lily-spirit " in the world to appreciate
and to give thanks for the experience, the flashes of
insight, the simple wisdom, the brave sincerity, the inner
certainty of the true World within the world we see, and
the spiritual message of " the way to the soul's native
Country," which he has given us.

CHAPTER XII

THE first appearance in English of any of the writings of Jacob Boehme was in 1645, when a tiny volume was issued with the title: *Two Theosophical Epistles, Englished.*

There had appeared a year earlier (1644) a seven-page biography of Boehme which was the first presentation of him to the English reader. This brief sketch contains the well-known incidents which became the stock material for the later accounts of his life.[1] It also contained the following quaint description of Boehme which was the model for all the portraits of the Teutonic philosopher in the English biographies of him: " The stature of his outward body was almost of no Personage ; his person was little and leane, with browes somewhat inbowed ; high Temples, somewhat hauk-nosed : His eyes were gray and somewhat heaven blew, and otherwise as the Windows in Solomon's Temple : He had a thin Beard ; a small low Voyce. His Speech was lovely. He was modest in his Behaviour, humble in his conversation and meeke in his heart. His spirit was highly enlightened by God, as is to be seen and discerned in the Divine Light out of his writings."

The slender volume of *Theosophical Epistles* was followed by another little book issued a year later (1646),

---

[1] " The Life of one Jacob Boehmen, who although he was a meane man, yet wrote the most wonderful deepe knowledge in Naturall and Divine Things, that any hath been known to doe since the Apostles' Times, and yet never read them or learned them from any other man, as may be seene in that which followeth."
—London, 1644, printed by L. N. for Richard Whitaker.

consisting of a Discourse delivered in Latin in the Schools at Cambridge by Charles Hotham, Rector of Wigan. This Discourse was translated into English by the author's brother, Justice Durant Hotham, and was published under the title : *Introduction to Teutonic Philosophy, or A Determination concerning the Original of the Soul,* Englished by D. F. [Durant Frater], 1650. This interesting little volume, full of quaint phrase and strange speculation, reflects throughout its pages the profound influence of Boehme on these two brothers. The Preface to the Englished edition written by Justice Hotham not only shows specific marks of Boehme's influence upon a high-minded and scholarly man, but it also reveals in an impressive way a type of thought that was very prevalent in England at this period of commotion. " There are," Justice Hotham says, " two islands of exceeding danger, yet built upon and inhabited and defended as part of the main continent of Truth. The first is called : ' I believe as the Church believeth.' Happy man whom so easie labour hath set on the shore of wisdom ! The other island is called : ' whatsoever the Church believes that will I not believe.' " Both these " islands " seem to him " exceeding dangerous." To adopt as truth what the Church has believed, solely because the Church has believed it, to forego the personal quest and to arrive at " the shores of wisdom " without the venturous voyage, is " too easie labour " for the soul. But, nevertheless, he feels that the opposite danger—the danger of negating a truth merely because the Church affirms it—is even more serious. It is wise to maintain an attitude of " much reverence " toward the " unanimous consent of good and pious men in sacred matters." He suggests that the way of wisdom consists in making the " I believe " of the Church " neither a fetter nor a scandel." " May I be," he says, " in the bed-route of those Seekers that, distrusting the known and experienced deceits of their own Reason, walk unfettered in the quest of truth, . . . not hunting those poor soules with Dogge and speare whose dimme sight hath led them into desert and unbeated paths." This was in all probability the Justice Hotham of whom George Fox wrote : " He was a pretty tender man yt had had some experiences of God's workeinge in his hearte : & after yt I had some discourse with him off ye things of God hee tooke mee Into his Closett & saide *hee had knowne yt principle* [of the Light] *this 10 yeere* : & hee was glad yt ye Lorde did now publish it abroade to ye people." [1]

Like his Teutonic master, Justice Hotham distrusts Reason and Sense as spiritual guides. They are at best, he says, " but guides of the night, dim lights set up, far distant from Truth's stately mansion, to lead poor groping souls in this world's affairs." The surer Guide is within the soul itself, for the soul of man, he insists, has " a noble descent from eternal essences " and " our nobel Genealogy should mind us of our Father's House and make us weary of tutelage under hairy Faunes and cloven-footed Satyres." [2] He shows that he has lost all interest in theological speculations that assume a God remote in time and space, a God who once created a world and left it to go to ruin. He reminds his readers that the God in whom he believes is " yet alive and still speaks." [3] In the light of this Preface, in which he declares that he has " suckt in truth from divinest philosophy " from his childhood, it is not strange that he welcomed Fox, when the latter appeared in Yorkshire in 1651, proclaiming an inward Light and a present God near at hand, nor is it surprising that Hotham said to the young prophet of the inward Guide : " If God had not raised uppe this principle of light and life, ye nation had beene overspread with rantism . . . but this principle of truth overthrew ye roote & grounde of there [*i.e.* the Ranters'] principle." [4]

The enthusiasm of Justice Hotham for his Teutonic master gets fervid expression at the end of his Preface as follows : " Whatever the thrice great Hermes [Hermes Trismegistus] delivered as oracles from his prophetical tripos, or Pythagoras spake by authority or

---

[1] *Journal of George Fox* (Cambridge edition, 1911), i. p. 18.
[2] Preface, A. 4.   [3] *Ibid.*   [4] *Journ.* i. p. 29.

Socrates debated or Aristotle affirmed ; yea, whatever divine Plato prophesied or Plotinus proved : this and all this, or a far higher and profounder philosophy is (I think) contained in the Teutonick's writings. And if there be any friendly medium which can possibly reconcile these ancient differences between the nobler wisdom which hath fixt her Palace in Holy Writ and her stubborn handmaid, Naturall Reason : this happy marriage of the Spirit and Soul, this wonderful consent of discords in one harmony, we owe in great measure to Teutonicus his skill ! "

The central problem of the *Discourse*, written by the brother, Charles Hotham, is the origin of the soul.   After the manner of his German teacher, the English disciple finds the origin of man's soul in " the bottomless, im- measurable Abyss of the Godhead," in " the great deep of the perpetually eternal God." Man is an epitome of the universe. He unites in himself all the contrary principles of the worlds visible and invisible, he is a unity of body and soul, a centre of light and darkness, and in him is a " supreme region," or " Divine Principle," " by the mediation of which man has direct fellowship with God." In man, who thus epitomizes all the spheres and principles of the universe, " God, as in a glasse, hath a lively and delightful prospect of His own lovely visage and incomprehensible Beauty." Finally, again, the disciple reflects the constant teaching of Boehme that everything in the visible world is a symbol of a funda- mental and eternal World.

Durant Hotham showed the full measure of his devotion to his German master in the *Life of Jacob Behmen* which he wrote in 1653.[1] It is, however, much more important for the insight which it gives of the inner life of the Yorkshire Justice than for any biographical information it furnishes of Boehme himself. Hotham thinks that in Boehme he has discovered a new type of Christian Saint— " one who led a saint-like life in much sweet communion

---

[1] *The Life of Jacob Behmen*, written by Durant Hotham, Esquire, November 7, 1653. Printed for H. Blunden, and sold at the Castle in Corn Hill, 1654.

with God," while he declares that many of those who
" get admission into the Calendar by the synodical
jurisdiction of those who claim also to hold the bunch of
keys to the bigger Heaven " are hardly ripe for canoniza-
tion—" As for many who in these last ages have termed
themselves saints—what shift God may make of them in
heaven, I know not (He can do much)—but if I may
speak unfeignedly, they are so unmortified and untrue
of word and deed that they are found untoward members
for a true Commonwealth and civil Society here on
Earth." [1]

The type of saint the Justice admires is one who
refuses utterly to choose the path of least resistance, one
who will not be " a messenger of eternal happiness at a
cheap rate," but rather one who comes to challenge the
easy world, to fight evil customs and entrenched systems
and to win " the Land which the Devil holds in possession " ; and, with the name of Jacob Boehme, he thinks
he can " begin a new roll of Civil Saints," hoping, he
says, that in these last generations " much company "
may be added to the bead roll thus happily started.

Two points stand out clearly as central ideas of Justice
Hotham's Christianity. The first one is that religion
is an inward affair. " God," he declares, " hath sent this
last Generation a plain, uncouth Message, bidding man
to fight, telling him that he shall have a Heaven, a Joy,
a Paradise, a Land, a Territory, a Kingship—but that
all this is in himself, the Land to be won is himself." [2]
The second one is that religion is a progressive movement,
an unfolding revelation of life. " What a height of
Presumption is it," he says, " to believe that the Wisdom
and fullness of God can ever be pent up in a Synodical
Canon ?   How overweening are we to limit the successive
manifestations of God to a present rule and light, persecuting all that comes not forth in its height and breadth ! "
It is through this " unnatural desire " to keep Christians
in " a perpetual infancy " that " our dry nurses " in the
Church have " brought us to such a dwarfish stature,"

---

[1] *Life of Jacob Behmen*, B. 2.   [2] *Op. cit.* B. 2.

and he prays that the merciful God may teach at least one nation a better way than that of " muzzling " the bringer of fresh light.

Much more important, however, for the dissemination of Boehme's ideas in England was the patient and faithful work of John Sparrow who, in collaboration with his kinsman, John Ellistone, translated into English the entire body of Boehme's writings, between the years 1647 and 1661.[1] Sparrow was born at Stambourne in Essex in 1615. He was admitted to the Inner Court in 1633 and subsequently called to the Bar. He was probably the author of a widely-read book, published in 1649, under the title of *Mercurius Teutonicus*, consisting of a series of " propheticall passages " from Boehme.[2] His outer life was uneventful ; his inner life is revealed in his Introductions to the Boehme Translations. He begins his long series of Translations with the testimony that the writings of this author have " so very much satisfied " his own soul that he wants others to be partakers of the same source of light, though he warns his readers that their own souls must come by experience into the condition Boehme himself was in before they can fully understand him.[3]   He is profoundly impressed,

[1] The writings were translated in the following order: In 1647, *Forty Questions* by Sparrow ; *The Clavis*, by Sparrow. In 1648, *The Three Principles*, by Sparrow ; *The Way to Christ* (including the Treatises, *On True Repentance ; On True Resignation ; On Regeneration ; The Supersensual Life ;* and *On Illumination*), by Sparrow. In 1649, *Of the Last Times*, by Sparrow ; *Epistles of Jacob Behmen*, by Ellistone. In 1650, *The Three-fold Life*, by Sparrow. In 1651, *De signatura rerum*, by Ellistone. In 1652, *Christ's Testaments*—Baptism and Supper,—by Sparrow. In 1654, *The Mysterium magnum*, by Ellistone and Sparrow ; *A Table of the Divine Manifestation*, by H. Blunden and Sparrow ; *A Table of the Three Principles*, H. Blunden and Sparrow ; *An Epitome of the Three Principles*, by Sparrow. In 1655, *On Predestination*, by Sparrow ; *A Short Compendium on Repentance*, by Sparrow. In 1656, *The Aurora*, by Sparrow. In 1659, The Treatise on the *Incarnation*, by Sparrow. In 1661, *The Great Six Points ; The Earthly and Heavenly Mystery ; The Four Complexions ; Two Apologies to Tylcken ; Considerations concerning Stiefel's Threefold State of Man ; An Apology concerning Perfection ; On Divine Contemplation ; An Apology for the Books on True Repentance and True Resignation ; 177 Theosophic Questions ; The Holy Week ; 25 Epistles*, by Sparrow.

[2] Sparrow refers to this book in his Introduction to *The Three Principles* as follows : " For a taste of the Spirit of prophecy which the author [Boehme] had, there is a little treatise of some prophecies concerning these latter times, collected out of his writings by a lover of the Teutonic philosophy and entitled *Mercurius Teutonicus*."

[3] Introd. to *Forty Questions*.

as his great contemporary, Milton, was, with the strange birth of new sects " now sprung up in England," but he hopes that " goodness will get the upper hand and that the fruits of the spirit will prevail," and his mind " is led to think " that through Boehme's message, which has been very beneficial in other nations, " our troubled, doubting souls in England may receive much Comfort, leading to that inward Peace which passeth all understanding, and that all disturbing sects and heresies . . . will be made to vanish and cease." [1]

Sparrow was deeply impressed with two of Boehme's central ideas, and he gives expression to them, in his own quaint and peculiar way, in almost every one of his Introductions—(1) the idea that the visible is a parable of the Invisible, and (2) the idea that God manifests Himself within men. In the very first of the Introductions both of these ideas appear : " This outward world," he says, " is the best outward looking-glasse to see whatever hath been, is, or shall be in Eternity, and our own minds are the best inward looking-glasse to see Eternity exactly in " ; [2] and he expresses the belief that any one who learns to read all the work of God in the world without, and in the mind of man within, will learn to know Him truly, will see Eternity manifested in time, will discover that the mind of man is a centre of all mysteries, and that heaven and hell are potentially in us, and he will be convinced that God is in all things and all things are in God ; that we live in Him and that He lives in us.[3]

This second idea—that God can be found in the depth of man's soul—is strongly emphasized in Sparrow's next Introduction, written in 1648—" *The Ground of what hath ever been lieth in man.*" [4]   All that is in the Scriptures has come out of man's experience and therefore can now be grasped by us. All that was in Adam lies in the ground and depth of any man. When the Apostle John wrote that there is an unction which teacheth all things and leadeth into all truth, he did not confine this possibility

---

[1] Introd. to *Forty Questions.*   [2] *Ibid.*
[3] *Ibid.*   [4] Introd. to *The Three Princ.*

to apostles, but intended to include all men in the class
of those who may be anointed, and all who know " what
is in man " realize that it is possible to attain to this
inward and apostolic guidance.[1]   In a passage of great
boldness Sparrow goes in his venturous faith in the inner
Spirit as far as the young Leicestershire preacher did who
was starting out, the very year this Introduction was
written, to proclaim the message of the inward Light.
" The ground," he says, " of all that was in Adam is in
us ; for whatever Ground lay in God, the same lieth in
Christ and through Him it lieth in us, for He is in us all.
And he that knoweth God in himself . . . may well be
able to speak the word of God infallibly as the holy men
that penned the Scriptures.   And he that can understand
these things in himself may well know who speaketh by
the Spirit of God and who speaketh his own fancies and
delusions." [2]

In the Introduction to the *Mysterium magnum*,
Sparrow returns to this idea of inward illumination,
though he balances it better than he did in the former
Introduction, with his estimation of " the antient Holy
Scriptures," and he does not again suggest that present-
day men speak " infallibly."   He thinks that the same
God who so eminently taught Moses by His Spirit that
he could describe the processes of creation, must have
also prepared the people by the instruction of the same
Spirit, so that they could understand what was written,
and so that the Spirit in one man could verify itself in
the experience of many men.   He declares that when the
Scriptures instruct and perfect the man of God, they are
effective, " not as a meer relation of things done," but
as the medium of the living Word which reaches the
inward Man, the hidden Man of the heart, the Christ in
us, so that we pass beyond " the history of Christ "
and rise to " the experience that Christ is born within
us." [3]

No other book, he says, but the Scriptures, teaches

---

[1] Introd. to *The Three Princ.*   [2] *Ibid.*
[3] " To the Reader " in *Myst. mag.*

man " with assured knowledge of all the things which concern the soule, the eternal part of man," for other writers have written from the observation of their outward senses, but these writers had " inward senses—their eyes saw, their ears heard, their hands handled the Word of Life." And yet for those in these days who can " look through the vayle or shell within which the Eternal Spirit works its Wonders," the visible things of the world prove to be " a glasse wherein the similitude of spirituall things are represented " and " the Minde of man is a most clear and undeceiving glasse wherein we may perceive the motions and activities of that Work-Master, the Spirit who hath created everything in the world." [1] In the most satisfactory of all his Introductions, the one to the *Aurora* in 1656, he undertakes to show that " the Light within " which has now arisen in England is not a substitute for the Christ of history. On the contrary, he insists that the Christ within and the Christ of history is one and the same Person who is not divided. He was once manifested in the likeness of sinful flesh, suffering, dying, rising, ascending in glory, and now, in an inward and spiritual manner, He is actually present within men so that they may become conformable in soul and spirit to Him and share in His life, sufferings, death, resurrection and glory, or they may, by their own choice, crucify Him afresh within themselves.[2] The Word of Life calls loudly within every man, urging the soul to forsake that which it perceives to be evil and to embrace that which it perceives to be good and holy and divine. This, he says, is the Eternal Gospel, and it brings to all men everywhere the good news that we live and move and have our being in God, and that the soul that gropes in sincerity after God will find Him, for He is very nigh, even in the heart of the seeker.[3] He deals in an interesting way with the important contemporary problem—raised by the prevalence of the emphasis on an inward Divine Presence— whether human Perfection is possible in this life. His

---

[1] " To the Reader " in *Myst. mag.*   [2] Preface to the Reader in *Aurora*.
[3] Preface for the *Aurora*.

conclusion is that the tendency to sin remains so long as
" the mortal body " lasts. No person will ever reach a
stage of earthly life in which the spur of the flesh is
eradicated, and so no person can be infallibly certain
that he is beyond sin, but when Christ is inwardly united
to the soul and His Spirit dwells in us and reigns in us
and we are risen in soul, spirit, and mind with Him, then
we live no longer after the flesh, or according to its thrust
and push, but share His life and partake of the conquering
power of His Spirit ; and thus, though " sown in imperfection we are raised in perfection." [1] The important
matter, however, is not that one call himself a " Per-
fectist," but that he actually live " in this earthly
pilgrimage and in this vale of sinfull flesh " in the power
of Eternity and by the Light of Christ, whose fulness
may be revealed in himself.[2]

John Ellistone, Sparrow's kinsman and able helper in
the work of bringing Boehme into English thought, holds
the same fundamental ideas as his co-labourer, though he
has his own peculiar style and his own unique way of
uttering himself. The stress of his emphasis is always
on first-hand experience—what he calls " an effectual,
living, essential knowledge and real spiritual being of it
in one's own soul " ;[3] and the brunt of his attack is

[1] Preface for the *Aurora*.

[2] A contemporary of Sparrow, probably Samuel Pordage, wrote an
Encomium on Sparrow in the Introduction to a long Behmenite Poem called
Mundorum explicatio (London, 1661). The passage is as follows :

> " And learned Sparrow we thy praises too
> Will Sing ; rewards too small for what is due,
> The Gifts of Glory and of Praise we owe :
> The English Behmen doth Thy Trophies show.
> Whilst Englishmen that great saint's praise declare,
> Thy Name shall join'd with his receive a share.
> The Time shall come when his great Name shall rise,
> Thy Glory also shall ascend the skies.
> Thou mad'st him English speak, or else what Good
> Had his works done us if not understood ?
> To Germany they beneficial prove
> Alone ; till we enjoyed them by thy Love.
> Their German Robes thou took'st from them, that we
> Their Beauties might in English Garments see.
> Thus has thy Love a vast rich Treasure showen,
> And made what was exotic now our own."

[3] Preface to Boehme's *Epistles* (1649).

always against a religion of " notions "—what he calls
" verball, high-flowne, contrived knowledge and vapouring
Notions," constructed from " the mental idolls of approved
masters." [1]   Religion, he maintains, can no more consist
of " the letter " or of " a talkative historicall account "
than music can consist of a row of written notes.   These
things are only signs for the direction of the skilful
musician who must himself *make* the sounds on his instrument before there is any music.   So, too, if there is to be
any real religion in the world, we Christians must do more
than read and approve " the deciphered writings of
illuminated men," we must *act* by the same Spirit that
inspired those men, we must be " practitioners of the
Divine Light," we must give " living expression to Divine
love and righteousness," we must " practice the way of
regeneration in the Spirit of Christ and *divinitize our
knowledge into an effectual working love and attaine the
experimental and essential reality of it in our owne soules !* " [2]
The way out of " the tedious Maze and wearisome
laborinth of discussions and opinions concerning God,
Christ, Faith, Election, the Ordinances and the Way of
Worship " is " to know the Word of Life, Light and
Love experimentally," to have " the fire of His love so
enkindled in our own hearts that it may breake forth in
our practice and conversation to the destroying of all
Thornes and tearing Bryars of vaine contentions ! " [3]

Like his kinsman, he has endless faith in the possibility
of man ; he thinks that the entire Scripture directs us to
the Word within us, and that the Book of all mysteries
is within ourselves.   " In our owne Book," he says,
" which is the Image of God in us, Time and Eternity
and all Mysteries are couched and contained, and they
may be read in our owne soules by the illumination of the
Divine Spirit.   Our Minde is a true mysticall Mirror
and Looking-glasse of Divine and Naturall Mysteries,
and we shall receive more real knowledge from one
effectuall innate essentiall beame or ray of Light arising
from the New Birth within us than in reading many

[1] Preface to Boehme's *Epistles*.   [2] *Ibid.*   [3] *Ibid.*

hundreds of authors whereby we frame a Babel of knowledge in the Nation." [1]

He goes so far with his faith in the soul's possibility
to return into " the Original Centre of all Reality " that
he declares that a man may sink deep enough into this
Original Principle that binds his own soul into union with
God so that he can penetrate by an inner Light and
experience into the secret qualities and virtues hid in all
visible and corporeal things, and may learn to discover
the healing and curative powers of metals and plants,
and may thus, by inward knowledge, advance all Arts
and Sciences. [2]

Ellistone returns to this inner way of arriving at a
knowledge of outward things in his Preface to *Signatura
rerum* in 1651. Man, he declares, is a microcosm, or
abridgment, of the whole universe, he is the emblem and
hieroglyphic of Time and Eternity, and he who will take
pains to push in beyond Solomon's Porch, or the Outer
Court of sense and natural reason, to the Inner Court
and Holy Place, where the immortal Seed abides and
where man can become one again with that which he was
in God before he became a creature, then he will have
the key that opens all mysteries both inner and outer.
Nature will be an open Book of Parables in which he can
read the truth of Eternity, the world will be a clear
mirror in which he can see the things of the Spirit and
he will know what will cure both soul and body. The
" Depth of God within the Soul," the Inner Light,
is the precious Pearl, the never-failing Comfort, the
Panacea for all diseases, the sure Antidote even against
death itself, the unfailing Guide and Way of all
Wisdom. [3]

Here, then, were two very enthusiastic disciples of
Boehme who took their master's teaching very seriously,
who on the whole grasped its essential meaning, were
possessed and penetrated by the *idea* of a deeper eternal
world manifesting itself in the temporal, and who gave
their lives to the difficult task of making Boehme's message

---

[1] Preface to *Epistles*.   [2] *Ibid.*   [3] Preface to *Sig. re.*

available to their own people and to their own perplexed
age. They were not " occultists." They did not run
into enthusiastic vapourings, nor did they strain after
psychic experiences which would relieve them of the
stress and strain of achieving the goal of life through the
formation of balanced character and the practice of social
virtues, though, as we shall see, some of the readers of
their translations took the risky course, and ended in the
fog rather than in the clear light.

The question has naturally been raised whether
Boehme exercised any direct influence upon the early
Quaker movement.[1] There is at present no way of
proving that George Fox, the chief exponent of the
movement, had actually read the writings of the Teutonic
philosopher or had consciously absorbed the views of the
latter, but there are so many marks of influence apparent
in the *Journal* that no careful student of both writers
can doubt that there was some sort of influence, direct
or indirect, conscious or unconscious. The works of
Boehme were, as we have seen, all available in English
during the great formative period of Fox's life, from 1647
to 1661. There can be no question that they were read by
the serious *Seekers* in the period of the Commonwealth.
Thomas Taylor, who was one of the finest fruits of the
Seeker movement, bears in 1659 a positive testimony to
the spiritual value of Jacob Bewman's (Behmen) writings.
Taylor received a letter from Justice William Thornton
of Hipswell in Yorkshire, warning him to beware of " the
confused Notions and great words of Jacob Bewman
and such like frothy scriblers." Taylor replies : " For
thy light expressions of Jacob Bewman, I know in most
things he speaks a Parable to thee yet, and so his writings
may well be lightly esteemed of by thee ; but there is
that in his Writings which, if ever thy eye be opened,
will appear to be a sweet unfolding of the Mystery of God
and of Christ, in divers particulars, according to his Gift.
And therefore beware of speaking Evil of that which thou

---

[1] This question was raised by Barclay in his *Inner Life of the Religious Societies
of the Commonwealth* (London, 1879), pp. 214-215.

know'st not." [1]   We have also seen how Boehme appealed
to such noble Seekers as Charles and Durant Hotham,
John Sparrow, and John Ellistone. [2]   One Quaker of
some importance, Francis Ellington, not only read the
writings of Boehme, but regarded " that Faithful Servant
Jacob Behme " as " a Prophet of the Lord." [3]   He
quotes from his German " Prophet " the words : " A Lilly
blossometh to you ye Northern Countries ; if you destroy
it not with sectarian contention of the learned, then it
will become a great Tree among you, but if you shall
rather contend than to know the true God, then the Ray
passeth by and hitteth only some ; and then afterwards
you shall be forced to draw water for the thirst of your
souls among strange nations."   Ellington regards Boehme
as a genuine " prophet," and the " Lilly " that was to
blossom in the North seems to Ellington plainly to be
George Fox and his Quaker Society, which the learned
have tried in vain to overthrow.   He cites many passages
from the Teutonic Prophet of the Lord to show the
parallelism between the prophesied type of spiritual religion and the Children of the Light who have exactly
fulfilled it. [4]

It would be natural to expect that the young Quaker
seeker, eager for any light on his dark path, would read
the *Forty Questions* and *The Three Principles of the
Divine Essence*, or at least that he would hear them dis-
cussed by the people among whom he moved in these
intense and eventful years.   In any case there are ideas
expressed and experiences described in the *Journal* which
look strangely like memories, conscious or subconscious,
of ideas and experiences to be found in the Boehme
writings.   The most striking single passage is one which
describes an experience which occurred to Fox in 1648.   It
is as follows : " Now was I come up in Spirit through the
flaming sword into the paradise of God.   All things were

---

[1] Thomas Taylor's *Works* (London, 1697), p. 86.
[2] The writings themselves constantly use the word " Seeker," and the Introductions emphasize the Seeking attitude.
[3] *Christian Information Concerning these Last Times*, by F. E. (London, 1664),
pp. 10-11.   [4] *Op. cit.* pp. 11-12.

new ; and all the Creation gave another smell unto me than before, beyond what words can utter. I knew nothing but pureness and innocency and righteousness, being renewed into the image of God by Jesus Christ, to the state of Adam before he fell. The creation was opened to me ; and it was showed me how all things had their names given them, according to their nature and virtue. I was at a stand in my mind, whether I should practise physic for the good of mankind, seeing the nature and virtue of things were so opened to me by the Lord. . . . The admirable works of creation and the virtues thereof may be known through the openings of that divine Word of Wisdom and power by which they were made." [1]

Jacob Boehme had, as we have seen, a similar experience of having " the nature and virtues of things opened " to him in the year 1600. The following account of it was given in Sparrow's Introduction to *Forty Questions*, printed in 1647 : " He went forth into the fields and there perceived the wonderful or wonder works of the Creator in the signatures, shapes, figures, and qualities or properties of all created things very clearly and plainly laid open. Whereupon he was filled with exceeding joy." The same incident is told in a slightly different way in Justice Hotham's *Life of Behmen* : " Going abroad into the Fields, to a Green before Neys-Gate, at Gorlitts, he there sate down, and viewing the Herbs and Grass of the Field, in his Inward Light he saw into their essences, use and properties." It was, further, a fundamental idea of Boehme's that the outward and visible world is a parable and symbol of the spiritual world within, and that by a spiritual experience which carries the soul down to the inner, hidden, abysmal Centre, the secrets and mysteries of the outward creation may become revealed. Hotham says that Boehme, by his divine Light, " beheld the whole of creation, and from that Fountain of Revelation wrote his book *De signatura rerum*." [2] Ellistone, in the Introduction to Boehme's *Epistles*, printed in 1649, predicts

---

[1] *Journal* (ed. 1901), 28. Unfortunately the Cambridge Journal does not contain any biographical incidents prior to 1652. [2] Hotham's *Life*, D. 4.

that an experience, like this one which Fox claimed, will come to those who receive the inner Divine Light. " This knowledge," he says, " must advance all Arts and Sciences and conduce to the attainment of the Universal Tincture and Signature, whereby the different secret qualities and vertues that are hid in all visible and corporeall things, as Metals, Minerals, Plants and Herbes, may be drawne forth and applied to their right naturall use *for the curing and healing* of corrupt and decayed nature." [1]

It was also a feature of Boehme's teaching that man must enter again into Paradise and return to the condition of the unfallen Adam. " The Noble Virgin " [*i.e.* Sophia or Spiritual Wisdom], Boehme writes, " showeth us the Gate and how we must enter again into Paradise through the sharpness of the sword," which, in a few lines previous, he calls " the flaming sword which God set to keep the Tree of Life." [2]   Fox's experience of the " new smell " of creation is an even more striking parallel. Mystic awakenings and spiritual openings generally impress the recipient of them with a sense of new and fresh penetration into the meaning of things and leave them with a feeling of heightened powers, but cases in which the experience results in a new sense of *smell* are fairly rare. Two persons might, no doubt, have such an experience quite independently, but one who has become familiar with the range of *suggestion* in experiences of this type will note with interest the large place which " new Smells and Odours " occupy in Boehme's writings. For example, he says, in the *Signatura rerum*, where he describes the coming of the Paradise-experience : " When Paradise springs up, the paradisaical joy puts itself forth with a lovely smell," [3] and in one of his Epistles he speaks of a spiritual awakening in his own life that was marked by a new smell—" A very strong Odour was given to me in the life of God." [4]

There is another passage in Fox's *Journal*, a few lines

---

[1] Preface to *Epistles*, p. 10.   [2] *The Three Princ.*, trans. 1648, xx. 40-41.
[3] *Sig. re.* viii. 23.
[4] *Ep.* xv. 18.   For another passage on " the new smell," see *The Three Princ.* iv. 27.

beyond this famous account of his Paradise-experience, that also bears the mark of Boehme's influence. In fact, it is difficult to believe that Fox could have got his phraseology anywhere else than from Boehme. The passage reads : " As people come into subjection to the Spirit of God and grow up in the Image and Power of the Almighty, they may receive the *Word of Wisdom that opens all things, and come to know the hidden Unity in the Eternal Being.*" [1] Everywhere in Boehme it is " Sophia, the Word of Wisdom," that " opens all things," and the goal of all spiritual experience and of all divine illumination for him consists in coming to " the hidden Unity in the Eternal Being, or the Eternal Essence." That is not a Biblical phrase, and it is not one which the Drayton youth would have heard from native English sources. It came to England with the Boehme literature. Further revelations along this same line of " opening " follow in the *Journal.* In the Vale of Beavor the Lord " opened " things to Fox, relating to " the three great professions in the world, physic, divinity and law." " He showed me," Fox says, " that the physicians were out of the Wisdom of God by which the creatures were made, and so knew not their virtue because they were *out of the Word of Wisdom.*" He saw that the priests were actuated by *the dark power*—a very suspicious phrase to one who knows what a place the " Dark Principle " holds in Boehme's writings—and he saw that the lawyers were out of the Wisdom of God. But it was opened to him that all these three professions might be " reformed " and " brought into the Wisdom of God by which all things were created," and " have a right understanding of the virtues of things through the Word of Wisdom " ; for " in the Light all things may be seen both visible and invisible." [2] The extraordinary use of Old Testament figures, by which Fox illustrates the condition of the Church, in the section of the *Journal* following the passages above quoted, is no less significant. The figures of Cain and Esau, of Korah and Balaam, and the types of Adam and Moses are given

[1] *Journal,* i. p. 29.   [2] *Ibid.* i. pp. 29-30.

quite in the style of *The Three Principles*, or of the *Mysterium magnum*.[1] One parallel is especially interesting. Fox says : " I saw plainly that none could read Moses aright without Moses' spirit, by which Moses saw how man was in the Image of God in Paradise, and how he fell and how death came over him, and how all men have been under this death." [2] The Preface to *Mysterium magnum* says : " I cannot but think that the same God that taught Moses so eminently by His Spirit had so fitted the people for whom he wrote that they were capable to receive instruction by his words." [3] This idea, so frequently expressed in the writings of Fox, that no one can understand the Scriptures except by the Spirit that gave forth the Scriptures,[4] is equally a fundamental idea of Boehme and his English interpreters. In many passages of the *Mysterium magnum* Boehme declares that the written word is only a witness to the living Word, which latter Word can be understood only by those who are in the Spirit that spoke in the Prophets and Apostles.[5] Sparrow, in his Introduction to the *Aurora*, declares that no person can understand the spiritual mystery of redemption, " though he reade of it in the Scriptures," unless the Holy Spirit in himself, the true Divine Light, enlighten him, and give him the word of faith in his heart ; " neither," he adds, " can any understand the Holy Scriptures but by the same Gifts of the Holy Spirit in the Soul." [6]

On one occasion the Lord showed Fox the nature of things that are in the human heart—" as the nature of dogs, swine, vipers, etc." [7] So, too, Boehme saw that there are many kinds of wild beast in man's nature— the lion, the wolf, the dog, the fox, and the serpent.[8] Fox frequently speaks of the two " seeds "—the Seed of God or the Seed of Christ and the seed of the serpent—and the victory of life in the Spirit consists in having the Seed of God conquer the seed of the serpent, or, as Fox

---

[1] See *Journal*, i. pp. 31-34.   [2] *Ibid.* i. p. 33.   [3] *Op. cit.* A.
[4] See, for specimen passages, *Journal*, i. pp, 36 and 124.
[5] See especially *Myst. mag.* xxxviii. sections 52-59.
[6] Preface to *Aurora*, B.   [7] *Journal*, i. p. 19.   [8] *Three Princ.* xvi. 31-37.

often expresses it, having " the Seed of God bruise the serpent's head," or having " the Seed of God atop of the devil and all his works " ; or having " the Seed reign." [1] This phraseology runs throughout Boehme's writings. The two " seeds " are everywhere in evidence, and " the Treader on the serpent " is the frequent name for Christ and for the victorious soul. God showed Adam, Boehme says, how " the Treader on the serpent " should once again be brought with virtue and power up into the Paradise of God, and live anew by the Word of God.[2]

Fox, in the account of his first great transforming opening in 1647, says : " I knew God by revelation as one who hath the key doth open." [3] This is a frequent figure in Boehme for a first-hand experience. " Where is Paradise to be found ? " he asks. " Is it far away or is it near ? One person cannot lend the key to another. Every one must unlock it with his own key or else he cannot enter," [4] and again he describes that " surpassing joy of the new regeneration," when the soul " gets the keys of the kingdom of heaven and may open for itself." [5]

Fox's " openings " about university-trained ministers and his references to " stone churches," or " churches of stone and mortar," have many parallels in Boehme. Dinah of the Old Testament, for example, is " nothing else but a figure of our stone churches and our colleges with their ministers ! " and Jacob's concubine, again, " signifieth nothing else but the stone churches in which God's word and testament are handled." [6]

Finally, Fox's great vision of an ocean of Darkness and an ocean of Light, while no doubt a real experience and expressed in his own words, is profoundly like Boehme's fundamental insight that there are two world-principles of Light and Darkness, and that Light is, in the end, victorious over Darkness.[7]

No attempt has been made to gather an exhaustive set

[1] See *Journal*, i. p. 13 ; pp. 190-191 and *passim*.
[2] *Three Princ.* iv. 5.   See also *ibid.* xv. 24 ; xvi. 42 ; and xviii. 24.
[3] *Journal*, i. p. 12.   [4] *Three Princ.* ix. 25-26.
[5] *Ibid.* xix. 33.   [6] *Myst. mag.* lxii. 17 and lxiii. 36.
[7] See Fox's *Journal*, i. p. 19.

of parallels between the experiences and ideas of these two religious teachers. Enough, however, is presented to show that this spiritual leader in England was distinctly a debtor to the Teutonic seer who died the same year in which the former was born. Fox himself never mentions Boehme by name, nor does he ever refer to the little sect of " Behmenists," which, springing into existence contemporaneously with the birth of the Quaker movement, had an interesting, though short-lived, history ; but a number of the followers of Fox went aggressively into the lists against their puny rival.

The so-called " sect of Behmenists " is thus described by Richard Baxter : " The fifth sect are the Behmenists whose opinions go much toward the way of the former [the Quakers] for the sufficiency of the Light of Nature, Inward Light, the salvation of the Heathen as well as Christians, and a dependence on ' revelations.' But they are fewer in number, and seem to have attained to greater Meekness and conquest of passions than any of the rest. Their doctrines are to be seen in Jacob Behmen's Books, by him that hath nothing else to do, than to bestow a great deal of time to understand him that was not willing to be easily understood ! " [1]

" The chiefest " of this " sect of Behmenists," Baxter says, was Dr. John Pordage. Pordage was born in 1607 ; was curate in 1644 of St. Lawrence's in Reading ; was made rector of the Church in Bradfield late in 1646 ; was charged in 1651 with heresies, comprised in nine articles, consisting apparently of a sort of mystical pantheism. He was at first acquitted, but was later charged again with heresies on these nine counts, with fifty-six more, and was deprived of his rectory in 1655. He valiantly defended himself in a book with the title, *Truth appearing through the Clouds of Undeserved Scandel*, and in other publications, and after the Restoration he was reinstated. As the Behmenists were definitely attacked by the Quaker, John Anderdon, in 1661, it is to be inferred that they existed as a society at least as early as the Restora-

[1] *Reliquiae Baxterianae* (London, 1715), i. 77.

tion, though the movement became much more prominent in the 'seventies, when Pordage discovered a remarkable woman named Jane Leade, and they " agreed to wait together in prayer and pure dedication." Jane Leade, whose maiden name was Jane Ward, was born of a good English family in 1623. She was a psychopathic child, and as a young girl " heard miraculous voices " which led her to devote herself to religion. She became profoundly impressed with the writings of Boehme, as Pordage had been still earlier, and under the *suggestion* of Boehme's experiences she received many " prophetic visions," which are recorded in her spiritual Diary, *A Fountain of Gardens*.[1] A few instances of her experiences in the early stages will be of some value to the reader. She was visiting, she says, in April 1670, in a quiet, retired place, and was " contemplating the happy state of the angelical world, much exercised upon Solomon's choice, which was to find out the Noble Stone of Wisdom." " There came upon me an overshadowing bright cloud, and in the midst of it the Figure of a woman, most richly adorned with transparent gold, her hair hanging down, and her face as terrible as chrystal for brightness, but her countenance was sweet and mild. At which sight I was somewhat amazed, and immediately this Voice came, saying, Behold, I am God's Eternal Virgin, Wisdom, whom thou hast been enquiring after. I am to unseal the Treasures of God's deep Wisdom unto thee. . . . Wisdom shall be born in the inward parts of thy soul." Three days later, " the same Figure in greater Glory did appear, with a crown upon her head, full of majesty, saying, Behold me as thy Mother and know thou art to enter into covenant, to obey the New-Creation laws that shall be revealed unto thee."[2] In her account of the following extraordinary experience there are many marks of Boehme's influence : " I retained no strength, my Sun of Reason and the Moon of my outward sense were folded up and withdrew. I knew nothing by myself, as

---

[1] *A Fountain of Gardens*, 4 vols., London, 1696–1701.
[2] *Op. cit.* i. pp. 17-19.

to those working properties from Nature and Creature, and the wheel of the Motion standing still, another [influence] moved from a central Fire, so that I felt myself transmuted into one pure flame. Then came that Word to me, ' This is no other than the Gate to my Eternal Deep.' " [1]

Pordage's main contribution to the exposition of " Behmenism " was a book published in 1683 and entitled, *Theologia Mystica, or the Mystic Divinitie of the Eternal Invisibles*. It is the work of a confused mind, and its spiritual penetration, as also its mastery of the English language, are of a low order. The marks of Boehme's influence appear everywhere in the book, though Pordage is quite incapable of comprehending the more profound and robust features of Boehme's philosophy. What he relates professes to be what he himself has *seen* in visions, or what he has heard from celestial visitants. It has, he says, been his privilege to taste much of that Tree of Life which grows in the midst of the Paradise of God ; to *smell* the difference between heaven and hell ; to have seen through the veil of nature into the spiritual glory of eternity, to have felt " the distillations of heavenly dew and secret touches of the Holy Ghost." Unlike his Teutonic master, he taught (and it was also the view of Jane Leade) that in the end Divine Love transmutes evil into good and even hell into Paradise. One passage in his book, written in his best style, will be sufficient to illustrate his glowing optimism : " Love is of a transmuting and transforming Nature. The great effect of Love is to turn all things into its own Nature, which is all goodness, sweetness, and perfection. This is that Divine Power which turns Water into Wine, Sorrow and Hellish Anguish into exulting and triumphing Joy ; Curse into Blessing ; where it meets with a barren heathy Desart it transmutes it into a Paradise of delights ; yea, it changeth evil to good and all imperfection into perfection. It restores that which is fallen and degenerated to its primary Beauty, Excellence and Perfection. It is

[1] *A Fountain of Gardens*, p. 25.

the Divine Stone, the White Stone with a Name written on it, which none knows but him that hath it . . . the Divine Elixir whose transforming power and efficacy nothing can withstand." [1]

His greater disciple, Jane Leade, " the enamoured woman-devotee of Pordage," the main exponent of the Behmenist movement of this period, was a far too voluminous writer.[2] She was a sincere, pure-minded woman, of intense devotion, but she was a strongly emotional type of person, and lived in a kind of permanent borderland of visions and revelations. Her language, like that also of Pordage, is ungrammatical, of involved style, and full of overwrought and fanciful imagination. Christopher Walton, who in many ways respected her, calls her writings "a huge mass of parabolicalism and idiocratic deformity!"[3] In her *Message to the Philadelphian Society* she reports a curious vision from heaven which assures her that the Quakers are not God's chosen people. There pass in review before her illuminated sight the various claimants to the lofty title of the true Church, the real Bride of Christ. There are Anabaptists, Fifth Monarchy Men, and many others. " Then," she says, " did I see a body greater than any of these come up with great boldness, as deeming themselves to have arrived to Perfection and so visibly distinguishing themselves from all the rest, and I said, Now surely the anointed of the Lord is before Him. But a Voice said, Neither are these they ; for the Lord seeth not as man seeth." [4]

A third and intellectually far greater member of this group of " Behmenists " was Francis Lee, a Fellow of St. John's College, Oxford, a student in Leyden University, and a man of splendid parts. He became acquainted with the movement while in Holland, and on his return home sought out Jane Leade, became her adopted son, and, later, on the strength of a " revelation " made to his

---

[1] *Theologia mystica*, p. 81.

[2] Christopher Walton, in his *Notes and Materials* (1854), gives a list of eighteen of her books. [3] *Ibid.* p. 238.

[4] *Op. cit.* p. 9. Pordage disliked the Quakers and speaks slightingly of them in *Theologia mystica*. He also wrote a Treatise against them. See Walton, p. 203.

spiritual mother, he married her daughter. Until the time of Jane Leade's death in 1704, he was her devoted disciple, writing for her in the period of her blindness, and editing and publishing many of her books. He was the moving spirit in the formation of " the Philadelphian Society " for the propagation of the mystical ideas of the followers of Boehme—a Society which existed from 1697 to 1703, and which had a far-reaching influence not only in England but still more on the Continent of Europe.[1]

John Anderdon, an interesting Quaker pamphleteer, born in 1624, convinced of the Truth of the Quaker Message by the preaching of Francis Howgil in 1658, and for many years a prisoner for his faith, for which he finally died in prison, furnishes in his attack on the " Behmenists " in 1661 the earliest data available for an estimate of their views and practices.[2] The writer has evidently read the works of Jacob Boehme, or at least some of them, and he contends that the " Behmenists " whom he is attacking have failed to understand the writings of their master and have never fathomed " the tendencie of his spirit " : " The Conclusion which you have drawn to yourselves from his Writings will not profit you ; neither doth it make you any jot the more excellent, that ye can talk much of him and his Books and Writings, being not come to the right Spirit in which is life, which brings men out of dead Forms." [3]

His main criticism of the little sect is that its members make use of " Mediums and borrowed Instruments for the conveyance of God's Grace and Virtue into the Soul," [4] and that they have " not come to the Light which gives

---

[1] Important material on this subject may be found in Walton's *Notes and Materials*, especially pp. 188-258.

[2] The full title-page of Anderdon's book is as follows : *One Blow at Babel.* In those of the Pepole called Behemnites, whose Foundation is not upon that of the Prophets and Apostles, which shall stand sure and firm forever ; but upon their own carnal conceptions, begotten in their Imaginations upon Jacob Behmen's writings : They not knowing the better part, the Teachings of that Spirit that sometime opened some Mysteries of God's Kingdom in Jacob, have chosen the worser part in Esau, according to the predominancy of that Spirit which ruled in them when they made choice of their Religion, as it doth in others the hearts of the children of disobedience.—By John Anderdon. (London, printed in the year 1662, written in 1661).

[3] *One Blow at Babel*, p. 3.   [4] *Ibid.* pp. 1 and 6.

a true understanding of the things of God," though he admits that there " was sometime " in them " a hungering and thirsting after Righteousness." [1] These " Mediums " are evidently the Water of Baptism and the Bread and Wine of the Supper—" Ordinances," he says, " as you call them." [2] It would seem from this Quaker Pamphlet that the " Behmenists " under review were much like the followers of Fox, except only that they continued to use the sacraments. This use of " Mediums " seemed to him to indicate that they were " out of the Light " and " trying to *cover* the serpent's head," instead of stamping on it, but Anderdon would not have written his *Blow at Babel* if he had not been impressed with the general marks of likeness in other respects between the " Behmenists " and his own people.

Another interesting Quaker document furnishes a glimpse of the " Behmenists " a dozen years later—at about the period when John Pordage and Jane Leade were beginning to " wait together in prayer and pure meditation." It is a Minute adopted by the London " Morning Meeting " of Friends, " the 21st of ye 7th Month 1674." The occasion for action was the reception of " an Epistle to the Behminists," written by Ralph Frettwell of Barbadoes, at an earlier period " one of the Chief Judges of the Court of Common-pleas " in the island. He had been stirred to write for the same reason that impelled Anderdon, and his " Epistle " called these partly spiritualized people, as he believed, to the fuller Light, and warned them against the use of Baptism, and Bread and Wine, and " the Pater Noster." The Minute of the Morning Meeting, which opens with the words : " Deare freind R. F. in the Truth that never changeth but changeth all who believe and obey it," records the decision of the Meeting not to publish the Epistle, " wee haveing well weighed it in the feare of God and in tender Care of Truth." The reason given in the Minutes for not publishing the " Epistle " is, first, that " the writings of J. B.

---

[1] *One Blow at Babel*, pp. 1-2.
[2] Jane Leade's writings give great importance to the outward sacraments.

reveal a great mixture of light and darkness," and indicate that he lived sometimes in the power of one and sometimes in the power of the other, that God Himself has tried and judged the Spirit of darkness, and that the Spirit of Light has already " come to its own Centre and flows forth again purely "—presumably in the Quaker movement.[1] As the Lord Himself has given judgment and has given victory to the Principle of the Light, the publication of the " Epistle " is unnecessary.

And, secondly, Frettwell, in calling the " Behmenists " from " the use of Mediums," admits that at an earlier period of his life, before he received the full Light, he " received light and peace " through these external things. This seemed to the Meeting " too much giveing them encouragement " to dwell in things which give " only drynesse and barrenness," and they fear that " the ffoxes among them would take advantage " of this aid and comfort.[2] It would appear that the gravamen of the Quaker attack on the little sect was the failure of its members to dispense with sacraments. At a later period, when the " Philadelphian Society " was in full flower, an old-time pillar Quaker, George Keith, then become a Churchman and " an apostate " in the eyes of Friends, attacked the writings of Jane Leade on the ground that " she wrote derogatory to the Humanity of Christ," *i.e.* the historical Christ. Francis Lee took up vigorously the defence, and told George Keith that he himself had taught again and again the same principle of inward Light and inward Religion, that he had never yet publicly renounced these early ideas of his, and that he of all men ought to understand the meaning of a Christ within and of a " Still Eternity." [3]

Traces of Boehme's influence appear in the terms and

---

[1] The use of the phrase " its own Centre," which became an important Quaker term, is an interesting relic of Boehme's influence.

[2] *Minutes of the Morning Meeting*, i. George Fox apparently asked to see Frettwell's MS., for in a Letter under date of eighth mo. 1st, 1674, Alexander Parker writes to George Fox : " I likewise spoke to Edw. Man [Edward Mann] to send down Ralph ffrettwells Book, I suppose he intends to see thee shortly and if he can find ye Book to bring itt with him."—*Journal* (Cambridge edition), ii. p. 305.   [3] Walton's *Notes and Materials*, pp. 227 and 231.

ideas of many English writers during the period under consideration, besides those specifically mentioned. Sir Isaac Newton read Boehme's books with great appreciation and meditated upon those strange accounts of the invisible universe which underlies and is in the visible world, but we need not take too seriously the claim of the " Behmenists " that " he was ploughing with Behmen's heifer " when he discovered the law of universal gravitation ! [1] Milton, without any doubt, had read the German mystic's account of the eternal war between the Light Principle and the Dark Principle, of the fall of Lucifer, of the loss of Paradise, and of the return of man in Christ to Paradise, and there are many passages in the great poet which look decidedly like germinations from the seed which Boehme sowed, but we must observe caution in tracing the origin of verses written by a poet of Milton's genius and originality and range of knowledge. One great Englishman of a later period, William Law, unmistakably owed to Jacob Boehme the main influences which transformed his life, and through the pure and lucid style of this noble English mystic of the eighteenth century, Boehme's insights found a new interpretation and a clearer expression than he himself or any other interpreter had been able to give them.[2]

---

[1] See Walton's *Notes and Materials*, pp. 3, 46, 72, and 404.

[2] William Law lies beyond the period to which this volume is devoted. It is customary to call the edition of Behmen's *Works*, published 1764–1781, " William Law's Edition." This is quite incorrect. This edition is in the main a reprint of the earlier Translations by Sparrow and Ellistone. It was edited by George Ward, assisted by Thomas Langcake, and printed at the expense of Mrs. Hutcheson, an intimate friend of William Law.

CHAPTER XIII

EARLY ENGLISH INTERPRETERS OF SPIRITUAL RELIGION :
JOHN EVERARD, GILES RANDALL, AND OTHERS

I

THE ideas developed by spiritual Reformers on the
Continent were brought into England by a great variety
of carriers and over many routes. Some of the routes
were devious and are difficult to trace, but some of them,
on the other hand, are obvious and easily found. One of
the potent and pervasive intellectual influences for the
formation of the " spiritual " type of thought in England
was the Platonic influence which came to England through
the Humanists. This strand of thought, inherited from
the remote past, is woven into the inner structure of all
these interpreters of the divine Life. The English revival
of Greek philosophy is closely connected with the work of
the early Italian Humanists, especially with that of the
Florentine scholar, Marsilio Ficino (1433–1499), who was
selected and educated by Cosimo de Medici to be the head
of the new Academy in Florence. It was a fixed idea of
Ficino that Philosophy and Religion are identical, and
therefore that Religion, if it is true Religion, is rooted and
grounded in Reason, since God is the source of all Truth
and all that is rational. Plato, in Ficino's eyes, *is* Philosophy. He was the divine forerunner of Christ in the
realm of intellect as John the Baptist was in the realm of
the law. In his mind Plato's Philosophy is the greatest
possible preparation for an adequate understanding of the
world of Truth which Christ has unveiled and of the way

of Life which He has revealed. Ficino translated Plato's Dialogues into Latin, and gave his own interpretation of the great philosopher in a Treatise on *Plato's Doctrine of Immortality of Souls*. He also translated Plotinus and the writings falsely attributed to Dionysius the Areopagite, and put them anew into spiritual circulation.

Ficino, though living in an age of corruption and debauchery, and though closely associated with Humanists who had hardly a thin veneer of Christianity, and who were bent on reviving paganism, yet himself maintained a positive Christian faith and a pure and simple life. He found it possible to be a priest in the Christian Church and at the same time to be a high-priest in the temple of Plato, because he found faith and reason to be indivisible and indissoluble. His influence was marked upon the early English Humanists, Linacre, Grocyn, Colet, and More, and he was a vital influence in the new revival, which occurred in the seventeenth century, of Plato and Plotinus as contributors to a virile religion based upon an inherent divine and human relationship.

Still another influence, of a very different sort, came to England by way of Italy—the intense interpretation of Faith as the way of salvation, expressed in the writings of the Spanish reformer, Juan de Valdès, and in the powerful sermons of his two Italian disciples, Bernardino Ochino (1487–1564) and Pietro Martire Vermigli (1500–1562), generally known as Peter Martyr. Juan de Valdès, twin brother of the Humanist, Alfonso de Valdès, the friend of the Emperor Charles V., was born of a distinguished Castilian family toward the end of the fifteenth century. He was splendidly prepared in his youth, both mentally and religiously, for the great work of his life, which was to be a spiritual mover of other souls. As his views of the needed transformation of Christianity broadened and intensified he concluded that he would be safer in Italy than in Spain, and he thus took up his residence in Naples in 1529. Here he became the centre of a remarkable circle of spiritual men and women who were dedicating themselves to the reform of the Church and to the propa-

gation of a more vital religion. Ochino, the most powerful
Italian preacher of the age ; the fervent scholar, Vermigli ;
the papal secretary, Carnesecchi, later a martyr to the new
faith ; Vittoria Colonna, the friend of Michael Angelo
Buonarotti, and the beautiful Giulia Gonzaga, were among
those who kindled their torches from his burning flame.
For the instruction of his friends—especially for Giulia
Gonzaga—de Valdès translated St. Paul's Epistles to the
Romans and Galatians and wrote commentaries on them,
and contributed the penetrating original works, *The
Christian Alphabet* and *The Hundred and Ten Divine
Considerations*.[1]

These writings present in vivid and powerful style the
way of salvation through Faith. The primary insight is
Lutheran, but it is everywhere coloured and tempered by
the author's Humanistic outlook. He insists, in all his
interpretations of salvation, upon the vital interior work
of the Holy Spirit and upon the necessity of re-living the
Christ-life in all its heights and depths. All the truths of
religion, he constantly urges, must be known and verified
in experience, and those who are to be effective ministers
of the Gospel in any age must know that they are divinely
sent and must be taught by the inward Word of God rather
than by human science. The attractive power of the
Cross is rediscovered in his profound experience and makes
itself felt as the dynamic principle of his entire moral
activity.

The Divine Considerations was put into English by
Nicholas Ferrar (1592–1637) of Little Gidding, and published
at Oxford in 1638, together with the Introduction to the
Commentary on Romans, under the name of " John
Valdesso." The English translation was submitted by
Ferrar to his friend, George Herbert, who wrote some inter-
esting critical notes which were printed with the original
edition. George Herbert expresses his great love for
" Valdesso," whose eyes, he says, God has opened, even in
the midst of Popery, "to understand and express so clearly

[1] The Italian titles of these two books are *Alfabeto Christiano* (1546) and
Le Cento et dieci divine Considerationi (1550).

and excellently the intent of the Gospell in the acceptation
of Christ's righteousness," but he " likes not " his slighting
of Scripture and his use of the Word of God for inward
revelation. He believed, though wrongly, that de Valdès
was a " mystic," and that he was advocating a religion of
" private enthusiasms and revelations." The fact was
rather that de Valdès was presenting or was aiming to
present a religion of universal validity, brought to birth
by the discovery of God in Christ as revealed in the Gospel,
and made continuously effective anew by personal experience of the same Christ as Divine Revealer in the lives of
men.

There is no question of the far-reaching influence of
Ferrar's translation of this vital message of de Valdès,
especially among scholars and literary men. It must also
have had a popular influence, for Samuel Rutherford in
1648 declared it to be one of the " poysonable " sources of
" Familisme, Antinomianisme, and Enthusiasme." [1] He
charges that " Waldesso," as he calls him, teaches men
that the Scriptures have been supplanted by the inner
Light, in fact that " Scripture shines only as a light in a
dark place until the Day-star arises in the heart, and that
then man hath no more need to seeke that of the holy
Scripture which departs of it selfe, as the light of a candle
departs when the Sunne-beames enter, even as Moses
departed at the presence of Christ and the Law at the
presence of the Gospel." [2]

Ochino and Vermigli spent six important years in
England from 1547 to 1553, when persecution under Mary
forced them to flee. They were far more under the
influence of Calvin at this period than under that of their
former friend de Valdès, but they both with the fire and
intensity of their Italian nature—especially Ochino in his
sermons—drove home to the hearts and consciences of
their hearers the way of salvation by faith and the absolute
necessity of inner experience and interior religion.

[1] *A Survey of the Spiritual Antichrist* (1648), p. 164.   [2] *Ibid.* p. 319.

II. John Everard

Dr. John Everard of Clare College, Cambridge, was clearly one of the earliest and one of the most interesting carriers of these ideas, and in his case it is not difficult to discover the influences which shaped the course of his thought and suggested the general lines of his message. He was born about 1575—the birth year of Jacob Boehme—though all early biographical details are lacking. He had a long student period at Clare College, receiving his degree of B.A. in 1600, M.A. in 1607, and D.D. in 1619. He was deeply versed in the great mystics, and always reveals in his sermons the influence of Plotinus and Dionysius the Areopagite, and no less the influence of Eckhart, Tauler, and the *Theologia Germanica*. But at some period of his life he tapped a new source and came into possession of a fresh group of live and suggestive ideas which influenced all the thinking of his later stage. His translations, some of which are in MS. and some in printed form, furnish a clue to the main sources of his ideas, which present a striking parallelism with those held by the continental spiritual Reformers of the sixteenth century. He was possessed of original power and of penetrating insight, with " eyes of his own," but no one can fail to see that he had read and pondered the writings of these submerged Reformers, and that in a country remote from theirs he has become a reincarnation of their ideas and a new voice for their message.

His public career, in the England of the first two Stuarts, was a stormy one. He was Rector of St. Martin-in-the-Field. In the early stage of his preaching he felt called upon to oppose the " Spanish Marriage " as " the great sin of matching with idolators," and he underwent a series of imprisonments for his attacks upon this precious scheme of King James, who wittily suggested changing his name from Dr. Everard [" Ever-out "] to " Dr. Never-out." Some time before his fiftieth year—the date cannot be exactly fixed—he reached

his new and deeper insight, and henceforth became the
bearer of a message which seemed to him and to his friends
like the reopening of the treasury of the Gospels, and in
this new light he felt ashamed of the barren period
of his life when he walked in " the ignorance of litteral
knowledge," when he was " a bare, literal, University
preacher," as he himself says, and had not found " the
marrow and the true Word of God." [1] The great *change*
which cleaves his public career into two well-defined parts
is impressively indicated by his friend and disciple, Rapha
Harford, in his " Dedicatory Epistle " to the Sermons
and in his preface " to the Reader," though he nowhere
gives any light upon the events and influences which
initiated the transformation. " In a special and extraordinary manner God appeared to him in his latter days,"
Harford says, " and after that, he desired nothing more
than to bring others to see what he saw and to enjoy what
he enjoyed." [2] He was, we are told, " a man of presence
and of princely behaviour " and was known " as a good
philosopher, few or none exceeding him," " endowed with
skill and depth of learning," but after his new experience,
when he " came to know himself," and to " know Jesus
Christ and the Scriptures *experimentally* rather than gram-
matically, literally or academically," he came to esteem
lightly " notions and speculation," " letter-learning " and
" University-knowledge," and he " *centred his spirit* on
union and communion with God " and turned his supreme
interest from " forms, externals and generals " to the
cultivation of " the inner man," and to " acting more
than talking." [3]

His new way of preaching—vivid, concrete, touched
with subtle humour, grounded in experience and filling
old texts with new meaning—appealed powerfully to the
common people and to an elect few of the more highly
privileged who had won a large enough freedom of spirit
to go with him into new paths.[4] Like his Master, he loved

---

[1] Epistle Dedicatory to *Some Gospel Treasures Opened* (London, 1653).
[2] *Gospel Treas.*, " To the Reader." [3] *Ibid.*
[4] Sometimes " Divers Earls and Lords and other great ones " were in his
audience.

the common people, " thinking it no disparagement to accompany with the lowest of men," " tinkers, coblers, weavers and poor beggarly fellows who came running " to hear him, and he poured out the best he had in his treasury to any, even the simplest and most ordinary, who cared to hear of this " spiritual, practical experiment of life." His preaching naturally brought him suffering and persecution. He was " often fetched into the High Commission," was forced to give " attendance from Court to Court and from Term to Term," was on one occasion fined a thousand pounds for his " heresies," and had many interviews with Archbishop Laud, but he always held that " Truth is strongest," and he declared that God had called him to be " a Sampson against Philistines and a David against the huge and mighty Goliath of his times," [1] and he was ready to pay the cost of obedience to the Light. His friend, Harford, who had " much ado " to keep the manuscript of his sermons " out of the Bishop's fingers," declares that though Everard clearly " distinguished the outward and killing letter from the Life and Spirit of the Holy Word," he was not an antinomian or in sympathy with ranterism. " Our author," the Dedicatory Epistle says, and says truly, " missed both rocks against which many have split their vessels. He carries Truth amain with Topsail set. He cuts his way clear between the meer Rationalist who will square out God according to his Reason, and the Familist who lives above all ordinances and by degrees hath turned licencious Ranter." Thomas Brooks added to Harford's Testimony a brief " Approbation " to the Volume, on Behalf of the Publishers, recommending all readers to receive its " heaven-born truths " into their homes and into their hearts, assuring them that as they read and open their inner eyes they will find their own hearts in the book and the book in their own hearts, *i.e.* the book will " find them."

Before turning to Everard's message, as it finds expression in the rare volume of his sermons—*The Gospel Treasures Opened*—we must consider the Translations

---

[1] *Gospel Treas.*, " To the Reader."

which he left unpublished. They are preserved in clearly written manuscripts in Cambridge University Library, under the title " Three Bookes Translated out of their Originall." [1] The first " Book " bears the following title-page : " The Tree of Knowledge of Good and Evil, And the Tree of Life in the Midst of the Paradise of God : Taken out of a Book called The Letter and the Life, or The Flesh and the Spirit. Translated by Dr. Everard." An interesting article on Dr. Everard in *Notes and Queries* [2] concludes that this first " Book " of Everard's is a free translation of the Second Part of Tentzel's *Medicina diastica*. This guess, however, proves to be incorrect, though there is a slight likeness between Tentzel's book and the English MS. Everard's book is, in reality, a translation of Sebastian Franck's *Von dem Baum des Wissens Gutes und Böses* (" Of the Tree of Know-ledge of Good and Evil "). The translation is made from a Latin edition of Franck's little book, which was published in 1561. The entire message of this treatise, written by the wandering chronicler and spiritual prophet of Germany, and here reproduced in English, is the *inwardness* of every-thing that concerns the religious life. The Tree of Life was in Adam's heart, and in that same inner region of the soul was the Tree of the Knowledge of Good and Evil. The story of Paradise is a graphic parable of the soul's experience. " That Tree which tested Adam was and is nothing else in truth but the Nature, Will, Knowledge, and Life of Adam, and every man is as much forbidden to eat of this Tree as Adam was." Franck's significant book contained passages from Hans Denck's *Widerruf* (" Con-fession "), and Everard translated them as an appendix to his first manuscript book. [3] They hold the very heart of Denck's message and deal, with Denck's usual sincerity and boldness, with the fundamental nature of spiritual religion. He here declares the primacy of the Word of God in the soul over everything else that ministers to man's life : " I prefer the Holy Scriptures before all Humane

---

[1] *Sig. Dd.* xii. p. 68.   [2] Fourth series, i. p. 597.
[3] Denck's name is used in its Latin form John Denqui, and he is called *magnus theologus.*

Treasure ; yet I do not so much esteem them as I do the Word of God which is living, potent, and eternal, and which is free from all elements of this world : For that is God Himself, Spirit and no letter, written without pen or ink, so that it can never be obliterated.   True Salvation is in the Word of God ; it is not tied up to the Scriptures. They alone cannot make a bad heart good, though they may supply it with information.   But a heart illumined with the Light of God is made better by everything." Franck declares, in comment on Denck's words : " I myself know at least twenty Christian Religions all of which claim to rest on the Holy Scriptures which they apply to themselves by far-fetched expositions and allegories, or from the dead letter of the text. . . . They can be understood rightly, however, only by the divine new-man, who is God-born, and who brings to them the Light of the Holy Spirit." There can be no doubt, I think, that Dr. Everard found in the writings of these two sixteenth-century prophets the body and filling of his own new conceptions of Christianity, and it was through his vigorous interpretations that this stream of thought first flowed into England.

It will not be necessary to make extended comment on Everard's other translations.   The second one was " The Golden Book of German Divinitie," rendered into English in 1628 from the Latin edition of "John Theophilus," who is Sebastian Castellio, and the third is a translation of Nicholas of Cusa's *De visione Dei* (" The Vision of God "), which is a profound and impressive piece of mystical literature and deserves to be much better known than it is.   Everard, further, translated the " Mystical Divinity " of Dionysius the Areopagite, selections from John Tauler and Meister Eckhart, and " The Divine Pymander [Poemander] of Hermes Trismegistus "—a book which nearly all the spiritual Humanists ranked in the very first list of religious literature.[1]

We must now turn to Everard's message as it is pre-

---

[1] *Hermes Trismegistus* was published in Everard's lifetime.   Large extracts from his manuscript translations are given in the *Gospel Treasures Opened* (1653). *The Vision of God* was edited and published in full by Giles Randall in 1646, and it is very probable that Everard and Randall did this work together.

sented in his Sermons, and endeavour to discover what he
told the throngs of people who came gladly to hear him in
the Kensington Meetings and the gatherings at Islington.
The central emphasis in every sermon is on personal
experience, or, as we should phrase it to-day, on a religion
of life and reality. He has had his own " scholastic "
period, but he looks back on it as a passage across an arid
desert, and he feels a mission laid upon him to call men
everywhere away from a religion of " notions and words " [1]
to a religion of first-hand experience and inwardly felt
realities.   Unless we know Christ, he says, experimentally
so that " He lives within us spiritually, and so that all
which is known of Him in the Letter and Historically is
truly done and acted in our own souls—until we experimentally verify all we read of Him—the Gospel is a meer
tale to us." It is not saving knowledge to know that
Christ was born in Bethlehem but to know that He is born
in us.   It is vastly more important to know experimentally
that we are crucified with Christ than to know historically
that He died in Jerusalem many years ago, and to feel
Jesus Christ risen again within you is far more operative
than to have " a notional knowledge " that He rose on the
third day.   " When thou begins to finde and know not
merely that He was conceived in the womb of a virgin,
but that *thou* art that virgin and that He is more truly and
spiritually, and yet as really, conceived in thy heart so that
thou feelest the Babe beginning to be conceived in thee by
the power of the Holy Ghost and the Most High overshadowing thee ; when thou feelest Jesus Christ stirring to
be born and brought forth in thee ; when thou beginnest
to see and feel all those mighty, powerful actions done in
thee which thou readest that He did in the flesh—here is a
Christ indeed, a real Christ who will do thee some good." [2]

---

[1] *Gospel Treasures Opened*, p. 393.

[2] Sermon on " The Starre in the East," *Gospel Treas.* pp. 52-54.   See also
pp. 586-587. Compare the famous lines of Angelus Silesius :

> " Had Christ a thousand times
> Been born in Bethlehem
> But not in thee, thy sin
> Would still thy soul condemn."

Angelus Silesius, edited by Paul Carus (Chicago, 1909), p. 103.

To have Christ born in the soul means also to "do the deeds of Christ," to grow and increase toward perfection as His life is more fully manifested in us, to be able to say as we read of divine events, "This day is this Scripture fulfilled in me," and to see Christ work all His miracles before our eyes to-day. It is the "key of experience" which unlocks all the drawers and cabinets and hidden and secret doors of Scripture.[1] We can discover, as we read, that there are whole armies of Philistines in us to be overcome, that there are Goliaths to be slain, and that there are Promised Lands to be won.[2] "When thou hast seen God and found Him for thyself; then thou mayest say: Now I believe, not only because it is written in Genesis, but because I have felt it and seen it written and fulfilled in mine own soul."[3] "Men should not so much trouble themselves," he says to those who are expecting a "Fifth Monarchy," "about a personal reign of Christ here upon earth, if they saw that the chief and real fulfilling of the Scriptures were *in them*; and that, whatever is externally done in the world or expressed in the Scriptures, is but typical and representative, and points out a more spiritual *saving*, and a more divine fulfilling of them."[4]

In almost the same figures used by Sebastian Franck he contrasts the letter and the Spirit, the outward and the inward, the word of the written Book and the living Word of God. This contrast is carefully worked out in four sermons, preached at Kensington, on "The Dead and Killing Letter, and the Spirit and the Life." Here he insists, often in quaint and curious phrases, that the Old Testament, "from the first of Genesis to the last of the Prophets," is an allegory, "woven like a beautiful tapestry" to picture forth to the eye a history whose real meaning is to be found within the soul; if you dwell upon it only as picture, only as history, it is a letter that kills; if you see your own selves in it and by it, then it gives life.[5] You may learn the whole Bible by heart and speak to any point in divinity according to text and letter, and yet *know*

---

[1] *Gospel Treas.* pp. 59, 72, and 98.   [2] *Ibid.* pp. 270-271.   [3] *Ibid.* p. 282.
[4] *Ibid.* p. 92.   [5] *Ibid.* p. 280

nothing of God or of spiritual life.[1] " If you be always
handling the letter of the Word, always licking the letter,
always chewing upon that, what great thing do you?
No marvel you are such starvelings ! "[2] The letter is the
husk ; the Word, the Spirit, is the kernel ; the letter is
the earthen jar, the Spirit is the hidden manna ; the letter
is the outer court, the Spirit is the inner sanctuary ;
the letter is the shadow, the Spirit is the substance ; the
letter is the sheath, the Spirit is the sharp two-edged
sword ; the letter is the hard encasing bone that must be
broken, the Spirit is inward marrow which nourishes the
soul ; the letter is temporal, the Word is eternal [3]—" if
ye once know the truth experimentally after the Spirit
ye will no longer make such a stir about Forms, Disciplines,
and Externals as if that were the great and only Reformation ! "[4] The real difficulty, the true cause of spiritual
dryness, is that " men strive and contend so much for the
letter and the external part of God's worship, that they
neglect the inward and internal altogether ; for where
is the man who is so zealous and hot for the internal as
he is for the external. If we press men to the inward
before the outward, or do as I do, lift up that ; either
how cold and heartless they are, or else how quarrelsome
and malicious they are ! "[5] When once the inward core
of things has been grasped and the transforming experience has occurred, making a new man—freed, illuminated,
sin-delivered, with " God the Life of the life and the Soul
of the soul "[6]—the outward forms and the external things
will fall into the right perspective and will receive their
proper emphasis. Imitating St. Augustine's great saying :
" Love God absolutely and then you may do as you
please," Everard says, " Turn the man loose who has found
the living Guide within him, and then let him neglect the
outward if he can ; just as you would say to a man who
loves his wife with all tenderness, ' you may beat her,
hurt her or kill her, if you want to ! ' "[7]

The conception of God which forms the foreground of

[1] *Gospel Treas.* pp. 310-311.   [2] *Ibid.* p. 286.   [3] *Ibid.* p. 468.   [4] *Ibid.* p. 343.
[5] *Ibid.* p. 344.   [6] *Ibid.* p. 341.   [7] *Ibid.* p. 344.

all Everard's teaching is one perfectly familiar to those
that have studied the great mystics who have formed
their ideas under the direct or indirect influence of Plotinus.
The conception is, of course, not necessarily mystical—it
is rather a recurring type of metaphysics—but it has
peculiarly suited the mystical mind and is often regarded
by Christian historians as synonymous with mysticism.
God, for Everard as for Dionysius and for Eckhart, Tauler,
and Franck, is unknowable, unspeakable, unnamable,
abstracted from all that is created and visible, an absolute
One, alone of all beings in the universe able to say " I am,"
since He alone is Perfect Reality ; but just for that reason
He is unrevealable in His inmost nature to finite beings
and incapable of manifestation through anything that
is finite.[1]

He is a permanent and unchanging Substance ; all
things that are visible are but shadow and appearance, are
like bubbles in the water which are now here and now
gone.[2]   Every created and finite thing, however—from
a grain of sand to a radiant sun and from a blade of grass
to the Seraph that is nearest God—is a beam or a ray or
expression of that eternal Reality, is an angel or messenger
that in some minute, or in some glorious fashion, reveals
God in space and time ; and all created things together,
from the lowest to the highest, from the treble of the
heavenly beings to the base of earthly things, form " one
mighty sweet-tuned instrument," sending forth one harmonious hallelujah to the Creator and revealing a single
organic universe, " acted and guided by one Spirit "—
the Soul of all that is.[3]   "Ask the craggy mountains what
part they sing, and they will tell you that they sing the
praise of the immutableness and unchangeableness of God ;
ask the flowers of the field what part they sing, and they
will tell you they sing the wisdom and liberality of God
who cloathes them beyond Solomon in all his glory ; ask
the sun, moon and stars what part they sing, and they will
say the constancy of God's promises, that they hold their
course and do not alter it ; ask the poor received sinner

---

[1] *Gospel Treas.* p. 81.   [2] *Ibid.* p. 630.   [3] *Ibid.* pp. 637 and 658.

what part he sings, and he will tell you he sings the infinite free mercy of a most gracious Father ; and ask the wicked, obstinate sinner what part he sings, and he will tell you he sings the praise of the patience and justice of God." [1]

In a very striking passage, Everard points out how the beings nearest in order to God are most free of matter and imperfection, while those lower in hierarchical scale are increasingly more material : " God is a pure Spirit, only Form without any manner of matter ; and all the Creatures, the further off from Him, the more matter [they have] and the nearer the less. For example, Angels are pictured with complete *bodies* ; yet to show they are further off from matter than men, therefore they have always *wings*. And Arch-angels, they being nearer the Nature of God than Angels, are pictured *with bodies cut off by the middle with wings*. But Cherubims, having less matter and nearer God Himself than either, are pictured *only with heads and wings, without bodies*. But Seraphims, being farthest off from man and nearest of all to God, *have no bodies nor heads nor wings at all* but [are] only represented *by a certain yellowish or fiery Colour*." [2]

We ourselves, we men, are both finite and infinite. We have come from an infinite source, and even in our apparent finiteness and independence we still remain inwardly joined to that central Reality.

He tells this in his parable of the water-drops : " Suppose two water-drops reasoning together, and one says to the other,

' Whence are we ? Canst thou conceive whence we are ? Dost thou know either whence we come or to whom we belong, or whither we shall go ? Something we are, but what will in a short time become of us, canst thou tell ? ' And the other drop might answer, ' Alas, poor fellow-drop, be assured we are nothing, for the sun may arise and draw us up and scatter us and so bring us to nothing.' Says the other again, ' Suppose it do, for all that, yet we are, we have a being, we are something.'

' Why, what are we ? ' saith the other.

---

[1] *Gospel Treas.* p. 411.   [2] *Ibid.* 2nd ed. ii. p. 345.

' Why, brother drop, dost thou not know ?   We, even we, as small and as contemptible as we are in ourselves, yet we are members of the Sea ; poor drops though we be, yet let us not be discouraged : *We belong to the vast Ocean.*' " [1]

The way back to this infinite Ocean from which we have come and in which we belong is through the tiny rivulet, the narrow inlet, of our own souls, for " the Sea flows into all the creeks and crannies of the World." [2]   But to find Him—this original Ground and Reality—we must " leave the outcoasts " and go back into " the Abysse."   Most of us are busy " playing with cockel-shells and pebble-stones that lie on the outcoasts of the Kingdom," and we do not put back to the infinite Sea itself, where we become united and made one with His Life. [3]

The process of return is a process of denial and sub-traction.   The " cockel-shells and pebble-stones " must be left, and one finite thing after another must be dropped, and finally " all that thou callest I, all that selfness, all that propriety that thou hast taken to thyself, whatsoever creates in us Iness and selfness, must be brought to nothing." [4]   If we would hear God, we must still the noises within ourselves.   " All the Artillery in the World, were they all discharged together at one clap, could not more deaf the ears of our bodies than the clamorings of desires in the soul deaf its ears, so you see a man must go into silence or else he cannot hear God speak." [5]   All " the minstrels " that are singing of self and self interests " must be cast out."   If " the creature " is to be loved and used at all, it must be loved and used rightly and in balance, which is hard to do.   " Thou must love it and use it as if thou loved it not and used it not, not appropriating it to thyself, and always being ready to leave it willingly and freely ; so that thou sufferest no rending, no tearing in thy soul to part with it, and so thou usest it for God and in God and to ends appointed by God." [6]

The result of this junction of finite and infinite in us is

---

[1] *Gospel Treas.* p. 753.   [2] *Ibid.* p. 418.   [3] *Ibid.* pp. 423-425.
    [4] *Ibid.* p. 230.   [5] *Ibid.* p. 600.   [6] *Ibid.* p. 308.

that a Christian life is bound to be a strenuous contest :
" you must expect to fight a great battel." " You are,"
Everard says again, " bidden to fight with your own
selves, with your own desires, with your own affections,
with your own reason, with your own will ; and therefore
if you will finde your enemies, never look without. If
you will finde out the Devil and what he is and what his
nature is, look within you. *There* you may see him in his
colours, in his nature, in his power, in his effects and in his
working." [1]

In a word, the way to God is the way of the Cross.
Christ Himself is the pattern and His way of Life is the
typical way for all who would find God—" Christ Jesus
is He that all visions tend to ; He is the substance of all
the types, shadows, and sacrifices. He is the *business*
that the whole Word was ever about, and only is, and shall
be about ; He hath been, is, and shall be the business of
all ages, in one kinde or other." [2] " The Book of God,"
he says in another sermon, " is a great Book, and many
words are in it, and many large volumes have been drawn
out of it, but Jesus Christ is the body of it ; He is the
Mark all these words shoot at." [3] It henceforth becomes
our *business* to find Christ's life and Christ's death in us,
to see that all His deeds are done in us. Christ's will
must become our will, Christ's peace our peace, Christ's
sufferings our sufferings, Christ's cross our cross, and then
we may know " the eternal Sabbath," and keep " quiet,
even if the whole fabrick of heaven and earth crack and
the mountains tumble down." [4]

Everard was always on the watch for those things
which prevent the growth, progress, and advance of the
soul into the deeper significance of religion. The true
Christian continually " grows taller in Christ," he does
not stop at " the child's stature," his growth is " not
stinted like a Dwarf." [5] He discovers one of the prevailing

---

[1] *Gospel Treas*. p. 142.   [2] *Ibid*. p. 648.   [3] *Ibid*. p. 642.
[4] *Ibid*. pp. 99 and 250. Everard's greater contemporary, Pascal, also held
the view that what happened to Christ should take place in every Christian.
He wrote to his sister, Madame Perier, Oct. 17, 1651, on the death of their father :
" We know that what has been accomplished in Jesus Christ should be accomplished also in all His members."   [5] *Ibid*. pp. 555-556.

causes of arrested development, the " stinting " of the
soul, to lie in the wrong use of externals, in the subtle
tendency to " rest " in the elements or beginnings of
religion, as he calls them, in " the lowest things in Christianity." This is " to cover oneself with fig-leaves as
Adam did." [1]   Men " turn shadows into substance,"
and instead of using ordinances and sacraments, " as
means, schoolmasters and tutors," " as steps and guides
to Christ who is the Truth and Substance," they so use
them that they stop the soul mid-way and hinder it from
going on to Christ.[2]   He cites the way in which St. Paul
" burst out into a holy defiance " of everything which
did not directly minister to the formation of a new creation
within the person, whether it were Moses and the law or
even Christ after the flesh, or any " outward Priviledges
and Ordinances " whatever.   Those who make these
things " the top and quintessence of religion " miss the
Apostle's " more excellent way."   Those who " stick in
externals " and " rest upon them as Crutches and Go-bies "
[i.e. become arrested there] prevent growth in religion,
" turn the ordinance into an Idol " and occasion disputes
and differences, "like children who quarrel about triffles." [3]
But Everard is, nevertheless, very cautious not to go too
far in this direction and he always shows poise and balance.
So long as the outward, whether letter or sacrament, is
kept in its place and is used as means or medium for the
attainment of a spiritual goal—the formation of Christ
within—he approves of its use and warns against a too
sudden transcendence of the outward helps to the soul.[4]

Here in England, then, during the tumultuous years
from 1625 to 1650 a solid scholar and a great preacher
was teaching the people the same views which the spiritual
Reformers of Germany had taught a century earlier.
Like them, Everard taught that the book of the Bible,
in so far as it consists of words, syllables, and letters, is
not the Word of God, for God's Word is not ink and paper,
but Life and Spirit, quick and powerful, illuminating the

---

[1] *Gospel Treas.* p. 315.   [2] *Ibid.* p. 558.
[3] *Ibid.* pp. 561-562.   [4] *Ibid.* pp. 563-565.

soul immediately, and demonstrating itself by its creative work upon the inward man until he becomes like the Spirit that works within him.[1] Like them, he insisted that Christ becomes Saviour only as He becomes the Life of our lives and repeats in us in a spiritual way the events of His outward and historical life. Like them, too, he had discovered that God is not a being of wrath and anger, needing to be appeased. On the contrary he says : " Beloved, were you once to come to a true sight of God, you would see Him glorious and amiable, full of love and mercy and tenderness—all wrath and frowns blown clean away. We should see in Him not so much as any shadow of anger."[2] Like them, he found heaven not far away but in the redeemed soul : " Heaven is nothing but Grace perfected, 'tis of the same nature of that you enjoy here when you are united by faith to Christ."[3] "I remember," he once said, " how I was taught as a child, either by my nurse, or my mother, or my schoolmaster, that God was above in heaven, above the sun, moon and stars, and there, I thought, was His Court, and His Chamber of presence, and I thought it a great height to come to this knowledge ; but I assure you I had more to do to unlearn this principle than ever I had to learn it."[4] He tries to call his hearers away from " the childish apprehensions " that heaven is a place of " visible ànd ocular glories," or that " it shall be only hereafter," or that its glory " consists in Thrones, and Crowns, and Scepters, in Music, Harps and Vyols, and such like carnal and poor things."[5]

He was a man of beautiful spirit, of saintly life, " courageous and discerning," " concerned not so much over self-sufferings as that truth should not in any way be obstructed through him," and he belongs in the list of those who saw through the veil of the outward, through the parable of the letter, and found the inward and eternal Reality.[6]

---

[1] *Gospel Treas.* pp. 310-315.   [2] *Ibid.* p. 361.   [3] *Ibid.* p. 365.
[4] *Ibid.* p. 736.   [5] *Ibid.* p. 552.
[6] It is not possible to tell whether the sermons of John Everard were generally known to the early Quakers or not. He held similar views to theirs on many points, and he reiterates, with as much vigour as does Fox, the inadequacy of

III. Giles Randall and his Translations

Another seventeenth-century interpreter of religion as direct and immediate experience of God was Giles Randall, who, like John Everard, was a scholar, a translator of religious books, and a powerful popular preacher. If one knew him only through the accounts of the heresy-hunters of the period, one would suppose him to have been a disseminator of the most " virulent poyson " for the soul ; but a careful examination of all the material available convinces me that he was a high-minded, sincere, and fearless bearer of the message of the present, living, inwardly-experienced Christ, as Eternal Spirit, Divine Light, and Word of God.

It is extremely difficult, from the fragmentary details at hand, to construct a biographical account of Randall, but the following sketch of him seems fairly well supported by facts :

He was the son of Edward Randall of Chipping Wycombe, Bucks, and received his B.A. from Lincoln College, Oxford, February 13, 1625–6.[1] He was probably the nephew of John Randall, B.D. (1570–1622), an eminent Puritan divine, a man of good scholarship and of large means, who bequeathed by will his house and garden to his " loveing Nephewe Gyles Randall." [2] He seems to have been for some years a minister in good odour and repute, and to have given no occasion of complaint against his doctrine before 1643. He probably was the Giles Randall who was arrested in 1637 and tried in the Star Chamber for

---

University learning as a preparation for spiritual ministry. One Quaker at least of the early time read Everard and appreciated him. That was John Bellers. In his " Epistle to the Quarterly Meeting of London and Middlesex," written in 1718, Bellers quotes " the substance of an excellent Discourse of a poor man in Germany, above 300 years ago, then writ by John Taulerus, and since printed in John Everard's Works, who was a religious dissenter in King James the First's time." He thereupon gives the " Dialogue between a Learned Divine and a Beggar " (which Everard ascribed to Tauler) to add force to his own presentation of " the duty of propagating piety, charity, and industry among men."

[1] Foster's *Alumni Oxonienses* (1500–1714), vol. iii. Early Series, p. 1231.
[2] 57, Savile, Probate Court of Canterbury, Somerset House.

preaching against "ship-money" as unjust and an offence against God, since it was, he declared in his sermon, "a way of taking burdens off rich men's shoulders and laying them on the necks of poor men." [1] He was again before the Star Chamber—this time it is certainly our Giles Randall—in 1643 charged with preaching "anabaptism," "familism," and "antinomianism," according to the usual labels of the time. He had been for some years preaching peaceably at "the Spital" in London with great multitudes of people flocking to hear him.[2] The charge of heresy was brought against Randall for a sermon which he was said to have preached in St. Martin Orgar's, a soundly orthodox church, in Candlewick ward, London—the charge being that he preached against "the mandatory and obligatory nature of the law as a Christian rule to walk by," and asserted that a child of God can live as sinless a life as Christ's was.[3] He was "removed" from the ministry "for his anabaptism" in the autumn of 1644, though he continued to preach after being "removed." [4] The famous drag-nets of heresy give us a few more details of Randall's "poysonous" doctrine. Edwards says that Randall taught that "our common food, ordinary eating and drinking, is a sacrament of Christ's death," and that "all creatures [i.e. everything in the visible creation] held forth God in Christ." [5] Samuel Rutherford charges him with teaching a possible perfection in this life : "Randall, the antinomian and Familist says, those persons are ever learning and never coming to knowledge who say that perfection is not attainable in this life." [6] He further charges that Randall in a sermon said that "Christ's Parables, from Sowing, a Draw-net, Leaven, etc., did prove that to expound the Scriptures by allegories was lawfull and that all the things of this life, as Seeds, the Wayside, a Rocke, the Sea, a

---

[1] Calendar of State Papers, Dom. Ser. Charles I.
[2] Robert Baillie's *Anabaptisme, the true Fountaine of Independency* (1646), p. 102.
[3] Thomas Gataker's *God's Eye on His Israel* (1645), Preface.
[4] *Journal of Commons*, August 9, 1644, pp. 584-585.
[5] *Gangraena* (1646), part iii. p. 25.
[6] *A Survey of the Spiritual Antichrist* (1647), chap. xi. p. 143.

Net, the Leaven, etc., were sacraments of Christ . . . and that a spiritual minde might see the mysteries of the Gospel in all the things of nature and of this life. This man who preacheth most abomnable Familisme is suffered in and about London publickly, twise on the Lord's Day, to draw hundreds of Godly people after him ! " [1]

John Etherington throws a little more light upon the nature of this " abomnable Familism," which so many godly people liked. He says that Randall taught in his sermons that when a person is baptized with the Holy Ghost he knows all things, and has entered into the deep mystery which is " like the great ocean where there is no casting anchor nor sounding the bottome " ; that perfection and the resurrection are attainable in the present time ; that " those who have the Spirit have nothing to doe with the law nor with the baptism of repentance which John preached " ; " he presumes to turn the holy writings of Moses, the Prophets, of Christ and His Apostles into Allegories," and gives " a spiritual meaning " to the same.[2] It is clear from the comments of these crumb-pickers of pernicious doctrine that Giles Randall, as a preacher, was teaching the views now quite familiar to us. He was teaching that the whole world is a revelation of God, that Christ is God fully revealed ; that the Divine Spirit, incarnate in Him, comes upon men still and brings them into the bottomless, unsoundable deeps of Life with God, and makes it possible for them to attain a perfect life ; that the Scriptures as outward and legal must be transcended, and that they must be spiritually discerned and experienced.

Nearly everything connected with Randall's name presents an historical puzzle to us. His biography, as we have seen, lies hid in obscurity and his books present baffling problems. There are three translations of religious classics which bear his name on the title-page, and which are introduced to the reader in Prefaces written by him, but it is far from certain that he actually made the transla-

---

[1] *A Survey of the Spiritual Antichrist*, chap. lxxvi. pp. 162-163.
[2] *A Brief Discovery*, etc. (1645), pp. 1-5.

tions. In 1646 he published a little book called the *Single Eye, or the Vision of God wherein is unfolded the Mystery of the Divine Presence.* Randall says that the book was written by " that learned Doctor Cusanus." It is in fact a translation of the *De visione Dei* of Nicholas of Cusa, and it is word for word a printed copy of the Cambridge MS. ascribed to John Everard. The other book, published in 1648, is an English edition of *Theologia Germanica*, the translation being made from the Latin of " John Theophilus," that is, Sebastian Castellio. It is called " a Little Golden Manuall briefly discovering the mysteries, sublimity, perfection and simplicity of Christianity in Belief and Practice." Everard, it will be remembered, also translated this " little golden book," but in this case there are very great variations between Randall's printed copy and the Cambridge MS., and they probably did not come from the same hand.[1] The English translation was evidently made some time before the appearance of this edition of 1648, for Randall says in his Introduction that " This little Book was long veiled and obscured (by its unknown tongue) from the eye of the illiterate and inexpert, until some years since, through the desires and industries of some of our own countrymen, lovers of Truth, it was translated and made to speak to thee in thine own dialect and language. But the time of its Nativity being under the late wise and wary Hierarchie who had monopolized and engrossed the discovery of others . . . it walked up and down the city in MSS. at deer rates from hand to hand of some well-wishers to truth, in clandestine and private manner ; like Moses in his Arke, or the little

---

[1] Contemporary writers held that the Giles Randall who preached in " the Spital " was the translator. Robert Baillie, Principal of Glasgow University, in his work on *Anabaptisme*, pp. 102-103, speaks of Randall who preached in " the Spital," and refers to his increasing temerity as shown by the fact that " he hath lately printed two very dangerous books and set his Preface before each of them, composed as he professes long ago by Popish Priests, the one by a Dutch Frier and the other by an English Capuchine." Baillie further refers to the " deadly poison " of these books as shown in Benjamin Bourne's *Description and Confutation of Mysticall Antichrist, the Familists* (1646), where " the dangerous books " are named, as *Theologia Germanica, the Bright Star, Divinity and Philosophy Dissected*. Edward's *Gangraena* also identifies Randall the preacher with the translator of " Popish Books written by Priests and Friers," citing as an example " The Vision of God by Cardinall Cusanus," *op. cit.* (1646), part iii.

Child fled and hid from Herod, never daring to crowd into the Presse, fearing the rude usuage of those then in authority." [1]

Both Robert Baillie and Benjamin Bourne had seen the treatise before their respective books against heresy appeared in 1646, and they were deeply stirred against Randall for sowing what to their minds seemed such dangerous doctrines and such regard for "Popish writings." [2] His critics further connect Randall with other books. Baillie speaks of two books : " the one by a Dutch Frier [evidently the *Theologia*] and the other by an English Capuchine." Bourne writes against those dangerous books *Theologia Germanica, The Bright Star, Divinity and Philosophy Dissected*, and Edwards couples with *the Vision of God* (the treatise by Nicholas of Cusa) " the third part of the Rule of Perfection by a Cappuchian Friar." [3]

John Goodwin, vicar of St. Stephen's in Coleman St., commenting on Edward's *Gangraena*, humorously says : " I marvaile how Mr. Edwards having (it seems) an authorized power to make errors and heresies at what rate and of what materialles he pleaseth, and hopes to live upon the trade, could stay his pen at so small a number as 180, and did not advance to that angelicall quotient in the Apocalypse, which is *ten thousand times ten thousand,"* and he adds that if Edwards had consulted with a book " printed within the compasse of his foure years, intitled *Divinity and Philosophy Dissected, set out by a mad man,* with some few others . . . He shall be able to increase his roll of errors from 180 to 280, if not to 500." [4]   Samuel

---

[1] Preface.

[2] Bourne's *Description and Confutation* and Baillie's *Anabaptisme.* It seems likely that there was an earlier edition of the *Theologia* than this of 1648, as the chapters and pages quoted by Bourne do not correspond with those of the 1648 edition, whose title-page has this clause : " Also a Treatise of the Soul and other additions not *before* printed."

[3] *Gangraena*, part iii.

[4] Goodwin's *Cretensis* (1646). The book, entitled *Divinity and Philosophy Dissected*, and attributed by implication to Randall, was published in Amsterdam in 1644, with the following title-page :

"Divinity & Philosophy Dissected, & set forth by a mad man.

"The first Book divided into 3 Chapters.

"Chap. I.   The description of the World in man's heart with the Articles of the Christian Faith.

Rutherford says: " So hath *Randel* the *Familist* prefixed an Epistle to two Popish Tractates, furnishing to us excellent priviledges of Familisme, the one called *Theologia Germanica*, and the other *Bright Starre*, which both advance perfect Saints above Law, and Gospel ". . .[1]

This treatise, called *A Bright Starre* (London, 1646), which so deeply disturbed the seventeenth-century guardians of orthodoxy, is a translation of "The Third Part of the Rule of Perfection," written by an English Capuchin Friar, and " faithfully done into the English tongue," apparently by Randall, "for the common good."[2] It is a profoundly mystical book, characterized by interior depth and insight. Its central aim is the exposition of a stage of spiritual life which transcends both " the active life " and " the contemplative life," a stage which the writer calls " the Life Supereminent." In this highest stage " the essential will of God is practiced," without strain or effort, because God Himself has now become the inner Life and Being of the person, the spring and power of the new-formed will.

Randall's preface, or " Epistle to the Reader," as he calls it, is a further revelation of his religious views, and his Christian spirit. He pleads for freedom and for variety in religious life and thought. God does not want one fixed and unvarying Christian form or doctrine ; He wants variety in the spiritual life as He has arranged for variety in the external world of nature : " As in the world all men are not of an equall height and stature of body, but some taller, some shorter ; some weaker, some stronger : so neither are all of one just and even proportion in spiritual light and strength of faith in the kingdome of Christ, some are dwarfs of Zacheus his pitch, some

---

"Chap. II. A description of one Spirit acting in all, which some affirme is God.

"Chap. III. A description of the Scripture according to the history and mystery thereof.

"Amsterdam, 1644."

[1] *Survey*, etc., part ii. chap. xlvii. p. 53.

[2] The only copy of Randall's *Bright Starre* which I have been able to locate is in the Lambeth Palace Library. A copy of it formerly belonged to the learned Quaker, Benjamin Furly, and was sold with his remarkable collection of books in 1714.

againe of Saul's port, taller by his head and shoulders than his brethren ; so, in the kingdome of Christ, some are babes, some are young men, some are fathers, every one according to the measure of the gift of Christ." God has something in His kingdom that fits each spiritual stature, something suited to each intellectual capacity. He does not want one and the same note struck by all— " harping blindly on one string." He does not want men to be " tyed to one forme and kept forever to one lesson, unable to top up their work "—He wants men to " go from strength to strength, from faith to faith and from height to height."

Randall declares that he has observed with deep sorrow " the *non-proficiency* of many ingenuous spirits who through the policie of others and the too too much modesty and timerity of themselves " have failed to progress " to the top and pitch " of their possible perfection—" poore soules after many years travelling being found in the same place and going the same pace ! " He hopes that this book on Perfection which he is now giving " common vulgar people in their own mother tongue," though it is a way that is " high and hard and almost unheard of amongst us," may help men to grow up into their full stature and to come to " the uttermost steps of Jacob's Ladder which reacheth into the heavens." The lower stages of the religious life consist (1) of external practices and exercises in conformity to the law of God, and (2) interior contemplation and meditation of a God thought of as outside and beyond the soul's real possession. But the true spiritual life, and " Sabbath rest of the soul," is reached only when God becomes the inner Life of our lives, when Christ is formed within and we see Light and have our wisdom through His divine anointing. At the highest stage of spiritual life man finds himself by ceasing to be himself. God can now reveal His beauty and glory through such a person and act and work in him and through him. This teaching, Randall admits, is only for " experienced Christians," but he believes that this book will have " good successe amongst *the Children of the Light,* who are taught of God and who run and read the hidden and deepe things of God." [1]

If we may judge Randall from his extant Prefaces he was a beautiful spirit and was, in fact, what he calls himself, "a lover of the Truth in the Truth." [2] He says that "Nothing is or ever was endeavored by most men, with more industry and less success than the true knowledge of God," but this perennial failure is due, he thinks, to the false ways which have been taken, especially to " the negative process of abstraction " by which men have tried in vain to find God. The only true way to Him is " the new and living way " through the concrete revelation of Him. "The sound and unerring knowledge of God standeth in your knowledge of your man Christ Jesus, and whoever hath seen Him hath seen the Father also, for He is not a dead image of Him, but a living Image of the invisible God, yea, the fulgor or brightness of His glory and character of His person. . . . He is an Immanuel, God with us, God in us. . . . But there is no true knowledge of God within us till He be in us formed in the face of Jesus Christ." [3] He declares that since " understanding " must be helped by " sense " and " sense is not available till it live in the light of the understanding," we must learn to find the infinite in the finite, the invisible in the visible, and thus in Christ we have God " finitely infinite and infinitely finite "—" He cloathes Himself with flesh, reason, sense and the form and nature of a servant, who yet is above all and Lord over all." " He that is infinitely above thee makes himselfe be to thee [visibly] what He is in thee." [4] Christ is the universal revealer of God to all who see Him, just as the portrait of a human face seems to fix and follow the beholder from any position in the room, while at the same time it does the same to all other beholders from whatever angle they may look. [5]

The Vision of God, whether Englished by Randall or

---

[1] This term, " Children of the Light," was the name by which Friends, or Quakers, first called themselves. It was plainly a term current at the time for a Christian who put the emphasis on inward life and personal experience.

[2] Preface to *Theologia.*

[3] Preface to *The Vision of God.*

[4] *Ibid.*

[5] Nicholas' Preface to *De visione Dei.*

by Everard, or by both working together, is translated into beautiful, often poetical and rhythmical English, and contains many vivid passages, such as the following : " Thou, O God, canst never forsake me so long as I am *capable of Thee.*" [1]   " I love my life exceedingly because Thou art the sweetness of my life." [2]   " No man can turn to Thee except Thou be present, for except Thou wert present and diddest solicit me I should not know Thee at all." [3]   " Restless is my heart, O Lord, because Thy love hath enflamed it with such a desire that it cannot rest but in Thee alone." [4]   " In the Son of Man I see the Son of God, because Thou art so the Son of Man that Thou art the Son of God and in the finite attracted nature I see the Infinite Attracting Nature."   " I see all things in thy human nature which I see in thy divine nature." [5]   " To come to God is Paradise ; to see God is to be in Paradise." [6] " The Word of God illuminateth the understanding as the light of the sun doth the world. I see the fountain of Light in the Word of God. . . . Christ is the Word of God humanified and man deified." [7]   " What is more easie than to believe God, what is more sweet than to love Him. . . . Thy Spirit, O God, comes into the intellectual spirit of good men, and by the heat of divine love concocts the virtuall power which may be perfected in us. . . . All Scriptures labour for nothing but to show Thee, all intellectual spirits have no other exercise but to seek Thee and to reveal Thee. Above all things Thou hast given me Jesus for a Master, the Way of Life, and Truth, so that there might be nothing at all wanting to me." [8]

The literary style of *Divinity and Philosophy Dissected* is unlike that of Randall's known writings, and yet it is not impossible for him to have written it. [9]   The ideas which fill the little book are quite similar to those which

---

[1] *The Vision of God*, p. 11.   [2] *Ibid.* p. 13.

[3] *Ibid.* p. 19. Compare this passage with Pascal's saying : " Thou wouldst not seek me if thou hadst not already found me."

[4] *Ibid.* p. 37.   [5] *Ibid.* p. 130.   [6] *Ibid.* p. 138.

[7] *Ibid.* pp. 151-152.   [8] *Ibid.* pp. 170-176.

[9] There is no author's name or initial in the book, only the statement that it is " put forth " by a " mad man," who " desires to be in my wits and right minde to God, although a fool and madman to the world."

Randall held and are in full accord with those which prevailed in this general group of Christian thinkers. The writer of the treatise, whoever he was, is fond of allegory and symbolic interpretation. He turns Adam into a figure and makes the Garden of Eden an allegory in quite modern fashion. " Doe you thinke," he writes, " that there was a materiall garden or a tree whereon did grow the fruit of good and evill, or that the serpent did goe up in the same to speake to the woman? Sure it cannot stand with reason that it could be so, for it is said that all the creatures did come to Adam, and he gave them names according to their natures : now it is contrary to the Serpent's nature to speake after the manner of men, unlesse you will alleadge that she understood the language of the beasts, and thought them wiser than God, and resolved to be ruled by them, which to me seems altogether against reason, that the woman should be so ignorant and unrationall, who was created rationall after the image of God to be ruler of all creatures : for at this day if a Serpent went up into a tree, and did speake from thence to men and women, it would make them afraid in so much that they would not doe what he bid them : or dost thou thinke that in Meso-potamia (a great way off beyond the seas) that there is a materiall garden wherein standeth the tree of life, and the tree of knowledge of good and ill, both in one place, and an angell, standing with a flickering sword to keep the tree of life from the man ! " [1]

The book contains a very striking confession of Faith quite unlike that which Rutherford or Baillie or Edwards would have allowed as " sound," but yet serious, honest, and marked with a clear note of experience. God is, for the writer, above everything a living God, a Spirit, " a perfect clear Light that reveals to man the Truth." God is, he says, Light, Life, and Love, and He is all these things to man. He instructs and convinces his conscience ; He disciplines and corrects him ; He raises condemnation in us for our sins, and " His Light persuades our hearts to have true sorrow and real repentance for our sins, with a

---

[1] *Divinity and Philosophy Dissected*, pp. 39-40.

broken and contrite heart and sorrowful spirit, and so
we begin to hate ourselves and our sins, and doe really
forsake them."[1] " There is," he maintains, in words that
sound strangely like the yet unborn Quakers, " an infallible Spirit, Jesus Christ, the power of God in us, which
directs, corrects, instructs, perswades, and makes us wise
unto salvation ; for He is the holy Word of life unto us
. . . and discovers all mysteries unto us, . . . if so be
we are obedient unto Him ; but if we are not obedient
unto Him, this infallible Spirit, Jesus Christ in us, then
we shall know nothing of God or of the Scriptures, but it
shall be a *sealed book*, a *dead letter, a seeming contradiction*
unto us."[2]

Samuel Rutherford declares the little treatise to be
" a rude, foolish and unlearned Pamphlet of late penned
and changing, as Familists and Antinomians doe, Scripture
and God and Christ into metaphores and vaine Allegories."[3] The comment of this good man is honest and
sincere, but of value only as revealing the mental attitude
of himself. Here the representative of the old system
was speaking out of the past and condemning a dawning
movement which with his apperceiving material he could
not understand, but which was in a few years to have
extraordinary expansion and which, when it should in
time become defecated through discipline and spiritual
travail, was destined to speak to the condition of many
minds to whom Rutherford's " notions " have become
only empty words.

IV

A beautiful little anonymous book of this period,
containing a similar conception of Christianity to that
set forth in the writings of Everard and Randall, must be
briefly considered here : *The Life and Light of a Man in
Christ Jesus* (London, 1646). The writer, who was a
scholarly man, shows the profound influence of the
Theologia Germanica, that universal book of religion which

---

[1] *Divinity and Philosophy Dissected*, p. 17.   [2] *Ibid.* p. 62.
[3] *A Survey of the Spiritual Antichrist*, chap. xiv. p. 163.

fed so many souls in the sixteenth and seventeenth centuries, and he has evidently found, either at home or abroad, spiritual guides who have brought him to the Day-star in his own heart.

Religion, he says, is wholly a matter of the " operative manifestation of Christ in a man—the divine Spirit living in a man." [1] To miss that experience and to lack that inner life in God is to miss the very heart of religion. " There be many and diverse Religions and Baptisms among many and diverse peoples of the habitable world, but to be baptized as a man in Christ—that is to be baptized into the living, active God, so that the man has his salvation and eternal well-being wrought in him by the Spirit and life of his God—is the only best." [2] Those who lack " this real spiritual business " never attain " the true Sabbath-rest of the soul." They go to meeting on " Sunday, Sabbath or First day [sic] merely to hear such or such a rare divine preach or discourse, or to participate in such or such Ordinances." [3] They have " an artificiall, historicall Divinity [Theology] which they have attained by the eye, that is by reading books, or by the ears, that is, by hearing this or that man, or by gathering up expressions "—their religion rests on " knowledge " and not on Christ experienced within.[4] This external religion is not so much wrong as it is inadequate and immature. " It is," he says, " like unto young children, who with shells and little stones imitate a real building ! " [5] The religion which carries a man beyond shadows to true realities and from the cockle-shell house to a permanent and eternal temple for the Spirit is the religion which finds Christ within as the Day-star in the man's own heart.[6]

There is throughout this simple little book a noble appreciation of love as the " supream good " for the soul. " The God of infinite goodness and eternal love " is a kind of refrain which bursts forth in these pages again

[1] *Life and Light*, p. 3.   [2] *Ibid.* pp. 99 and 101 quoted freely.
[3] *Ibid.* p. 19. It should be noted that this use of " First-day " for Sunday antedates the Quaker practice.
[4] *Ibid.* pp. 26-27.   [5] *Ibid.* p. 35.   [6] See *ibid.* p. 36.

and again. Love in *us* is, he thinks, " a sparkle of that immense and infinite Love of the King and Lord of Love." [1] Salvation and eternal well-being consist for him in the formation of a life " consecrated and united unto the true Light and Love of Christ."   The man who has this Life within him will always be willing and glad when the time comes " to returne againe into the bosome of his heavenly Father-God." [2]   And not only is the man who has the Life of Christ in him harmonized in love upwardly toward God ; he is also harmonized outwardly towards his fellows.   " He is a member with all other men, with the good as a lowly-minded disciple to them ; with those that are not in Christ, as a deare, sympathizing helper, doing his utmost to do them good." [3]   He has written his " little Treatise," he says, " as a love-token from the Father " to help lead men out of the " darke pits of the world's darkness " into the full Light of the soul's day-dawn.

The book lacks the robustness and depth that are so clearly in evidence in most of the writings that have been dealt with in this volume, but there is a beauty, a simplicity, a sweetness, a sincerity born of experience, which give this book an unusual flavour and perfume.   The writer says that there is " an endless battle between the Seed of the woman and the seed of the serpent," but one feels that he has fought the battle through and won. He says that " a man should be unto God what a house is to a man," *i.e.* a man should be a habitation of the living God, and the reader feels that this man has made himself a habitation for the divine presence within.   He says if you want spiritual help you must go to a " man who has skill in God," and one lays down his slender book feeling assured that, out of the experience of Christ in his own soul, he did have " skill in God," so that he could speak to the condition of others.   There was at least one man in England in 1646 who knew that the true source and basis of religion was to be found in the experience of Christ within and not in theological notions of Him.

[1] *Life and Light*, p. 11.   [2] *Ibid.* p. 38.   [3] *Ibid.* p. 34.

CHAPTER XIV

SPIRITUAL RELIGION IN HIGH PLACES—ROUS, VANE, AND STERRY

THE spiritual struggles which culminated in the great upheaval of the English Commonwealth were the normal fruit of the Reformation spirit, when once it had penetrated the life of the English *people* and kindled the fire of personal conviction in their hearts. Beginning as it did with the simple substitution of royal for papal authority in the government of the Church, the English Reformation lacked at its inception the inward depth, the prophetic vision, the creative power, the vigorous articulation of newly awakened personal conscience, which formed such a commanding feature of the Reformation movement on the Continent. It took another hundred years in England to cultivate individual conscience, to ripen religious experience, to produce the body of dynamic *ideas*, and to create the necessary prophetic vision before an intense and popular spirit of Reform could find its voice and marching power. The contact of English exiles and chance visitors with the stream of thought in Germany, in Switzerland, and in Holland, and the filtering in of literature from the Continent, together with the occasional coming of living exponents, sowed the seeds that slowly ripened into that strange and interesting variety of religious thought and practice which forms the inner life of the Commonwealth. The policy of the throne had always opposed this steadily increasing tide of thought which refused to run in the well-worn channels, but, as usual, the opposition and hindrances only served to

deepen personal conviction, to sharpen the edge of conscience, to nourish great and daring spirits, to formulate
the battle-ideas and to win popular support. The inner
life and the varied tendencies of the Commonwealth are
too rich and complicated to be adequately treated here.[1]
The purpose of this chapter is to show how the type of
inward and spiritual religion, which the Reformation in
its kindling power everywhere produced, finds expression
in the writings of three men who came to large public
prominence in the period of the Commonwealth, Francis
Rous, Sir Harry Vane, and Peter Sterry.

I

Francis Rous was born in Cornwall in 1579. He
graduated B.A. at Oxford in 1597 and at the University
of Leyden in 1599. He entered the Middle Temple in
1601, with the prospect of a legal and public career
before him, but soon withdrew and retired to Cornwall,
where in a quiet country retreat he became absorbed in
theological studies. His later writings show an intimate
acquaintance with the great Church Fathers, especially
with St. Augustine, St. Ambrose, Clement of Alexandria,
Origen and the two Gregorys, and with the mystics,
especially with the writings of Dionysius the Areopagite,
St. Bernard, Thomas à Kempis, and John Tauler. He
was intensely Puritan in temper and sympathies in his
earlier period of life, and much of his writing at this stage
was for the purpose of promoting the increase of a deeper
and more adequate reform in the Church. He translated
the Psalms into " English Meeter," and his version was approved by the Westminster Assembly, authorized for use by
Parliament, and adopted by the estates in Scotland, "whose
Psalms," Carlyle says, " the Northern Kirks still sing." [2]
He was a member of Charles I.'s first and second
Parliaments, and again of the Short Parliament and of

[1] I have studied the " Familists," the " Anabaptists," the " Seekers," and
" Ranters," and some of the interesting religious characters, such as John Salt-
marsh, William Dell, and Gerard Winstanley, in my *Studies in Mystical Religion*
(London, 1908).

[2] *Oliver Cromwell's Letters and Speeches* (New York, 1900), i. p. 103.

the Long Parliament. He was also a member of the
Little Parliament, often called " Barebones Parliament,"
of which he was Speaker, and of the Parliaments of 1654
and of 1656, and he was, too, a member of Oliver's Council
of State. He was one of many thoughtful men of the
time who passed with the rapid development of affairs
from the Presbyterian position to Independency, and he
served on the Committee for the propagation of the
Gospel which framed a congregational plan for Church
government. He was a voluminous writer, but his type
of Christianity can be seen sufficiently in his three little
books : *Mystical Marriage* (1635), *The Heavenly Academy*
(1638), and *The Great Oracle* (1641).[1]

He, again, like so many before him, influenced by
Plato as well as by the New Testament and Christian
writers, made the discovery that there is something
divine in the soul of man, and that this " something
divine " in man is always within hail of an inner world
of divine splendour. " I was first breathed forth from
heaven," he says, " and came from God in my creation.
I am divine and heavenly in my original, in my essence,
in my character. . . . I am a spirit, though a low one,
and God is a Spirit, even the highest one, and God is the
fountaine of this spirit [of mine]." [2]

The possession of this divine " original," unlost even
in the mist and mystery of a world of time and sense,
enables man, he holds, to live in that higher world even
while he sojourns in this lower world. Human reason,
i.e. reasoning, is sufficient to guide in the affairs of this
life, but it is blind to the world of the Spirit from which
we came. " The soule has two eyes—one human reason,
the other far excelling that, a divine and spiritual Light.
. . . By it the soule doth see spiritual things as truly as
the corporall eye doth corporal things." [3] "Human reason
acknowledges the sovereignty of this spiritual Light as a
candle acknowledges the greater light of the sun," and,

---

[1] These three books were issued together in Latin under the title, *Interiora
Regni Dei*, in 1655 and in 1674, and in an English Collection of Rous' Works
under the title, *Treatises and Meditations* (1657).
[2] *Mystical Marriage*, pp. 1-2. [3] *Treatises and Meditations*, pp. 230-231.

by its in-shining, the soul passes " beyond a speculative and discoursing holiness, even beyond a forme of godliness and advances to *the power of it.*" [1]   But this inward Light does not make outward helps unnecessary. " The light of the outward word [the Scriptures] and the Light in our soules are twinnes and agree together like brothers," [2] and again he says, " It is an invaluable [inestimable] Loss that men do so much divide the outward Teacher from the Inward," though he insists that the ministry of the Spirit is above any ministry of the letter.[3]

This eye of the soul which is a part of its original structure and is responsive to the Light of the spiritual world, so that " soule and Light become knit together into one," is also called by Rous, as by his predecessors, " Seed " or " Word." Sometimes this divine Seed is thought of as an original part of the soul, and sometimes, under the assumption that " man has grown wild by the fall of Adam " and is " run to weeds," it is conceived, as by Schwenckfeld, as a saving remedy supernaturally supplied to the soul—" Christ entering into our spirits lays in them an immortal seed." [4]   In any case, whether the Seed be original, as is often implied and stated, or whether it be a supernatural gift of divine Grace in Christ, as is sometimes implied, it is, in Rous' conception, essential for the attainment of a religious experience or a Christian life : " A Christian man hath as much need of Christ's Spirit [called in other passages Seed or Word] to be a Christian and to live eternally, as a natural man hath of a spirit [principle of intelligence] to be a man and to live temporally, so Christ's Spirit and a man together are a Christian, which is a holy, eternal and happy thing." [5]   He shows, as do so many of those who emphasize the inner experience of Christ as a living presence, an exalted appreciation of the historical revelation in Christ.   Christ is, he says, both God and man, and thus being the perfect union of divinity and humanity

---

[1] *Treatises and Meditations*, pp. 240 and 258.   [2] *Ibid.* p. 235.
[3] *The Heavenly Academy*, pp. 110-111.   [4] *Mystical Marriage*, p. 10.
[5] *Treatises and Meditations*, p. 496.

can be our Saviour.[1] Here in the full light of His Life and Love we may discover the true nature of God, who was " great with love before we loved Him." [2] The outer word answers to the inner Light as deep calls unto deep, and the two are " knit together " not to be sundered. The eye must be on Christ the Light, and the wise soul " must watch the winde and tide of the Spirit, as the seaman watcheth the naturall winde and tide. When the tide of the Spirit floweth then put thy hand to the oar, for then if thou row strongly thou maiest advance mightily." [3]

He quaintly says that he has written about these spiritual things, about the world of divine splendour and the " soule's inner eye," because he wants to exhibit " some bunches of grapes brought from the land of promise to show that this land is not a meere imagination, but some have seene it and have brought away parcels, pledges and ernests of it. In these appears *a world above the world*, a love that passeth human love, a peace that passeth naturall understanding, a joy unspeakable and glorious, a taste of the chiefe and soveraigne good." He has, further, written because he wanted to " provoke others of this nation to bring forth more boxes of this precious ointment." [4]

His little books are saturated with a devotional spirit rising into words like these : " Let my love rest in nothing short of thee, O God ! " " Kindle and enflame and enlarge my love. Enlarge the arteries and conduit pipes by which Thou the head and fountaine of love flows in thy members, that being abundantly quickened and watered with the Spirit I may abundantly love Thee." [5] They contain bursts of intense prayer—" Put thy owne image and beauty more and more on my soule." He went through all the Parliamentary storms of that great epoch ; he was Provost of Eton College ; he was Cromwell's friend ; but his main ambition seems to have been to be " knit to God by a personal union," to have " the day-

---

[1] *Mystical Marriage*, p. 10. [2] *Ibid.* p. 16. [3] *Ibid.* p. 193.
[4] Preface to *Mystical Marriage*. [5] *Mystical Marriage*, p. 322.

spring in his own heart," and to be taught in " the heavenly Academy—the High School of Experience." [1]

II

The story of Sir Harry Vane's life, adequately told, would involve the entire history of the great epoch of the Commonwealth. Next to Cromwell, he was the most influential shaper of events from the time of the meeting of the Long Parliament in 1640 until his " retirement " on the occasion of the expulsion of the members of Parliament in 1653. In his views of constitutional government and of human liberty he was one of the most original and one of the most modern men of the seventeenth century. Richard Baxter, who had no love for Vane, is only stating an actual fact when he says : " To most of our changes he was that within the House that Cromwell was without." [2] Clarendon, who loved him still less, said of him : " He was indeed a man of extraordinary parts, a pleasant wit, a great understanding which pierced into and discerned the purposes of men with wonderful sagacity." [3] What Milton thought of him he has told in one of the noblest sonnets that a poet ever wrote on a great statesman :

> Vane, young in years, but in sage counsel old,
> Than whom a better senator ne'er held
> The helm of Rome, when gowns not arms repelled
> The fierce Epirot and the African bold :
> Whether to settle peace, or to unfold
> The drift of hollow states hard to be spelled,
> Then to advise how war may best upheld
> Move by her two main nerves, iron and gold,
> In all her equipage ; besides to know
> Both spiritual power and civil, what each means,
> What severs each, thou hast learned, which few have done :
> The bounds of either sword to thee we owe ;
> Therefore on thy firm hand religion leans
> In peace, and reckons thee her eldest son.[4]

---

[1] *The Heavenly Academy*, Preface, and *ibid.* p. 57.
[2] *Reliquiae Baxterianae*, i. p. 75.
[3] Clarendon, *History of the Rebellion and Civil Wars* (Oxford, 1827), p. 1581.
[4] Milton's sonnet *To Sir Henry Vane the Younger.*

Vane was quite naturally selected at the Restoration as one of the actors in the historical drama who could not be allowed to live any longer. The day after Vane's trial began, Charles II. wrote to Clarendon : " He is too dangerous a man to let live, if we can honestly put him out of the way." [1] His death brought out the loftiest traits of his character, and gave him a touch of beauty and glory of character which for posterity has done much to cover the flaws and defects which were not lacking in him. " In all things," writes Pepys, who saw everything in those days, " he appeared the most resolved man that ever died in that manner." [2]

It is, however, not Vane the statesman, the maker of covenants with Scotch armies, the creator of sinews of war for the battles of Marston Moor and Naseby, the organizer of a conquering navy, the man who dared withstand his old friend Cromwell in the day of the great soldier's power, that concerns us in this chapter ; it is Vane, the religious Independent, the exponent of inward religion ; the man whom Milton calls " religion's eldest son." Even in his early youth he passed through a decisive experience which altered his entire after-life. " About the fourteenth or fifteenth year of my age," he said in his dying speech, " God was pleased to lay the foundation or ground-work of repentance in me, for the bringing me home to Himself, by His wonderful rich and free grace, revealing His Son in me, that by the knowledge of the only true God and Jesus Christ whom He hath sent, I might, even whilst here in the body, be made a partaker of eternal life, in the first fruits of it. . . . Since that foundation of repentance was laid in me, through grace I have been kept steadfast, desiring to walk in all good conscience toward God and toward men, according to the best light and understanding God gave me." From this early period on through his life, he always emphasized the importance of first-hand experience, of inward revelation, and of Christ's reign in the kingdom of the

---

[1] Burnet, *History of his Own Times* (Airy ed.), i. p. 286.
[2] Pepys, *Diary* (ed. by H. B. Wheatley, London, 1893), ii. p. 242.

human soul. He was still a very young man, when, under
the impelling guidance of his conscience, he felt himself
called to intermit, as Schwenckfeld and others had done,
the practice of the sacraments of the Church. His
attitude toward the sacraments at this time, and, apparently ever afterwards, was that of the " Seekers." He
had reached the insight that religion is a spiritual relationship with a spiritual God, and on the basis of this position
he questioned the divine " commission " of those who
administered the external ceremonies of the Church. It
is, however, perfectly clear that these views were not
" original " with him, but that he had come under the
influence of the teachings of the men whom I am calling
" spiritual Reformers."

How inward and mystical his type of Christianity
really was, may be gathered from a short passage of an
Epistle which he wrote in 1661 : " The Kingdom of God
is within you and is the dominion of God in the conscience
and spirit of the mind. . . . This Kingdom of Christ
is capable of subsisting and being managed inwardly in
the minds of His people, in a hidden state concealed from
the world. By the power thereof, the inward senses, or
eyes of the mind are opened and awakened to the drawing
of them up to a heavenly converse, catching and carrying
up the soul to the throne of God and to the knowledge of
the life that is hid with Christ in God. Those that are
in this Kingdom, and in whom the power of it is, *are
fitted to fly with the Church into the wilderness, and to
continue in such a solitary, dispersed, desolate condition
till God call them out of it. They have wells and springs
opened to them in this wilderness, whence they draw the
waters of salvation,* without being in bondage to the life
of sense." [1]

He was only twenty-two years of age when, " for
conscience' sake " and " in the sweete peace of God,"
he left England and threw in his lot with the young
colony in Massachusetts Bay. At twenty-three he was

---

[1] *An Epistle to the Mystical Body of Christ on Earth.* The lines which I have
put in italics in the text clearly show the " seeker "-attitude.

Governor of the Colony and found himself plunged into a maelstrom of politics, Indian wars, and ecclesiastical quarrels which would have tried even a veteran like John Winthrop. It was here in Massachusetts that the lines of his religious thought first come clearly into view, if any of Vane's religious ideas can ever properly be called " clear." The controversy in the Massachusetts Colony (1636–1638) was initiated and led by Anne Hutchinson, and was, in the phraseology of that period, an issue between " a Covenant of Works " and " a Covenant of Grace," which was a seventeenth-century way of stating the contrast between a religion historically revealed and completely expressed in an infallible Book on the one hand, and, on the other, a religion primarily based on the eternal nature of God and man, and on the fact of immediate revelation and communication between the God of Grace and the needy soul.[1] Governor Vane aligned himself with the Hutchinson party and was in sympathy with this second type of religion, the religion of inward experience, the immediate conscious realization of God, which, in the terminology of the times, was called " the Covenant of Grace." [2] Absorbed as he was for the next fifteen years after his return from America in momentous public affairs, he had no opportunity to give expression to the religious ideas which were forming in his mind. During his " retirement " after his break with Cromwell, he wrote two books which give us the best light we can hope to get on his religious views—*The Retired Man's Meditations* (1655), and *A Pilgrimage into the Land of Promise* (1664), written in prison in 1662.

Baxter complained that his Doctrines were " so clowdily formed and expressed that few could understand them," [3] and the modern reader, however much time and patience he bestows upon Vane's books, is forced to agree with Baxter. Vane acknowledges himself that his

---

[1] See my *Quakers in the American Colonies* (1911), pp. 1-25.

[2] In his *Retired Man's Meditations* he speaks of " Christ's rule in the legal conscience " and " Christ's rule in the evangelical conscience," by which he means to contrast a religion founded on external performances or historical events, and a religion founded on *events transacted in the soul of the man himself*.

[3] *Reliquiae Baxterianae*, i. p. 75.

thought is " knotty and abstruce." In religious matters his mind was always labouring, without success, to find a clear guiding clue through a maze and confusion of ideas, which fascinated him, and he allowed his mind to get lost in what Sir Thomas Browne calls " wingy mysteries." He had no sound principle of Scripture interpretation, but allowed his untrained and unformed imagination to run wild. Texts in profusion from Genesis to Revelation lie in undigested masses in his books. He had evidently read Jacob Boehme, but, if so, he had only become more " clowdy " by the reading, for he has not seized and appreciated Boehme's constructive thoughts, and, at least in his later period and in his last book, he is floundering under the heavy weight of millenarian ideas, which do not harmonize well with his occasional spiritual insights of an ever-growing revelation to man through the eternal Word who in all ages voices Himself within the soul. He was an extraordinary complex of vague mysticism and astute statesmanship.

In one matter he was throughout his life both consistent and clear, namely, in the advocacy of freedom of conscience in religion. He put himself squarely on a platform of toleration in his early controversy with Winthrop.[1] His friend Roger Williams in later life heard him make " a heavenly speech " in Parliament in which he said : " Why should the labours of any be suppressed, if sober, though never so different ? We now profess to seek God, we desire to see light ! " [2] Throughout his parliamentary career he stood side by side with Cromwell in the difficult effort, which only partly succeeded, to secure scope for all honest religious opinion. Finally, in *The Retired Man's Meditations*, he wrote : " We are bound to understand by this terme [the Rule of Magistracy] the proper sphere, bounds and limits of that office *which is not to intrude itself into the office and proper concerns of Christ's inward government and rule in the*

---

[1] See Vane's *A Brief Answer to a certain Declaration made of the Intent and Equity of the Order of Court*, etc., in Hutchinson's Collection of Original Papers.
[2] Preface to Williams' *Bloudy Tenet*.

conscience." After defining the magistrate's proper functions in the affairs of the external life, he then adds : " The more illuminated the Magistrate's conscience and judgment is, as to natural justice and right, by the knowledge of God and communications of Light from Christ, the better qualified he is to execute his office." [1]

The central idea of his religious thought—though it never completely penetrated the fringes of his mind—was the reality of the living Word of God, the self-revealing character of God, who is an immediate, inward Teacher, who is His own evidence and demonstration, and who has, Vane testifies, " experimentally obtained a large entrance and reception in my heart as a seed there sown." [2] This living Word is not to be confused with the Scriptures, which are an outward testimony to the inner Word—an external way to the " unveiled and naked beauty of the Word itself," who is Spirit and Life.[3]   In the long process of self-revelation through the living Word a temporal universe has been created by emanations in time, a universe double in its nature, first a deeper, invisible universe of light, of angels and exalted spirits, then a visible and material and " animalish " world, a shadow of the invisible world.[4]   At the top of the order, man was created, uniting both the visible and the invisible worlds in one being.   Man thus in himself is in miniature a double world, a world of light and spirit and a world of shadow.   Two seeds, as Boehme had already taught, are always working in man, and his native free-will determines the course of his destiny.   In his first test, man fell, though " the tree of life," which was a visible type of Christ, was before his eyes in Paradise, but this event was only the beginning of the long human drama, and the real history of the race is the story of the stages and dispensations of the living Word of God, educating, regenerating, and spiritualizing man, and bringing him to the height of his spiritual possibilities.

---

[1] *The Retired Man's Meditations.* p. 388.   Italics mine.
[2] *Ibid.* Preface.   [3] *Ibid.* chap. ii.
[4] *Ibid.* ii. chaps. iii. and iv.   See also *A Pilgrimage into the Land of Promise*, pp. 1-3.

In the first stage of this divine pedagogy, man has the Word of God within himself " as a lampe or light in his mind, manifesting itself to inward senses, assisted by the ministry of angels." This is the period of " conditional covenant," under which man's spiritual life depends on " obedience to the inward operations of this Word," and those that obey are made " Children of the Light," and attain a forward-looking apprehension of the coming Son.[1]

The second degree of glory—" a more excellent and near approach to the sight of the Son Himself "—is the training stage under the written word, which makes wise unto salvation. This is a dispensation of discipline, reproof, correction, instruction in righteousness, and it culminates in the manifestation of Grace in Jesus Christ, who is the Root of a new race. There are two ways of using the ministry of Grace in Jesus Christ—on the lower level as mere " restoration-work " and on the higher level as " re-creation into new life." Those who apprehend Christ on the lower level, as simply a new law-giver, do not get beyond the spirit of bondage and do not succeed in attaining an immutable and incorruptible nature. Those, however, who are born from within by the immortal and incorruptible Seed of God are " changed from their wavering unstable power " into an inward likeness to God, into a love that binds man's spirit into union with God's Spirit, into " steadfast and unmoveable delight in goodness " and " fixed and unshaken averseness to sin and evil." [2]

The third and final stage of glory, the full dispensation of the Spirit—when " the whole creation will be restored to its primitive purity and to the glorious liberty of sons of God "—will be the thousand years' reign of Christ to which, Vane believed, both the outward and inward Word testify.[3]

It is not easy to see how a man of Vane's mental and moral calibre, who had himself, as he tells us in his scaffold speech, been " brought home to himself by

---

[1] *A Pilgrimage into the Land of Promise*, pp. 51-52.
[2] *Ibid.* pp. 55-56.   [3] *Retired Man's Meditations*, chap. xxvi.

God's wonderful, rich and free Grace, revealing His Son in me that I might be a partaker of eternal life," and who had all his life held that there is an eternal Word and Seed of God working both without and within to bring men to their complete spiritual stature, should be unwilling to trust the operation of this divine Word to finish what He had begun, and should resort to a cataclysmic event of a new order for the final stage. We of this later and more scientific age must, however, speak with some caution of the idealistic dreams and visions and glowing expectations of men, who in their deepest souls believed that God was a living, acting God who, in ways past finding out, intervened in the affairs of men and fulfilled His purposes of good. "God is almighty," Vane said once in a Parliamentary speech. "Will you not trust Him with the consequences? He that has unsettled a monarchy of so many descents, in peaceable times, and brought you to the top of your liberties, though He drive you for a while into the wilderness, He will bring you back. He is a wiser workman than to reject His work."

George Fox, in 1657, was "moved of ye Lord to speake to him of ye true Light," having heard that "Henery Vane has much enquired after mee." Fox told him, in his usual fashion, "howe yt Christ had promised to his disciples to sende ym ye holy ghoast, ye spiritt of truth which shoulde leade ym into all truth which wee [Friends] witnessed and howe yt ye grace of God which brought salvation had appeared unto all men and was ye saintes teacher in ye Apòstles days & soe it was nowe." Vane's comment on the Quaker's message was : "None of all this doth reach to my experiens," and Fox, in his plain straightforward manner, said : "Thou hast knowne somethinge formerly ; but now there is a mountaine of earth & imaginations uppe in thee & from that rises a smoake which has darkened thy braine : & thou art not ye man as thou wert formerly. . . . I was moved of ye Lord to sett ye Seede Christ Jesus over his heade ! " [1]

[1] *Journal of George Fox* (Cambridge ed.), i. pp. 313-314.

Clarendon was more charitable toward Vane than was Fox, who never deals gently with persons who approach his point of view and yet miss it. The former, declaring that Vane's writings lack " his usual clearness and ratiocination," and that " in a crowd of very easy words the sense was too hard to find out," yet concludes to give the furnace-tried statesman the benefit of the doubt : " I was of opinion that the subject was of so delicate a nature that it required another kind of prepara- tion of mind, and perhaps another kind of diet, than men are ordinarily supplied with ! " [1]

There can, at any rate, be no doubt of Vane's honesty or of his loyalty to the Light within him. Standing face to face with death, he told his strange audience that he had put everything that he prized in the world to hazard for the sake of obeying the best Light which God had granted him, and he added these impressive words : " I do earnestly persuade all people rather to suffer the highest contradiction from men, than disobey God by contradicting the Light of God in their own conscience."

III

Peter Sterry was born in Surrey, early in the seven- teenth century, and entered Emmanuel College, Cam- bridge, in 1629, graduating B.A. in 1633 and M.A. in 1637. Emmanuel College had been founded during Elizabeth's reign (1584) by one of her statesmen, Sir Walter Mildmay, for the especial encouragement of Calvinistic theology, and it was the most important intellectual nursery of the great Puritan movement in England. During Sterry's University period there was a remarkable group of tutors and fellows gathered in Emmanuel College. Foremost among them was Tuckney, who was tutor to Benjamin Whichcote the founder of the school of Cambridge Platonists, or " Latitude-Men," and Whichcote himself was at Emmanuel College through-

[1] *Animadversions on Cressy's Answer to Stillingfleet* (1673), p. 59.

out Sterry's period, graduating M.A. the same year that Sterry graduated B.A.

Sterry was a thorough-going Platonist in his type of thought and had much in common with Henry More, whose writings were " divinely pleasant " to him and whom he calls " a prophet " of the spiritual unity of the universe, and with Ralph Cudworth, the spiritual philosopher, though he finds "somewhat to regret " in the work of both these contemporary Cambridge Platonists.[1] Sterry is not usually reckoned among the Cambridge Platonists, but there is no reason why he should not be included in that group. He was trained in the University which was the natural home of the movement, he read the authors most approved by the members of this school, and his own message is penetrated with the spirit and ideals of these seventeenth-century Platonists. His writings abound with references to Plato and Plotinus, with occasional references to Proclus and Dionysius the Areopagite ; and the world-conceptions of this composite school of philosophers, as they were revived by the Renaissance, are fundamental to his thought. He was thoroughly acquainted with the writings of Ficino, and quotes him among his approved masters. He had also profoundly studied the great mystics and was admirably equipped intellectually to be the interpreter of a far different type of Christianity from that of the current theologies.

He became intimate in his public career with Sir Harry Vane, and there are signs of mutual influence in their writings, which gave occasion for Richard Baxter's pun on their names : " Vanity and sterility were never more happily conjoined." [2] Upon the execution of Charles I., Sterry was voted a preacher to the Council of State with a salary of one hundred pounds a year, which was soon after doubled and lodgings at Whitehall added. He generally preached before Cromwell on Sundays, and on every other Thursday at Whitehall, frequently before

---

[1] See *A Discourse of the Freedom of the Will* (1675), pp. 31-32.
[2] *Reliquiae Baxterianae*, i. p. 75.

the Lords and Commons. A number of his sermons were printed " by Order of the House," and enjoyed a wide popularity, though their great length would make them impossible sermons to-day. Cromwell evidently appreciated his preaching very highly and felt no objection to the mystical strain that runs through all his sermons. He had many points of contact with Milton, and may have been for a period his assistant as Latin Secretary.[1] He was devotedly fond of music, art, and poetry, and he held similar views to Milton regarding the Presbyterian system. He naturally fell out of public notice after the Restoration, and quietly occupied himself with literary work, until his death in 1672. The main material for a study of his " message " will be found in his three posthumous Books : *A Discourse of the Freedom of the Will* (1675) ; *Rise, Race and Royalty of the Kingdom of God in the Soul of Man* (1683), and *Appearance of God to Man in the Gospel* (1710).[2] His prose style is lofty and often marked with singular beauty, though he is almost always too prolix for our generation, and too prone to divide his discourse into heads and sub-heads, and sub-divisions of sub-heads. Here is a specimen passage of his dealing with a topic which Plato and the great poets have often handled : " Imagine this Life as an Island, surrounded by a Sea of Darkness, beyond which lies the main Land of Eternity. Blessed is he who can raise himself to such a Pitch as to look off this Island, beyond that Darkness to the utmost bound of things. He thus sees his way before and behind him. What shall trouble him on his Twig of Life, on which he is like a bird but now alighted, from a far Region, from whence again he shall immediately take his flight. Thou cam'st through a Darkness hither but yesterday when fhou wert born. Why then shouldst thou not readily and cheerfully return through the same Darkness back again to those everlasting Hills ? "[3]   I will give one more

---

[1] A Mr. Sterry was appointed Sept. 8, 1657, to assist Milton as Latin Secretary (*Nat. Dict. of Biog.* Art. " Sterry ").

[2] Besides the above named I have also used his Sermons on *The Clouds in which Christ Comes* (1648) and *The Spirits' Conviction of Sinne* (1645).

[3] *Rise, Race and Royalty*, p. 8.

specimen passage touching the divine origin and return of the soul : " At our Birth, which is the morning of life, our Soul and Body are joined to this fleshly Image as Horses are put into a Waggon, to which they are fastened by their Harnes and Traces.[1] The Body is as the fore-horse, but the Soul is the filly which draws most and bears the chief weight. All the day long of this life we draw this Waggon heavy laden with all sorts of temptations and troubles thorow deep ways of mire and sand. This only is our comfort that the Divine Will, which is Love itself in its perfection, as a Hand put forth from Heaven thorow a Cloud, at our Birth put us into this Waggon and governs us all the day. In the evening of our life, at the end of the day, Death is the same Divine Will as a naked Hand of pure Love, shining forth from an open Heaven of clear light and glory, taking our Soul and Body out of the Waggon and Traces of this fleshly Image and leading them immediately into their Inn." [2]

Everything in the universe, he believes, is double. The things that are seen are copies—often faint and shadowy—of That which is. Every particular thing " below " corresponds to an eternal reality " above." Even those things which appear thin and shallow possess an infinite depth, or we may just as well say an infinite height. " Didst thou ever descry," he asks, " a glorious eternity in a winged moment of Time ? Didst thou ever see a bright Infinite in the narrow point of an Object ? Then thou knowest what Spirit means—that spire-top whither all things ascend harmoniously, where they meet and sit connected in an unfathomed Depth of Life." [3] And the immense congeries of things and events, even " the jarring and tumultuous contrarieties," " through the whole world, through the whole compass of time, through both the bright and the black Regions of Life and Death," consent and melodize in one celestial music

---

[1] There is, he thinks, an inner " body " which is as immortal as the soul and which together with the soul is united to the body of flesh—" the fleshly Image."

[2] *Rise, Race and Royalty*, p. 435.

[3] *Ibid.* p. 24. See also *ibid.* p. 5, and *Discourse*, p. 55.

and perfect harmony of Divine purpose.[1] " The stops
and shakes make music as well as the stroaks and sounds,"
even Death and Hell " are bound by a gold chain with
shining links of Love " to the throne of God.[2]

He outdoes even the " pillar " Quakers, his contemporaries in later life, in his proclamation of a Divine Root
and Seed in the soul of man. In words almost precisely
like those which Barclay used later in his *Apology*, he
says : " There is a spiritual man that lies hid under the
natural man as seed under the ground,"[3] or, again, " go
into thyself beyond thy natural man, and thou shalt meet
the Spirit of God."[4] There is " something eternal,"
" a seminal infiniteness," in the soul, its native Root and
Bottom, consubstantial with it and inseparable from it.
" It lasts on through all forms, wearing them out, casting
them off for new forms, through which it manifests itself,
until it finally brings us back into Itself and becomes our
only clothing."[5] But though " native," it is not a part
or function of the natural, psychical man, it is not of
the " finite creature." It is from above, a transcendent
Reality ; it belongs to the eternal world and yet it is a
Root of God within, a point in the soul's abyss (or apex)
unsevered from God, so that one who knew the soul to its
depths would know God.[6] Beneath all the wreck and
ruin and havoc of sin it is still there, with its " glimpses
of immortal Beauty." The prodigal who would return
" home " must first return to himself, to that divine
Seed, " hid deep beneath the soil and dung, beneath
the darkness, deformity and deadness of its Winter-
Season and rise up in its proper Spring into pleasant
flowers and fruits, as a Garden of God."[7] There is thus
" a golden thread " which is always there to guide the
soul back home, through all the mazes of the world, or,
to use another of his figures, " Thou hast but to follow
the stream of Love, the Fountain of the Soul, if thou

---

[1] *Discourse*, pp. 30-35. Also p. 161.
[2] *Ibid.* Preface, p. c 8, and *Rise, Race and Royalty*, p. 164.
[3] *Rise, Race and Royalty*, p. 126.   [4] *Ibid.* p. 96.
[5] *Ibid.* pp. 4, 5, 6, 18-19.   [6] *Discourse*, pp. 67 and 77.
[7] *Rise, Race and Royalty*, Preface, p. b 2. See also pp. 362 and 512-513.

wouldst be led to that Sea which is the confluence of all the waters of Life, of all Truth, of all Goodness, of all Joy, of all Beauty and Blessedness." [1]

The *Fullness* of the juncture of God and Man is seen only in Christ. In Him, " God and Man are one, one Love, one Life, one Likeness." [2] He is the Pattern, the unspoiled Image, the Eternal Word, and He is, too, the Head of our race. In Him the Divine Spirit and the human spirit " are twined into one." " If you want to see God, then see Christ." [3] If you want to see what the Seed in us can blossom into when it is unhampered by sin, again, see Christ.[4] He is a Life-giving Spirit who can penetrate other spirits, who broods over the soul as the creative Spirit brooded over the waters, and who, when received, makes us radiant with *Love, which is the only truth of religion.*

Sin is the mark and brand of our failure—it is our aberration from the normal type as it is fully revealed in Christ. " Nothing is so unnatural as sin," [5] nothing is so irrational, nothing so abnormal—it is always a break from the unity of the divine Life, a movement towards isolation and self-solitariness, a pursuit of narrowing desires, a missing of the potential beauty and harmony of the Soul.[6] But in every case, whether it be Adam's or that of the last man who sinned, it is always an act of free-will—" even in its most haggish shapes sin is the act of free-will." Some strange contrary principle in us, something from a root alien to the divine Root, makes civil war within us,[7] and though the Word of God's eternal Love is ringing in our ears and though the gleams of divine Beauty are shining in our eyes, we still walk away into " the barren dessert of the world and forsake our proper habitation in the paradise of God." [8] There is no way back from the " barren dessert," without a complete reversal of direction, a conversion : " He that will pass

---

[1] *Discourse,* Preface, pp. a and c 6, and *Rise, Race and Royalty,* p. 101.
[2] *Rise, Race and Royalty,* p. 78.   [3] *Ibid.* p. 68.
[4] *Ibid.* pp. 95 and 184. Also *Appearance of God,* pp. 239 and 251.
[5] *Rise, Race and Royalty,* p. 73.
[6] *Ibid.* pp. 16-18 and 141, and *Discourse,* pp. 141-142.
[7] *Appearance of God,* p. 91.   [8] *Rise, Race and Royalty,* p. 359.

from the dismal depths of sin to the heights of strength
and holiness must make his first motion a conversion, a
change from a descent to an ascent, from going outward
toward the circle to go inward towards the centre ";
there must be an *awakening* so that the soul comes to see
all things in the light of their first Principle ; a Birth
through the Spirit and a newness of life through the
bubbling of the eternal Spring.[1]

The mighty event of re-birth is described by Sterry
very much after the manner of Schwenckfeld. The new
Seed, Christ Jesus, the divine Life itself, comes into
operation within the man, and the new-made man, raised
with Christ, is joined in Spirit with Him and lives henceforth not after Adam but after Christ the Head of the
spiritual Race.[2] The shift of direction, the complete
reversal, however, does not mean " parting with delights,"
or " putting on a sad and sour conversation "—on the
contrary, it means enlargement of soul and " a gainful
addition of joy," the discovery within of another world
and a new kingdom.[3]

Like all this group of thinkers to whom he is kindred,
Sterry makes a sharp contrast between the Spirit and the
letter, between what happens within the soul and what
is external to it. The early stage of religion is characterized by externals, and only after long processes of
tutorship and discipline does the soul learn how to live
by the Seed of life and Light of truth within. The early
stage is legalistic, during which the person is " hedged
about " with promises and threats, " walled in " with
laws and ordinances, " living in a perpetual alarm of
fears," " shut up to rules, retirements and forms "—but
it is far better to serve God from fear and by outward
rules than not to serve Him at all. The true way of
progress is to move up from fear and law to love and
freedom, and from outward rules to the discovery of a
central Light of God, a Heavenly Image, in the deeps of

---

[1] *Rise, Race and Royalty*, pp. 2, 23, and 466.
[2] See especially *Appearance of God*, pp. 74-75 and 480.
[3] *Rise, Race and Royalty*, pp. 107-109.

one's own spirit—" real knowledge comes when the Day Star rises in the heart." [1] We pass from " notions " and " words " to an inward power and a bubbling joy. He calls the period of law and letter a " baby-stage," " when we see truth as blear-eyed beholders." Legal religion compared with the religion of the Spirit is " like a spark struck from flint at midnight " compared with the sun ; it is like " drawing the waters of Grace, a bucketful at a time," when we might have " the Spirit gushing as a living and perpetual Fountain." [2] But God is so good that He speaks to us in a variety of ways, and He lets us " spell His name " with the alphabet, until we learn to know His own Voice. Nature, in the elements of visible creation, tells us of Him ; Reason compels us to recognize One who is First and Best, the All in all ; the written word cries in our ears that God is Love ; but above these voices there is a Principle within our own souls by which " God propagates His Life " in us, and he who, in this love-way, has become a son knows God as *Abba-Father*.[3] We pray now with power, when this new Life of the Spirit has come into us, and we pour our spirits out in self-forgetfulness, " as a River pours itself into the sea, where it loseth its own name and is known only as the waters of the Sea." [4]

He is always gentle in his account of other religions and other stages of faith, and he sees good in all types, if only they help the soul to hunger for the Eternal and do not cramp it. " O that I had a hundred mouths," he writes, " an hundred tongues, a Voice like the Voice of God that rends Rocks, to cry to all sorts of Persons and Spirits in this Land and in all the Christian World through the whole creation : ' Let all that differ in Principles, Professions, Opinions and Forms, see the good there is in each other ' ! " [5]

The world, busy with action and choosing for its historical study the men who did things, has allowed

---

[1] *Rise, Race and Royalty*, pp. 46-47 and 467.
[2] *Ibid.* pp. 56-60.   [3] *Ibid.* pp. 63-67.
[4] *Appearance of God*, pp. 130-131.   [5] *Discourse*, Preface, p. a 6.

Peter Sterry to drop into oblivion and his books to gather dust and cobwebs, but there was, I think, a Seed of God in him, and he had a message for his age. He sincerely endeavoured to hand on the torch which in his youth at Cambridge had been kindled in him by some other flame. " When one candle is lighted," he beautifully says, " we light many by it, and when God hath kindled the Life of His glory in one man's Heart he often enkindles many by the flame of that." [1]

---

[1] *Rise, Race and Royalty*, p. 39.

CHAPTER XV

BENJAMIN WHICHCOTE, THE FIRST OF THE
" LATITUDE-MEN " [1]

THE type of Christianity which I have been calling
" spiritual religion," that is, religion grounded in the
nature of Reason, finds, at least in England, its noblest
expression in the group of men, sometimes called " Cambridge Platonists," and sometimes " Latitude-Men," or
simply " Latitudinarians." These labels were all given
them by their critics and opponents, and were used to
give the impression that the members of this group or
school were introducing and advancing a type of Christianity too broad and humanistic to be safe, and one
grounded on Greek philosophy rather than on Scripture
and historical Revelation.[2]

They were, however, undertaking to do in their generation precisely what the long line of spiritual interpreters
had for more than a century been endeavouring, through
pain and suffering, misunderstanding and fierce persecution, to work out for humanity—a religion of life and
reality, a religion rooted in the eternal nature of the
Spirit of God and the spirit of man, a religion as authoritative and unescapable " as mathematical demonstration." [3]

It is not possible to establish direct connection between
the leaders of this school and the writings of the successive

[1] This interesting phrase occurs in *A Brief Account of the New Sect of Latitude-Men*, by S. P. (probably Simon Patrick), 1662.

[2] S. P. in his *Sect of Latitude-Men* says : " A Latitude-Man is an image of Clouts [a man of straw] that men set up to encounter with, for want of a real enemy ; it is a convenient name to reproach a man that you owe a spite to."

[3] Letters of Tuckney and Whichcote in the Appendix to Whichcote's *Aphorisms* (London, 1753), p. 2.

spiritual Reformers on the Continent whom we have been studying in this volume, though the parallelism of ideas and of spirit is very striking. Both groups were powerfully influenced by the humanistic movement, both groups drew upon that profound searching of the soul which they found in the works of Plato and Plotinus, and both groups read the same mystical writers. These things would partly account for the similarities, but there was almost certainly a closer and more direct connection, though we cannot trace it in the case of Whichcote as we can in that of John Everard of Clare College. There has been a tendency to explain Whichcote's views through the influence of Arminius and Arminians; but he himself denied that he had been influenced by Arminius,[1] while his disciple, Nathaniel Culverwel, speaks disapprovingly of Arminianism.[2] There are no distinct allusions in Whichcote to Jacob Boehme, and the former's conception of the Universe is vastly different from the latter's, but their vital and ethical view of the way of salvation is almost exactly the same, and the constant insistence of Whichcote and his disciples that Heaven and Hell are primarily conditions of life in the person himself has, as we know, a perfect parallel in Boehme.

The Cambridge scholars were much better equipped for their task than any of the men whom we have so far studied, their gravest difficulty being an overweighting of learning which they sometimes failed to fuse with their spiritual vision and to transmute into power. But with all their propension to learning and their love of philosophy, they were primarily and fundamentally *religious*—they were disciples of Christ rather than disciples of Plato and Plotinus. Bishop Burnet's testimony to the positive spiritual contribution of this movement, now under consideration, and to the genuineness of the religious life of these men is well worth quoting. After describing the arid condition of his time, the prevailing tendency of ministers to seek pomp and luxury, and the apparent thinness of the preaching of the day, he adds: " Some

---

[1] *Aphorisms*, Appendix, p. 53.   [2] Culverwel, *Elegant Discourses* (1654), p. 6.

few exceptions are to be made ; but so few, that if *a new set of men had not appeared of another stamp*, the Church had quite lost her esteem over the nation." He then designates this group of Cambridge scholars. Speaking particularly of Whichcote, he says : " Being disgusted with the dry systematical way of those times, he studied to raise those who conversed with him to a nobler set of thoughts, and to consider religion as *a seed of a deiform nature* (to use one of his own phrases). In order to this, he set young students much on reading the ancient philosophers, chiefly Plato, Tully and Plotin, and on considering the Christian religion as a doctrine sent from God, both to elevate and sweeten human nature, in which he was a great example, as well as a wise and kind instructor. Cudworth carried this on with a great strength of genius and a vast compass of learning." [1]

These " Latitude-Men " were Puritan in temper and in intensity of conviction ; they were all trained in the great nursery of Puritan faith, Emmanuel College, and they were on intimate terms with many of the men who were the creators of the outer and inner life of the Commonwealth, but in their intellectual sympathies they went neither with the sectaries of the time—" the squalid sluttery of fanatic conventicles," as S. P. puts it—nor with the prevailing Puritan theology. They read Calvin and Beza with diligence, at least Whichcote did, but their thought did not move along the track which the great Genevan had constructed. They discovered another way of approach which made the old way and the old battles seem to them futile. Instead of beginning with the eternal mysteries of the inscrutable divine Will, they began with the fundamental nature of man, always deep and difficult to fathom, but for ever the ground and basis of all that can be known in the field of religion. Their interest was thus psychological rather than theological. It is their constant assertion that nothing is more intrinsically rational than religion, and they focus all their energies to make this point clear and evident.

[1] Burnet, *History of His Own Times* (London, 1850), p. 127.

They came to their intellectual development in the period when Hobbes was formulating one of the most powerful and subtle types of materialism that has ever been presented. They were, too, contemporaries of Descartes, and they followed with intense interest the attempt of the great Frenchman to put philosophy in possession of a method as adequate for its problems as the method of geometry was for the mathematical sciences. None of the " Platonists " was possessed of the same rare quality of genius as either of these two great philosophers, but they saw with clear insight the full bearing of both systems. They heartily disapproved of Hobbes' materialism and shuddered at its nakedness. They were too much committed to the ideals of Humanism to be positive opponents of Descartes' rational formulation of all things outer and inner, but they never felt at home with the vast clock-like mechanism to which his system reduced the universe, and they set themselves, in contrast, to produce a religious philosophy which would guarantee freedom, would give wider scope for the inner life, would show the kinship of God and man and put morality and religion—to their mind for ever one and inseparable—on a foundation as immovable as the pillars of the universe.

The first of this group, the pathbreaker of the movement, was Benjamin Whichcote, though it must not be forgotten that he had noble forerunners in John Hales, William Chillingworth, and Jeremy Taylor. The biographical details which have survived him are very limited. A great teacher's life is so largely interior and so devoid of outward events that there is usually not much to record.[1] He was descended from " an ancient and honourable family," and was born at Whichcote-Hall, in the parish of Stoke, the 11th of March, 1609. He was admitted in 1626 to Emmanuel College—"which was looked on from its first foundation as a Seminary of Puritans"—and was there under the tutorship of two great Puritan teachers, Dr. Anthony Tuckney and Thomas Hill,

---

[1] We are dependent, for the few facts which we possess concerning Whichcote's life, on the Sketch of him written by Dr. Samuel Salter, as a Preface to his edition of Whichcote's *Aphorisms*, published in 1753.

both of whom were for a time associated with John Cotton, afterwards the famous preacher of colonial Boston. He was ordained both deacon and priest in 1636, was made Provost of King's College, Cambridge, in 1644, " went-out " Doctor of Divinity in 1649, and for twenty years gave the afternoon Lecture on Sundays at Trinity Church, Cambridge. At the Restoration he was deprived of the Provostship by order of the King, which brought his university career to an end. He was made curate of St. Anne's, Blackfriars, in 1662, and later received from the Crown the vicarage of St. Laurence Jewry, where he preached twice each week until his death in 1683.

He once said in one of his sermons : " Had we a man among us, that we could produce, that did live an exact Gospel life ; had we a man that was really gospelized ; were the Gospel a life, a soul, and a spirit to him . . . he would be the most lovely and useful person under heaven. Christianity would be recommended to the world by his spirit and conversation." [1] Dr. Whichcote himself was, as far as one can judge from the impression which he made on his contemporaries, such a " gospelized " man. He " recommended religion," as Dr. Salter says, by his life and writings, and showed it " in its fairest and truest light as the highest perfection of human nature." [2] He seemed to be " emancipated " when he came back to Cambridge as Provost of King's College, and he devoted himself to " spreading and propagating a more generous sett of opinions " than those which were generally proclaimed in the sermons of the time, and " the young Masters of Arts soon cordially embraced " his message.[3]

This " new sett of opinions," proclaimed in Trinity Church with vision and power, soon disturbed those who were of the older and sterner schools of thought.   " My heart hath bin much exercised about you," his old friend and tutor, Dr. Tuckney, wrote to him in 1651, " especially since your being Vice-Chancellour, I have seldom heard you preach, but that something hath bin delivered

---

[1] *Select Sermons* (1698), p. 30.
[2] Salter's Preface, pp. xxii-xxiii.   [3] *Ibid.* p. xx.

by you, and that so authoritatively and with big words, sometimes of ' divinest reason ' and sometimes of ' more than mathematical demonstration,' that hath much grieved me." [1]   The novelty of Dr. Whichcote's " opinions " comes more clearly into view as the letter proceeds : " Your Discourse about Reconciliation that ' it doth not operate on God, but on us ' is Divinity [theology] that my heart riseth against. . . . To say that the ground of God's reconciliation is from anything in us ; and not from His free grace, freely justifying the ungodly, is to deny one of the fundamental truths of the Gospel that derives from heaven." [2]

The correspondence which followed this frank letter supplies us with the clearest light we possess, or can possess, upon Whichcote's inner life and type of religion. He replied to his old friend, whom he had always held " in love, reverence and esteem," that he had noticed of late that " our hearts have not seemed to be together when our persons have bin," [3] " but," he adds, " your letter meets with no guilt in my conscience." " My head hath bin possessed with this truth [which I am preaching] these manie years—I am not late nor newe in this persuasion." [4] He then proceeds to quote from his notes exactly what he had said on the subject of reconciliation in his recent Discourse. It was as follows : " Christ doth not save us by onely doing for us *without* us [*i.e.* historically] : yea, we come at that which Christ hath done for us with God, by what He hath done for us *within* us. . . . With God there cannot be reconciliation without our becoming God-like. . . . They deceeve and flatter themselves extreamly ; who think of reconciliation with God by means of a Saviour acting upon God in their behalfe and *not also working in or upon them to make them God-like*," and he says that he added in the spoken sermon, what was not in his notes, that a theology which taught a salvation without inward moral transformation was " Divinity minted in Hell." [5]

---

[1] Appendix to *Aphorisms* (1753), p. 2.   [2] *Ibid.* p. 4.
[3] *Ibid.* p. 7.   [4] *Ibid.* pp. 8 and 13.   [5] *Ibid.* pp. 13 and 14.

Dr. Tuckney in his second letter becomes still more specific. He admits that Whichcote's " persuasion of truth " is not " late or newe " ; he remembers, on the latter's first coming to Cambridge, " I thought you then somwhat cloudie and obscure in your expressions." What he now notices with regret is the tendency in his old pupil to " cry-up reason rather than faith " ; to be " too much immersed in Philosophy and Metaphysics " ; to be devoted to " other authours more than Scripture, and Plato and his schollars above others " ; to be producing " a kinde of moral Divinitie, onlie with a little tincture of Christ added " ; to put " inherent righteousness above imputed righteousness " and " love above faith," and to use " some broad expressions as though in this life wee may be above ordinances " ; and finally he notices that since Whichcote has " cast his sermons in this mould," they have become " less edifying " and " less affecting the heart." [1] He thinks, too, that he has discovered the foreign source of the infection : " Sir, those whose footsteppes I have observed [in your sermons] were the Socinians and Arminians ; the latter whereof, I conceive, you have bin everie where reading in their workes and most largely in their Apologie." [2]

" In a thousand guesses," Whichcote answers this last charge, in his second letter, " you could not have bin farther off from the truth of the thing." " What is added of Socinians and Arminians, in respect of mee, is groundless. I may as well be called a Papist, or Mahometan ; Pagan or Atheist. And trulie, Sir, you are wholly mistaken in the whole course of my studies. You say you find me largelie in their *Apologia* ; to my knowledge I never saw or heard of the book before ! . . . I have not read manie bookes ; but I have studied a fewe : meditation and invention hath bin my life rather than reading ; and trulie I have more read Calvine and Perkins and Beza than all the bookes, authors and names you mention. *I have alwaies expected reason for what men say* ; less valuing persons and authorities in the stating and resolv-

[1] Appendix to *Aphorisms*, pp. 37-38.   [2] *Ibid.* p. 27.

ing of truth, therefore have read them most where I have found itt. I have not looked at anie thing as more than an opinion which hath not bin underpropt by convincing reason or plaine and satisfactorie Scripture." [1]

As to the charge that he has become immersed in philosophy, Whichcote modestly replies : " I find the Philosophers that I read good as farre as they go : and it makes me secretlie blush before God when I find eyther my head, heart or life challenged by them, which I must confess, I often find." To the criticism that he " cries-up reason," he answers that he has always found in his own experience that "that preaching has most commanded my heart which has most illuminated my head." " Everie Christian," he insists, " must think and believe as he finds cause. Shall he speak in religion otherwise than he thinks ? Truth is truth, whoever hath spoken itt or howsoever itt hath bin abused. If this libertie be not allowed to the Universitie wherefore do wee study ? We have nothing to do butt to get good memories and to learn by heart." [2] Finally, to the impression expressed by Dr. Tuckney that his sermons are less edifying and heart-searching, he replies with dignity and evidently with truth : " I am sure I have bin all along well understood by persons of honest heartes, but of mean place and education : and I have had the blessing of the soules of such at their departure out of this world. I thanke God, my conscience tells me, that I have not herein affected worldlie shewe, but the real service of truth." [3]

We need not follow further this voluminous correspondence in which two high-minded and absolutely honest men reveal the two diverging lines of their religious faith. To the man whose mind found its spiritual footing alone on the solid ground of Calvin's unmodified system, the new " persuasion " was sure to seem " cloudie and obscure " ; and no number of letters could convince him that the new message presented a safe way of faith and life. And no amount of criticism or advice could change the other man who found it necessary for him to have

[1] Appendix to *Aphorisms*, pp. 53-54.   [2] *Ibid.* p. 57.   [3] *Ibid.* p. 60.

reasonable cause for what he was to believe and live by. Whichcote closes the friendly debate with some very positive announcements that for him religion must be, and must remain, something which guarantees its reality in the soul itself : " Christ must be inwardlie felt as a principle of divine life within us." [1]   " What is there in man," again he says, " more considerable than that which declares God's law to him, pleads for the observation of it, accuseth for the breach and excuseth upon the performance of it ? " [2]   And finally he informs his friend that each of them must be left free to follow his own light : " If we differ there is no help for it : Wee must forbear one another. . . . If you conceeve otherwise of me than as a lover and pursuer after truth, you think amisse. . . . Wherein I fall short of your expectation, I fail for truth's sake." [3]

The central idea in Whichcote's teaching, which runs like a gulf-stream through all his writings, is his absolute certainty that there is something in the " very make of man " [4] which links the human spirit to the Divine Spirit and which thus makes it as natural for man to be religious as it is for him to seek food for his body.   There is a " seminal principle," " a seed of God," " something that comes immediately from God," in the very structure of man's inner nature, [5] and this structural possession makes it as natural and proper for man's mind to tend toward God, " the centre of immortal souls," as it is for heavy things to tend toward their centre. [6]   " God," he elsewhere says, " is more inward to us than our own souls," and we are more closely " related to God than to anything in the world." [7]   The soul is to God as the flower is to the sun, which opens when the sun is there and shuts when the sun is absent, [8] though this figure breaks down, because, in Whichcote's view, God never withdraws and is never absent.   This idea that the spiritual life is absolutely rational—a normal function

---

[1] Appendix to *Aphorisms*, p. 125.   [2] *Ibid.* p. 127.   [3] *Ibid.* pp. 133-134.
[4] *Select Sermons* (1698), p. 149.   [5] *Ibid.* pp. 131-133.
[6] *Ibid.* p. 88.   [7] *Ibid.* p. 109.   [8] *Ibid.* p. 74.

of man's truest nature—receives manifold expression in Whichcote's *Aphorisms*, which constitute a sort of seventeenth-century Book of Proverbs, or collection of Wisdom-sayings. He had absorbed one great saying from the original Book of Proverbs, which he uses again and again, and which became the sacred text for all the members of the school—" the spirit of man is a candle of the Lord." [1] This Proverb is for Whichcote a key that fits every door of life, and the truth which it expresses is for him the basal truth of religion, as the following Aphorisms will sufficiently illustrate :

" Were it not for light we should not know we had such a sense as sight : Were it not for God we should not know the Powers of our souls which have an appropriation to God." [2]

" God's image is in us and we belong to Him." [3]

" There is a capacity in man's soul, larger than can be answered by anything of his own, or of any fellow-creature." [4]

" There is nothing so intrinsically rational as Religion is." [5]

" The Truths of God are connatural to the soul of man, and the soul of man makes no more resistance to them than the air does to light." [6]

" Religion makes us live like men." [7]

" We worship God best when we resemble Him most." [8]

" Religion is intelligible, rational and accountable : It is not our burden but our privilege." [9]

Something is always wrong, he thinks, if Religion becomes a burden : " It is imperfection in Religion to *drudge* in it, and every man drudges in Religion if he takes it up as a task and carries it as a burden." [10] The moment we follow " the divine frame and temper " of our inmost nature we find our freedom, our health, our power, and our joy ; as one of the Aphorisms puts it :

---

[1] Proverbs xx. 27. [2] *Aphorism* 861. [3] *Aphorism* 934.
[4] *Aphorism* 847. [5] *Aphorism* 457. [6] *Aphorism* 444.
[7] *Aphorism* 87. [8] *Aphorism* 248. [9] *Aphorism* 220.
[10] *Several Discourses* (1707), iv. p. 259.

" When we make nearer approaches to God, we have more use of ourselves." [1]

This view is beautifully expressed in Whichcote's Prayer printed at the end of the *Aphorisms* : " Most Blessed God, the Creator and Governor of the World ; the only true God, and Father of our Lord Jesus Christ. We thy Creatures were made to seek and find, to know and reverence, to serve and obey, to honour and glorify, to imitate and enjoy Thee ; who art the Original of our Beings, and the Centre of our Rest. Our Reasonable Nature hath a peculiar Reservation for Thee ; and our Happiness consists in our Assimilation to, and Employment about, Thee. The nearer we approach unto Thee, the more free we are from Error, Sin, and Misery ; and the farther off we are from Thee, the farther off we are from Truth, Holiness, and Felicity. Without Thee, we are sure of nothing ; we are not sure of ourselves : but through Thee, there is Self-Enjoyment in the mind, when there is nothing but Confusion, and no Enjoyment of the World."

Religion is thus thought of as the normal way of life, as the true fulfilment of human nature and as complete inward health. " Holiness," he says, " is our right constitution and temper, our inward health and strength." [2] Sin and selfishness carry a man below the noble Creation which God made in him, and Religion is the return to the true nature and capacity of God's Creation in man : " The Gospel, inwardly received, dyes and colours the soul, settles the Temper and Constitution of it and is restorative of our Nature. . . . It is the restitution of us to the state of our Creation, to the use of our Principles, to our healthful Constitution and to Acts that are connatural to us." [3]

As soon as man returns to " his own healthful Constitution " and to " the state of his Creation," he finds that Religion has its evidence and assurance in itself. God made man for moral truths, " before He declared

---

[1] *Aphorism* 709.   [2] *Several Discourses*, iv. p. 192.
[3] *Select Sermons*, pp. 55 and 62

them on Sinai," or " writ them in the Bible," [1] and so soon
as the soul comes into " conformity to its original," [2] that
is " into conformity to God according to its inward
measure and capacity," [3] and lives a kind of life that is
" self-same with its own Reason," [4] the Divine Life manifests itself in that man and kindles his spirit into a blazing
candle of the Lord.   Those who are spiritual " find and
feel within themselves Divine Suggestions, Motions and
Inspirations ; . . . a light comes into the Mind, a still
Voice." [5]

This direct and inward revelation is, however, for
Whichcote never " a revelation of new matter," never
a way to the discovery of truths of a private nature.
The revelations which the guidance of the Divine Spirit
breathes forth within our souls are always truths of
universal significance, truths that are already implicitly
revealed in the Bible, truths that carry their own self-
evidence to any rational mind.   But these revelations,
these discoveries of what God means and what life may
become, are possible only to those who prepare themselves
for inward converse and who centre down to the deeper
Roots of their being : " Unless a man takes himself sometimes out of the world, by retirement and self-reflection,
he will be in danger of losing *himself* in the world."[6]
Where God is not discovered, something is always at fault
with man.   " As soon as he is abstracted from the noise of
the world, withdrawn from the call of the Body, having the
doors of the senses shut, the Divine Life readily enters and
reveals Itself to the inward Eye that is prepared for it." [7]
" Things that are connatural in the way of Religion,"
he once said, " the Illapses and Breakings in of God upon
us, require a mind that is not subject to Passion but is
in a serene and quiet Posture, where there is no tumult
of Imagination. . . . There is no genuine and proper
effect of Religion where the Mind is not composed,
sedate and calm." [8]

[1] *Select Sermons*, p. 7.   [2] *Discourses*, iv. p. 191.   [3] *Ibid.* p. 171.
[4] *Ibid.* p. 259.   [5] *Select Sermons*, p. 111   [6] *Aphorism* 302.
[7] Quoted almost literally from *Select Sermons*, p. 72.   [8] *Ibid.* pp. 32-33.

There is no tendency in Whichcote to undervalue
Scripture. Inward revelations are for him not a substitute
for the Bible nor an appendix to it. Through the Divine
Light in the soul and through Scripture, Divine communications are imparted to men. These he calls respectively "truth of first inscription" and "truth of
after-revelation," [1] and they no more conflict than two
luminaries in the physical world conflict. "Morals," he
says, "are inforced by Scripture, but they were before
Scripture : they were according to the nature of God," [2]
and, as he always claims, according to the deiform nature
in man's reason.[3] As soon as a person interprets the Light
within him—the candle of the Lord in his own heart—by
the Light of revelation his inward illumination becomes
clearer ; and contrariwise, as soon as one brings an enlightened spirit to the Bible its message becomes clarified—
"the Spirit within leads to a right apprehension of those
things which God hath declared." [4] But Truth is always
vastly more than " Notions," or conceptual formulation
of doctrine. "Religion," as he says in his wisdom-proverbs,
" is not a System of Doctrine, an observance of Modes or
a Form of Words "—it is " a frame and temper of mind ;
it shows itself in a Life and Action conformable to the
Divine Will " ; it is " our resemblance to God." [5] Bare
knowledge does not sanctify any man ; "Men of holy
Hearts and Lives best understand holy Doctrines."[6] We
always deceive ourselves if we do not get beyond even such
high-sounding words as conversion, regeneration, divine
illumination, and mortification ; if we do not get beyond
names and notions of every sort, into a real holiness of
life that is a conformity of nature to our original. His
most important passage on this point is one which is
found in his Sermon on the text : " Of this man's seed
hath God, according to His promise, raised up unto

---

[1] *Select Sermons*, p. 6. He also says in *Aphorism* No. 109, " God hath set up
two Lights to enlighten us in our Way : the Light of Reason, which is the Light of
His Creation ; and the Light of Scripture which is After-Revelation from Him."
[2] *Aphorism* 587.   [3] See *Several Discourses*, iv. p. 173.
[4] *Ibid.* ii. p. 275.   [5] *Aphorisms* 1127, 853, and 1028.
[6] *Select Sermons*, p. 79 ; and *Aphorism* 285.

Israel a Saviour, Jesus " (Acts xiii. 23). " Religion,"
he says in this passage, " is not satisfied in Notions ; but
doth, in deed and in reality, come to nothing unless it be
in us not only matter of Knowledge and Speculation, but
doth establish in us a Frame and Temper of Mind and
is productive of a holy and vertuous Life. Therefore let
these things take effect in us ; in our Spirituality and
Heavenly-mindedness ; in our Conformity to the Divine
Nature and *Nativity from above.* For whoever professes
that he believes the Truth of these things and wants the
Operation of them upon his Spirit and Life doth, in fact,
make void and frustrate what he doth declare as his
Belief. He doth receive the Grace of God in vain unless
this Principle and Belief doth descend in his Heart and
establish a good Frame and Temper of Mind and govern
in all Actions of his Life and Conversation." [1] This translation of Light and Truth and Insight into the flesh and
blood of action is a necessary law of the spiritual life :
" Good men spiritualize their bodies ; bad men incarnate
their souls " ; [2] or, as he expresses it in one of his Sermons :
" To be [spiritually] well and unactive do not consist
together. No man is well without action." [3]

Religion is, thus, with him always a dynamic principle
of Life, working itself out in the frame and temper of the
man and producing its characteristic effects in his actions.
It does not operate " like a charm or spell "—it operates
only as a vital principle [4] and we become eternally the
self which we ourselves form. " We naturalize ourselves,"
to use his striking phrase, " to the employment of
eternity." [5] We are lost, not by Adam's sin, but by our
own ; and we are saved, not by Christ's historical death,
but by our own obedience to the law of the Spirit of Life
revealed in Him and by our own death to sin ; [6] and
the beginning of Heaven is one with the beginning of conformity to the will of God and to our nativity from above.
" Heaven is a temper of spirit, before it is a place." [7]

---

[1] *Select Sermons,* p. 350. [2] *Aphorism* 367.
[3] *Select Sermons,* p. 71. [4] *Aphorisms* 243 and 625.
[5] *Aphorism* 290. [6] *Aphorisms* 525, 612. [7] *Aphorism* 464.

There is a Heaven this side of Heaven and there is as certainly a Hell this side of Hell. The most impressive expression of this truth is given in one of his Sermons : " All misery arises out of *ourselves*. It is a most gross mistake, and men are of dull and stupid spirits who think that the state which we call Hell is an incommodious place only ; and that God by His sovereignty throws men therein. Hell ariseth out of a man's self. And Hell's fewel is the guilt of a man's conscience. It is impossible that any should be so miserable as Hell makes a man and as there a man is miserable by his own condemning of himself : And on the other side, when they think that Heaven arises from any place, or any nearness to God or Angels, that is not principally so ; but Heaven lies in a refined Temper, in an inward Reconciliation to the Nature of God. So that both Hell and Heaven have their Foundation within Men." [1] The evil and punishment which follow sin are " consequential " and inseparable from sin, and so, too, eternal life is nothing but spiritual life fulfilling itself in ways that are consequential and necessary in the deepest nature of things : " That which is our best employment here will be our only employment in eternity." [2]

The good old Puritan, Tuckney, suspected that Whichcote was promulgating a type of Christianity which could dispense with ordinances—" as though in this life wee may be above ordinances,"—and it must be confessed that there was some ground for this suspicion. He was no " enthusiast " and he in no way shared the radical antisacramentarian spirit of the small sects of the Commonwealth, but it belonged to the very essence of this type of religion, as we have seen in every varied instance of it, to hold lightly to externals. " The Spirit," as Whichcote once said, " makes men consider the Inwards of things," [3] and almost of necessity the grasp slackens on outward

---

[1] *Select Sermons*, p. 86. This will be recognized as in perfect parallelism with Jacob Boehme's teaching, and the parallel is even more striking in the passage where Whichcote says that " Religion must inform the Judgment with Truth and reform the Heart and Life by the *Tincture* of it " (*Select Sermons*, p. 157).

[2] *Aphorism* 51. [3] *Select Sermons*, p. 42.

forms, as the vision focusses more intently upon inward and eternal realities. It is one of his foundation principles that "we worship God best when we resemble Him most,"[1] and if that is true, then the whole energy of one's being should concentrate upon the cultivation of "the deiform nature," "the nativity from Above." The real matters of religion, as he keeps insisting, are matters of life and inner being, the formation of disposition and the right set of will. But these vital things have been notoriously slighted, and "men's zeal is employed in usages, modes and rites of parties"; in matters that are divisive and controversial rather than in "things that are lovely in the eyes of all who have the Principles of Reason for their rule."[2] The great differences in religion have never been over necessary and indispensable Truth; on the contrary the disturbing differences have always been and still are "either over Points of curious and nice Speculation, or about arbitrary modes of worship."[3] Just as fast as men see that religion is a way to fullness of life, a method of attaining likeness to God, and just as soon as they realize that God can be truly worshipped only by acts and attitudes that are moral and spiritual, *i.e.* acts and attitudes that attach to the deliberate consent of the inner spirit, Whichcote thinks that "rites and types and ceremonies, which are all veils," will drop away and religion will become one with a rich and intelligent life.[4]

We can well understand how this presentation of Christianity as "a culture and discipline of the whole man—an education and consecration of all his higher activities"[5]—would seem, to those accustomed to dualistic theologies, "clowdie and obscure." It was, however, "no newe persuasion." In all essential particulars it is four-square with the type of religion with which the spiritual Reformers of Germany and Holland had for more than a century made the world acquainted. But,

---

[1] *Aphorism* 248.   [2] *Select Sermons*, p. 153.
[3] *Ibid.* p. 21.   [4] *Several Discourses*, ii. p. 329.
[5] John Tulloch's *Rational Theology in the Seventeenth Century*, ii. p. 115.

in the words of the Epistle to the Hebrews, somewhat adapted : " all these, having had the witness borne to them through their faith, received not the promise in full, God having provided some better, *i.e.* fuller, thing, that they should not be made complete, apart from those who succeeded them and fulfilled their hopes."

CHAPTER XVI

JOHN SMITH, PLATONIST—" AN INTERPRETER OF THE SPIRIT "[1]

PRINCIPAL TULLOCH, in his admirable study of the Cambridge Platonists, declares that John Smith was " the richest and most beautiful mind and certainly by far the best writer of them all."[2]

There can be no doubt, in the thought of any one who has come into close contact with him, of the richness and beauty of his spirit. He leaves the impression, even after the lapse of more than two hundred and fifty years, of having been a saint of a rare type. Those who were nearest to him in fellowship called him " a good man," " a Godlike man," " a servant and friend of God," " a serious practicer of the Sermon on the Mount " ; and we who know him only afar off and at second hand feel sure nevertheless that these lofty words were rightly given to him. His scholarship was wide—he had " a vastness of learning," as Patrick says ; but his main contribution was not to philosophy nor to theology, it consisted rather of an exhibition of religion wrought out in the attractive form of a beautiful spiritual life : " He was an Exemplar of true Christian Vertue of so poized and even a life that by his Wisdom and Conscience one might live almost at a venture, walking blindfold through the world."[3]

The details of his life are very meagre. We are in the

---

[1] Simon Patrick uses this phrase in his funeral sermon on his friend John Smith. *Select Discourses* (1673), p. 472.   [2] *Rational Theology*, ii. p. 122.
[3] Patrick's Sermon, *Select Discourses*, p. 496.

main dependent on the literary portraits of him drawn by
two of his affectionate friends—John Worthington who
edited his Discourses, and Simon Patrick who delivered
the remarkable sermon on the occasion of his funeral.[1]
From these sources we learn that John Smith was born at
Achurch near Oundle about the year 1618, " of parents
who had long been childless and were grown aged." It
appears incidentally that his parents were poor, and that
Benjamin Whichcote, who was Smith's college Tutor,
made " provision for his support and maintenance " in
his early student days.[2] He entered Emmanuel College
in 1636, and here he came under the profound religious
and intellectual influence of Whichcote, for whom " he
did ever express a great and singular regard." He became
a Master of Arts in 1644, and that same year was elected
Fellow of Queens' College. It was about this time that
Whichcote returned to Cambridge, " spreading and propagating a nobler, freer and more generous sett of
opinions," which " the young Masters of Arts soon cordially embraced." Among those who formed this group of
awakened and kindled students Smith was an enthusiastic
member, and he himself soon became a powerful exponent
in the Chapel of Queens' College of a similar message,
which, a contemporary writer says, " contributed to
raise new thoughts and a sublime style in the members
of the University." He was smitten, while still young,
with a painful lingering illness, which he bore " without
murmuring or complaining," " resting quietly satisfied
in the Infinite, Unbounded Goodness and Tenderness of
his Father," hoping only that he might " learn that for
which God sent the suffering," [3] and he died August 7,
1652, " after God had lent him to the world for about
five and thirty years." [4] " I was desirous," his friend
Patrick says at the opening of his funeral sermon, " that
I might have stai'd the wheels of that Triumphant Chariot
wherein he seemed to be carried ; that we might have

---

[1] Worthington's Sketch is given in the Preface to the Reader in *Select Discourses*, pp. iii-xxx, and Patrick's Sermon is given as an Appendix to the same
volume, pp. 471-512.

[2] Preface, p. vi.   [3] Patrick, *op. cit.* p. 498.   [4] Preface, p. xxviii.

kept him a little longer in this world, till by his holy
breathing into our souls, and the Grace of God, we had
been made meet to have some share in that inheritance of
the saints in light " ; but now, he adds, " we are orphans,
left without a father." [1] Patrick adapts to his own
departed teacher the beautiful words which Gregory
Thaumaturgus used of his great instructor, Origen : " He
hath entangled and bound up my soul in such fetters of
love, he hath so tyed and knit me to him, that if I would
be disengaged, I cannot quit myself. No, though I
depart out of the world, our love cannot die, for I love him
even as my own soul, and so my affection must remain
forever." [2] The whole sermon throbs with intense love,
and while it is somewhat overweighted with quotations
and learned allusions, it yet expresses in an impressive
way the sincere affection of a disciple for a noble master
who has " begot another shape in his scholar and has
made another man of him." [3] " Such men," he says,
" God hath alwaies in the world, men of greater height
and stature than others, whom He sets up as torches on
an hill to give light to all the regions round about." [4]
Such men " are the guard and defense of the towns where
they reside, yea of the country whereof they are members ;
they are the keepers and life-guards of the world ; the
walls and bulwarks of the Nation," [5] and when they leave
the world everybody soon feels that a glory has departed
—" when Elijah goes away you shall have fifty men go
three days to seek him ! " [6]

This disciple, who declared that whatever " heavenly
life " there was in himself had been " hatched " by the
fostering care, the nurturing love and the brave conduct
of his teacher, has left a few very clear traits for the
creation of a true portrait of this saintly interpreter of
the Spirit : He was a Fountain running over, Worthington
says, " an ever bountifull and bubbling Fountain." [7] Love
was bubbling and springing up in his soul and flowing out
to all. He would have emptied his soul into others. He

---

[1] Patrick, *op. cit.* pp. 471 and 472. [2] *Ibid.* p. 484.
[3] *Ibid.* p. 477. [4] *Ibid.* p. 474. [5] *Ibid.* pp. 480-481.
[6] *Ibid.* p. 486. [7] Preface, p. iii.

was dipped into Justice as it were over head and ears ;
he had not a slight tincture but was dyed and coloured
quite through with it. He cared only for those substantial and solid things of a Divine and Immortal Nature,
which he might carry out of the world with him. He was
a living library, a walking study, a whole college in himself, that carried his learning about with him ; a man of
great industry, indefatigable pains, and herculean labours.
His learning was so concocted that it lay not in notions in
his head, but was wrought out and formed in his very
soul so that a man came away always better after converse
with him. His faith did not busy itself about fine notions,
subtilties, and curiosities, but it was firmly set and fixed
in an experience of the mercy and goodness of God, seen
in Jesus Christ. He lived in a continuous enjoyment of
God and perpetually drew nearer to the Centre of his
soul's rest and always stayed God's time of advancement.
His spirit was absorbed in the business and employment
of becoming perfect in his art and profession—which was
the art *of being a good man*.[1] The devoted scholar's highest
wish, as he closes his glowing account of his beloved
master, who " enshrined so much Divinity that everything
about him had a kind of sacredness," was that those who
had enjoyed his presence and inspiration and had formed
their lives under his instruction might " so express his
life " in theirs, that men would say as they saw these
disciples of his, " There walks at least a shadow of Mr.
Smith ! " [2]

It would be difficult to find any one, in the long list of
those who have interpreted Christianity, who has been
more insistent than was John Smith that religion is the
normal function of the soul and the surest evidence of
its health and sanity. But religion of this normal and
spiritual type must be sharply differentiated both from
superstition and from legalistic religion. The mark of
superstition in his mind is the apprehension of God as
capricious, a hard Master, and of such a character that his

---

[1] This portrait is made up entirely of passages gathered out of Patrick's
Sermon, and but slightly altered.   [2] *Op. cit.* p. 509.

favour can be gained only by servile flattery or bribery
or by spells of magic. Superstition is "a brat of
darkness" born in a heart of fear and consternation. It
produces invariably "a forced and jejune devotion";
it makes "forms of worship which are grievous and
burdensome" to the life; it chills or destroys all free and
joyous converse with God; it kills out love and inward
peace, and instead of inspiring, heightening, and purifying
man's soul, it bends all its energies in the vain attempt
to alter the capricious attitude of the superior Being who
scares and terrifies men. It is, however, a very subtle
spirit and one hard to eradicate. It invades our religion
even when we are least aware of it : "it enters into our
chambers, creeps into our clothes, twines about our secret
devotions, and actuates our forms of belief and orthodox
opinions." [1]

Legalistic religion, or the "covenant of works," is
much of a piece with superstition. It, again, is always
a burden to be borne. Its mark is "drudgery and
servility." It is a "lean and lifeless form of external
performances." Its "law" is always something outside
the soul itself. It is a way of acquiring "merit," of
getting reckoned among "heaven's darlings," but it is
not a way of life or expansion or power or joy.[2]

This "dead" legalistic form of religion is, however,
not merely a thing of antiquity, of some early "dispensation" in the long stretch of years called "B.C." Like
superstition, legalistic religion also has "crept into our
clothes" and "twined about our secret devotions." The
"gospel" can be made, and·has often enough been made,
"as legal as ever the religion of the Jews was." The
gospel becomes legal, in Smith's sense, wherever it is
treated "as something onely without us," "as a meer
historical story or account," or as a collection of book-
facts, or "as *credenda* propounded for us to believe,"
or when we attempt to "make Christ's righteousness
serve onely as our outward *covering*."[3] "Some of our

---

[1] "A Short Discourse on Superstition," in *Select Discourses*, pp. 24-36.
[2] "Discourse on Legal Righteousness, etc.," *ibid.* pp. 273-338.
[3] Smith uses this phrase in precisely the same manner as Jacob Boehme.

Dogmata," he thinks, " and Notions of Justification puff
us up in far higher and goodlier conceits of ourselves than
God hath of us ; and we *profanely* make the unspotted
righteousness of Christ serve only as a *covering* to wrap
up our foul deformities and filthy vices in." [1]   This tendency, wherever it appears, is but legal religion.   Men
adopt it because it does not " pinch their sins."   It gives
them a " sluggish and drowsie Belief, a lazy Lethargy to
hugg their supposed acceptation with God " ; it enables
them " to grow big and swell with a mighty bulk with
airy fancies and presumptions of being in favour with
Heaven," and it fans up " a pertinacious Imagination
that their Names are enrolled in the Book of Life, or
crossed off in the Debt-Book of Heaven."   But it is all
" a meer Conceit or Opinion," for such men are " never
the better in reality in themselves and God judges all
things as they are."   " While men continue in their
wickedness, they do but vainly dream of a device to
tie the hands of Almighty Vengeance." [2]

True religion, on the other hand, is absolutely another
thing, sundered by the width of the sky from either
superstition or legalistic religion.   It is a reception and
assimilation of the Life of God within the soul of man
which is predisposed by its fundamental nature to the
influx and formative influence of the Spirit of God, who
is the environing Life and inner atmosphere of all human
spirits : " *Spiritual Life comes from God's breath within
us and from the formation of Christ within the soul.*" [3]

Like all of his kind, Smith begins with what to him is
an axiomatic fact, that the human soul has a " royal
pedigree and noble extraction," that, " as the best philosophers have alwaies taught, we must enquire for God
within ourselves," that " Principles of Divine Truth have
been engraven on man's Heart by the finger of God,"
that we can find " a clear impression of some Eternal
Nature and Perfect Being stamped upon our own souls,"
that there are " Radical Principles of Divine Knowledge "

---

[1] *Select Discourses*, p. 316.   [2] *Ibid.* pp. 319-321, quoted freely.
[3] *Ibid.* p. 21, quoted freely.

and " Seeds of Divine Nature " hidden within us and
that a Divine Spirit blows and breathes upon men's hearts,
assisting the soul to participate in the Life of God.[1]   In
one of his bold sayings this position is summed up as
follows : " Religion is a Heaven-born thing, the Seed of
God in the spirits of men, whereby they are formed to
a similitude and likeness of Himself.   A true Christian is
every way of a most noble extraction, of an heavenly and
divine pedigree." [2]

He finds the mark of man's excelling dignity in the
inexhaustible depth of his nature and in his noble dis-
content with every finite and mutable thing.   The soul
of man is " too big for earthly designs and interests."
There is forever a restless appetite within man for some
infinite Good without which he can never be satisfied.
Everything which he attains or achieves still leaves him
in " pinching penury," unsatiated with " the thin and
spare diet which he finds in his finite home."   His soul,
" like the daughters of the Horseleach is always crying :
' Give, give.' "   No happiness worth having ever arises,
nor through a whole eternity could arise, for any soul
sequestered like a hermit in the narrow confines of its
own private cell, sundered from " the Fountain-Goodness,"
for which it was created.   The immortal Principle within
forever drives it to seek its Original, and it lives only when
it " lives above itself," and follows " its own proper
motion upward." [3]

The real Gospel in contrast to the " legal gospel," is
" the formation of a Christlike Nature in a man's soul by
the mighty power of the Divine Spirit." [4]   It is no new
set of opinions ; no body of Notions about Truth ; " no
system of saving Divinity, cast in a Pedagogical mould " ;
it is, from its Alpha to its Omega, Spirit and Life, or, to
put it in Smith's own words, it is " a vital or energetical
Spirit or Power of Righteousness," " a Principle of Life
working in man's spirit," " a quickening ministration,"
" a Seed of God," " a vital Influx, spreading through all

[1] *Select Discourses*, pp. 13, 14, 57, 61, and 118.   [2] *Ibid.* p. 370.
[3] *Ibid.* pp. 375, 393, 395, 403, 407-408.   [4] *Ibid.* p. 311.

the powers of the soul and bringing it into a Divine Life." [1]
There are many close imitations of this real Gospel which
on the outside look exactly like it, but they only assume
" the garish dress and attire of religion," they put on
" the specious and seemingly-spiritual Forms " without
the inward Life and Power which are always the mark
of true religion. These " mimical Christians " reform
their looks, instruct their tongues, take up the fitting set
of duties and system of opinions, underprop their religion
with sacred performances ; " chameleon-like, they even
turn their insides to whatever hue and colour " is
demanded of religion ; they " furnish this domestick
Scene of theirs with any kind of matter which the history
of religion affords them " — only, however they " cun-
ningly fashion out their religion by Book-skill," they
cannot get " the true and living thing," which creates a
new spirit and produces a new inward joy: "True Religion
is no piece of artifice ; it is no boiling up of our Imaginative powers nor the glowing heats of Passion ; though
these are too often mistaken for it, when in our jugglings
in Religion we cast a mist before our eyes. But it is a new
Nature informing the souls of Men ; it is a Godlike frame
of Spirit, discovering it self most of all in serene and clear
Minds, in deep Humility, Meekness, Self-denial, Universal
Love of God and all true Goodness, without Partiality
and without Hypocrisie ; whereby we are taught to know
God, and knowing Him to love Him and conform ourselves
as much as may be to all that Perfection which shines
forth in Him." [2]

Heaven and Hell for John Smith, as for Boehme and
for Whichcote, " have their foundation laid in Men's own
souls." [3] They are rather something within us than
something without us. Sin and hell have the same
origin, " the same lineage and descent." " The Devil
is not only the name of one particular thing, but a *nature*.
He is not so much a particular Being designed to torture
wicked men in the world to come as a hellish and diabolical

[1] *Select Discourses*, pp. 303, 305, and 315.
[2] *Ibid.* p. 364. For Smith's view of mimical Christians see pp. 359-364.
[3] *Ibid.* p. 144.

nature seated in the minds of men. . . . Could the Devil change his foul and impure nature, he would neither be a Devil nor miserable. . . . All Sin and Wickedness in man's spirit hath the Central force and energy of Hell in it, and is perpetually pressing down towards it as towards its own place. There needs no fatal necessity or Astral influences to tumble wicked men down forcibly into Hell : No, Sin itself, hastened by the mighty weight of its own nature, carries them down thither with the most swift and headlong motion." [1] " Would wicked men dwell a little more at home, and *descend into the bottom of their own Hearts* they would soon find Hell opening her mouth wide upon them, and those secret fires of inward fury and displeasure breaking out upon them." [2] So, too, the Kingdom of Heaven is within. It lies not so much in external things, golden streets and crowns, as in the quality and disposition of a man's mind. The enjoying of God consists not so much in a change of place as in participation in the nature of God and in assimilation to God. Nothing can stand firm and sure, nothing can have eternal establishment and abiding permanence that " hath not the everlasting arms of true Goodness under it." [3]

In a very fine passage, in the noble discourse on " True Religion," Smith says : " I wish there be not among some such a light and poor esteem of Heaven, as makes them more to seek after *Assurance of Heaven onely in the Idea of it as a thing to come than after Heaven it self* ; which indeed we can never be well assured of untill we find it rising up within ourselves and glorifying our own souls. When true Assurance comes, Heaven it self will appear upon the Horizon of our souls, like a morning light chasing away all our dark and gloomy doubtings before it. We shall not then need to light up our Candles to seek for it in corners ; no, it will display its own lustre and brightness so before us that we may see it in its own light, and our souls the true possessours of it." " Should a man hear a Voice from Heaven or see a Vision from the Almighty to testifie unto him the Love of God towards him [and the

[1] *Select Discourses*, p. 452.   [2] *Ibid.* p. 456.   [3] *Ibid.* pp. 452 and 445.

Assurance of his Salvation] ; yet methinks it were more desirable to find a Revelation of all *from within*, arising up from the Bottome and centre of a man's own soul, in the Reall and Internal impressions of a Godlike nature upon his own spirit ; and thus to find the Foundation and Beginning of Heaven and Happiness within himself ; it were more desirable to see the crucifying of our own Will, the mortifying of the meer Animal life and to see a Divine life rising up in the room of it, as a sure Pledge and Inchoation of Immortality and Happiness, the very Essence of which consists in a perfect conformity and cheerful compliance of all the Powers of our Souls with the Will of God." [1]

The consciousness of Immortality rises or falls with the moral and spiritual height of the soul. Nothing makes men doubt or question the Immortality of their souls so much as their own " base and earthly loves," and so, too, inward goodness " breeds a sense of the Soul's Immortality " : " Goodness and vertue make men know and love, believe and delight in their Immortality. When the soul is purged and enlightened by true sanctity it is more capable of those Divine irradiations whereby it feels it self in conjunction with God. It knows that Almighty Love, by which it lives, is stronger than death. It knows that God will never forsake His own life which He has quickened in the soul. Those breathings and gaspings after an Eternal participation of Him are but the energy of His own breath within us." [2]

Smith finds the world in which he lives a fair world, everywhere full of " the Prints and Footsteps of God," the finite creatures of which are " Glasses wherein God reflects His glory." There are many " golden links that unite the world to God," and good men, " conversing with this lower world and viewing the invisible things of God in the things that are made in the outward Creation, may many times find God secretly flowing into their souls and leading them silently out of the Court of the Temple into the Holy Place." [3]

---

[1] *Select Discourses*, p. 416.   [2] *Ibid*. pp. 97-98. Quoted freely.
[3] *Ibid*. pp. 419-420.

The outward world is thus not something stubbornly foreign to the spirit ; it is not the enemy's country, but every finite good and everything of beauty is " a Blossom of the First Goodness, a Beam from the Father of Lights." The spiritual person discovers that the whole creation is spiritual. He learns to " love all things in God and God in all things, and he sees that God is All in all, the Beginning and Original of Being, the Perfect Idea of their goodness and the end of their motion." In the calming illumination of this clarified vision, the good man, in whose soul religion has flowered, " is no longer solicitous whether this or that good thing be mine, or whether my perfections exceed the measure of this or that particular Creature, for whatever good he beholds anywhere he enjoys and delights in as much as if it were his own, and whatever he beholds in himself he looks upon not as his *property* but as *a common good* ; for all these Beams come from one and the same Fountain and Ocean of Light in whom he loves them all with an universal Love. When his affections run along the stream of any created excellencies, whether his own or any one's else, yet they stay not here but run on until they fall into the Ocean ; they do not settle into a fond love and admiration either of himself or any other's excellencies, but he owns them as so many Pure Effluxes and Emanations from God, and in any particular Being loves the Universal Goodness. Thus a good man may walk up and down the world as in a Garden of Spices and suck a Divine Sweetness out of every flower. There is a twofold meaning in every Creature : a Literal and Mystical ; a good man says of everything that his Senses offer to him : it speaks to his lower part but it points out something above to his Mind and Spirit. . . . True Religion never finds it self out of the Infinite Sphere of Divinity and wherever it finds Beauty, Harmony, Goodness, Love, Ingenuity, Wisdom, Holiness, Justice, and the like, it is ready to say : *Here is God.* Wheresoever any such Perfections shine out, an holy Mind climbs up by these Sunbeams and raises up it self to God. . . . A good man finds every place he treads upon *Holy Ground* ; to him the world is God's Temple."[1]

The supreme instance of the revelation of the Universal through the particular, of the invisible through the visible, the Divine through the human, is seen in Christ. It was precisely such an event as might have been expected, for " the Divine Bounty and Fulness has always been manifesting Itself to the spirits of men." Those who have lived by inward insight have perpetually found themselves " hanging upon the arms of Immortal Goodness." At length, in this One Life the Divine Goodness blossomed into perfect flower and revealed its Nature to men. In Him divinity and humanity are absolutely united in one Person. In Christ we have a clear manifestation of God and in Him, too, " we may see with open face what human nature can attain to."[2] This stupendous event, however, was no " gracious contrivance," no scheme to restore lapsed men in order that God might have " a Quire of Souls to sing eternal Hallelujahs to Him " ; it was just " the overflowing fountain and efflux of Almighty Love bestowing itself upon men and crowning Itself by communicating Itself."[3] The Christ who is thus divine Grace become visible and vocal is also at the same time the irresistible attraction, " strongly and forcibly moving the souls of men into a conjunction with Divine Goodness," which is what Smith always means by the great word, *Faith*. It is something in the hearts of men which by experience " feels the mighty insinuations of Divine Goodness " ; complies with it ; perpetually rises into co-operation with it, and attains its true " life and vivacity " by partaking of it.[4] Christ is thus the Node, or Centre, of both Grace and Faith.

With this apprehension of Faith as a vital thing—a new and living way—Smith thinks very lightly of " notions " and what he calls " a knowledge of Divinity [Theology] which appears in systems and models."[5] This is but a poor way, he thinks, to " the Land of Truth."

---

[1] *Select Discourses*, pp. 421-423.   [2] *Ibid.* pp. 332 and 336.
[3] *Ibid.* p. 398.   [4] *Ibid.* p. 325.   [5] *Ibid.* p. 2.

" It is but a thin and aiery knowledge that is got by meer speculation." " This is but spider-like to spin a worthless web out of one's own bowels." " Jejune and barren speculations may unfold the Plicatures of Truth's garment, but they cannot discover her lovely Face." " To find Truth," he says in another figure, " we must break through the outward shell of words and phrases which house it," and by *experience and practice* discover the " inward beauty, life and loveliness of Truth." [1]

This hard " shell of words and phrases " which must be broken before Truth is found, is one of Sebastian Franck's favourite sayings, and we find Smith also repeating Franck's vivid accounts of the weakness of Scripture when it is treated only as external history, or as words, texts, and phrases. " Scripture," he says, in the exact words and figures of the German Humanist, " is a Sealed Book which the greatest Sophist may be most acquainted with. It is like the Pillar of fire and cloud that parted between the Israelites and Egyptians, giving a clear and comfortable light to all those that are under the manu-duction and guidance thereof [*i.e.* those who have the inner experience] but being full of darkness and obscurity to those that rebel against it.[2] " The dead letter," he says, " is a sandy foundation " for religion, because it is never in books and writings but rather in the human soul that men must seek for God.[3] Action and not words ; life and not motions ; heart and not brain, hold the key to Truth : " They cannot be good at Theorie that are bad at Practice." [4] " Our Saviour," he says, " would not draw Truth up into any System, nor would He lay it out into Canons or Articles of Faith, because He was not so careful to stock the world with Opinions and Notions as to make it thrive with true piety, Godlike purity and spiritual understanding " ; and in a very happy passage, he reminds us that there are other ways of propagating religion besides writing books : " They are not alwaies the best Men who blot the most paper ; Truth is not so

---

[1] *Select Discourses*, pp. 4, 7, and 8.   [2] *Ibid.* p. 278.
[3] *Ibid.* pp. 3 and 288.   [4] *Ibid.* p. 12.

voluminous nor swells into such a mighty bulk as our
Bookes doe.   Those minds are not alwaies the most chaste
that are the most parturient with learned Discourses." [1]

I have, I believe, now given a true account of Smith's
type of Christianity,   It was no new message.   It was a
re-expression of ideas and ideals that had already been
often proclaimed to the dull ears of the world.   He,
however, is never a repeater of other men's ideas.   What
he offers is always as much his own as was the life-blood
which coursed through his heart.   He fed upon the
literature which was kindred to his growing spirit, and his
books helped him find the road which he was seeking;
but he was nobly true to his own theory that the way of
Life is discovered by spiritual experience rather than by
" verbal description," and this quiet, sincere scholar and
prophet of the soul found it thus.   He once said that
" Truth is content, when it comes into the world, to wear
our mantles, to learn our language and to conform itself
as it were to our dress and fashions "; [2] that is to say,
prophets speak in their own dialect and use the modes of
their own culture, but they are prophets through their
own temporal experience of that one eternal Reality which
shines into their souls in its own Light. [3]

What impressed his contemporary friends most was the
beauty of his spirit, and that is what still most impresses
the reader of his Discourses.   He has succeeded in pre-
serving some of the strong elixir of his life in the words
which survive him, and we know him as a valiant soldier
in that great army of soldier-saints who have fought with
spiritual weapons.   " This fight and contest," he himself
has told us, " with Sin and Satan is not to be known by
the rattling of Chariots or the sound of an alarm : it is
indeed alone transacted upon the inner stage of men's
souls and spirits—but it never consists in a sluggish kind
of doing nothing that so God might do all." [4]   Life is
always battle, and the true Christian is always "a Champion
of God " clad in the armour of Light for the defeat of

[1] *Select Discourses*, p. 12.   [2] *Ibid.* p. 165.   [3] *Ibid.* p. 260.
[4] *Ibid.* pp. 461 and 458.

darkness and the seed of Satan. In this battle of Armageddon John Smith took a man's part, and his affectionate
disciple Simon Patrick was quite right in saying, as the
master passed away, " My father, my father, The chariot
of Israel and the horsemen thereof."

The other members of this impressive group of Cambridge Platonists, especially Ralph Cudworth, Henry
More, Nathaniel Culverwel and John Norris, might well
be studied, and they would furnish some additional
aspects of religious thought, but the teachings of the two
exponents whom I have selected as representative of the
school have brought the central ideas and the underlying spirit of this seventeenth century religious movement
sufficiently into view. Their intimate connection with
the currents of thought which preceded them has also
been made adequately clear. This volume does not
pretend to be exhaustive, and it cannot follow out all the
interesting ramifications of the complicated historical
development which I have been tracing. I have been
compelled to limit myself to the presentation of typical
specimens and examples of this continuously advancing
spiritual movement which found one of its noblest figures
in John Smith.

CHAPTER XVII

THOMAS TRAHERNE AND THE SPIRITUAL POETS OF THE SEVENTEENTH CENTURY

I

THE powerful religious upheaval in England which reached its culmination during the two middle decades of the seventeenth century, profoundly stirred both the upper and lower intellectual strata of society. It fused and organized men on the one hand, and carried them beyond themselves ; and on the other hand it broke up settled habits of thought, swept away many customs and practices which had become almost irresistible subconscious influences, and left those who were in any way morally and intellectually defective at the mercy of chance currents and eddies. As a result there appeared a strange medley of tiny sects. These groups, seething with enthusiasm, scattered pretty much over England, unorganized or loosely organized, generally gathered about some influential psychopathic leader, were lumped together in the public mind and named " Ranters." [1] They are by no means a negligible phenomenon of the period. They reveal the back-wash of the spiritual movement, which in the main went steadily onward. They exhibit, in their loose and unmoralized freedom, the inherent dangers which attach to the proclamation of spiritual liberty, and they furnish a clear historical illustration of the truth that progress toward a religion grounded upon the inner life of man can only be slowly and painfully achieved.

[1] See my *Studies in Mystical Religion*, chap. xix.

The religious poets of this period, on the other hand, furnish clear evidence of the constructive, organizing and fusing power of these newly dawning spiritual insights, as they worked upon the minds of highly gifted and endowed persons. Poets are not Reformers. They do not consider themselves " commissioned " to reconstruct old systems of thought, old forms of faith and old types of church-organization, or to re-interpret the Gospel, the way of salvation and the communion of saints. Their mission is a different one, though it is no less spiritual and, in the best sense of the word, no less practical. The poets are always among the first to feel the direction of spiritual currents, and they are very sure voices of the deeper hopes and aspirations of their epoch. All the religious poets of this particular period reveal very clearly the influence of the ideas which were central in the teaching of the spiritual leaders whom we have been studying. The reader of Milton needs no argument to convince him of the fact that, however far removed the great poet was in most points of view from the contemporary Quakers, he nevertheless insisted emphatically, as they did, on the illumination of the soul by a Light within ; " a celestial Light," he calls it in *Paradise Lost*, which shines inward and irradiates the mind through all her powers, and supplies an inward sight of things invisible to sense [1]—a Light which steadily increases as it is used by the obedient soul.[2] The origin of this inward Light, according to Milton's thought, is the eternal Word of God, who is before all worlds and who is the source of all revelation, whether inward or outward : the Spirit that prefers

Before all temples the upright heart and pure.[3]

The minor religious poets of the period had not, however, formed their intellectual outlook under the imperial sway of theological systems of thought in anything like

---

[1] Book III. lines 51-55.   [2] Book III. lines 194-197.
[3] Book I. line 18. Since this chapter was written, Alden Sampson's *Studies in Milton* (New York, 1913) has been published. His valuable chapter on " Milton's Confession of Faith " reveals in Milton a very wide acquaintance with the ideas which I have been tracing, and shows by a vast number of quotations how frequently the poet used these ideas sympathetically.

the degree that Milton had. They reflect the freer and
less rigidly formulated currents of thought. " All divinity
is love, or wonder," John Donne wrote in one of his
poems. No phrase could better express the intense
religious life of the group of spiritual poets in England
who interpreted in beautiful, often immortal, form this
religion of the spirit, this glowing consciousness that the
world and all its fulness is God's and that eternity is set
within the soul of man, who never is himself until he finds
his Life in God.

> E'en like two little bank-dividing brooks,
> That wash the pebbles with their wanton streams,
> And having rang'd and search'd a thousand nooks,
> Meet both at length in silver-breasted Thames,
> Where in a greater current they conjoin :
> So I my best beloved's am ; so He is mine.
>
> E'en so we met : and after long pursuit,
> E'en so we joined ; we both became entire :
> No need for either to renew a suit,
> For I was flax and He was flames of fire.
> Our firm united souls did more than twine ;
> So I my best beloved's am ; so He is mine.[1]

Whatever these poets, Herbert, Vaughan, Traherne,
Crashaw, Quarles, say of the soul and its fuller life, they
say quite naturally in terms of love and wonder. Religion
has become for them the flowering of the soul ; the flooding of the whole being with health and joy ; the consum-
mation of life ; and they tell of it as lovers tell of their
discovery and their joy.

> Oh mightie love ! man is one world and hath
> Another to attend him.[2]

We have here in these poets, as in the writings of
Whichcote and Smith, a type of religion which is primarily
concerned with the liberation and winning of the whole
of life, a thing which, they all tell us, can be done only in
conscious parallelism with the set of eternal currents.

These minor prophets of seventeenth century English
literature have often been treated as mystics, and there

---

[1] Francis Quarles' " My Beloved is Mine."   [2] George Herbert's poem " Man."

is in all of them, except George Herbert, a rich strand of mystical religion, but their mysticism is only an element, a single aspect, of a very much wider and completer type of religion which includes all the strands that compose what I have been calling " spiritual religion "—an inner flooding of the life with a consciousness of God, a rational apprehension of the soul's inherent relation to the Divine, and a transforming discovery of the meaning of life through the revelation in Christ, which sets all one's being athrob with love and wonder.

> Eternal God ! O thou that only art
> The sacred fountain of eternal light,
> And blessed loadstone of my better part,
> O thou, my heart's desire, my soul's delight,
> Reflect upon my soul and touch my heart,
> And then my heart shall prize no good above thee ;
> And then my soul shall know thee ; knowing, love thee.[1]

II

Thomas Traherne is one of the best and most adequate representatives, in this literary group, of this type of religion. He was profoundly influenced by the revival of Plato and Plotinus, and by the writings of the religious Humanists and he had absorbed, consciously or unconsciously, the ideas and ideals which appear and reappear in the widespread movement which I have been tracing. He was a pure and noble soul, a man of deep experience and fruitful meditation, the master of a rare and wonderful style, and we shall find in his writings a glowing appreciation and a luminous expression of this type of inner, spiritual religion.

He was born about the year 1636, probably at Hereford, the son of a poor shoemaker, but of a notable and well-endowed family line. He took no pains to inform the world of his outward history and we are left with guesses as to most of the details of his earthly career, but he has himself supplied us with an unusually full account of his

[1] Francis Quarles' " Light."

inward life during the early years of it. " Once I remember," he says, " I think I was about four years old
when I thus reasoned with myself, sitting in a little obscure
room of my father's poor house : If there be a God
certainly He must be infinite in Goodness, and I was
prompted to this by a real whispering instinct of Nature." [1]
Whereupon the child wonders why, if God is so rich, he
himself is so poor, possessed of " so scanty and narrow
a fortune, enjoying few and obscure comforts," but he
tells us that as soon as he was old enough to discover the
glory of the world he was in, and old enough for his soul
to have " *sudden returns into itself*," there was no more
questioning about poverty and narrow fortunes. All the
wealth of God was his—

> I nothing in the world did know
> But 'twas divine.[2]

As nobody has better caught the infinite glory of being
a child, and as nobody in literature has more successfully
" set the little child in the midst," than has Traherne, it
may be well to let him tell us here in his splendid
enthusiasm what it is to be a child and what the eyes of
a child can see. He shall do it, first in his magnificent
prose and then in his fine and simple verse.

" Certainly Adam in Paradise had not more sweet and
curious apprehensions of the world, than I when I was a
child. All appeared new, and strange at first, inexpres-
sibly rare and delightful and beautiful. I was a little
stranger, which at my entrance into the world was saluted
and surrounded with innumerable joys. My knowledge
was Divine. . . . My very ignorance was advantageous.
I seemed as one brought into the Estate of Innocence.
All things were spotless and pure and glorious : yea, and
infinitely mine, and joyful and precious. I knew not
that there were any sins, or complaints or laws. I
dreamed not of poverties, contentions or vices. All tears

---

[1] *Centuries of Meditations* (London, 1908), iii. 16. For details of his life and
for the story of the discovery of his writings, see the Introduction to *The Poetical
Works of Thomas Traherne* (1903) by Bertram Dobell.
[2] Traherne's poem " Wonder," iii.

and quarrels were hidden from mine eyes. Everything was at rest, free and immortal. I knew nothing of sickness or death or rents or exaction, either for tribute or bread. In the absence of these I was entertained like an Angel with the works of God in their splendour and glory, I saw all the peace of Eden ; Heaven and Earth did sing my Creator's praises, and could not make more melody to Adam, than to me. All Time was Eternity, and a perpetual Sabbath. Is it not strange, that an infant should be heir of the whole World, and see those mysteries which the books of the learned never unfold ?

" The corn was orient and immortal wheat, which never should be reaped, nor was ever sown. I thought it had stood from everlasting to everlasting. The dust and stones of the street were as precious as gold ; the gates were at first the end of the world. The green trees when I saw them first through one of the gates transported and ravished me, their sweetness and unusual beauty made my heart to leap, and almost mad with ecstasy, they were such strange and wonderful things. The Men ! O what venerable and reverend creatures did the aged seem ! Immortal Cherubims ! And young men glittering and sparkling Angels, and maids strange seraphic pieces of life and beauty ! Boys and girls tumbling in the street, and playing, were moving jewels. I knew not that they were born or should die. But all things abided eternally as they were in their proper places. Eternity was manifest in the Light of the Day, and something infinite behind everything appeared ; which talked with my expectation and moved my desire. The city seemed to stand in Eden, or to be built in Heaven. The streets were mine, the temple was mine, the people were mine, their clothes and gold and silver were mine, as much as their sparkling eyes, fair skins and ruddy faces. The skies were mine, and so were the sun and moon and stars, and all the World was mine ; and I the only spectator and enjoyer of it. . . . So that with much ado I was corrupted, and made to learn the dirty devices of this world. Which now I unlearn, and become, as it were, a little child again that I may enter into the Kingdom of God." [1]

> How like an Angel came I down !
> How bright are all things here !
> When first among His works I did appear
> O how their Glory did me crown !
> The World resembled His *Eternity*
> In which my soul did walk ;
> And everything that I did see
> Did with me talk. [2]

> Long time before
> I in my mother's womb was born,
> A God preparing did this glorious store,
> The world, for me adorne.
> Into this Eden so divine and fair
> So wide and bright, I come His son and heir. [3]

Like Vaughan, who, in his "angel - infancy," could

> In these weaker glories spy
> Some shadows of eternity,

and who

> Felt through all this fleshly dress
> Bright shoots of everlastingness, [4]

Traherne not only saw, in his paradise-innocence, the glory of the earth and sky—the streets paved with golden stones, and boys and girls with lovely shining faces—but he also felt that he was part of a deeper world which lay about his infancy and wooed him with love.

> O Lord I wonder at Thy Love,
> Which did my Infancy so early move. [5]

And out of this childhood experience, which many a meditative child can ·match, he insists that God visited him.

> He did Approach, He did me woo ;
> I wonder that my God this thing would do.
>
> He in our childhood with us walks,
> And with our thoughts Mysteriously He talks ;
> He often visiteth our Minds. [6]

---

[1] *Centuries of Meditations*, iii. 1, 2 and 3.
[2] "Wonder," i.   [3] "The Salutation"   [4] Vaughan's "The Retreat."
[5] Traherne's "The Approach."   [6] *Ibid.*

I know of no one who has borne a louder testimony than Traherne to the divine inheritances and spiritual possibilities of the new - born child, or who has more emphatically denied the fiction of total depravity : " I speak it in the presence of God," he says, " and of our Lord Jesus Christ ; in my pure primitive Virgin Light, while my apprehensions were natural and unmixed, I cannot remember but that I was ten thousand times more prone to good and excellent things than to evil." [1]   And he adds this impressive word on the doctrine of inheritance : " It is not our parents' loins, so much as our parents' lives, that enthrals and blinds us." [2]

After a happy childhood, during which " The Earth did undertake the office of a Priest," [3] and when his soul was

> A living endless eye
> Just bounded with the sky,
> Whose power, whose act, whose essence was to *see*, [4]

he entered Brasenose College, Oxford, in the year 1652, being made B.A. in 1656, M.A. in 1661, and Bachelor of Divinity in 1669.   He was admitted in 1657 to the Rectory of Credenhill, near Hereford, where he remained for about ten years, and in 1667 he was made chaplain to Sir Orlando Bridgman, in whose service he died in 1674, and was buried " under the reading-desk " in the church at Teddington near Hampton Court.

During his lifetime he published *Roman Forgeries* (1673), an unimportant work, and had begun the publication of his *Christian Ethics*, which appeared, after his death, in 1675.   His *Poems* and his *Centuries of Meditations* remained in MS. unknown until they were discovered in a London bookstall about the year 1897, and their authorship was proved by Bertram Dobell who published the *Poems* in 1903, and the *Centuries of Meditations* in 1908.   There still remains in MS. an octavo volume of meditations and devotions.

Traherne's poems show that he always dwelt near the

---

[1] *Centuries of Meditations*, iii. 8.   [2] *Ibid.*
[3] " Dumbness."   [4] " The Preparative."

gate of Heaven and was easily aware of the " ancient Light of Eden." An accidental bit of gossip, reported in John Aubrey's *Miscellanies*, indicates that he was subject to psychical experiences of an unusual sort, and the poet himself has reported an impressive crisis-experience when he chose his destiny and settled his preference for inward treasures, even though it meant, as with George Fox, the wearing of a leather suit.

" When I came into the country, and being seated among silent trees, and meads and hills, had all my time in mine own hands, I resolved to spend it all, whatever it cost me, in the search of happiness, and to satiate that burning thirst which Nature had enkindled in me from my youth. In which I was so resolute, that I chose rather to live upon ten pounds a year, and to go in leather clothes, and feed upon bread and water, so that I might have all my time clearly to myself, than to keep many thousands per annum in an estate of life where my time would be devoured in care and labour. And God was so pleased to accept of that desire, that from that time to this, I have had all things plentifully provided for me, without any care at all, my very study of Felicity making me more to prosper, than all the care in the whole world. So that through His blessing I live a free and a kingly life as if the world were turned again into Eden, or much more, as it is at this day." [1]

Like his predecessors in this faith, Traherne is never tired of declaring the infiniteness of the human soul. Eternity is in the human heart, if only the way of the open door is taken, if only the eyes are opened to see. God, he says, has made our spirits " centres in eternity," opening upon " innumerable infinities." The Ocean is but a drop of a bucket to the immensity of the soul, with its abysmal deeps and its immeasurable capacities. It is the very essence and being of the soul to feel infinity, for " God is ever more near to us than we are to ourselves, so that we cannot feel our own souls without feeling Him." [2] " You are never," he says, " your true self, till you live

---

[1] *Centuries of Meditations*, iii. 46.   [2] *Ibid.* ii. 81.   See also ii. 70 and 83.

by your soul more than by your body, and you never
live by your soul until you feel its incomparable excellence." [1]   Its nobility is revealed by its insatiable hungers,
its surpassing dignity is declared by its endless wants, its
inability to live by bread alone.   " As by the seed we
conjecture what plant will arise, and know by the acorn
what tree will grow forth, or by the eagle's egg what kind
of bird ; so do we by the powers of the soul upon earth,
know what kind of Being, Person, and Glory will be in the
Heavens, where its latent powers shall be turned into
Act, its inclinations shall be completed, and its capacities
filled." [2]

Not only in a primitive Eden, but in the world as we
know it, with its black and white, man always bears within
himself the mark of a heavenly origin, and has the quickening Seed of God in the depth of his soul :   " The Image of
God is seated in the lineaments of the soul."   Man is the
greatest of all miracles ; he is " a mirror of all Eternity." [3]
His thoughts run out to everlasting ; he is made for
spiritual supremacy and has within himself an inner,
hidden life greater than anything else in the universe.[4]
We are " nigh of kin to God " and " nigh of kin

> To those pure things we find
> In His great mind
> Who made the world." [5]

There is

> A Spiritual World standing within
> An Universe enclosed in Skin.[6]

With the same enthusiasm with which he proclaims
the divine origin and the heavenly connections of the soul,
Traherne also proclaims the glory and beauty of the
visible world as a revelation of God.

> Eternity stooped down to nought
> And in the earth its likeness sought.[7]

The world is not God, for He is Spirit, but the world is
" a glorious mirror " in which the verities of religion are

---

[1] *Centuries of Meditations*, ii. 92.   [2] *Ibid*. iv. 70.
[3] *Ibid*. i. 19, and iv. 81.   [4] *Ibid*. ii. 23.
[5] "My Spirit."   [6] "Fullness."   [7] "The Choice."

revealed and in which the face of God is at least partially unveiled.[1] It is here in this " mirror " that the clairvoyant eye discovers God's being, perceives His wisdom, goodness, and power, guesses out the footsteps of His love, and finds promises and pledges of the larger fulfilment of that love. Here in the world, which is full of " remainders of Paradise," is surely the visible porch or gate of Eternity.[2] It is easy to believe that God has given us His Son when once we have seen the richness of the world which He has given us.[3] But the world is never " ours " until we learn how to *see* it and enjoy it in its beauty, even in the most common things, and until we discover that all its service and all its excellency are spiritual : " Pigs eat acorns, but neither consider the sun that gave them life, nor the influences of the heavens by which they were nourished, nor the very root of the tree from whence they came. This being the work of Angels who in a wide and clear light see even the sea that gave them [the acorns] moisture : And feed upon that acorn spiritually while they know the ends for which it was created, and feast upon all these as upon a World of Joys within it : while to ignorant swine that eat the shell it is an empty husk of no taste nor delightful savour." [4]

Men, as well as angels, can learn to use the world spiritually—can learn to see how rough, common things are part of " the divine exchequer " ; how a grain of sand exhibiteth the wisdom of God and manifesteth His glory.[5] With this prelude, Traherne gives his glowing account of the true, spiritual way to enjoy the world.

" Your enjoyment of the world is never right, till every morning you awake in Heaven ; see yourself in your Father's Palace ; and look upon the skies, the earth, and the air as Celestial Joys : having such a reverend esteem of all, as if you were among the Angels. The bride of a monarch, in her husband's chamber, hath no such causes of delight as you.

" You never enjoy the world aright, till the Sea itself

---

[1] *Centuries of Meditations*, ii. 17.   [2] *Ibid.* ii. 1 and 17.
[3] *Ibid.* ii. 6.   [4] *Ibid.* i. 26.   [5] *Ibid.* i. 25. and 27.

floweth in your veins, till you are clothed with the heavens, and crowned with the stars : and perceive yourself to be the sole heir of the whole world, and more than so, because men are in it who are every one sole heirs as well as you. Till you can sing and rejoice and delight in God, as misers do in gold, and Kings in sceptres, you never enjoy the world.

" Till your spirit filleth the whole world, and the stars are your jewels ; till you are as familiar with the ways of God in all Ages as with your walk and table ; till you are intimately acquainted with that shady nothing out of which the world was made ; till you love men so as to desire their happiness with a thirst equal to the zeal of your own ; till you delight in God for being good to all ; you never enjoy the world. Till you more feel it than your private estate, and are more present in the hemisphere, considering the glories and the beauties there, than in your own house ; till you remember how lately you were made, and how wonderful it was when you came into it : and more rejoice in the palace of your glory, than if it had been made but to-day morning.

" Yet further, you never enjoy the world aright, till you so love the beauty of enjoying it, that you are covetous and earnest to persuade others to enjoy it. And so perfectly hate the abominable corruption of men in despising it, that you had rather suffer the flames of Hell than willingly be guilty of their error. . . . The world is a mirror of infinite beauty, yet no man sees it. It is a Temple of Majesty, yet no man regards it. It is a region of Light and Peace, did not men disquiet it. It is the Paradise of God. It is more to man since he is fallen than it was before. It is the place of Angels and the Gate of Heaven. When Jacob waked out of his dream, he said, ' God is here, and I wist it not. How dreadful is this place ! This is none other than the House of God, and the Gate of Heaven.' " [1]

But notwithstanding his exuberant and overflowing joy in creation, Traherne is conscious that the world has

---

[1] *Centuries of Meditations*, i. 28-31.

its "dreggy parts," that it has been "muddied" by man's misuse of it, and that the havoc of sin is apparent. The light which shined in infancy becomes eclipsed as the customs and manners of life close down over it and cover it. Men's mouths are full of talk of fleeting, vulgar, and worthless things, and they speak no syllable of those celestial and stable treasures which form the only wealth of life. The emphasis in education is on the wrong things. So with much ado the innocent child is "corrupted and made to learn the dirty devices of the world," which he must again unlearn and become a little child once more in the Kingdom of God.[1] The taint, however, is not in the native structure of the soul, it is not through a biological transmission, it is due to false training—it is from the parents' lives rather than their loins. Let parents, he says, who desire holy children learn to make them possessors of divine things *betimes*. It is "deadly barbarous and uncouth" to "put grubs and worms" into little children's minds, to teach them to say this house is mine, this bauble is a jewel, this gew-gaw is a fine thing, this rattle makes music, when they ought to be made instead to see the spiritual glory of the earth and sky, the beauty of life, the sweetness and nobility of Nature, and to live joyously, like birds, in union and communion with God. I am sure, he concludes, that barbarous people that go naked come nearer to Adam, God, and the Angels, in the simplicity of their wealth, than do many among us who partake of what we nick-name civility and mode.[2] The entire work of redemption is, thus, to restore man to himself, to bring him once more to the Tree of Life, to enable him to discover the glory all about him, to reveal to him the real values of things, and to bring to birth within him an immortal love. The true healing of the soul is always through the birth of love. Before a soul loves, it lives only to itself ; as soon as love is born it lives beyond itself and finds its life in the object of its love. It is Christ who first reveals the full measure of love, who makes us see the one adequate Object of love, and who

[1] *Centuries of Meditations*, iii. 7 and 3. [2] *Ibid.* iii. 11-13.

forges within our human spirits the invisible bonds of a
love that binds us forever to Him who *so* loved us. Here
in Him—" a Man loving all the world, a God dying for
mankind " [1]—we see that we are infinitely beloved, that
the foundations of an eternal Friendship are laid, that
God is infinitely prone to love, and that true love spares
nothing for the sake of what it loves—" O miraculous
and eternal Godhead suffering on a Cross for me ! " [2]
" That Cross is a tree set on fire with invisible flame
which illuminateth all the world. The flame is love :
the love in His bosom that died upon it." [3]

But there is no salvation for us in the Cross until it
kindles the same flame of love in us, until that immeasurable love of His becomes an irresistible power in us, so
that we henceforth live unto Him that loved us. It
must, if it is to be efficacious, shift all our values and set
us to loving as He loved—" He who would not in the same
cases do the same things Jesus Christ hath done can never
be saved," for love is never timorous. [4] The love of Christ
is to dwell within us and every man is to be the object
of it. God and we are to become one spirit, that is, one in
will and one in desire. Christ must live within us. We
must be filled with the Holy Ghost, which is the God of
Love ; we must be of the same mind with Christ Jesus
and led by His Spirit, and we must henceforth treat every
man in respect to the greatness of Christ's love—this is
salvation in Traherne's conception of it, and holiness
and happiness are the same thing. [5] The Cross has not
done its complete work for us until we can say : " O
Christ, I see thy crown of thorns in every eye ; thy bleed-
ing, naked, wounded body in every soul ; thy death
liveth in every memory ; thy crucified person is em-
balmed in every affection ; thy pierced feet are bathed
in every one's tears and it is my privilege to enter with
thee into every soul." [6]

However contemplative and mystical the bent of
Traherne's mind may have been, he always finds the

---

[1] *Centuries of Meditations,* i. 59.   [2] *Ibid.* i. 67 and 62.   [3] *Ibid.* i. 60.
[4] *Ibid.* iv. 59.   [5] *Ibid.* iv. 28. See also iv. 31.   [6] *Ibid.* i. 86.

terminus of spiritual life in action, indeed, in brotherly
service, in what he calls " blessed operations." Speaking
apparently of himself, he finely says : " He thought it a
vain thing to see glorious principles buried in books,
unless he did remove them into his understanding ; and
a vain thing to remove them into his understanding
unless he did revive them and raise them up with continual
exercise. Let this therefore be the first principle of your
soul—that to have no principles or to live beside them
is equally miserable. Philosophers are not those that
speak but do great things." [1] " It is," he writes in words
which sound like those of his contemporary Winstanley,
" it is an indelible principle of Eternal truth, that practice and exercise is the Life of all. Should God give you
worlds and laws and treasures, and worlds upon worlds,
and Himself also in the Divinest manner, if you will be
lazy you lose all. The soul is made for action and cannot
rest till it be employed. . . . If therefore you would be
happy, your life must be as full of operation as God of
treasure." [2]

Love, once kindled in the soul, is the mother of all
heroic actions ; love knows how to abound and overflow
—the man who has lighted his life from Christ's love is
constant in trials, patient in sufferings, courageous in
assaults, prudent in difficulties, victorious and triumphant
in action.[3]

Traherne shares with Boehme and with the Cambridge
Platonists the view that Eternity is as much here as
anywhere. Those Christians, he thinks, who put off
felicity and defer their enjoyment with long delays " are
to be much suspected." [4] " 'Tis not," so he states his
law, " change of place, but glorious principles well practised that establish Heaven in the life and soul. An
angel will be happy anywhere and a devil miserable,
because the principles of the one are always good, of the
other, bad. From the centre to the utmost bounds of the
everlasting hills all is Heaven before God, and full of

[1] *Centuries of Meditations*, iv. 2.   [2] *Ibid*. iv. 95.
[3] *Christian Ethics*, chapter on " Charity."
[4] *Centuries of Meditations*, iv. 9.

treasure ; and he that walks like God in the midst of them
is blessed." [1]   " You are in Heaven everywhere." [2]   The
real business of life, as he elsewhere declares, is to
" piece this life with the life of Heaven, to see it as one
with all Eternity, a part of it, a life within it," [3] which
reminds us of Vaughan's great words :

> I saw Eternity the other night
> Like a great ring of pure and endless light,
>> As calm as it was bright :
> And round beneath it, Time in hours, days, years,
>> Driv'n by the spheres,
> Like a vast shadow mov'd ; in which the world
> And all her train were hurl'd. [4]

And with much penetration Traherne tells us that
Eternity is not an endless addition of " times "—a weak
infinite series of durations, but rather a Reality in which
all true realities abide, and which retains in a present
now all beginnings and all endings. [5]   Eternity is just the
real world for which we were made and which we enter
through the door of love.

> It is a spiritual world within,
> A living world and nearer far of kin
>> To God than that which first He made.
>> While that doth fade
> This therefore ever shall endure
> Within the soul as more divine and pure. [6]

---

[1] *Centuries of Meditations*, iv. 37.   [2] *Ibid.* iv. 38.
[3] *Ibid.* iv. 93.   [4] Vaughan's poem, " The World."
[5] *Centuries of Meditations*, v. 7-8.   [6] Traherne's poem, " Thoughts."

CHAPTER XVIII

FEW words are needed in conclusion to point out the historical significance of the movement which we have been studying, and to indicate its connection with the rise and development of seventeenth century Quakerism. These chapters have presented sufficient historical evidence to show that from the very beginning of the Reformation there appeared a group of men who felt themselves commissioned, like the prophets of old, to challenge the theological systems of the Reformers, and to cry against what proved to be an irresistible tendency toward the exaltation of form and letter in religion. They were men of intense religious faith, of marked mystical type, characterized by interior depth of experience, but at the same time they were men of scholarship, breadth and balance.

Their central loyalty was to the invisible Church which in their conception was the Body of Christ, forever growing and expanding through the ages under the guidance of the ever-present Spirit ; and they esteemed but lightly the established Churches which seemed to them formed not after the pattern in the mount but after very earthly and political models. Challenging, as they did, the formulated doctrines of the Reformation, the type of Church which was being substituted for the Roman Catholic Church, and the entire body of ceremonial and sacramental practices which were being put in place of the ancient sacraments of the Church, these " prophets " found themselves compelled to discover the foundations

336

for a new type of Church altogether, and to feel their way down to a new and fundamental basis of religious authority. That would be a momentous task for any age, or for any spiritual leaders, and we must not demand the impossible of these sixteenth century pathbreakers. What they did do consistently and well was to proclaim the spiritual character of God as revealed in Christ, the native capacity of the human soul for God, the intimate and inherent relationship of the divine and human, the progressive revelation of God in history, the priority of the inward Word, the august ethical aspect which must attach to any religion adequate for the growing race, and the folly of losing the heart and spirit of Christianity in contentions over external, temporal, and pictorial features of it.

They themselves were not founders of sects or churches. Their sole mission was the propagation of a message, of a body of truth and of spiritual ideals. They were from the nature of the case destined to be voices crying in a wilderness-world, and they were obliged to trust their precious cause to the contagion of their word and life and truth. The Quakers of the seventeenth century are obviously one of the great historical results of this slowly maturing spiritual movement, and they first gave the unorganized and inarticulate movement a concrete body and organism to express itself through. The modern student, who goes to the original expositions of Quakerism to find what the leaders of this movement conceived their message and their mission to be, quickly discovers that they were not radical innovators setting forth novel and strange ideas, but that they were on the contrary the bearers, the interpreters, the living embodiment of ideas which have now become familiar to the reader of these chapters.

No one has given us a clearer statement of George Fox's mission and of the creation of the new " Society " than has the writer of the " Epistle to the Reader " in Fox's strange book *The Great Mystery of the Great Whore* (1659). This " Epistle to the Reader " was

written by Edward Burrough and was printed, also
under the same title, in Burrough's *Works* in 1672.[1]
In this striking document the writer gives his account
of the existing Church, and over against this dark
background he sets God's new Reformation that is
just beginning, of which he feels himself to be the divinely
sent herald and prophet. " As our minds became turned,
and our hearts inclined to the Light which shined in
every one of us," he writes, " we came to know the perfect
estate of the Church ; her estate before the apostles' days,
and in the apostles' days and since the days of the apostles.
And her present estate we found to be as a woman who
had once been clothed with the sun, and the moon
under her feet, who brought forth Him that was to
rule the nations ; but she [the Church] was fled into
the wilderness and there sitting desolate, in her place
that was prepared of God for such a season, in the
very end of which season, when the time of her sojourning
was towards a full end, then *we* [Friends] were brought
forth." [2]

In the Light which broke in upon them, he says,
they saw that " the world was in darkness " and that
" anti-Christ was set up in the temple of God, ruling over
all, having brought nations under his power, and having
set up his government over all for many ages ; even
since the days of the apostles and true churches hath he
reigned. . . . As for the ministry, first, looking upon it
with a single eye in the Light of the Spirit of God which
had anointed us, we beheld it clearly *not to be of Christ,
nor sent of Him, nor having the commission, power, and
authority of Christ, as His ministry had in the days of true
churches ; but in all things, as in call, practice, maintenance,*

---

[1] This document, though, as stated above, not written by Fox, had his
approval, and may be taken as exactly expressing his views and his position.
Many of the early Quaker books show how remarkable was the corporate character and the group-spirit of the " Society " at this period. Whatever any
individual could contribute was given for the common cause and went into the
life of the whole. I have given the passages, which I have quoted from this
" Epistle," in modern English.

[2] *The Great Mystery of the Great Whore* (London, 1659), p. B1. Jacob Boehme
had already set Fox the example of calling the existing Church by this opprobrious name. See *The Threefold Life of Man*, vii., 56-58.

*and in everything else, in fruits and effects we found it to
disagree, and to be wholly contrary to the true ministry of
Christ in the days of the apostles."* [1] His charge against
the ministers of his day is one now very familiar to us :
" You preach to people what you have studied out of
books and old authors, and what you have noted down
you preach by an hour-glass and not as the Spirit of God
gives you utterance. You preach other men's words
which you have collected." [2] The " call " to ministry,
he urges, is based upon learning acquired in schools,
colleges, and universities, and is not of the Spirit, and
ministers' lives are obvious signs that they are not in the
true " apostolic succession." [3] " As for all churches
(so called)," he continues, " we beheld you all in the
apostasy and degeneration from the true Church, not
being gathered by the Spirit of the Lord, nor anointed
thereby as the true members of Christ ever were, but to
be in forms of righteousness without power, and imitations without life. All the practices of religion we beheld
to be without power and life. . . . We beheld all professions [of religion] to be but as coverings of fig-leaves,
while the [inner] nature stood uncondemned and not
crucified." [4]

He insists that no true and radical reformation of the
Church has taken place, that the churches of his day still
bear the marks of apostasy as did the churches before
the Reformation occurred : " Do not professors and
sects of people have the form without the power of
godliness ? Are not all people still covetous and earthly-
minded, and given to the world, and proud and vain,
even such as profess religion ? Are not professors as
covetous and proud as such as do not profess ? Are
they not given to the world, and doth it not show that
they are not changed nor translated ? And is it not
manifest that they have taken up the *form* of the apostles'
and Christ's words and practices, and are without the

---

[1] *The Great Mystery of the Great Whore*, p. B3.
[2] *Ibid.* p. A6. [3] *Ibid.* pp. A5-A7.
[4] *Ibid.* p. B4. This is almost word for word Boehme's view.

life, and not guided by the Spirit of Christ and the apostles in their praying and preaching ? " [1]

Here, with an air of prophet-like boldness and infallibility, we have once again an announcement of the inadequacy of the Reformation, the formal and external character of prevailing types of religion, and the unapostolic nature of the existing churches. The language describing the visible church is throughout the language of a " Seeker." " We ceased," he says in words that exactly describe the " Seeker," " from the teachings of all men, and their words and their worships, and their temples, and all their baptisms and churches, and we ceased from our own words and professions and practices in religion. . . . We met together often, and waited upon the Lord in pure silence from our own words, and harkened to the voice of the Lord and felt His Word in our hearts." [2]

The striking difference between him and the contemporary " Seeker " lies in the fact that he profoundly believed that the time of " apostasy " was now at an end, that a new " commission " had come, that a real Reformation was being set into operation, and that the apostolic Church—the Church of Christ, the Church of the Spirit—had appeared as though let down from heaven. He relates how the " Lord raised us [Friends] up and opened our mouths in this His Spirit," and how " the Light of Christ revealed and made known to us all things that pertain to salvation, redemption, and eternal life, needful for man to know," and how through the outpouring and anointing of the Spirit " the true Church," " the true worship," " the true ministry " have come again to the world. He makes such exalted claims as these : we received the pouring out of the Spirit upon us ; the gift of God's eternal Spirit was bestowed upon us as in the days of old ; the deep things of God were revealed to us ; the Lord Almighty brought us out of captivity and bondage and put an end to sin and death ;

[1] *The Great Mystery of the Great Whore*, p. C3.
[2] *Ibid.* p. B1.

the babe of glory was born in us ; we entered into ever-lasting union, fellowship, and covenant with the Lord, and we were raised from death to Life. And, finally, he announces the new " commission " in positive words of glowing faith : " Then having armed us with power, strength, and wisdom and dominion, according to His mind, and having taught us in all things, and having chosen us unto His work, God put His sword into our hand and gave us a perfect *commission* to go forth in His name and authority, giving us the Word from His mouth what to cut down and what to preserve, and giving us the everlasting gospel to preach." [1]

In the absolute certainty of his divine " commission," he challenges the Churches which are defending their authority " with jails and prisons and whips and stocks and inquisitions—all Cain's weapons "—to a " trial " of faith and spirit and power, like that on Mount Carmel in the days of Elijah, " whether it be they or we that are of the true faith and true worship of God that the apostles were in." [2]

There can be no doubt, I think, that the writer of this " Epistle to the Reader " in *The Great Mystery*, has come out of the " Seeker " movement, or that he has " come out " of it only because he believes that he with others have found what they sought, and are the seed and nucleus of the true, restored, apostolic Church of God. They refuse absolutely to be called a sect ; and they assume in all their early writings that they are the restored Church of Christ, though they seldom use that word " Church " because in their thought it was a name associated with the " apostasy," and they preferred to call themselves " the Seed," or " the Children of the Light." These were, as I have sufficiently shown, names already in use.

It is an interesting fact that this " Epistle " dates the beginning of the new era as 1652—" it is now

---

[1] *The Great Mystery of the Great Whore*, p. B2. I have taken some liberty in correcting the grammatical form of the passage quoted, but the original sense is preserved.   [2] *Ibid.* p. C2.

about seven years since the Lord raised us up in the
North of England and opened our mouths in this His
Spirit "[1]—and that it locates the springing forth of " the
Seed " in the North of England. It was, we are now
well aware, out of the Seeker-groups of the northern
counties of England that the new " Society " was actually
born, and it grew, like a rolling snowball, as it gathered
in the prepared groups of " Seekers," both north and
south in England, and a little later in America.[2]

The creation of the Quaker " Society " was not the
work of any man ; the groups were there before the
formative leader appeared on the scene. In fact the
very term " Quaker," which was soon fixed upon the
new movement as the popular name for it, had already
been in use—at least as far back as 1646—for the members
of some of these highly emotional communities. As soon
as these groups—intense in their expectations—found a
leader who was already raised to an impelling conviction
of immediate contact with God and of definite illumination by the living Christ, and possessed of an overmastering *sense of mission*, the effect was extraordinary. The
account of what happened is, we may be sure, none too
strong : " The gift of God's eternal Spirit was poured
upon us as in days of old, our hearts were made glad, our
tongues were loosed, and we spake with new tongues as
the Lord gave us utterance and as His Spirit led us." [3]
Profound psychological experiences occurred ; they felt
themselves baptized together, fused and formed into one
group-spirit, swept into trembling as by a mighty rushing
wind, and carried beyond their common ordinary range
of thought and power and utterance. Their group-
experiences of a common divine Spirit coming upon their
lives from beyond themselves, their discovery that God
was in their midst, that gifts were conferred upon them,
and, above all, Fox's compelling sense of apostolic mission
—a conviction which was, as it always is, contagious—

[1] *The Great Mystery of the Great Whore*, p. B.
[2] For evidence of Seeker-groups in America, see my *Quakers in the American Colonies*.
[3] *The Great Mystery of the Great Whore*, pp. B1-B2.

were grounds enough to change these Seeker-groups into the seed and nucleus of a Body possessed of the faith that the long-expected Church of the Spirit had at last come. They rose to the group-consciousness that they were the beginners, in modern times, of a Church of the spiritual order, and a community-loyalty was born which gave the movement great conquering power and an amazing capacity for endurance and suffering.

In Fox we have a person of extraordinary psychical experiences and of dynamic leadership, and in him the " prophetical " and " enthusiast " traits of the movement are strikingly in evidence. He reveals in a variety of ways his connections with the great body of spiritual ideas that had been accumulating for more than a century before his time, but for the most part these influences worked upon him in sub-conscious ways, as an atmosphere and climate of his spirit, rather than as a clearly conceived body of truth which he got by reading authors and which he apprehended through clear intellectual processes. He can be rightly appreciated only as he is seen to be a potent member of an organic group-life which formed him as much as he formed it.

The expositions, however, of the more trained and scholarly Quakers show an explicit acquaintance with the writings of these men whom we have been studying, and they cannot be adequately understood in isolation. The fruits of reading and of contact with a wider intellectual world are clearly in evidence, and the ideas and the peculiar phrases of the spiritual reformers " pass and come again " in their voluminous works. Robert Barclay is the chief literary exponent of Quakerism. His range of familiarity with religious and theological literature is very extensive, and he shows intimate acquaintance with contemporary thought. For him, as for his spiritual predecessors, the existing Church is " in apostasy " ; it has departed from " the simplicity and purity of the gospel as it was in the apostles' days." Christian faith has become " burdened with manifold inventions and traditions, with various notions and opinions " which have been " substituted instead " of the true religion of Christ.[1]

The Quaker interpreters all unite in treating " notions and opinions "—or, to use their sweeping phrase, "notional religion "—as barren *substitutes* for a true religion of spiritual reality, which for them is always born in a first-hand experience of Christ as the inner spirit and life and power of one's entire being and activity. A good specimen instance of this position is found in William Penn's Tract, " A Key opening the Way to every Capacity," etc.[2] He says : " It is not Opinion, or Speculation, or Notions of what is true ; or Assent to or Subscription of Articles or Propositions, tho' never so soundly worded, that makes a Man a true Believer or a true Christian." " Phrases of Schoolmen," " notions of Father, Son, and Holy Ghost," " conceptions of man's meer Wit," " superfining interpretations of Scripture texts," he declares to be very chaffy substitutes for a consciousness of Christ's Life and Light within, conformity of mind and practice to the will of God, and the actual formation of Christ in the inner self.[3] The further Reformation, upon the necessity of which he insists, is one that will take Christianity not only beyond and beneath outward ceremonies, but beyond and beneath all formulations of creed and doctrine, and that will ground and establish it in the experience and attitude and verifying power of the person's life.[4] This is precisely what all these teachers of spiritual religion have all the time been demanding.

The Quaker view of the moral and dynamic character of saving faith, the view that justification is a vital process and not merely a forensic scheme, is, in heart and essence, indistinguishable from the central teaching of these spiritual predecessors of the Quakers. No Quaker has presented this view in a more compact, and at the same time adequate way than has Barclay in one of his

---

[1] Preface to *A Catechism and Confession of Faith*.
[2] *Works* (London, 1726), ii. p. 781.
[3] *Ibid.* ii. pp. 781-783.
[4] " Salvation lieth not in literal but in experimental knowledge."—Barclay's *Apology*, Props. V. and VI. sec. 25.

important early Tracts : " The manner and way whereby
Christ's righteousness and obedience, death and sufferings,
become profitable unto us and are made ours, is by
receiving Him, and becoming one with Him in our hearts,
embracing and entertaining that holy Seed, which as it
is embraced and entertained, becometh a holy birth in
us . . . by which the body of sin and death is done
away, and we cleansed, and washed, and purged from our
sins, *not imaginarily*, but really ; and we are really and
truly made righteous. . . . Christ Himself revealed in
us, indwelling in us, His life and spirit covering us—*that*
is the ground of our justification." [1]

The root principle of Quakerism is belief in a divine
Light, or Seed of God, in the soul of man. All of the multitudinous Quaker books and tracts bear unvarying testimony to that, and all their contemporary accounts make
that faith, that principle, their *organizing idea*. What they
all say is that there is a Light in man which shines into
his darkness, reveals his condition to him, makes him
aware of evil and checks him when he is in the pursuit of
it ; gives him a vision of righteousness, attracts him
toward goodness, and points him infallibly toward Christ
from whom the Light shines. This Light is pure, immediate, and spiritual. It is of God, in fact is God
immanently revealed.[2]

Then, again, the figure is changed and what was called
Light is now called " Seed," and it is thought of as a
resident germ of divine Life which, through the active
co-operation of the individual, produces a new creation
within, and makes the person through and through of a
new nature like itself.[3] It is also frequently called " the
Word of God," or " Grace of God," or " That of God in
you," or " Christ within," or " the Spirit," or " the
Kingdom within you." " By this Seed, Grace, and Word
of God, and Light wherewith every one is enlightened,"

---

[1] Barclay, " Truth cleared of Calumnies," *Works* (London, 1691), i. pp. 1-48.
[2] This view appears *passim* in the works of Isaac Penington.
[3] See Penington's Tract, " Concerning the Seed of God," *Works* (edition of
1761), ii. pp. 593-607.

Barclay says, " We understand a spiritual, heavenly, and invisible Principle in which God, as Father, Son, and Holy Spirit, dwells ; a measure [*i.e.* a portion] of which divine and glorious Life is in all men as a Seed, which of its own nature draws, invites, and inclines to God. This some call *vehiculum dei*, or the spiritual Body of Christ, the flesh and blood of Christ, which came down from heaven, of which all saints do feed and are thereby nourished unto eternal life." [1] But under whatever name it goes, it is always thought of as a *saving Principle*. He who says yes, responds, obeys, co-operates, and allows this resident Seed of God, or Christ-Light, to have full sway in him becomes transformed thereby and re-created into likeness to Christ, by whom the inner Seed was planted and of whose nature it is. The spiritual predecessors of the Quakers, as we have seen, all held this view with individual variations of phrase and experience. All the Quaker terms for the *Principle* were used by Sebastian Franck and by Caspar Schwenckfeld ; and all the men who taught the dynamic process of salvation presuppose that something of the divine nature, as Light or Seed or Spirit, or the resurrected Christ, is directly operative upon or within the human soul. That is, salvation is for them more than a moral change, it is a birth-and-life-process, initiated and carried through by the *real presence* of the Divine in the human.[2]

The Quakers are perhaps somewhat more emphatic than were their spiritual forerunners, with the exception

[1] *Apology*, Props. V. and VI. sec. 13. This passage could be exactly paralleled in the writings of Schwenckfeld.

[2] It is interesting to see how closely William Law, the great exponent of " Spiritual " Christianity in the eighteenth century, carrying on this train of thought in another channel, approaches the Quaker position : " Thou needest not run here or there saying, ' Where is Christ ? ' Thou needest not say, ' Who shall ascend into heaven, that is, to bring Christ down from above ? ' or, ' Who shall descend into the deep, to bring up Christ from the dead ? ' For, behold, the Word, which is the Wisdom of God, is in thy heart. It is there as a bruiser of thy serpent, as a Light unto thy feet and Lanthorn unto thy paths ; it is there as an Holy Oil, to soften and overcome the wrathful fiery properties of thy nature, and change them into the humble meekness of Light and Love ; it is there as a speaking Word of God in thy soul ; as soon as thou art ready to hear, this eternal, speaking Word will speak wisdom and peace in thy inward parts, and bring forth the birth of Christ, with all His holy nature, spirit, and temper within thee."—" Spirit of Prayer," *Works*, vii. p. 69.

of Schwenckfeld, in their declarations that this Seed, this Light, is not *natural*. " We assert," William Penn wrote, " the Light of Christ not to be a Natural Light, otherwise than as all men born into the world have a Measure of Christ's Light, and so in a sense it may be called Natural to all Men. But this Light is something else than the bare Understanding which Man hath as a Rational Creature." [1] What man does naturally have, in William Penn's view, is a *capacity* for the Light, but the Light itself is from a source wholly heavenly and divine. Barclay, in quite Cartesian fashion, interprets it to be " a real spiritual Substance," " a substantial Seed " from another world, hidden away within man's soul at birth, lying there " like naked grain in stony ground," until the child is old enough to feel its stirrings and to determine by his own free choices of obedience or disobedience to its movings whether it shall grow and develop or not.[2] We plainly have here a double world. The once-born man is " natural," though he carries buried deep in the subsoil of his nature a Seed of God, a germ of Life drawn from the higher, spiritual world. He may live in and under the dominion of either world, but he must choose which it shall be. By response to and participation with the divine Seed of radio-active spiritual energy, he can become transformed—utterly and completely—into a new nature, and can belong here and now to the spiritual World which Christ by His victorious Life has brought across the chasm and planted in our soil. On the other hand, by negligence or by disobedience he can live a mere empirical, natural life, and keep his inestimable Seed of God buried and forgotten in a region of himself which he seldom or never visits.

The Quakers, however, as a consequence of their heightened group-consciousness, and as a result of the intense experiences enjoyed in their gatherings, exhibited a far greater degree of *enthusiasm* than had appeared in the earlier exponents of the inner Word ; and they showed a heightened element of *prophetism*, both in their faith

---

[1] *Works*, ii. p. 780. [2] *Apology*, Props. V. and VI. sec. 13.

and practice. They devoutly believed that in them the prophecy of Jeremiah had found fulfilment : God had written His Word in their hearts, so that they were recipients of His will and His message. The more sure Word of prophecy, announced by Peter, had come and the Day Star had risen in their hearts. Their Light was to them not only a principle of connection with a higher world, a germ of a new nativity, it was also a principle and basis for continuous revelation, and for definite openings of light and guidance on all matters that concern present-day life and practice. " The inward command," Barclay says, " is never wanting in the due season to any duty." [1]

Like their predecessors, they did not slight the importance of the outward word, the Scriptures. They had an immense reverence for them and were diligent in the study and skilful in the use of them, though of course they used them in a thoroughly uncritical and unhistorical way, as did also their opponents. But they would never allow the Scriptures to be called the Word of God or to be treated as God's only revelation of Himself to man without a challenge. " The Word of God," Barclay says, " is, like unto Himself, spiritual, yea, Spirit and Life, and therefore cannot be heard and read with the natural external senses as the Scriptures can." Our Master, he adds, is always with us. " His letter is writ in our hearts and there we find it." [2] " There is," William Penn declares, " something *nearer to us* than Scriptures, to wit, the Word in the heart from which all Scriptures came," though he is very emphatic in his claim that Friends never slight the Scriptures and believe in their divine authority. [3]

It is not necessary to prolong the exposition of early Quakerism farther. The similarity of its fundamental position with that of the preceding spiritual reformers is perfectly clear. Quakerism is, thus, no isolated or sporadic religious phenomenon. It is deeply rooted and embedded in a far wider movement that had been accumu-

---

[1] " Truth Cleared of Calumnies," *Works*, i. p. 13. [2] *Ibid.* i. pp. 13-15.
[3] *Works*, ii. p. 782.

lating volume and power for more than a century before George Fox became a " prophet " of it to the English people. And both in its new English, and in its earlier continental form, it was a serious attempt to achieve a more complete Reformation, to restore primitive Christianity, and to change the basis of authority from external things, of any sort whatever, to the interior life and spirit of man.

That the *formulation* of this vast spiritual Reformation, as presented by the men who are studied in this volume, was adequate, I do not for a moment assert. The views here expounded in their historical setting are plainly hampered by inadequate philosophical and psychological presuppositions. They need reconstructive interpretation and a fresh re-reading, in terms of our richer experience, our larger historical perspective, and our truer psychological conceptions. That work of re-examination and reinterpretation, especially of the Quaker movement and the Quaker message, is a part of the task undertaken in the historical volumes which follow this one in this series. It must suffice for the present to have reviewed here the story and the struggles of these brave, sincere men and their heroic endeavours to proclaim a spiritual Christianity. It has been a privilege to live for a little while with this succession of high-minded men, to review for our time their type of spiritual religion, and to retrace their apostolic efforts to bring the world, with its sins and its tragedies and its inner hungers, back to the Father's Love and to the real presence of the eternal Christ. They may have failed in their intellectual formulation, but at least they succeeded in finding a living God, warm and tender and near at hand, the Life of their lives, the Day Star in their hearts ; and their travail of soul, their brave endurance, and their loyal obedience to vision have helped to make our modern world.

INDEX

THE END